A Treasury *of*
Jewish Holiday Baking

A Treasury of

Jewish Holiday Baking

MARCY GOLDMAN

DOUBLEDAY

New York   London   Toronto   Sydney   Auckland

PUBLISHED BY DOUBLEDAY
a division of Bantam Doubleday Dell Publishing Group, Inc.
1540 Broadway, New York, New York 10036

DOUBLEDAY and the portrayal of an anchor with a dolphin are
trademarks of Doubleday, a division of Bantam Doubleday Dell
Publishing Group, Inc.

Some of the bagel recipes appeared originally in Eating Well magazine, March 1996.

*Filo Honey Cheesecake, Frozen Cherry Brandy Cheesecake used with
permission of Bon Appétit magazine from "Fabulous Cheesecakes," 1988. The recipes for
Halvah Filo Cheesecake, White Chocolate Truffle and Raspberry Cheesecake, and Fudge Top
Marble Cheesecake first appeared in the May 1988 issue of Bon Appétit. BON APPÉTIT is a
registered trademark of Advance Magazine Publishers Inc., published through its division,
the Condé Nast Publications Inc. Copyright © 1997 by the Condé Nast Publications Inc.
Reprinted with permission.*

BOOK DESIGN BY LEAH S. CARLSON
ILLUSTRATIONS BY CATHERINE ROSE CROWTHER

Library of Congress Cataloging-in-Publication Data
Goldman, Marcy.
A treasury of Jewish holiday baking/Marcy Goldman. — 1st ed.
p.   cm.
Includes bibliographical references and index.
1. Baking.   2. Cookery, Jewish.   3. Fasts and feasts—Judaism.   I. Title.
TX763.G566   1998
641.8'15'089924—dc21

97-44137
CIP

ISBN 0-385-47933-6
October 1998
First Edition
3 5 7 9 10 8 6 4 2

In memory of my grandmothers,
Annie Marks Goldman and *Iliena (Annie) Pertsofsky Ilieff*,

and to my father,
Nathan Goldman,

and to my mother, *Ruth Ilieff Goldman*,
who gave me freedom in the kitchen and offered my brothers
and me a taste of everything along with the best culinary advice:
"If you start with good ingredients, even if it doesn't exactly
turn out, it can't taste bad."

Especially dedicated, with love, to those fabulous baker
brothers, my sons, *Jonathan*, *Gideon*, and *Benjamin*,
my own crop of spring wheat.

ACKNOWLEDGMENTS

TESTERS (AKA THE SISTERHOOD)

I am often asked the same questions about my recipes. One is, do you make up your own recipes? In most cases, yes. I have more than a hunch about what makes a recipe "correct": it should be technically balanced, authentic from both historical and culinary point of view, and easy for someone else to reproduce. Another question I am asked is if the recipes work. A strange question, but one I am asked frequently nonetheless. Again, the answer is yes. First of all, I test recipes many times, refining and modifying them so that someone else will have success with them, and trying to make it as easy as possible to achieve this. For newspaper and magazine feature work, this is particularly important, for once a recipe hits the (usually) Wednesday food section and people run out to get ingredients, you just cannot have any doubt about a recipe's worthiness. It is unethical to waste people's time and money with improperly tested recipes. Readers loathe being fooled—and who can blame them. It is in a food writer's best interest to care about his or her work—for nothing invalidates you more quickly than a reputation for recipes that do not turn out. Some newspapers, fortunately, have test kitchens (all food magazines have them) and that is another insurance policy.

For a cookbook, the task of recipe testing is even more important. Number one, there is no back-up test kitchen to confirm your efforts. Secondly, unlike a newspaper that can print recipe corrections (a dreaded, but practical reality), a cookbook cannot alter an error until the next printing (if indeed there is one). So, recipes really have to be tested by others. Where to find these benevolent test bakers?

When I first started putting this cookbook together, I would create and test recipes and deliver samples of finished prototypes to friends. Little white confectioners' bags containing samples of honey cake, fluden, strudel, mandelbrot, etcetera would be left on door knobs, exchanged at carpool, or hand-delivered to any friend or acquaintance I might meet in the course of my day. "Try this, try that," I would implore. "Should it go in the book? What do you think? More sugar? Less vanilla? Add some chocolate, increase the apples? Would you make this for Shabbat or for Rosh Hashanah? Would you add raisins or not? Should it be a nine by thirteen-inch pan or a ten-inch spring-form?"

When you bake around the clock, you can lose your sense of taste. Letting friends sample the recipes restored some of my perspective.

Eventually, as time marched on, the do-you-think-it-should-go-in-the-book refrain became a plea for help. I was determined to get the whole book retested inside out and trouble-free. As the deadline for the manuscript drew even closer, this goal became overwhelming. Sensing a drowning baker in their midst, friends stepped in.

Linda Sidel set to work baking—squeezing recipe-testing into her own busy schedule, beguiling her three sons and husband with a myriad of challahs, loaf cakes, and kuchens. Very soon another dear friend, Janet Goldstein, heard my s.o.s. and quickly joined the baker's militia. Armed with a draft copy of the cookbook, she approached the project in a very pragmatic way. She sat down with friends Mona Abrams and Cheryl Birenbaum over coffee one day, and these good ladies expediently divided up recipes into equal portions. Janet also engaged Rebecca Freedman. Then came Cynthia Kerr, a known-to-be-competent baker in the community. When I felt I was imposing on the "foundation" test recipe team too much (i.e., more recipes cropped up and I paled at the thought of asking for more help from those already knee-deep in bubka and schnecken), others volunteered, including Mayda Dubman and Barbara Kling. And then Heidi Cooney, AKA "The Cake Queen," a friend with a new, second daughter to tend to, as well as her own cake company to run, entered the picture. She graciously threw her oven mitts into the ring (it must be said, that Heidi, as well as Janet Goldsteen, did the lion's share of the Passover test baking—no mean feat in the off season), and joined the baking frenzy.

With each person's help and interest, I was rescued from my writer/baker vacuum. Volunteer testers made short work of a task that had seemed insurmountable. They set about retesting recipes immediately, comparing my baking times with theirs, as well as confirming pan sizes, methods, ingredients, and directions. Copies of recipes flew back and forth (left in nursery school cubby boxes, as well as faxed and emailed to and fro) as the huge task got distributed among several capable pairs of hands and kitchens. My phone began ringing as questions arose: "You never said what temperature. You left out the second half of the directions for the strudel! My oven baked it in less time than yours. Can I use a tube pan instead of an angel cake pan? You called for lemon zest but don't say in the recipe where it goes!" And so on and so forth. One day, one tester casually said to me, "You know, no matter how perfect you intend to make it, everyone bakes in different ways, ovens are different, eggs are different, personal methods vary—you can make yourself crazy over this!" True enough, but I was (and am) determined that in this era of nonbakers, anyone using this book should find success.

Overall, the recipes worked. But having other people bake them meant they were checked for errors and stripped of ambiguity—all because of the efforts of this special baker's task force. It was also a good way of gauging if something was too hard, or an ingredient too uncommon to bother with, or if a recipe was less than stellar. Since everyone has different mixers, ovens, and baking pans, the unofficial test-bake team offered insights into how well recipes worked out in a variety of conditions. If these recipes are easy, trouble-free, failure-proof, and taste wonderful, much of the thanks belongs to these women.

THE BAKER'S SISTERHOOD

Mona Abrams
Cheryl Birenbaum
Heidi Cooney
Mayda Dubman
Rebecca Freedman
Janet Goldstein
Heather Ingberg
Cynthia Kerr
Barbara Kling
Linda Beck Sidel

TORCH LIGHTS

Thanks to my neighbors, Brenda and Kenny Bernamoff and family. Kenny and Brenda have the most refined, caring palates a baker could hope for. They couple this with their sensitive commentary (Kenny and Brenda make even the negative sound not so bad) and loads of hearty encouragement.

Thanks to Doris Leibovitch, our surrogate bubbie, the daughter of a Jewish baker herself. Who else could help me manage three wild boys, translate Yiddish words and expressions, and occasionally assist as my sous chef so seamlessly? Without Doris around for physical and moral support, I doubt this book would have been published.

Thanks to the legions of Jewish food writers who have preceded me. These fine people have been the keepers of the flame, documenters of a culture, and generous sharers, in ways they may not even have realized, of their knowledge and expertise. All have forged the path to which I now humbly add my own footprints.

SOME PROFESSIONAL NOTES: THE "GREEN LIGHTS"

Writers can write all they want to but it just doesn't mean as much unless your words get published. An editor has to give you the go-ahead green light—that is, accept your work. I have been fortunate to have contributed to many well-respected newspapers and magazines in the United States and Canada. This has given me the best possible training (aside from my training as a pastry chef and baker) to become a cookbook author. Several editors have been very helpful at different points in my career, validating my work by publishing my byline in their pages, allowing me to share my passions as a baker and a writer with their readers. My thanks to:

Elizabeth Baird, *Canadian Living*
Mark Bittman, *Cook's Illustrated*
Susan Bonne, *Coffee Journal*
Cynthia David, *Toronto Sun*
Christine Diemert, *London Free Press*
Patty Doten, formerly *Boston Globe*
Barbara Fairchild, *Bon Appetit*
Ellie Tesher, *Toronto Star*
Felicia Gressette, *Miami Herald*
Frances Litwin, *Better Health*
Carol Meighen Haddix, *Chicago Tribune*
Martha Holmberg, *Fine Cooking*
Evelyn Kramer, formerly *Boston Globe*
Cecilia MacGuire, *Montreal Gazette*
Karol Menzie, *Baltimore Morning Sun*
Tim Moriarty, *Pastry Art and Design*
Renee Murawski, *Newsday*, formerly *Detroit Free Press*
Janice Okun, *Buffalo News*
Russ Parsons, *Los Angeles Times*
Susan Pucket, *Atlanta Journal-Constitution*
Irene Saxe, *Disney,* formerly *Newsday*
Margot Slade, formerly *New York Times*
Susan Stuck, formerly *Eating Well Magazine*
Toni Tipton, *Cleveland Plain Dealer*

And a special thank you:

Nancy McKeon and Stephanie Witt Sedgwick, of the *Washington Post*. These women, are, without doubt, the most encouraging editorial duo an out-of-town freelancer could ever encounter. They have given me the honor of consistently being part of their food section pages and testing a great number of the recipes in this book. And Donna Nebenzahl, *Montreal Gazette*, *Elm St.* magazine. Donna has long been a bright light. I consider myself honored to be in her stable of writers and a friend.

SPECIAL THANKS TO:

My sponsors at my web site, Baker Boulanger, *The Online Magazine for Bakers Who Cook* (www.betterbaking.com):
Ares Restaurant and Kitchen Equipment
All Clad Metal Crafters
Black and Decker, Canada and U.S.
Five Roses
fermipan (Lallemand) Inc., in particular for their technical assistance in understanding yeast
Garland Range, Canada and U.S.
Hodgson Mill
Hollingsworth Custom Wood Products
Saco Foods
Weber Stephen Products Company

As well as the following people and companies, Rabbi Lionel Moses, Congregation Share Zion, Montreal, for his scholarly expertise.

The Quebec Hotel Institute (officially, l'Institut d'hotellerie et tourisme de Quebec) for the best training a pastry chef and baker could receive on this side of the Atlantic.

Jim Birchall, Jim Birchall Associates
Boyijian's of Boston, Inc.
Eggology
King Arthur Flour
Marc Fowler
The Lodge
Brian Maynard, Kitchenaid
Matt Nielsen, Nielsen Massey Vanillas
Nordic Ware Inc.
Penzey's Spice House
Theresa Stahl, Weber Stephen Products
Julia Stambules, Patricia Tanaka and Company
White Lily Flour Company

The readers of the following newspapers and magazines—for allowing me in their kitchens and the many kind letters I have received from them over the years:

Atlanta-Journal Constitution, Baltimore Morning Sun, Bon Appetit, Boston Glove, Buffalo News, Canadian Living, Chicago Tribune, Chocolatier, Cleveland Plain Dealer, Coffee Journal, Cook's Illustrated, Detroit Free Press, Eating Well, Fine Cooking, Food and Wine, Newsday, New York Times, Ft. Lauderdale News and *Sun Sentinel, King Arthur's Baking Sheet, London Free Press, Miami Herald, Montreal Gazette, Oregonian, Ottawa Citizen, Pastry Art and Design, San Diego Union, Sacramento Bee, Toronto Star, Toronto Sun, Vancouver Sun,* and in particular, to the readers of the *Montreal Gazette* and *Washington Post.*

My agent, Susan Ginsberg, for bringing me to Doubleday.

My Editor, Judith Kern (as well as the editorial staff at Doubleday), who painstakingly went through mounds of very raw manuscript and an Old Testament's worth of Jewish holiday recipes, and for keeping a new author focused—in my case, no mean feat.

Paul Berg, a fine lawyer and a prince in the truest sense of the word.

My brother, Mark Goldman; every sister should be this lucky.

Yvan Huneault, broadcaster, Templar Knight, Web master, and collaborator of Baker Boulanger, where this book got its first electronic plug. My heartfelt thanks for managing a newly launched Web site while I completed this book, for his editorial skills and innate craftsmanship in copyediting as well as stringent proofreading of the manuscript, and for his support, both as a colleague and as a friend.

To My Grandmother on Shabbat

In my grandmother's blind eyes
I have seen
The paths of many before.
The wandering of others
Somehow stops with us.
Here, in this house,
We settle.
And for a time,
The endless trek ceases.

I help her with the candles
And turn her to face the light
Of the Sabbath candles—
A glow she can sense,
But cannot see.
My grandmother's face
Reflects the light of gold and mellow.
Reflects tradition
Generations old . . .
Almost timeless.

My grandmother's voice rises and falls,
With the tones of prayer.
It is the music
That will haunt and comfort me forever.
I listen,
As she sings songs
That are heard,
Far away from Russia.

—M.G.

CONTENTS

In Montreal, one has access to some outstanding, sophisticated, international bakeries and pâtisseries. I have learned much from working with fellow chefs, but when I want comfort food, I turn to what is familiar: "Jewish baking." Around holiday time, this style of baking is my first choice. It is what I want to offer my family and friends, sharing with them not only a piece of apple cake, but the taste of nostalgia. Even when it is not holiday time, I like the basic appeal of a lightly sweet poppy seed cookie or my grandmother's sour cream chocolate cake. I take pleasure in watching guests sink their teeth into something freshly baked and old-fashioned. Maybe the cake or cookie tastes great, but more important, it is a style of baking that is comforting. The Yiddish word for this is *haimish*—implying homey or informally cozy. When I give someone a slice of something just out of the oven, I love seeing that little smile of contentment. They may think they're eating just a piece of cake, but they are tasting memories. Perhaps, for a moment, they can capture that fleeting, warm spirit of an adored bubbie or nona, or balabosta grandma.

Seeing my own children dive into a fresh, warm challah or having them implore me to make a certain hamantaschen or vanilla-scented marble cake, is another level of joy. Not all our experiences are about food, but some of our best family moments come mingled with something from the kitchen.

For me, as a baker, a mother, a friend, what is important as giving someone something fresh from the oven is the thrill of sharing a recipe or technique, or letting a friend or reader know how to make something taste better. I can't feed everybody—though I try! Failing that, I am dedicated to passing on what I have learned. I am a big believer in sharing, and handing a recipe to someone is a wonderful way to share. It is the original gift that keeps on giving.

JEWISH HOLIDAYS AT THE TABLE: CELEBRATIONS IN BAKING

When we think of holidays, we reflect on our religious traditions and ceremonies. Every holiday on the Jewish calendar brings us back to our heritage in a unique, vital way, for each celebration is a chapter in our history. Each is fortified with rites, customs, family times, and special foods. Our observance of the Jewish festivals seems, in light of the distractions of modern living, almost designed to anchor us to Judaism.

Holidays are a time when we strengthen the special bonds of family and friends. Watching our children grow and experience the holidays in new ways, we remember being the youngest at the Seder, fretting over being relegated to the bridge table. Now we are at the head table—perhaps even the hosts, graciously welcoming back the aunts and uncles, and (if we are very lucky) a grandmother or grandfather. These are the guests who first set those holiday examples—our role models. We honor them by following their examples and having them at our own tables.

"Shabbat shalom," "Happy Chanukah," "A good *Yom tov*," "*Shana tova*," "Happy New Year," "I wish you an easy fast," or simply, a toast of "*L'chaim! (To Life!)*" ...At holiday time, the blessings are many and heartfelt. Heady stuff, holidays are. Warm, nostalgic, and glad—tinged with a touch of the bittersweet as well as the sweet.

To a baker, holidays are as much about holiday foods as they are about family and religious heritage. It is something the Jewish culture shares wholeheartedly with all others—celebration through special dishes and treats. Without these, the holidays are less complete, and nowhere near as memorable. A New Year's synagogue sermon may contain wishes for a good and fruitful year ahead, but a honey cake makes the point in its own way! A slightly sweet, spiral-shaped challah, studded with raisins, reinforces the continuity of life, as do bagels, round and sturdy, welcomed at every Jewish holiday table (except Passover, of course). These are edible symbols. They start on the tongue but they stay in the heart and the mind.

Some foods are holiday musts. Families may joke about them, but the truth is, they are always welcome. We count on seeing them on the table. Tradition, always, tradition. And yet . . . "on the other hand," as Tevye, the wise but fallible patriarch of *Fiddler on the Roof* would say, there is little dispute that innovation, especially when it tastes delicious, is also part of the picture. In accepting innovation we broaden the notion of what is traditional. Innovation, adaptation, modification—these are the hallmarks of Jewish culture. If a raisin challah is tasty, might not an apple studded challah work as well? Could not that wonderful sweet red kosher wine also find its way inside the batter of a crisp mandelbrot, transforming it from your grandma's cookie into your own unique creation? Consider too, that Passover products, in particular, have evolved substantially. "Kosher for Passover" now includes vanilla powder and brown sugar, just two items that make for more creative Passover baking. So the tradition expands and, along with it, our judgment and appreciation of what constitutes "holiday baking."

So Nu? Who Has Time to Bake?

The odd thing is that even people who do not bake regularly will find time to make something "for the holidays." The busiest, least domestic among us, somehow feel that urge to make at least one pan of apple cake or a batch of mun cookies. Because, as wonderful as professional bakeries and pastry shops are, they cannot reproduce that special home-baked taste. And homemade foods, regardless of the expertise of the baker, are still the hallmark of caring and craftsmanship. Making something with love for those you love has a value beyond pragmatism.

It's silly and pointless to argue that time is short, or that it may, in fact, be more economical to purchase than to bake yourself. We are talking about another level of investment. Moreover, no matter how advanced the world becomes, making something our forefathers made and ate still feels innately right. My grandmother (my dad's mother), Annie Marks Goldman, may not be here, but her sour cream chocolate layer cake and delicious roly-poly pastry remind me of her often.

THE LAWS OF KASHRUTH, AND SOME NOTES ON KOSHER INGREDIENTS

The Laws of Kashruth, in Brief

There are certain ingredients that you will find cropping up again and again in this book. But before I get to them, a word about Kashruth in general.

When foods are prepared in accordance with the laws of Kashruth, they are said to be kosher, or simply translated, "fit" or "proper." The Torah does not really go much beyond presenting the laws of Kashruth as a divine command guiding Jews toward holiness. However, generations of rabbis and Jewish scholars have offered a rationale for Kashruth based on a foundation of ethics and spirituality. Detailed and in depth, the counsel and cautions on what and how we eat, found in these ancient laws, govern us on levels that transcend the mere function of eating. Some scholars postulate that the laws of Kashruth were designed this way for a purpose. For if we are always conscious and aware of what and how we eat and how this relates to other levels of daily Jewish being, our association to our faith remains strong. If the longevity of the Jews is anything to go by, this theory makes a lot of sense. In any case, the observation of Kashruth has left a unique imprint on the development of Jewish cuisine.

In the laws of Kashruth, there are a number of basic tenets. First, certain foods, such as shellfish and pork, are forbidden. Second, there are specific laws on how to slaughter those animals permitted for consumption. The emphasis is always on being merciful and avoiding at all costs any undue pain or cruelty to the animal. Trained for this task are professional, ritual slaughterers, known as *shochtim,* who also ensure that the animal is healthy. Once the animal has been slaughtered, considerable care is taken to remove as much blood as possible.

In the Jewish kitchen, food is divided into three groups: meat, dairy, and pareve or neutral foods. Of these, meat and dairy dishes are served separately. Pareve or neutral foods, such as eggs, fish, fruits, nuts, grains, sugar, coffee, tea, spices, oils, and vegetables can be eaten with either meat or dairy foods. Utensils (pots and pans, plates, cutlery, et cetera) used for either meat or dairy, are also kept separate from one another.

Processed foods which are certified kosher, have been prepared under rabbinical supervision to ensure that meat and dairy products are not mixed and that all ingredients come from sources which are certifiably kosher. Kosher certification by a reliable Kashruth supervising organization is indicated by a symbol on the package.

Ensuring Kashruth at Passover is another level of keeping kosher, and the rules get more specific (see The Passover Pantry page 274).

How Kashruth Affects Baking

What is significant about Kashruth insofar as it relates to Jewish baking is the use of pareve fats and non-dairy liquids in the preparation of cakes and pastries. For instance, to serve a cake that accompanies a meat meal, the cake must be prepared as pareve or neutral. To do this means using a number of ploys geared to impart flavor to a dessert that is generally butter and milk free. This also serves to explain why a traditional Friday night challah is made with oil, not melted butter, as another rich egg bread might be, or why the richest honey cake is traditionally made with oil, and not butter. The neutral nature of these ingredients gives a dish flexibility—it may be served with either meat or dairy.

The result of Kashruth observance has been to inspire a whole genre of baking that is a salute to the ingenuity of Jewish bakers. A cup of coffee or cup of orange juice, the use of vegetable oil and flavors such as chocolate and cinnamon, toasted nuts, fresh apple and plum slices, citrus zests, a dash of kosher wine—generously used in cake and pastry baking—are all strategies to add wonderful flavor. Some cakes, such as a typical oil and orange juice–based apple cake, have become so popular that mainstream cultures have adopted them. Often, I have seen a "bubbie"-style apple cake referred to as "Jewish Apple Cake" in a community church cookbook!

A Note on Kosher Baking Ingredients

Authentic Jewish recipes are created with kosher ingredients. Most baking ingredients and related packaged items (such as pudding powders) are certified kosher. The larger, national flour millers, extract manufacturers, nut and raisin packers, and makers of canned and packaged goods offer the kosher certification on their products. There are also kosher product companies that offer a broad line of kosher goods throughout North America. Depending on the city or community, the symbol may be a small or large **K** in a circle, a **U** in a circle, the words "Kosher" or "Certified Kosher," or one of many other designations (you can contact the Orthodox or Conservative Council of Rabbis or your own rabbi for guidance).

Confectionery products, such as sugars, chocolates, and candies such as gummie bears, are also usually kosher. Haddar, Lieber's, Streits, Manischewitz, Horowitz, Rokeach are just some of the more familiar names in kosher food products. If you require a certain product and do not know if it is available (or want to know the full range of Passover products) you can contact these companies by mail. Generally, they manufacture far more items than any supermarket can stock.

But Is It Fat Free?

When I began writing this book, every so often someone would ask: "Is it fat free?" or, "Is it low fat?" Well, yes and no. The recipes in this book are no more or less fat laden or fat free than any other collection of traditional baking recipes (unless they are billed as "fat free" or "low fat"). Baking, unless it is bread, is generally the pursuit of sweet temptations—and by its nature, is not particularly a low-fat affair. But then, no cake or pastry is supposed to be devoured as a main dish or whole meal nor by one person. Baking for the holidays is baking for a special occasion—it is supposed to be a treat. To me, classic Jewish baking (in fact, all classic baking) should be uncompromisingly delicious. Fiddle with it too much and the effect is lost. Besides, one slice of a classic babka or honey cake every couple of months is not going to make the difference if you maintain an otherwise reasonable diet and lifestyle.

My best advice is to find a place for treats in the overall scheme of things. Have a small piece of something terrific—not a huge piece of something that is tasteless. Share with others. Use good, wholesome, natural ingredients and take pleasure in knowing your baking is freshly made by you and full of good things like whole eggs, calcium and vitamin–enriched unbleached flour, pure orange juice or milk, fiber-laden raisins and nuts. Besides, you can always walk to shul the next day!

Remember that the term *nutrition* encompasses a lot more than digestion. Nutrition is also about taking pleasure in life. Food, particularly dessert, is not the whole of life; it is an incidental indulgence that brings enjoyment. Enjoyment, whether it be from a good book, a coffee with a friend, or one perfect hamantaschen, is part of the overall quality of life and health.

MY MISHEGOSS,* OR JUST THE WAY I DO THINGS

I put a lot of labor, energy, and love into my baking. This being the case, I can think of no reason to compromise this investment with inferior ingredients. The way I see it, you can't necessarily have the largest diamond in the world or keep a couple of luxury cars in your garage, but you can certainly have the best flour (which is still one of life's better deals), real butter, pure vanilla, quality chocolate, and unblemished fruits (save bananas, which are at their baking best in a beat-up state) to bake with. In short, if you are not fussy about the foundation—quality ingredients that are properly handled—you are tossing out your best efforts. People often ask me why

* MISHEGOSS—from the Yiddish language, meaning "craziness," "peculiarity."

their recipes don't turn out as mine do. The fact is, they all turn out a bit different—that's part of the magic and charm of baking. When things don't pan out well, it's time to look to the basics.

Much of my technique comes from the ingredients I use and how I handle them. A second component is the proper tools and equipment.

Three Ingredients to Better Baking

There are three essentials to better baking: The first two are simple. They are your own two hands and your refrigerator. The third is less obvious but equally attainable.

HANDS. Your hands are the original mortar and pestle. They can also slice, dice, mix, and stir; cut fat into flour; press out cookies; and knead bread. Respect them and take care of them. Remember, those wonderful men and women who came before us did not have food processors, so never apologize if you lack some sort of electrical appliance. You own the original tool of any trade.

THE REFRIGERATOR. When I was in pastry school, I soon learned that nothing was unsalvageable as long as there was a refrigerator nearby. A too-soft cookie dough that spread miserably on the cookie sheet somehow behaved once it was allowed a brief respite in the fridge. A dough that could not be cajoled in any way to line a quiche or springform pan turned magically obedient after being chilled. When in doubt about how to handle something, or if you fear a dough or batter is unmanageable, consider using your fridge as your kitchen assistant.

Recipes that look hopeless are often revitalized when chilled. The fridge is also your best friend when it comes to slowing down a rising challah—allowing you flexible scheduling in yeast baking. So, before you even consider changing a recipe or throwing up your hands in frustration, head for the refrigerator.

PATIENCE. It's something we are not all born with but which is certainly attainable and free of charge. Patience is that wonderful trait that is behind every careful, caring baker. Rushing things rarely results in perfection. Patience also implies a certain respect for craftsmanship and belief in yourself. Never, ever give up! With patience comes the bonus of confidence. With confidence, comes increased success and hours of enjoyable, satisfying baking. Or at least, the mastering of a few, choice recipes. For the record, anyone who knows me well will attest to the fact that I am not terribly patient. But I have acquired patience and have learned not to panic. I have been rewarded for my efforts and you will be too.

INGREDIENTS

Flour—"White Gold"

Whenever I reach into a bin of flour, I feel like I've come home. The silky feel and velvety softness of flour is irresistible. For artists, the bait is new paints and an unblemished canvas; for musicians, it might be a Steinway grand piano; for gardeners it could be new earth, good weather, seeds, and flower bulbs; but for me, it is flour that courts my imagination with its promise of unlimited baking potential. Add a little salt, water, and yeast and a simple mound of flour becomes bagels, baguettes, brioche, or a velvety challah. Throw in some butter, vanilla, and sugar and you have legendary chocolate chip cookies, a buttery coffee cake, or tender strudel. Flour, even in this day and age, is relatively inexpensive, so there is no reason not to insist on the best and be loyal to it.

The two flours used extensively in this book are unbleached all-purpose and unbleached bread flour. Recipe testing for this cookbook consumed some

2,400 pounds of flour. Just imagine how much strudel, rugekish, and poppy-seed cookies that made!

HOW I MEASURE FLOUR

Professional bakers weigh ingredients, rather than measure them, because weighing is far more accurate. Most British home bakers as well as North American perfectionist bakers will also weigh ingredients. Most of us, however, are in the habit of measuring ingredients. It may be less accurate but when done with care and respect, measuring can be relied on to result in fine baking. So that your recipes turn out as mine do, use my method for measuring flour. I do not sift flour, since it is already quite refined and consistent. But flour does get packed or compacted, sitting in a canister or in a bag on the store shelf. Before I measure a cup, I stir the flour in the canister, aerating it somewhat, using a wire whisk. *Then,* I measure out the flour in my dry measure cup. This prevents me from measuring a couple of extra ounces in my cup (which incidentally, weighs in at 4½ ounces). So, remember, stir to aerate, then measure.

UNBLEACHED ALL-PURPOSE FLOUR

All-purpose flour is exactly that, a flour created for the home baker to suit a multitude of purposes. It is not a dedicated flour, as are pastry, cake, or bread flours. All-purpose is a good choice for most home baking.

I always use *unbleached* all-purpose, simply because it makes more sense to me. Unbleached really means "naturally aged" as opposed to having added chemicals, such as chlorine, which prematurely age, whiten, and strengthen the flour as well as strip it of its vitamins. "Naturally bleached" or "naturally aged" is probably a more accurate term. When a flour is naturally aged, it lightens in color and acquires strength. Unbleached flours are a lovely cream color as opposed to the more pristine white of regular, bleached, enriched flours. (Unbleached flours are usually also enriched with extra vitamins and minerals.)

I tested many of these recipes with Hodgson Mill unbleached all-purpose and unbleached bread flour as well as King Arthur flour (check the source guide in the back of the book). Hodgson Mill, in particular, is an exceptional product. Other well-known flours—reputable, unbleached brands, such as Gold Medal, Pillsbury—are also fine, and when I have used them, I have been rewarded with good baking results. In Canada I rely on CSP's Great Plains flour, an all-purpose flour I adore as well as CSP's Diamond unbleached bread flour, both of which are the pride of the wheat fields of Saskatchewan. I also recommend Five Roses flour, a fine flour I grew up with, as well as Robin Hood flour, both easily available in Canadian supermarkets. One other flour I like very much, especially for superb biscuits, tender cakes, flaky pies, or spectacular scones is White Lily. This flour is the pride of the South and is available via mail order (see Sources) and worth the effort to get it. Try it for the Sconalah recipe (page 350) for incredible results.

If you are still not sold on using unbleached flour, you should feel comforted in knowing all these recipes turn out very well using enriched, bleached flours as well. In fact, when it comes to cake making, even fans of unbleached flour, give the nod to a bleached flour because of its performance and the tender-crumbed cakes that result.

The main thing is to get to know a flour brand in order to achieve consistency in your baking. You care about your baking; so look for flour companies who are equally caring about their product because it's going to be the very body of everything you bake.

This doesn't mean you can't maintain a few brand loyalties or prefer one brand for one type of baking and another for other sorts of baking, but it does mean you shouldn't take this precious ingredient for granted. It is not just "white powdery stuff" to dump into a cake. It is literally white gold.

BREAD FLOUR, UNBLEACHED AND BLEACHED

These days, bread flour can be found just about anywhere, and for most bread recipes, this is the right choice. It has a slightly higher percentage of protein than all-purpose flour (approximately 12.5 to 14.5 grams versus all-purpose's 11.5 to 12.5 grams, depending on the brand of flour). Although millers try to teach home bakers that it is also a matter of the "quality" of the protein—not just the quantity—these higher levels usually indicate that a flour has more body, and consequently, will produce a bread with more elasticity. If you are hand-kneading, as opposed to using an electric mixer with a dough hook or a bread machine, you might have to knead a dough made with bread flour longer than you are accustomed to, in order to develop the dough's structure.

Bread flour makes for high-rising, expansive loaves, with hearty crusts and good inner crumb structure. Bread flour has the strength necessary to hold up rye flour in a pumpernickel roll and makes for rustic, chewy bagels. I prefer challah made with bread flour because it produces a wonderful crust and a gently chewy interior, preventing this rich bread from crossing the line into denseness. However, challah is such an amenable bread that it will also work reasonably well with all-purpose flour, especially if you are baking with a quality, unbleached all-purpose such as Hodgson Mill, King Arthur, or, Canada's Five Roses, for example.

King Arthur's bread flour, called "Special," is also recommended for breads although you will generally find you require less of this flour than of the usual bread flours such as Gold Medal, Pillsbury, Robin Hood's Better For Bread flour, or Five Roses bread flour. Definitely opt for bread flour in recipes that call for it. Yeast coffee cakes can be made with either all-purpose or bread flour. Yeast coffee cakes can also be made with a combination of the two—usually in a fifty-fifty or one third to two thirds ratio. This combination of two flours is what I prefer for these recipes. Traditional style stretch strudel should always be made with bread flour for the proper elasticity, (once the dough is developed) to be stretched into the huge, thin sheets that are required.

WHITE WHOLE WHEAT FLOUR

A relative newcomer to supermarket flour choices, white wholewheat flour is an all-purpose flour which King Arthur introduced to the consumer market. It is now also offered by Hodgson Mill. Advertised as having all the nutrition of regular whole wheat with a sweet, nutty taste, white whole wheat is a good choice for adding flavor, fiber, and extra nutrition to your baking. If you are not using this flour, you can substitute regular whole wheat flour. When you can, buy stoneground whole wheat. Many supermarket whole wheat flours are, in fact, referred to in the trade as "restored" whole wheat. These are regular white all-purpose flours to which bran has been reintroduced. They look the part but they are not truly 100 percent whole wheat flour—they are more a cosmetically correct whole wheat. True *whole* wheat flour has the entire wheat berry milled *and* includes the bran and germ along with the flour. The result is a dense but hearty and flavorful flour.

CAKE FLOUR

This flour is dedicated to cakes and, used properly, makes for outstanding, light cakes and scones (check out the Sconalah recipe, page 350). However, cake flour is not included in this book because not many merchants keep it in stock. Sometimes, in lieu of cake flour, I have used a tablespoon or two of corn starch to tenderize a dough or batter. Cornstarch does a good job of adding a delicate quality to a cake—not quite the same as a good cake flour, however.

RYE

Rye flour comes in various granulations. Varieties that are called "light" or "medium" are pretty well interchangeable in rye bread recipes, particularly for light rye breads and sour ryes. A more rustic-tasting rye flour is "pumpernickel," sometimes called "dark rye" or "rye meal." As with whole wheat flour, this includes more or all of the rye berry. I find that pumpernickel has the most robust flavor, and offers a lot of character in traditional Jewish breads, buns, and bagels. It is a must for pumpernickel bread. Rye flour is flavorful and distinct but it has little body. It is usually combined with white flour, preferably bread flour, to help hoist it up. The more rye you use (in proportion to white flour) the denser the bread will be. The less rye you use, the lighter (and less rye-tasting) the bread will be. I prefer medium or dark rye flour for optimal flavor and texture, and I combine it conservatively with white bread flour. Store rye flour in the refrigerator or freezer.

STONEGROUND CORNMEAL

Good stoneground cornmeal tastes buttery, slightly sweet, and fully "corn-ish". It is bright yellow and slightly waxy, with traces of corn bran and residual corn oil. There are many good mail order sources for cornmeal. I like Hodgson Mill best. It's available in American supermarkets or by mail order if you cannot find it. If you are used to store-brand cornmeal, which can be dry and flat stoneground cornmeal will be a revelation to you. Using it makes all the difference in a corn cake or quick bread. Store stoneground cornmeal in the refrigerator or freezer.

Yeast

Ah yeast, the baker's soul mate. How I love this ingredient! Every living cell of this microorganism is filled with potential. In fact, I think every bakery and kitchen should have a sign posted saying: "Yeast is our friend." Experienced bakers adore yeast; but many home cooks are mystified by this miraculous product. Yet yeast, given a little respect, is relatively easy to work with. Using yeast is the only way you are going to get a homemade, outstanding challah or a buttery, mouthwatering, better-than-a-bakery babka, so it is worth learning about.

YEAST BASICS

1. Many of the recipes have been tested with both instant yeast and active dry yeast. For home baking, I prefer *instant yeast,* for its reliability and durability. However, when I use the term "dry yeast" in these recipes, that is an indication to you, the home baker, that *either* product will be fine. Items made with active dry yeast might rise a bit more slowly, but that is all.

2. Yeast is commonly activated with water (although instant yeast can be dissolved in liquid first *or* put in with the flour). Depending on the baker and the recipe, the temperature of the water can vary. Bread bakers may like cooler water for slow-rising loaves (and to compensate for the increase in dough temperature generated by the friction of mechanical mixing, such as a dough hook); sweet-yeast pastries profit from slightly warmer water to kick-start the process. When I call for "warm water," I mean about 110°F. If you do not have a thermometer to verify the temperature, the water should be comfortably warm, not hot, when you test it on your wrist.

3. Whenever I call for yeast to be mixed with warm water and a pinch of sugar (to start it off) I have used the phrase "allow to sit until the yeast swells or appears dissolved." Some cookbooks use the phrase "until the yeast foams or bubbles." This doesn't always happen with yeast, depending on the type or the brand, and I have seen people become confused and uncertain, waiting for a big song and dance from the yeast. Just expect a slight froth or a swollen look after a few minutes of rehydration.

4. Yeast can respond somewhat sluggishly in milk. Since many recipes are enriched with milk, I usually start the yeast in a small amount of warm water; warm milk will be added later in the recipe, once the yeast has been activated. In this way, richer recipes are still largely milk-based and flavorful, but have been jump-started with warm water to ensure the dough is responsive. Many professional bakers use warm water to begin their sweet-yeast recipes, and call for dry milk powder later on (See Better Than the Bakery's Babka, page 328). In this way, bakers get good yeast activity but do not lose the full flavor of the dairy ingredients in their cakes and pastries. Dry skim milk powder also strengthens a rich dough.

5. Regardless of which type you use, make sure the yeast does not come in direct or prolonged contact with salt. It "burns" the yeast. Second, do not allow yeast to come in direct contact with the recipe's fat (usually oil) before the yeast is properly dissolved in the sugar and water. Fat coats the yeast, preventing it from becoming properly active.

TYPES OF YEAST

I love all yeast and have learned to appreciate the characteristics of each kind. Some bakers disdain one or another. A really good baker, home-based or professional, respects all types of yeast and is successful with them all. There is no such thing as the "wrong yeast." There are only misconceptions about one yeast product or another and/or poor handling. Besides, even if we all agreed that fresh yeast is best, if you were sitting in the middle of an Alaskan snowstorm and your dogsled was on the fritz and in your pantry you had a nice vacuum packet of instant dry yeast, you would be very, very, grateful. You would also be able to make yourself some wonderful bread to go with your hot chocolate. Point is, all yeast is worthy of respect and can be used to produce fine baking.

Years ago, there was only compressed fresh yeast (actually before that there were sourdough starters made with wild yeasts), something our grandmothers, great-grandmothers, and professional bakers knew about. Then came the convenience of active dry yeast, a product geared to bakers who could not regularly get fresh yeast or for home bakers, who did not consume enough fresh yeast to turn it over before it got old.

After *active dry* came *quick,* then *rapid rise* or *rapid mix.* Following that came *instant,* made from a different yeast strain, and different in its manufacture than its predecessors. But the evolution of yeast begins with wild or natural yeast spores.

Wild Yeast- Natural wild yeast spores have been flying around the world since time immemorial. They are the foundation of sourdough starters and countless bakers' myths. The fact is, the more you bake, regardless of which yeast you depend on, the more you invite yeast spores into your environment. Eventually, whatever yeast you bake with most often becomes "native" to your kitchen. Over time, the more you bake with yeast, the better your baking becomes, as your recipes ingest the yeast spores that live in your kitchen, gracing all your batters and doughs.

Fresh Compressed Yeast- For the longest time, I feared fresh yeast. When I was growing up, I thought the only yeast in the world was Fleischmann's active dry yeast in packets and cans. As a young baker, most recipe books I read had already abandoned fresh yeast; the great majority called for one packet of active dry yeast. I had heard that professional bakers preferred fresh yeast, but I had very good results with active dry yeast. Later on, as a professional baker, I worked successfully with the newer, European instant yeasts, such as fermipan (the primary yeast used to test many of the recipes in this book) and Saf, as well as their American counterparts, Red Star and Fleischmann's.

Then I got curious and procured some fresh yeast to try out in challah recipes. It transformed outstanding challah into sublime, phenomenal challah! Doughs made with it are remarkably supple, bouncy, and responsive. How does a dough know it has fresh yeast in it? I'm not sure, but it knows!

Fresh yeast is inherently more active. This is the result of two factors. According to yeast technologists at fermipan Lallemand Inc., a yeast company that is a large supplier to the professional baker (Eagle Bakers Yeast in the United States), the yeast strains used to make fresh yeast are different from those used for dry yeasts. Dry yeast strains are selected for their stability under stress (being dried, rehydrated, et cetera) rather than their activity or liveliness. The second way fresh yeast differs from its dry yeast cousins is in something called "lag time." Dried yeast contains only 5 to 8 percent moisture, compared to the 70 to 72 percent it contains in its normal state (that is, before being processed into dry form). After rehydration (i.e., adding some warm water to the yeast to proof it) there is a short period of time, the "lag time," that the yeast requires in order to become active again. Fresh yeast does not have this lag time and this is another reason for the responsiveness of doughs made with it.

However, wonderful things have their drawbacks. Fresh yeast is delivered every other day to commercial bakers. A good thing, since it cannot be proofed quite the same way as dry yeasts, to see if it is active or lively enough with which to bake. Fresh yeast keeps, under refrigeration, for one to two and a half weeks.

FREEZING FRESH COMPRESSED YEAST: Many cookbooks advise home bakers to hack a block of fresh yeast into one-ounce chunks (almost impossible, because it shatters and splinters all over the place) and then freeze it for a couple of months. Fresh yeast fares well enough in the freezer, but not as well as if stored in the refrigerator and used within two to three weeks. The longer the yeast is frozen, the more likely it will lose potency.

If you do try freezing fresh compressed yeast, know that once it is frozen it should be used within a couple of months. When I use frozen, fresh yeast, I throw it out after ten weeks rather than take the chance that it is not sufficiently active. When I first started using fresh yeast, I noticed that the first breads made with it were explosive and floated out of the oven like golden pillows. A month or two later, using the same batch of frozen-and-defrosted yeast, I noticed a difference in performance.

To freeze fresh yeast properly, wrap it first in wax paper, then in plastic wrap. It is important to keep the yeast from drying out. The best results are obtained from frozen fresh yeast if you allow it to defrost in the refrigerator the night before you are planning to bake.

For fresh yeast baking I use Lallemand yeast, (known as Eagle brand in the States), because that is the brand bakers in my area use and I have learned to rely on it.

What I recommend, if you become as besotted with fresh yeast as I am, is to buy a half or whole block of fresh yeast (you can always share with friends) when you think you will be putting in a particularly big week of baking. Keep it well wrapped, in a Ziploc bag, and refrigerated. Take out what you need when you need it. After two to three weeks, throw out what you have left. Most bakeries sell a block of yeast for a couple of dollars. Better to throw out old, possibly inactive yeast than to take the chance that it won't perform its magic.

TO SUBSTITUTE FRESH YEAST FOR DRY: I generally use ³/₄ to 1 ounce of fresh yeast to replace four teaspoons of active dry or instant yeast. If a recipe is quite rich with eggs, sugar, and fat (such as babka), I use 1 to 1¹/₄ ounces of fresh yeast. For larger recipes, exceeding seven cups of flour, I use 1¹/₄ to 1¹/₂ ounces of fresh yeast to replace two tablespoons of dry. It varies, too, depending on the season and the freshness of the yeast. If you need assistance, you can contact the toll-free consumer line at Fleischmann's, Red Star, or fermipan.

Fleischmann's 1 (800) 964–8663 ext. 3047
fermipan 1 (800) 432–1090
Red Star 1 (800) 445–4746 ext. 2
SAF 1 (800) 641–4615

Just once, in spite of these cautions and your own reservations, try fresh yeast to make a challah (see the recipe for "This Tastes Like Cake" Fresh Yeast Challah, page 78).

Active Dry Yeast- As with fresh compressed yeast, active dry yeast is a live culture, but it needs water or another moistening agent for activation. If you are using active dry yeast, mix the yeast with warm water and a pinch of sugar and allow the yeast to soften and dissolve. It may even bubble somewhat. If your packet of active dry yeast is vacuum sealed, it can sit in your pantry. Once opened, exposed to air, moisture, and warmth, it should be used soon. Yeast can be sealed well and refrigerated or placed in the freezer and should fare well. Always take note of the expiration date.

Rapid Rise or Rapid Mix Yeast- Quick Rise or Rapid Rise, or Rapid Mix yeasts are finer granulations of active dry yeast. They are small "i," *instant* (as opposed to capital "I," *Instant*) insofar as they act more quickly than active dry yeast because they dissolve faster. Some of these yeasts can tolerate higher temperatures, and doughs made with them rise quickly. But you are less likely to find this variety of yeast because the marketplace is overrun with two other dry yeasts: instant (bread machine yeast) and active dry.

If you are using Quick or Rapid Rise/Mix yeast, you may add it directly to the dry ingredients or, as for active dry yeast, mix it first with warm water and a pinch of sugar to activate it. The recipes in this book use any and all dry yeasts the traditional way—with warm water and sugar first, to activate the yeast.

Instant Yeast, Bread Machine Yeast- Probably the most confusing thing the yeast companies could ever have done for home baking was to bring out a great product and call it "instant" yeast. Worse, they complicate the whole issue by having a variety of names for similarly performing yeast products such as Quick Rise, instant active Dry Yeast, and/or Bread Machine yeast. Here are the facts.

After active dry and Rapid Rise yeasts, come the newer breed of instant yeasts. These are both biologically and technologically different from their active dry yeast predecessor and are notably durable or "damage proof," making them good choices for home bakers. Instant yeast also dissolves or activates rapidly in warm water and blends readily into a recipe. Because instant yeasts ferment breads quickly, bread machine companies often recommend this variety (they know consumers want fresh bread as fast as possible and for the most part, manufacturers have timed their bread machine cycles to go with instant yeast). "Bread machine yeast" is in fact, an instant yeast.

Instant yeast is particularly good for home baking because it suits a variety of bakers with a variety of skills. It is wonderful for rich, sweet yeast baking. The very resilience of instant yeast is a quality that makes it a good choice for inexperienced bakers, as it compensates, for the baker's lack of skill. What is meant by resilience in talking about yeast? It means that if you overload the recipe with too much fat or sugar—ingredients that can impede fermentation—instant yeast has a higher threshold. Was your water too cold or too hot? Again, instant yeast is more tolerant. Also, instant yeast is remarkably "active,"

meaning there are fewer inactive or dead yeast cells in each teaspoon than in other types of yeast. It is a yeast that is mistake proof. Almost.

TOO MUCH OF A GOOD THING: If instant yeast has a drawback, it is the following. Because it is quite active and bred to be very resilient, it can also be very powerful. Using too much of it can be detrimental to a recipe. How do you know if this is the case? Three ways: 1. You will see evidence of this in a premature rise (i.e., a proofed dough rising out of the bread machine before the dough cycle is complete). 2. You'll smell a yeasty fragrance that is very pronounced. Or, 3. You'll have a refrigerated dough actually rising and pushing open your fridge door! Overfermented doughs will taste too yeasty and/or will become stale prematurely. *The solution is very simple: Use less, decreasing the amount by half-teaspoon increments.*

Incidentally, overfermentation can be caused by too much yeast, no matter which type you use. BUT . . . it can also be caused by allowing a dough to rise too long. Make sure you do not allow doughs to rise to almost double their original size. Beyond the tell-tale yeasty, beery fragrance, an overrisen dough will also not bake up as well because much of its kick will have been spent.

The one time you have no leeway when interchanging active dry yeast with instant yeast (or using too much of either) is when you are *baking* in the bread machine. If you use too much instant yeast and are baking in the bread machine, there is a good chance your bread will bake up and fuse to the inside window of your machine! This is not a problem when you use your bread machine only to prepare dough. You can take out a dough that is rising too much or too fast and punch it down before it gets too far.

MEASURING DRY YEAST

If you bake frequently, consider buying a four-ounce jar or tin of yeast. It is far easier to scoop and measure out of the jar than to play around with half packets of yeast. Also, for challah, a rich bread, you will find that you use substantial amounts of yeast, so a four-ounce can makes sense and is convenient. If you are used to the packets or sachets of dry yeast, remember that one packet is equal to about two and a quarter teaspoons.

Sugar

Where would a baker be without sugar? Sugar has many functions in baking aside from adding sweetness. The little crystals help fluff up and introduce air into butter (when you are creaming butter and sugar together); sugar is a moisture agent (it turns partially into a syrup in the baking process); sugar helps provide texture, tenderness of crumb, flavor, and shelf life.

Yes, one can reduce the sugar in a recipe, but only to a certain point, say 10 to 20 percent. After that, the quality of the recipe begins to change. If you are concerned about sugar, try any one of the mandelbrot recipes or sweet yeast coffee cakes. These are your best bets if you want a not-too-sweet dessert or wish to experiment with reducing the sugar (start by taking out two to four tablespoons). I do not recommend baking with sugar substitutes unless you have special recipes for these.

BROWN SUGAR, LIGHT, DARK, AND GOLDEN

Mostly, as a matter of personal taste, I use *light brown or golden* sugar, although dark brown will work just as well. With its light caramel taste and color, brown sugar lends an extra touch to recipes that are milk and butter–free, so I consider it a big asset to Jewish

baking. Unless otherwise stated in the recipe, I always pack brown sugar *firmly* in the measuring cup.

Kosher Salt

You might assume a book on Jewish baking would recommend kosher salt, and you would be right. Usually I use Haddar brand, mostly because I like the sprightly yellow canister it comes in, but other brands are absolutely fine. Aside from the obvious, kosher salt is iodine free and infinitely pure of taste, which makes it wonderful with which to bake. It is also a little less salty than regular salt. Now, about the whole issue of salt in baking. Years ago a male friend asked me the point of using salt in baking. "Why add something salty to something sweet?" At that time, I agreed with him. His argument against salt seemed quite logical. Thankfully, as I learned to bake better, I began to understand the special balance of flavors in a recipe, as well as that special relationship between sugar and salt. Salt, in judicious amounts, does not make something taste salty, it lets taste shine through. Without it, breads are just starchy rounds (also they do not rise properly, but that is another story), cakes are sweet and insipid, cookies are bland, pastries are flat. Add a little salt and the whole picture changes. Even if you are on a reduced-salt diet, most recipes here do not call for that much salt. In a twelve-portion cake, much of that salt is distributed into modest amounts (although leaveners offer their own salt).

The point is, salt offers a lot of bang for its buck, giving anything you bake a few more layers of taste. Leaving salt out takes away the punch and flavor of a dessert. I am fanatical about testing for just the right salt quotient in a recipe. That said, I also happen to be conservative in my salt requirements and use it quite carefully. This is one ingredient that you can adjust incrementally—up or down—to suit your own taste.

One last word on salt that goes beyond taste and nutrition: Salt regulates yeast activity. Without it, yeast cakes, coffee cakes, breads, and rolls would just rise, indiscriminately, sprawling out, without any sort of discipline, all over the place. Salt makes sure a yeast dough behaves in a controlled manner, making for a nice, steady, consistent rise and no wild, ungainly bulges.

Eggs

All recipes in this book were tested with grade A, size large eggs. Extra large eggs, at least in this collection of recipes, are not more of a good thing—they might upset the balance, as would a medium or small egg.

For all baking, but especially yeast baking, do not use ice-cold-from-the-refrigerator eggs. Cold eggs make for a sluggish dough or a slightly denser cake. If you haven't had a chance to let your eggs sit on the counter to warm for about twenty minutes, put them in a bowl (still in their shells), cover them with very warm water for one or two minutes, then drain. Avoid any eggs that are suspect or have hairline cracks; this is a good place for bacteria to creep in.

Unsalted Butter

Nothing rivals butter for taste. Substitutions may not be so noticeable in an intensely chocolaty double fudge cake but they would really be apparent in a vanilla pound cake, rich rugelach, or a majestic streusel coffee cake. Because it is a dairy fat, butter contributes to browning, and adds moisture, flavor, and a wonderful aroma. Baked goods made with butter also freeze and keep better (even the Sara Lee company discovered this years ago in their frozen cake line). It is also a natural, not overly processed, ingredient. Use salted butter for toast, not baking.

When I see unsalted butter on sale, I buy several pounds and freeze it—it's like having gold in the bank.

Salted butter is too salty for use in baking. Using it, and leaving out salt (as I am often asked about), is not recommended. Salt gives flavor to butter and helps preserve it. It also masks butter that is not fresh. Sometimes, when creaming butter and sugar, your mixture will look curdled. A baker's trick is to add a tablespoon or two of the flour called for in the recipe to the creamed butter/sugar mixture to hold it together. This also will help when you add the dry ingredients.

Measuring Butter- When using butter, note that:

2 cups equal 1 pound or 16 ounces
1 cup equals 1/2 pound or 8 ounces
1/2 cup equals 1/4 pound or 4 ounces
1/4 cup equals 1/8 pound or 2 ounces
2 tablespoons equal 1 ounce

For stick-portioned butter:

4 sticks equal 1 pound or 2 cups
2 sticks equal ½ pound or 1 cup
1 stick equals ¼ pound or ½ cup

To be absolutely accurate in preparing butter for a recipe, use a small portion scale or follow the grid marks usually supplied on the wrapping or box of a one-pound block of butter.

Unsalted Margarine, Pareve or Nondairy

When I refer to "unsalted margarine" in this book, I am referring to a kosher margarine that is nondairy or pareve. Some margarines are indeed kosher but still contain dairy components. *Pareve* margarine is a "neutral" fat—something to be aware of when shopping for margarine for nondairy baking.

Next, and just as important, *do not use a whipped, salted margarine.* This is not a product that is good for baking. Whipped means there is air in it (and it is probably substantially processed), less fat and more water and air. What you want is a hard block of unsalted margarine for baking.

Incidentally, if you want to bake with margarine, and you do not require it to be pareve or dairy-free, you can simply opt for a block or stick of kosher, unsalted margarine.

Finally, taste the margarine you are planning to use. If it does not taste good plain, it will not undergo any marvelous transformation in the final baked product.

During Passover, the scenario changes a bit (check out The Passover Pantry, page 274). Margarine for baking is not only required to be pareve (not whipped and not salted), but also "kosher for Passover." The only margarine I use is a brand from New York called Migdal Unsalted, Sweet Margarine. It comes in a carton of four 4-ounce sticks. It is one of the best Passover margarines I have tested. If your retailer does not stock Migdal (sometimes it is brought in for Passover), check out the Source Guide on page 353.

Margarine is measured as butter, above.

Vegetable Shortening

Vegetable shortening, a relatively modern invention in American convenience products and one that many kosher cooks have embraced, has many attributes. It is neutral in taste, can be found with the kosher designation, is pareve, and makes for especially crisp cookies, light cakes, and flaky pies. Vegetable shortening has enabled kosher homemakers to create all sorts of great recipes—particularly where one requires a solid, but nondairy fat. As far as authenticity goes, oil is generally more traditional in *nondairy* Jewish baking, and you will note that most recipes (when not using unsalted butter or margarine) call for this ingredient. When I have opted for shortening, it is either required (for a pie pastry dough, for example) or simply better in the recipe for one reason or another. If you like shortening, feel free to substitute it, in equal proportions, for unsalted butter or unsalted margarine.

Vegetable shortening is measured as butter and margarine, above.

Oil and Nuts

Nuts and oil turn up frequently in Jewish recipes and both can make or break a cake. I tested a great marble cake for this book—it looked and smelled divine, until I tasted it. Something was not right—the oil. It does not happen often but it does happen—the oil had turned rancid. Nuts, unless fresh and stored in the freezer, can also make for a rude awakening. Taste your oil before using it. Never assume all is well. Ditto for the nuts. Taste them before using them and store them in the freezer.

Acidic Dairy Ingredients

I use a lot of acidic dairy ingredients in my baking in addition to regular sweet milk, because of the pleasant interactions that occur in the baking process. Here is an overview of their definitions and substitutions.

SOUR CREAM

Sour cream is a dream ingredient. Rich, smooth, creamy, it enriches every dough, cake, and pastry it comes in contact with. It acts as a dough and pastry tenderizer and helps color a cake, cookie, or pastry in the baking process. You can substitute a lighter fat sour cream if you prefer, as well as yogurt or buttermilk. You will still wind up with good baking, but the results will not be as rich. Sour cream is very luxurious and has a unique taste.

YOGURT

Yogurt is made from milk into which a lactic culture has been introduced. This results in a dairy substance that is thick—generally thicker than buttermilk but not as thick as sour cream. Yogurt, which varies in fat content (depending on brand, type, and additions), can be a good substitute for buttermilk or sour cream. As with its acid cousins, yogurt adds a certain tang to baked goods.

BUTTERMILK AND BUTTERMILK POWDER

Buttermilk is a low-fat, creamy dairy liquid. Lightly acidic, it is an ideal ingredient for use in many cakes, breads, and cookies. Buttermilk used to be the sour milk leftover from butter-churning. These days, commercial buttermilk is pasteurized skim milk (making it comparatively low fat) to which a culture is added to assist in thickening the product.

Buttermilk is a must in almost all the muffins, quick breads, and coffee cakes I make. Because it is acidic, it naturally tenderizes flour's tougher gluten strands—a bonus for achieving an extra-delicate cake crumb. However, when I don't have fresh buttermilk on hand, I am quite devoted to and grateful for natural buttermilk powder. I discovered Saco Cultured Buttermilk Blend, a buttermilk substitute in the form of a dairy powder, years ago, on holiday in New England. I rarely have less than a couple of cans stashed away. Over the years I have corre-

sponded with the Saco company and was thrilled to find a really nice bunch of people behind it, and a wealth of special, buttermilk-powder-based recipes.

When substituting buttermilk powder, add three to four tablespoons of powder to the *dry ingredients* for each cup of buttermilk. Don't attempt to reconstitute it. Use one cup of water, or orange juice, to replace the one cup of liquid.

Look for Saco brand buttermilk powder in the baking aisle of your supermarket or contact the company as listed in the Source Guide (page 356). You can also find bulk buttermilk powder at health food or bulk food stores as well as baking supply companies.

SOURED MILK

The important thing to remember about soured milk, and using it as a substitute for either buttermilk or yogurt, is that it is—soured, not spoiled. To make soured milk, mix one cup of regular milk with one to two tablespoons of something acidic, such as vinegar or lemon juice. Let it stand a couple of minutes, until it develops curds or looks cloudy and the milk seems to be separating. It can now be used as a handy replacement for buttermilk or plain yogurt.

COTTAGE CHEESE AND OTHER ALIASES

No ingredient has caused so much confusion in my food-writing career as cottage cheese. For baking, I use a no-curd, or dry cottage cheese. It is a cottage cheese that is relatively low in fat (1, 2, 4, to 8 percent, depending on the brand and style of manufacture). Here are some aliases: baker's cheese, pot cheese, dry cottage, no-curd, and small curd cottage cheese. Try to find a cottage cheese that looks like a drier version of cream cheese—no curds, not wet or floating in dairy whey. It is the ideal ingredient for danish and coffee cake cheese fillings, blintzes, or strudels, and cheesecake. It is not as rich as cream cheese, but it does an awful lot of nice things in baking.

HALF AND HALF, LIGHT CREAM, AND EVAPORATED MILK (CREAM'S "UNDERSTUDY")

Half and half and light cream, for these recipes, are interchangeable. Half and half generally means the product is, indeed, half milk and half cream. Light cream can be marked as 10 or 12 percent fat, although I have seen 5 percent as well. Any of these products is richer than milk, and both add an extra level of tenderness and flavor to cakes and cookies. When I do not have half and half or light cream on hand, I use evaporated milk.

Evaporated milk tastes superb in baking and performs like a light cream or half and half. Evaporated milk can also be diluted with water if you like. Economical and always in my pantry on standby, it extends my dairy supply if I don't have a lot of milk on hand in the refrigerator. When I use it to replace milk in baking, I dilute it with one cup of water for each cup of milk.

Vanilla and Other Extracts I Have Known

Jewish baking is about simple tastes. Thus quality extracts really shine through. Years and years ago, when I first began baking and didn't know better, I would use anything I had on hand as vanilla. At one point, I even tried making my own vanilla by soaking dried-up, old vanilla beans in vodka for a couple of weeks. I got "vanilla-ish" scented vodka for my efforts but not what I would now accept as vanilla extract, suitable for baking.

Then I tried inferior-but-pure vanillas—weak, alcoholic, and without dimension. I then went through a stage where, as a commercial baker, double-strength (extra-strong) artificial vanilla was the norm. For a while, I got used to the heavy, sweet fragrance that overpowered everything. And then I began to research vanilla and the companies that specialize in making it. Real, pure vanilla, made by vanilla specialists, knows no rival.

One of my favorite gourmet brands of vanilla is Neilsen Massey. This family-owned company is a supplier to bakeries, pastry shops, hotel kitchens, and food service manufacturers who demand the best. For the consumer, the product can be purchased from gourmet shops, such as Williams Sonoma, or by contacting the company for an outlet in your region (1-800-525-7873). I like all the Neilsen Massey vanillas, Madagascar Bourbon, Tahitian, and Mexican, all of which offer their own, unique bouquet and are produced in single or double strength (more concentrated) preparations.

If I am using a vanilla from the supermarket shelves, I generally choose McCormick Pure Vanilla (in Canada, look for the same product under the Club House name). Here is another company that cares about its extracts and can offer you consistency, as well as recipes and advice.

Once you invest in better vanilla, you will begin to notice a difference in your baking. Pure vanilla is quite subtle and delicate, yet able to pull together the separate flavor elements in a recipe. Coffee cakes thrive on a healthy teaspoonful or two of vanilla; whereas just a dash of vanilla is all you need in a yeast babka to make the buttery dough shine without being overpowered. Pareve or dairy-free cakes really rely on the use of superior vanilla. Think too, of combining extracts in cakes and cookies. A touch of almond extract and some vanilla make a subtle difference. For a more bakery-style danish-tasting yeast cake, consider using a touch of lemon, orange, and almond extracts along with a tad more vanilla. Be conservative, but try to play around a little with flavorings. You will be surprised by the results.

At Passover, however, regular liquid vanilla, because it is alcohol-based and therefore has fermentable components in it (restricted at Passover) cannot be used. Instead, you may use Passover Vanilla Sugar (See The Passover Pantry, page 274), easily available in supermarkets before and during Passover.

Get to know the vanilla you use. As with flour, do not take it for granted. You have choices, and the more you respect your ingredients, especially foundations such as extracts, the better your baking will be.

BOYIJIAN'S LEMON AND ORANGE OIL

These natural oils, which I use instead of lemon or orange extract, are available from a wonderful company called Boyijian's, Inc. Packaged in five-ounce bottles, these oils are the essence of pure, fresh citrus, bottled up for a baker's delight. Similar oils are offered to commercial bakers by supply companies, but they do not compare at all with the quality of Boyijian's (available also from King Arthur Flour and Williams-Sonoma). You can substitute supermarket extracts—orange or lemon—and the results will be good, although these extracts are not as intense or natural-tasting as the citrus oils. Lime oil is also part of the Boyijian repertoire, along with some savory products. When a recipe calls for orange juice and I am out, I substitute water and Boyijian orange oil (say one half teaspoon per cup of water) and the results are exceedingly good.

CITRIC ACID

This ingredient is a mainstay of the Jewish cuisine. I rarely make cabbage soup without it. It is available in the kosher food section of most supermarkets. A granular substance resembling salt, this ultra-zesty, acidic ingredient provides a powerful lemony jolt to lemon cakes. I like citric acid when I want something that is boldly lemony or need to enhance the lemony taste in a cake and yet not upset the liquid balance by adding too much lemon juice.

CITRUS ZESTS

Zest is the colorful outer skin of lemons, limes, etrogs, and oranges without the white pith. It is rife with flavor and essential oils. To use zest, wash the fruit first, scrubbing away chemical residues and waxy coatings. Then, using either a vegetable grater or special zester tool made for this purpose, scrape off the colorful, outer strips. Mince this finely—no one wants to bite into a long strip of chewy zest in the middle of a cake. That aside, finely minced zest ensures equitable distribution of flavor throughout the cake or cookie. I often zest lots of oranges and lemons at once and store the minced zest in the freezer.

Cinnamon

Until I investigated further, I thought all cinnamon came either in a little bottle from the supermarket or in a huge five-kilo, red drum from my bakery supplier. I also thought all cinnamon tasted the same. Not true. Some cinnamons are warm and sweet, almost syrupy and mellow. Some are harsh and acrid, almost medicinal. Penzeys Spice House supplies a choice of cinnamon (and great vanilla, and a zillion others spices and herbs too). Since so much Jewish baking relies on this spice, it is worth checking out.

Smell cinnamon before you buy it. It won't be long before your nose can categorize and file different cinnamon bouquets, and you will become very choosy. I use Penzeys cinnamons and rely on their excellent service, but if you have another favorite spice house, mail order or local, think seriously about getting your basic spices from this source, rather than the supermarket. When you do purchase supermarket spices, smell and taste them before you purchase them to verify their freshness, if possible.

Cocoa

I go through a lot of cocoa and I use many brands—Saco, Droste, Ghirardelli, Van Houten, and Hershey's, as well as Fry's (in Canada). Cocoa is far more drying an ingredient than flour, so measure it properly. Generally, use a dry measure cup to scoop out gently what you need. Then sift it, or use a small wire whisk to free it of lumps and make it more blendable. Cocoa releases its flavor when in contact with liquid. A trick used by bakers I have worked with is to mix cocoa with either melted butter or warmed vegetable oil before adding it to a cake to get maximum flavor.

Chocolate

The general understanding among pastry chefs when it comes to chocolate is that the best ones are usually imported—Callebaut, Lindt, Suchard, and Tobler are some renowned brands. When it comes to chocolate, taste, taste, taste. If it doesn't taste smooth and rich and clear when you snack on it, it will not improve in the recipe. My first choice in chocolate for cookies is Saco chunks. They are excellent. I also use Van Houten chocolate chips, which are manufactured in Vermont. I like using coarsely chopped semisweet chocolate to replace chocolate chips—just for the change. Above all, trust your own palate. Chocolate

can be melted in the traditional way—in a double boiler (usually I set a stainless-steel bowl over a one-quart saucepan filled one third of the way with water) on a low burner. You can also microwave chocolate to melt it—usually one cup of chopped chocolate or chips takes two to three minutes to melt. Stir to smooth out the chocolate and cool before incorporating it in recipes.

White Chocolate Despite its name, white chocolate, is more of a baker's confectionery product, and is made of cocoa butter, sugar, and dry or whole milk. Different brands taste remarkably different from one another, ranging from bland and sweet to waxy and tasteless to smooth and creamy. Because white chocolate contains dairy solids, I use it in recipes that are either pareve or dairy-based, depending on the meal they will follow (if they are following a meal). White chocolate, melted and drizzled, is the easiest way to glitz up anything. Just the name, "white chocolate" has an upscale sound. But before you bake with it, taste it and make sure you like it plain. Inferior white chocolate doesn't transform itself in any positive way through baking.

Baking Powder

The biggest tip I can give about this core baking product is *not to assume* it is fresh. Baking powder should be turned over every four to six months. To test, simply mix a little baking powder with warm water. It should bubble quite vigorously. As with yeast, get into the habit of checking the expiration date on your baking powder. I am always amazed at the extra volume a cake or loaf will have when made with *fresh* baking powder. A fresh can is worth every penny. I tested my recipes with Clabber Girl and

Rumford and have used both for years because I find that they give increased volume, a tender crumb, and no baking powder aftertaste. In Canada, one can also choose the "national" baking powder, Magic brand. I have also used Davis brand with good results but have had the most volume & best overall results when using Clabber Girl. Baking powders can be made of a few different chemical combinations. Once you get used to a certain brand, you get to know what to expect in your baking.

Baking Soda

Baking soda is an ingredient that turns up in preparations that feature acidic ingredients (such as cocoa, orange juice, sour cream, or buttermilk) and usually in conjunction with baking powder. Baking soda balances the acid present in a cake, ensuring proper leavening. Too much baking soda will make a cake taste soapy. Soda is said to have an indefinite shelf life but still, since it can absorb odors from the air, turn it over every three months or so (or pour it down the sink to freshen the pipes). Baking soda brands are pretty interchangeable, but I am used to Arm & Hammer (formerly Cow Brand in Canada).

Baker's Caramel—A Must for Pumpernickel Bread and Bagels

Baker's caramel or blackjack is a natural coloring agent that gives pumpernickel rolls, bagels, and dark rye breads their hearty hue. Essentially it is carbonized sugar—resembling dark brewed coffee in appearance. A runner-up ingredient if you don't have baker's caramel on hand is Kitchen Bouquet—found in supermarkets everywhere. It is a similar potion used to deepen the color of gravies and stews. Kitchen Bouquet is adequate, but it does contain salt and, overall, is less dark than real baker's caramel. Incidentally, a small bottle of baker's caramel should last a home baker quite some time or several hundred bagels. It keeps indefinitely. It may be obtained via the King Arthur catalogue.

Raisins—Treat Them Kindly

I like yellow raisins for some recipes, dark raisins for others, especially when the raisins are going to be part of a dark, fruit filling. But I treat all raisins alike—I plump them first. Nothing is worse than a hard, dry, little raisin nugget, shriveled and tasteless, sitting inside an otherwise moist and delicious cake.

So, always plump raisins before using them. To do this, cover them with boiling or extremely hot water and let them stand for a couple of minutes. Drain well and dry, blotting well with paper toweling, and then use in the recipe. You can also plump raisins in hot orange juice, rum, wine, or any other liquid whose flavor will marry well with the recipe and the raisins.

Sour and Sweet Cherries, Cranberries

Once an exotic, expensive ingredient, sour and sweet dried cherries, as well as dried cranberries, are here to stay. These fruits are like sweet rubies, adding their wonderful flavor, color, and texture to so many Jewish delicacies, and instantly updating old-fashioned favorites. For a change of pace, use either dried sour or sweet cherries, and dried cranberries instead of raisins. I often use both dried and fresh cranberries in a recipe for a spectacular burst of flavor. If the dried fruits you purchase are very fresh, you do not need to refresh them by plumping with hot water. If they seem a little dry, plump them briefly, then dry with paper towels, and proceed with the recipe. Available in supermarkets, and from mail order companies such as American Spoon Foods; see Source Guide, page 353.

Poppy Seeds—Ground

Ground poppy-seed filling, or *mun,* is a mainstay of European-style Jewish baking. For years, I fiddled with grinding my own (See The Quest for Homemade Poppy Seed Filling, page 252) and commercial poppy seed paste. Then I found *both* a proper grinder and a source (Penzey's Spice House), of ground poppy seeds. Homemade filling is far better than canned, but you need to start with a good grinder (I use a Czech grinder—Porkert). Also, some years poppy-seed harvests are good and plentiful and the seeds are fragrant and sizeable (comparatively). Other times, it seems you can barely find poppy seeds (even for bagel making) and when you do, they are not too healthy looking (smaller, less perfumed when crushed). So be picky about poppy seeds, they are not all equal. Again, your safest bet is to order them from a reliable spice store.

EQUIPMENT, OR NAMING NAMES

When you bake with good ingredients, it makes sense to use cookware and bakeware befitting the batters that go into them. Good bakeware that will last and provide superb results is not expensive. As a food writer and baker, I have gone through more than my share of cookware, bakeware, appliances, and gadgets—testing and evaluating a lot of different brands and qualities. Below are some of my recommendations.

The Baker's Basic Batterie de Cuisine

Whenever possible, consider commercial baking pans (particularly loaf pans), available from mail-order sources or restaurant supply stores. Commercial bakeware is durable and baked goods are less likely to burn when made in these heavy-duty pans.

In some cases, regular domestic pans found in gourmet and houseware stores, especially in the case of more decorative, lighter-duty pans such as springform or layer cake pans, are fine. Here is a basic list of the pans called for in this book.

> two large baking or cookie sheets, 15″ × 21″
> two small baking or cookie sheets (also known as jellyroll sheets), 15″ × 11″
> one 9″ × 13″ rectangular pan
> one 9″ × 2″ square pan
> one 9″ pie pan
> one 9″ springform or cheesecake pan
> one 10″ springform or cheesecake pan
> one 9″ or 10″ quiche pan
> one 12″ × 5″ loaf pan
> two 9″ × 5″ loaf pans
> two 8″ × 4″ loaf pans
> one 9″ or 10″ tube pan
> one 9″ or 10″ angel cake pan
> one 12-cup bundt pan or 9″ gugelhupf
> (or turk's head pan, a round fluted pan with a center post and high sides)
> two 9″ round layer cake pans

Bakeware Picks and Pans

For loaf pans, as well as cookie or baking sheets and muffins tins, I use glazed, commercial pans such as Lockwood Brand as well as Chicago Metallic and Ecko. I fell in love with Lockwood after reading James Beard and Burt Wolf's description of them in their great book on cooking equipment, *The Cook's Catalogue,* New York: Harper & Row, 1975, (if you cannot find this book, check out a secondhand bookstore or Internet book search or Strand Books in New York). I use a 12 by 5-inch loaf pan for breads—especially loaf-style (aka "bubka" style) challahs. I use 9 by 5-inch and 8½ by 4-inch pans for cakes and quick breads.

Generally, commercial pans are made of aluminum or tin with a specially glazed reinforced steel frame. Glazed pans are not coated with a surface such as silverstone or teflon but are *treated* pans. These pans are easy to clean and maintain. Breads glide out and, with a little extra nonstick cooking spray, they can be relied on to release your cakes and quick breads without sticking. Hillside Metal Ware in New Jersey makes superb, high-sided springform (or cheesecake) pans of aluminum, and I have had much success with them. The sides on these pans are higher than most and the clip on them is quite hardy. Hillside is generally available in the States and Canada in better houseware departments or kitchen shops. I do not recommend nonstick cheesecake pans since the nonstick sides make it difficult for a slippery cream cheese batter to cling. In Canada, a good option in push-up bottom cheesecake pans (no clip, rather, the bottom of the pan can be pushed up and out) is Blue Bird bakeware. A good source for quality bakeware is the Wilton company and Parrish heavy-duty, aluminum cake pans. I depend on many pans from both these extensive lines, including the classic 9 by 13-inch rectangular pans, round layer pans, and brownie pans. Wilton is widely available throughout the States and Canada and also features many different qualities within the same size and style pan. Parrish's Cake Decorating Supplies Inc. in Gardenia, California, stocks many specialty baking pans. One particular favorite, is a 9 by 4-inch round pan (also stocked by King Arthur) which is ideal for big babkas or soda breads and large, single layer cakes (especially if your 9-inch springform pan is in use). For tart and quiche pans with removable bottoms, especially odd sizes, try any of the mail order sources described in the back of this book. Most of these pans are imported from France.

Many of the recipes in this book call for an angel cake pan, a tube pan, or a large Bundt cake pan. Each cake mold gives a different look to a finished cake. It is worth noting that the Bundt cake pan was first manufactured in response to a request, in 1950, from the Minneapolis Chapter of the Hadassah Society. H. David Dalquist, founder of Nordic Ware, graciously accommodated the local Hadassah chapter, and the result is a bakeware success story. This fluted pan is an ideal choice for just about any coffee cake, honey cake, or babka. Nordic Ware, the originator, still makes the best bundt pans on the market (I have tried them all) in a variety of weights and finishes. I like their cast aluminum pan because it is extra heavy. Angel or tube pans have a center post that helps pull up cake batters. Angel pans are quite high and make for statuesque cakes. I really like these pans for honey cakes. Tube pans are not as high as angel food pans, but feature a wider base—a good choice for quick breads (such as Harvest Zucchini Loaf, page 200), babkas, honey cakes, and coffee cakes. Sometimes you can find a springform pan that offers a tube insert as well as a flat-bottomed insert, giving you two pans in one, so to speak. Hillside makes one of these.

I like Pyrex pans for many reasons but am careful when baking in them. Although you can see how a cake is progressing when you use glass, you must remember to reduce the heat 25 degrees as recommended by Corning. On the other hand, Everybody's Jewish Apple Cake, page 106, would not look the same in any pan other than a 9 by 13-inch Corning dish. Similarly, my Aunt Helen's Cortland apple pies would not look the same in anything other than Corning's 10-inch scalloped edge pie dish.

Electrics

Everyone who visits me assumes I will have a kitchen that is wall-to-wall electric appliances. I have some, but not many. No toaster oven, no electric can opener, no blender. I jealously guard every extra bit of clear, uncluttered counter space. But there are three appliances I could not do without: the food processor, the stationary mixer, and the bread machine. These are my baker's triumvirate—my sous chefs, as it were. If they could talk, they would be my closest friends!

For food processors I tested these recipes with a big-capacity (11 cup) KitchenAid KFP600. I like this model for its extra bit of horsepower, its clear work bowl, near-instant response buttons, the mini-bowl that is a standard component (this allows me to chop nuts and chocolate—becoming a small processor for a smaller job), and a wonderful, trouble-free feed tube that enables me to add eggs, vanilla, liquids—without any cumbersome maneuvering. This machine is a baker's delight. I also have used a large Cuisinart for many years. Mine is an older model and still has the narrow feed tube, which I prefer to the newer models. Nowadays, you will have to find a Cuisinart parts supplier to get this old-fashioned work bowl and feed tube. Both KitchenAid and Cuisinart processors are very reliable, heavy-duty machines that are a baker's right hand—for cutting fat into flour, making coffee cakes, hamantaschen doughs, pie doughs, cookies, rugelach—you name it. That quality, along with capacity (*buy the largest capacity you can*) make these great baker's tools. The larger capacity Cuisinarts are the DCL Food Prep Center (which I have) or the Pro Custom 11, taking 14 cups and 11 cups of ingredients respectively. I also like the Braun processor for its pulse button, range of grating discs, and ease of use. It is a fine choice, offering a lot of flexibility for the baker who is just starting out and perhaps is more budget conscious.

For mixers, I use two different brands—which I adore for different reasons. KitchenAid most closely resembles the commercial Hobart mixers I have worked with. The larger capacity machine is as solid a mixer as you'll ever encounter in a home kitchen. It also looks good, has the three standard attachments (dough hook, paddle, and whisk), can take a lot of punishment, and makes easy work of sponge cakes. The KitchenAid comes in 5-quart and 4½-quart sizes and has a range of options and other attachments. The Rival (known as Kenwood in Canada and Great Britain) is another quality mixer I have tested and rely on. It also comes in a 5-quart as well as a wonderful, professional-duty, 7-quart capacity, which is best for very large families or for those making big batches of bread. The Rival offers a lot of flexibility with its slow first speed (ideal for creaming fussy, dusty ingredients such as cocoa and confectioners' sugar) and a tilt-back head (in the KitchenAid, the smaller mixer has the tilt-back head). One thing is certain—if you are making sponge cakes, a top-of-the-line, heavy-duty mixer is essential. Other stationary mixers and hand mixers are just not the same in capacity, motor strength, or even the mixing/beating action they generate (for more, see Sponge Cakes Made Sublime, page 280). For breadmakers who want a lot of capacity, consider the Swedish Magic Mill. With a generous 8-quart capacity, this mixer is well-known in Mormon and Orthodox Jewish communities, where the bigger bakers in the nation often dwell. A good mixer can be a life-long investment. Consider all the features and options carefully before you decide which one is right for you.

When it comes to bread machines, I have tested about two dozen or more. I use bread machines to prepare yeast doughs, as well as strudels (for more, see The Bread Machine—My Sous Chef, page 36). In fact, every recipe in this book that calls for yeast (and does not exceed six cups of flour) can be made on the dough cycle of a bread machine (method explained in the Bread Chapter). After testing many machines, I am still most at home with Black and Decker's line or my old Zojirushi BBCCs-15A. Black and Decker in particular manufactures very reliable, high-performing bread machines, with many features, and solid company support. Compact and sleek, the Black and Decker does not impose on my counter space (although I now keep my machines just beside my baking counter on a separate "baker's table" or hutch, commonly available at any catalogue store). Zojirushi's bread machines offer flexibility with a helpful "homemade" cycle.

Since I do not generally use the bread machine to bake in—*only to knead the dough*—other bread machines can also do the trick. I have been pleased with results in a Regal and I use it for test baking (the newer Regals even have a "Bagel" cycle!)—and I like the full range of bread machines this company has developed. Other good choices in bread machines include those from Hitachi, Proctor Silex, and Sunbeam Oster. Bread machines are *constantly* evolving.

If you are considering a bread machine (most of the yeast recipes in this book were tested in them, as well as with a regular mixer) *do not* consider a machine whose capacity is less than 1½ pounds (there are still 1-pound and 1¼-pound units on the market.) You want a machine that can knead upward of 5 cups of flour. But, if you have one of the smaller, older bread machines, you can still use it to make babkas and breads. Divide your dough in half and knead a portion at a time (more on this in the Bread and Babka chapters.)

Rolling with the Best

If you are serious about baking, or simply want your efforts to result in better baking, a good rolling pin is a must. I am always on a rolling pin mission (in fact, at one point, I had my own custom pins made, based on a pin crafted for me as a special, treasured gift). If you are lucky, you may have inherited an incredible pin from a loving relative. If not, check out these companies that specialize in American-made, heirloom-quality rolling pins. Each manufactures several models and styles for everyone from new pastry chefs to "master bakers." The finishes are very smooth, so the pins easily release the dough. Poorly sanded, improperly finished pins inhale flour and fat and stick terribly.

Banton, a relatively new company, specializes in outstanding pepper mills of all descriptions and also produces wonderful, well-made, metal-bearing rolling pins of hard Maine maple. A sprightly, classic "best pie in the county," red enamel–handled fifteen-inch pin makes a stunning, and serviceable addition to your collection. Bantom Pins are among my absolute favorites to work with—their slick finish makes dough-sticking problems rare and their design and weight are, for me, ideal. Thorpe Rolling Pin Company, based in Connecticut, makes old-fashioned metal-bearing, steel-center-rod, hardwood maple rollers that are the choice of discerning home bakers and pastry chefs all over the continent. I have several Thorpe pins in my collection. J. K. Adams makes a fine collection of top-quality rollers with rust-free plastic bearings that ensure an easy glide. The Tarla Pin is the design of Tarla Fallgatter, pastry chef, teacher, and restaurant consultant. Unsatisfied with what she found in the market in the way of pins, this pastry chef designed and patented her own. Fallgatter's criteria for "the perfect pin" resulted in "The Tarla Pin," a patented, copper-and-wood pin that is as striking as it is functional. The hardwood pin is wrapped in a heavy-gauge, mirror-finish copper jacket that serves as a stay-cool, naturally nonstick surface. Superb for confectionery work, very thin poppy-seed cookies, and rugelach.

Last, but not least, and certainly unique, is the Kuchenprofi Stainless Steel Pin. Imported from Germany by King Arthur Baker's Catalogue, this unique and sleek stainless pin is exceptional. Weighing nearly four pounds (double the weight of traditional wood pins) this is a particularly good choice for springy, yeast doughs such as danish, thin California-style pizza, or classic strudel, but it can be used for all doughs in between. Chill the pin for a stay-cool surface—perfect for ultra-thin poppy-seed cookies. Pricey but useful.

For the thinnest *mun* cookies and the most delicate hamantaschen, use a pastry or rolling pin stocking available in kitchenware stores and from companies such as Fox Run or Progressive International.

Wood Butcher Blocks for Better Baking, Trouble-Free Rolling

I always roll pastry on wood—sometimes marble, but mostly wood. And I am very fussy about my butcher block counter. It comes from a company I found years ago and continue to rave about, Hollingsworth Custom Wood Products.

You would think butcher blocks are much the same as each other but a well-made, premier quality one is in its own league and earns its way with every baking and pastry task it assists with. Poor ones are made of indifferent maple and sometimes, inappropriate soft woods, and often poorly glued together to make the run-of-the-mill butcher block chopping board. Most of these products are indistinguishable from each other and you'd hardly think to shop for one by brand name. But it is worth it. I visited the plant where my butcher block was made up in "the Soo," Sault Ste. Marie, Ontario. Hollingsworth has been manufacturing their product since 1932. Consumers are just becoming aware of Hollingsworth's line (and now they do mail order) but the restaurant and hotel trades have known about them for years. The sheer density of the hardwood maple (the yield of maple trees that grow in extremely cold northern woods) ensures that rich doughs such as bubka and rugelach rarely stick to the work surface, whereas more porous woods necessitate diligent flour dusting to prevent sticking. But what about the sanitation of wood?

Some years ago, they told us wood boards collected bacteria. Out went butcher block cutting and steak boards and in came plastic and polyurethane substitutes. We hated them, but hey, at least they were cleaner and food service supplies assaulted us with color-coded plastic cutting boards. If nothing else, plastic is pristine. Right? Wrong. Recent, and thorough research at the University of Wisconsin-Madison confirms that mysteriously, bacteria on wood surfaces disappear—up to 99.9 percent in as little as three minutes, while on plastic, bacteria not only remain but multiply. The results, concluded by researchers Cliver and Ak, are not yet scientifically explainable, but they are absolutely conclusive. The good news, however, is that wood— wonderful, honest, easy-to-work-on, and attractive— is also hygienic. To rid wood boards of onion and garlic and other strong odors, clean with a solution of two parts water and one part chlorine bleach or a mild soap. Rinse clean with water, then re-oil with a non-toxic wood oil or a light vegetable oil. However, I suggest you do as I do. Use one smaller butcher board for savory work, such as carrot chopping and garlic smashing or preparing meat. Use another, larger board for all your pastry and baking tasks so there is no transfer of taste from one item to another.

Cookware

Yes, even bakers have to use pots and pans sometimes. I prefer commercial-quality, heavy-bottomed pans that will not scorch cream, butter, or chocolate. In general, aside from some specialty pans, I choose stainless steel because of its looks, durability, and performance. I like deep pots with long handles. I also recommend a couple of extra-small pans—such as 1-quart, 1½-quart, and 2-quart pots or pans— since they come in handy when you are baking. I mix and match a collection of stainless pots, primarily built around All-Clad and Padinox Chaudier. Cast iron is great for baking and serving. Sitram and Bourgeat are other good choices in commercial cookware. Some of these brands are available from commercial mail order companies; sometimes your local restaurant supply store can order them for you.

Little Stuff

I always have extras of the items I use frequently. It makes no sense to have only one set of measuring spoons or one Pyrex measuring cup. I have a couple of sets of stainless-steel measuring cups for dry measuring and several sets of long-handled, stainless-steel measuring spoons. Both my cups and spoons are by Progressive International, a brand widely available in housewares and gourmet shops as well as in mail order catalogues.

These are just about the best measuring cups and spoons you can find. I also stock more than a half dozen Rubbermaid spatulas. Rubbermaid's spatulas (the ones they sell to the trade), are the most hygienic and durable. Wood and rubber spatulas are not the most hygienic. First, you cannot put these combination spatulas in the dishwasher, and because wood-and-plastic cannot offer a totally closed seal, there is room for bacteria to grow and fester. I also keep several paring knives, and a stack of nested stainless-steel bowls.

I would also be lost without my two dough cutters, also known as bench scrapers. This is a wide-bladed tool that can smash garlic, clean a doughy work surface, cut raw dough neatly in portions. My favorite is one made by Lamson & Goodnow, an excellent knife company located in Massachusetts. This company also crafts incredible wood boards that make fine challah boards. I would be lost without my wire whisk collection (many of my recipes call for ingredients to be "whisked" together). Vollrath and Best (both available in restaurant supply stores) are among the best. Before I went to pastry school, I was used to wooden spoons (which I still use), but for blending and whisking and incorporating, a good wire whisk can't be beat. A zester, for all that flavorful citrus zest, is a must, and cheap ones never last. Victorinox makes a fine, durable zester that will last a lifetime and save your knuckles. Some of my favorite knives include Edgecraft, Lamson & Goodnow, Victorinox, and Wustoff Trident. I have a variety of knives—for each company excels in various ways, and each knife is different in heft, grip, blade, and overall design. You may like the parer in one line but adore the 8-inch chef's knife in another. Start with a foundation of solid craftsmanship—particularly for knives—and you should have no problems. Aside from a good zester, your knife collection should include an 8-inch chef's knife, a serrated 10-inch bread knife (a must for homemade challahs and ryes), a 6-inch chef or utility knife, and at least one, if not two paring knives—a regular 3½-inch paring knife and/or a "bird's beak" or curved paring knife to make short work of all those apples you are going to go through at Rosh Hashanah. Lamson & Goodnow also manufactures an irreplaceable "bench scraper"—just the tool you need for bread-making, cleaning your work surface, or making icing smooth and slick on the sides of a layer cake. For cutting fresh bread, I really like Edgecraft's 9-inch bread knife—the grip is good and the knife stays sharp for a very long time.

When it comes to *mun* cookies, rugelach, and hamantaschen, and cutting any sort of shape you want, a company from France, but with warehouses here, called Matfer, makes incredible nested cookie cutter sets—either in tin or a new, durable synthetic called Exoplast. These are not inexpensive but they are irreplaceable. For specialty cutters, try Sweet Celebrations (for a graduated set of star of David cutters) or a unique clay cookie stamp company, the Rycraft company, which manufactures a beautiful star of David cookie stamp—perfect for Yom Kippur or Purim butter cookies.

When it comes to timers, I am very fussy—I like them to be loud, persistent, and accurate. Terraillon makes a round on-a-rope timer that is easy to use and can go with you as you leave the kitchen while your cake is baking. Cooper timers, from Cooper Instrument company, are available in some houseware stores, but certainly in restaurant supply stores and mail-order catalogues. These are king of the heap as far as timers go. I have a small one that also hangs on a cord, as well as a larger, wall- or counter-mounted timer that can be programmed in a number of ways. It does not stop ringing (and you can adjust the volume—very helpful) until you get back to the kitchen and check on your cake or bread. It also will show how many minutes of accumulated extra time a recipe requires (i.e., if you see your cake is not done, the timer will continue counting the extra time the cake takes to bake completely),

making it easier to note in a recipe for the next time you bake it.

Parchment Paper

This product, also known as baking parchment or silicone paper, is something you will never be without once you have tried it. Available on a roll (but it is expensive this way) or in stacked sheets that fit baking pans, parchment paper makes everything easier, cleaner, faster, and generally trouble free. It is available from any baking supply company and can be ordered from companies mentioned in the Source Guide, page 353. I use so much of it that I purchase it in ten- and twenty-pound stacks of some 500 sheets (I often share this with friends.) Most parchment paper is kosher. You should be able to get five and six uses out of the same sheet—providing you are buying a good-quality parchment paper.

Parchment paper is nonstick paper that does not burn. When you line a baking sheet with it, you do not have to grease the baking sheet. Baked goods slide off parchment when they are done. Rugelach does not stick, neither does strudel, or any other sticky pastry. I also cut parchment paper in circles and line tube and springform pans with it to make cakes, particularly honey and chocolate cakes. Parchment paper ensures that I do not lose my cake in the pan when I unmold it. If you do not use parchment paper, make sure you properly grease and flour your bakeware (even nonstick pans) before using. *Do not* substitute wax paper or greased brown paper for baking parchment.

Oven Thermometers and Ovens

So often, we bakers speak of our ovens' "hot spots" or declare our ovens to be "hot" or "fast" ovens. While we like to think we all know (and even like) our ovens' idiosyncrasies, the truth is that ovens are, in fact, about heating coils, thermostats, and inner cavity design.

A "fast" oven probably means your oven's 350° is closer to 375°. Many people grow accustomed to this and learn to compensate with either shorter bakes or lowering the preheat temperature. A better way is simply to invest in a three-dollar oven thermometer and finally know with certainty what you have in the way of heat. If the oven thermostat is off or inaccurately calibrated, it can be adjusted by a service person, and then the mystery is solved. The same is true for a "slow" oven—one whose 350° is closer to 325°. On the other hand, poor oven cavity designs can make for uneven, inconsistent heating (some ovens are really well sealed and designed to the point of being naturally convective; others may suffer from heat leakage or have hot and cold spots). If you have that problem, you may well have to learn to live with this by choosing where you bake certain items (which shelf or rack and at which section of the shelf) or by changing shelf positions.

Using a reliable oven thermometer (brands to rely on are Cooper, Taylor, Pelouze) will guide you toward getting your oven properly calibrated and being able to verify the calibration every few months. Temperature can vary from shelf to shelf, so place the oven thermometer near where the baking dish will be placed.

As far as what type of oven you use is concerned, regular gas or regular electric can be good provided it is properly calibrated. I happen to depend on a commercial-for-the-home Garland range, (aka, a residential commercial range) because I do *a lot* of baking and it is a solid, big-capacity range that has seen more than its share of challahs, cheesecakes, and chocolate chip cookies. Years ago,

when I first started baking professionally and converting my home kitchen into a test kitchen, I chose a single-oven, electric Garland.

More recently, I opted for a gas Garland. My first range was a commercial model which I had to retro fit. Nowadays, commercial range companies (such as Garland, Wolfe, and Dynasty) have come up with a line of "commercial-for-home" ranges that have all the bells and whistles and safety features along with the big look and performance of their restaurant counterparts.

If you are dedicated to baking (and cooking), these ranges are treasures and worth every penny. I particularly like the Garland's ability to bake everything evenly and find I get an extra rise on cakes and muffins. At holiday time, one of the ovens is chockful of honey cakes and mun cookies and hearty French breads and challahs. The other side is roasting the brisket or potatoes, or big pans of chickens and kugel. I love the fact that I do not have to jostle cakes and jiggle roasting pans or schedule the cooking and baking as I have enough room to accommodate my holiday needs without fuss. The rest of the time, my Garland is the heart of my test kitchen. It is a range I can wholeheartedly recommend to any serious home cook and baker. I spent many years with regular ovens (in fact, I even ran a small cake catering company using a General Electric Range as my main oven), making wonderful cakes and cookies, and these recipes have been tested successfully by many friends in their home ovens. If you are interested in commercial-for-home ranges, aside from Garland, there are brands such as Wolfe, Dynasty, Viking, and Thermador. Check a major appliance store in your area or your local restaurant supply store for more information.

I used a small convection oven for a short time and while it was good for some baked items, it made a crusty, sugary top or finish on others. The heat is supposed to be more even in a convection oven, but just turning a cookie sheet around midway through baking does the trick. Professional or commercial convection ovens work better in my opinion, since they are substantially different in design. If you have a convection oven, you might find you have to reduce the baking times for some recipes. Always check on your foods—don't abandon them.

Which Rack to Bake On?

Unless it is mentioned specifically, I bake most things on the bottom or middle rack of the oven. When baking on the bottom rack I *always* use doubled-up baking sheets—even if I am using a loaf pan, I put it on the doubled up baking sheets. I tend to use the bottom rack when baking two batches of cookies at the same time, or for pastry, such as rugelach or tarts, where I want a nice crisp bottom. I also use the bottom rack if I am making an especially tall challah that might, baked on the middle rack, hit the top of the inner oven cavity. I use the middle rack for cakes, squares, and other items that do not require a more intense heat.

Freezing Cakes

For major family holidays (excluding Passover), I often bake ahead. I always have a variety of bakery boxes on hand (available from bakeries for a nominal price) that fit cakes, pies, tortes, batches of cookies, and so on very nicely. Just box and label, and you're all set. Having bakery boxes greatly simplifies things, especially if you are going to be toting a honey cake as a gift. Boxed up, it looks professional, and no one has to worry about getting a pan or a piece of Tupperware back. I also keep decorative bakery bags to store mun cookies, hamantaschen, and rugelach. Again, baked goods stored and offered this way make for neat, professional, and appetizing gifts. Honey cakes can be made a couple of days ahead, covered well in plastic wrap, and left to mature. They need not be frozen. I also suggest you use a "cake liner" when making loaf cakes. These are made of silicone paper and are shaped to fit a 9 by 5-inch or 8½ by 4½-inch loaf pan. Usually white, with accordion pleating that expands as the batter fills the liner, these are something every Jewish bakery has in great supply. I purchase mine by mail from Sweet Celebrations. Aside from looking clean and neat, honey cake easily releases from the loaf pan in which it was baked if you use a cake liner.

Winning Recipes for the Bakery Challenged

Some people are new at baking—"bakery challenged," if you will. Some of us are great cooks but hesitate to work with flour and dough. Personally, despite my classical training, I have always been a "minimal effort, maximum effect" chef, so I like things easy. It leaves me more time to bake other treasures and better yet, be with people I love.

Easy means:

- ingredients are always on hand— in the pantry
- little preparation or special techniques
- no special tools or pans
- can be mixed by hand
- fool-proof results

Winning Recipes for the Bakery-Challenged

Majestic and Moist New Year's Honey Cake, page 128

Double Chocolate Chip Cookies, page 300

Layered Apple Cinnamon Cake, page 160

Friday Night Bread Machine Challah, page 44

Melt-in-Your-Mouth Mun Cookies, page 103

Double Fudge Chocolate Tube Cake, page 110

Apple Strudel in the Round, page 142

Frozen Cheesecake with Brandied Cherries, page 236

Caramel Matzoh Crunch, page 278

Blitz Cherry Cake, page 91

Malai Romanian Cottage Cheese Cornmeal Kugel, page 321

Incredible Cinnamon Chip Cake, page 97

Chanukah Gelt Double Fudge Chocolate Layer Cake, page 230

Decadent Fudge Brownies, page 298

Quick-and-Easy Cinnamon Apple Strudel, page 88

Free-Form Apple or Plum Tart, page 150

Triple-Toned Mandelbrot, page 95

1. Breaking Bread

Celebrating the Jewish Seasons with Flour and Yeast

Di libeh iz zis, mit broit iz zi besser.
"Love is sweet, but it's nicer to have bread with it."

A groiser oiven—a kleine challah!
"A big oven—a small loaf!"

—YIDDISH PROVERBS

Jewish Bread at the Table

As far back as I can remember, bread has played an important role in my home. Store-bought sliced challah, onion rolls, pungent rye bread, dense, rustic Russian black breads with cracked wheat, and sour, seeded corn breads were always to be found on our kitchen counter. Bagels brought back from a pilgrimage to our favorite, legendary shop, never lasted very long. It seemed the same in the homes of my friends and relatives. Households and families differed in many ways, but in the ways of bread we were the same. A slice of challah with soft butter was a typical snack. Smooth-as-silk chopped liver topped with caramelized onions, on a small slice of rye bread made a meal. Onion rolls or pletzels hastily filled with a slice of deli salami were easily devoured by my brothers and myself. Always, bread figured in some way in the meal.

Jews, along with many cultures throughout the world, revere bread. The simplest meal is made special by the presence of a humble loaf. Bread is so special that there is a Hebrew blessing over all breads. And though the blessings on Friday night over the wine and candles precede the blessing over the challah, it is only after the prayer for the bread has been performed does the meal begin.

The luncheon that follows a joyous kiddish after a *brith,* starts with the blessing over the bread. A bar mitzvah feast waits until the rabbi blesses the ceremonial challah. A couple in a new home receives a first gift of a loaf of bread and some salt—edible symbols for *mazel,* or good luck, in the new abode. Bagels, served at times of mourning and at times of rebirth, such as at the birth of a new child or at the end of the Yom Kippur fast, are another indication of bread's integral place in the meaning of Jewish life. Round bagels—unending circles of the life cycle—so much meaning in a good munch!

For any Jewish family celebration, be it the high holy days or a life passage such as an engagement supper, or simply a big Sunday brunch with friends, there is one phrase, pertaining to planning, that will be uttered at some point or another.

It is this: *"Did you remember the bread?"*

Bread is never an afterthought. It is focal.

Bread Basics

As a kid, I recall making bread as quite an ordeal. Usually bread was store-bought. I saw making a loaf as a noble, weekend pursuit that was intriguing. But I didn't know much about yeast, was terrified by it, in fact. I didn't know much about water temperature, or when a loaf was done, or how much was enough kneading (let alone how to knead). I knew nothing about rising times, only that letting it rise until doubled in bulk took *forever!* Who even knew when it was risen enough? And this business about punching down the dough, for years, I thought this meant to re-knead the dough. When all along it simply meant to deflate the gases out of it before forming the loaf. Who knew?

But the more I baked, the better I got. Also, I had my grandmother, who lived with us, praising all my efforts. It was a great incentive. Who wouldn't want to please a bubbie?

In the meanwhile, I began to get more informed about bread tools and ingredients. I discovered mixers with dough hooks. I found a source for bread flour. Instant yeast arrived, and then came bread machines. New cookbooks that illuminated the mystique of yeast and gluten filled the bookstore shelves. Homemade bread-baking was getting ever easier. I thrived on these new inventions, and aspired to be a better baker.

These days, bread is still an art, but easier, and

success is more attainable than ever. Whether or not you are an experienced baker and an accomplished breadmaker, you can make outstanding breads utilizing any one of a number of methods: by hand, bread machine, or an electric mixer with a dough hook. There are also fool-proof ingredients, such as heartier-bred yeasts and terrific flours on the market, and heavy-duty baking pans for better-crusted breads.

The most important thing to remember about bread is that no matter how dismal it seems, it will turn out. Either the loaf will be a high-rising success and you will get challah, or it will stay put and not rise and you will get matzoh or pita bread. *But it will all still be edible, as well as fresh and warm and fragrant.* You really cannot fail, and you are always on your way to better. Once you realize that it will be okay, no matter how it turns out, you will lose your fear. The truth is, more often than not it works out. So drop your fear of yeast and adopt a cowboy attitude—there's a whole frontier out there to discover.

Food Processors and Bread Kneading

Some cookbooks and cooks enjoy the food processor as a bread-making tool. I adore the processor and would find it hard to run my kitchen without one—in fact, I think of my food processor and mixer as the "dynamic duo" of my kitchen. I like the processor for a number of jobs, such as cutting fat into flour, making streusel topping, and whipping up a batch of mandelbrot or hamantaschen dough, or any one of many oil-based or butter cakes. But I am less drawn to the idea of the processor as a dough kneader. I know some colleagues who would use nothing but the food processor for bread doughs, especially very slack, wet doughs, but I see the blade as cutting through, rather than manipulating the dough, and severing the gluten strands. The blade also gets quite warm and that heat

can be transferred to the dough, increasing it to a temperature that might cause premature fermentation. How could something that whirls the dough around for thirty seconds (usually the time needed to shape bread dough into a ball in the food processor) replicate the same eight-to-twelve-minute kneading process other methods provide? Also, how could a whizzing blade replicate the gentle under and over maneuver of kneading?

With so many methods available, home bakers have some solid choices. If you like this method and have spent years making your breads successfully, by all means, do what works for you. One's own experience is always the higher truth. But do consider some other options.

HANDS-ON BREAD-MAKING

It goes almost without saying that hand-made anything is better. Hands are just not replaceable by machines. Hands feel and perceive, and we rely on our sense of touch to transmit messages about the dough. Machines rely on the baker's sense of sight to receive these same messages. As with anything else, hands-on bread is wonderful, but not all of us have the time or inclination to hand-knead. Fortunately, there are options available— noble options—which I talk about later in this chapter.

True, bread-making, any hand work in fact, is therapeutic and contributes to health. But you might prefer to work at your loom or easel or sketch pad while your bread machine does the dough. Or you might be more inclined to cradle a tired toddler who of course, gets priority over dough! But no matter what method you choose, even if you are not using your hands alone—you still must always finish a dough by hand, deflating it, shaping it, and finishing it with a glaze or some other wash, to make it ready for the oven.

If I could, I would do everything by hand, but that would mean giving up something else. In other words, if I am making our daily bread (and I do), cookies would have to go, or I would have to forget another household task or activity. So I preserve my hands for where nothing else will do—pastry-making and French breads (which require exceedingly slack, wet doughs), for example. And I respect the inventions, such as dough hooks and bread machines, that, *used with judgment and discretion,* have become my assistants in the baking process. But I never turn the whole job over to them. I think the main point is not to be such a purist that you do not make bread at all unless it is all hand-done. That attitude probably results in more store-bought bread than any lack of expertise.

The rewards of eclecticism, if you embrace it, are great.

Bread-Making by Hand

Without a machine, your hands are the horsepower. To develop the gluten properly in higher protein bread flour, you must give the dough a more ample knead than perhaps you are used to if you are habituated to kneading doughs made with all-purpose flour. Slap the dough around once in a while and let it rest for a couple of minutes (giving you a rest) between kneading. This is probably the best way to find out how dough functions and behaves. You can feel with your hands how the dough's nature changes and matures. Kneading dough by hand, much like pie pastry–making, is still a satisfying and relaxing activity. As with bread machines and dough hooks, add additional flour if the dough is too sticky. Time will take care of much of the stickiness, but add

some flour—judiciously—if you need it. If you are a purist devoted to this method, carry on. Breads made by hand are outstanding and have a very personal touch.

THE BREAD MACHINE— MY SOUS CHEF

I often joke with friends that my bread machine is as close to having help in the house as I will ever get. Designed to manufacture completely baked, warm, ready-to-eat-bread-for-breakfast from start to the finish, bread machines really have another manifest destiny. Rather than using a bread machine for *baking,* use one for making and proofing or rising dough. Then bake the bread in your own, conventional oven. You will be surprised how creative you can get when you have already-proofed dough, ready to work with.

When used for the whole process, dough mixing, kneading, and baking, bread machines are quite limited. First of all, you can only bake as big a bread as your machine can accommodate, which is generally a bread based on three- or four cups of flour. *But . . .* if you use the bread machine as a dough kneader and proofer, you can use five to six, even seven cups of flour in that same one-and-a-half-pound unit. This amount of flour makes a considerably bigger bread or babka or batch of bagels.

Next, bread *made-and-baked* in the machine is very good but not exceptional. The restrictive cavity of the bread-machine baking pan prevents the bread from enjoying the expansiveness it deserves and needs. In the oven, bread can stretch out and be as expansive as it wants. Oven temperatures can be adjusted; the bread machine temperature cannot—it is always around 350°F. Bread in the machine is always that weird shape. Machine-made dough but *regular-oven* baked means you have an opportunity to shape the bread into a babka or braided challah. And face it, challah baked in a vertical loaf, straight out of the bread machine, is not challah—it is vertical egg bread. In shaping the dough, you also have a chance to play and work with it. This is satisfying and helps you feel more connected to the bread and the baking process.

I know waking up to fresh bread, baked while you sleep, is beguiling stuff. I don't dispute the appeal, nor the impressive technology behind it. As a baker, I also know, however, that the bread machine's best, unsung, unexploited attribute is its two other functions, kneading and proofing. I use my bread machine for lots of doughs, and really rely on it for things I make all the time—such as Friday night challah dough or countless batches of bagel dough.

If you have carpal tunnel syndrome or any discomfort using your hands from whatever cause, bread machines are a blessing. You can still have homemade-tasting bread without imposing on your hands—so don't wave good-bye to yeast baking because of muscular ache. And for those of you who are terrified of yeast and bread-making itself, I also advise investing in a bread machine. Bread machines offer a wonderful, safe way to get used to working with yeast, since you can count on some sort of success, no matter how much of a novice you are. As one friend said, "If all I ever did with it was make Friday night challah dough, it would be worth its weight in gold." If you love to bake and are knowledgable about baking, a bread machine will make you soar. You can use your hands for rugelach rolling and pastry-making and creating slack, French-style sour doughs; your mixer for cakes and tortes; and your bread machine for yeast doughs. Believe me, you will not have sold out—you will be busier than ever. Your whole kitchen will be buzzing with baking activity! One success will lead to another.

Your interest will grow as you move with ease from one recipe to another.

Bread Machine Method

Pretty well every bread and yeast coffee cake or babka recipe in this book can be made on the Dough cycle of a one-and-a-half pound bread machine. Only larger recipes should be done by hand or with a mixer with a dough hook (usually recipes exceeding six cups of flour).

For making challah, as well as most other breads, I generally put the warm water called for in the recipe in the machine first. Next comes the yeast and a pinch of sugar. I wait a couple of minutes and allow the yeast to dissolve or swell. Then I add the remaining sugar or honey, oil, eggs, flour, and last the salt.

I kick-start the yeast's activation with the water and a pinch of sugar before adding other ingredients. My main focus is to avoid having the salt in the recipe in direct contact with the yeast.

For using the bread machine to make babka doughs, consult the Bread Machine Method for Babka Dough (page 329). For a unique experience that will leave you incredulous, check out Stretch Strudel dough from the bread machine (page 152). Yes, you can even make strudel dough in the bread machine.

Bagels are especially superb done in the bread machine, as the nonstick sides of the pan allow you to produce a very slick, dense dough that is a requirement of great bagels.

As your machine is working the dough (during its knead cycle), check on it once in a while. It may need more flour. If so, dust in about a tablespoon at a time. The dough should form a soft ball and clear the bottom of the bread machine pan. As dough is kneaded, it develops somewhat, and time, along with additional flour, will help it reach the proper consistency.

If your dough seems to be having trouble getting mixed, carefully poke the flour and liquids together, using a rubber spatula, thus encouraging the ingredients to combine. Sometimes things need a little extra help getting started, particularly when you are using more than four cups of flour.

Take the dough out when the cycle is over and continue on with the recipe for rising and forming the bread, and later, baking in your traditional oven. Properly risen dough is usually flush, or a bit higher than the top of the bread machine pan.

Bread machine brands are discussed in the Equipment section on page 23.

DOUGH HOOK WITH ELECTRIC MIXER METHOD

After hands and chef's knives, dough hooks are probably one of the best inventions to come out of kitchen appliance history. (Although the dough hooks we speak about here have to be attached to the best standing mixers, such as KitchenAid.) When using a stationary mixer with a dough hook attachment, you can start by hand-mixing the ingredients together as prescribed in the recipes. Once this mixture can no longer be easily mixed, it is time to use the dough hook and knead for the amount of time stipulated in the recipe. Use the slow speed since too rigorous a kneading speed will oxidize a dough (it will look whiter in color) and later on result in a fine-grained, rather than airy, crumb. To start a dough, you can also use the paddle attachment until the dough is too thick to be handled this way. Then, attach the dough hook and, on low speed, knead the dough for the time prescribed in the recipe. Dust in more flour as required to get the dough to a soft, elastic consistency.

Dough hooks and stationary mixers are great tools with which to make bread. A stationary mixer has a larger capacity than a bread machine (bread machines can take three to six cups), and the larger mixers (five-quart KitchenAid, for example), can accommodate up to eight cups of flour. Essentially, stationary mixers can outdo bread machines in the range of tasks they perform (cakes to breads to pastries, et cetera) and in capacity. But I find I require both appliances to keep my kitchen humming.

BAKING SHEETS AND DOUBLE SHEETING— OR NO MORE BURNT BOTTOMS

Use heavy-duty commercial baking sheets, if you can get them. Usually these are glazed at the factory where they are manufactured to be permanently "nonstick." Made of tin or aluminum and reinforced with steel rods, these sheets never buckle or warp and offer even heat distribution. I recommend you use two baking sheets (whether you are using commercial sheets or regular ones) stacked together for baking free-form or braided loaves. The bread will bake properly, without risking a burnt bottom. This is a ploy I also use for baking cookies. Cookies baked on the bottom rack of the oven are more protected this way (I use only a single sheet for the upper-rack batch of cookies). Double-sheeting gives you a few extra minutes if you are delayed getting back to remove something from the oven. Another good occasion to use double sheeting is when baking cakes, such as honey or chocolate, that can scorch easily. I double-sheet habitually these days, but for recipes that really profit from this tactic, I have included a reminder in the baking instructions.

Plastic Bag Proofing Tent—
The Easy Way to Get
Bread to Rise

For yeast doughs to rise properly, they should be in a moist, warm environment. Some books counsel one to cover rising doughs with greased plastic wrap and a damp tea towel. Often, this method produces doughs that rise beyond their limits and stick to the plastic wrap or tea towel (which dries out as the dough is rising, thus becoming a dough magnet).

Instead, I place the dough and baking sheet or loaf pan *entirely* in a large supermarket plastic bag (for cake pans or loaf pans) or in an oversized, clear, plastic bag such as Hefty. I loosely seal the bag with a twistie or knot it closed. Placing the whole affair in a plastic bag is like making your own proofer (or proofing tent) for the rising dough. The bread is safe from drafts and humidity forms inside the bag (doughs love humidity). An extra precaution to ensure that the dough does not dry out or form a crust or skin while it is rising is to spray the dough with a mister before inserting it in the plastic bag. I find that spraying the top of the dough, then water-misting a plastic drawstring bag and sealing it up, works best and is the neatest method of all.

Large, drawstring bags are usually found in the supermarket where plastic trash bags are kept. Clear ones are often available and certainly make things easier (you can see how the dough is rising) but if not, use the more common black or green ones. Smaller clear bags (if you can find them) are ideal for yeasted coffee cakes that are in tube or angel cake pans. I keep small amounts of dough—yeasted or not—in Ziploc bags. You can also use painter's plastic, found on the roll or in packages, from hardware stores. These are large sheets of clear plastic used to protect furniture from paint splatters. Drape these plastic sheets lightly over rising dough.

When dough has its first rise (and this is something to look out for, especially when you are using an instant or "bread machine" yeast), take care not to let it rise too much—only two thirds of the way, not the traditional "until doubled." You want the dough to rise but not overferment. It will have another chance to rise the second time around.

Adventures in Challah

Although they're supposed to be unbiased, the plain truth is that most professional bakers do play favorites. For one of my colleagues from pastry school days, it's French bread—chewy, crusty, rife with holes. Another baker friend's daily mission is to confect countless whipped cream and ganache triple layered tortes, only to go home to experiment with his organically grown wheat berries and festering sour dough starter to make rustic hearth breads. As for myself, I admit it, as a professional pastry chef and baker who happens to be Jewish, I am a challah freak. As soon as I try one challah recipe, I invent another one. Frankly, it doesn't take much to motivate me; the idea of another great "concept" challah always seems to be lurking around the corner. Further still, elusively out of reach on my baker's horizon, beckons "The Definitive Challah"—a lifetime quest.

What baker would not be drawn to the silky, cream-colored dough, the supple, accommodating texture, the rich yeasty fragrance that emanates as a challah bakes? Slightly sweeter than most breads, richly eggy, sometimes featuring a hint of honey, with a sesame or poppy-seed topping, wonderful fresh or several days later, challah is a bread with fans far beyond its ethnic boundaries. As with French bread and European rye, challah is internationally appealing. Who doesn't agree that it is the foundation for superlative French toast, the throne for sweet butter, or the natural habitat for late summer sliced tomatoes?

Friday nights are delegated to elegant, not-too-rich, not-too-sweet, bulka, or loaf-style challahs. Nicely sweet and best warm-from-the-oven challah rolls make for great snacks, while butter-based challahs make outstanding sandwich bread.

It seems unnecessary to confess that when the Jewish New Year rolls around, I am more than casually anticipatory. The Jewish New Year brings the season of honey and apples, raisins and pomegranates. It is also big challah territory, and the historically ceremonial bread, fashioned into a rounded spiral shape, almost like a turban, is the crowning centerpiece of the festive table. Rosh Hashanah challahs, also known as *faigeles* (See page 120 for the New Year's Sweet Round Raisin Challah recipe) are traditionally circular, as well as a bit sweeter than the usual homemade or regular supermarket challah. When cut, the Rosh Hashanah challah reveals a host of plump raisins, symbolizing the holiday's signature wish for sweetness in the New Year. After the New Year drifts into other autumnal Jewish festivals, you can similarly segue to any one of the recipes from this challahs-for-all-seasons collection.

Challah Basics

Fresh yeast makes the most incredible challahs, but dry yeast, generally the first choice of home bakers, properly used, will still make outstanding loaves. Since challahs are rather rich, I find much success when I make them with the very durable, so-called instant yeasts. (For more about yeast, check out the Ingredients section, page 7.)

EGGS

Large, not extra-large, are the size eggs to use for these recipes. Warmed-up eggs work best, for challah is considerably richer than most breads and needs all the support it can get. Ice-cold eggs really impede any dough's development, but in challah, they are not recommended. Cover the eggs, still in their shells, with very warm water for one to two minutes before using them. Your reward for this minor, extra step will be a good inch or two more height in your bread.

HONEY VERSUS SUGAR

In challahs, I use honey for flavor, sugar for convenience and for sweetness without too distinct a flavor. A combination of the two, in some recipes, sometimes works for me; other times, such as during Rosh Hashanah, I use more honey for that special New Year's touch. For sandwich challahs, I often use sugar alone. If you want to substitute honey for sugar, do so in equal amounts. You might have to add a bit more flour to compensate for the added liquid. Also, challahs made with honey brown more and faster, so watch them at the end of their baking.

Challah Braiding

The easiest braid, and the one I usually do, is a simple three-strand one. I know many people who are proficient at braiding and it seems almost everyone can produce a family member: an aunt, a bubbie, a great grandmother, who could do a multitude of braids. Much as I admire such talent, I have just never devoted myself to this task, focusing instead on developing yet another quintessential challah. But make no mistake, visually, six and five braids are stunning and at the core of challah craftsmanship, in itself a culinary art form. The more braids you have, the more peaked the challah looks. There are countless books about both Jewish and non–Jewish braided breads that illustrate, in numerous, imaginative ways, the ease of braiding.

But there are also some easier ways to get some very pretty challahs.

Some commercial bakers simply make a large, three-strand braided challah and a "mini" three-braided one, which they place on top of the first one. My favorite way of making our Friday night challah is to make a large challah, braid it with the three strands, and place it in a nine by twelve-inch loaf pan. In this way I get a loaf-shaped bottom with a twisted or braided top, which is very attractive. Best of all, the deep loaf pan supports the rich challah dough, preventing it from spreading out sideways (although multi-braided breads are also a good insurance against this.) Made in this fashion, even slack challah doughs rise mile high. Another preferred method I use is to simply take three or four balls of challah dough and place them side by side in the loaf pan. As the balls rise, they fuse together and produce a triple or quadruple humped loaf that looks like a fancy bakery bread. The laziest method, which results in an absolutely gorgeous bread, is to cut the dough, using a dough cutter or a very sharp, large chef's knife, into four or five large chunks. Stack these side by side in the large loaf pan. Glaze, seed, and bake. Stunning and unique!

NOTE: **New Year's challah and a specialty apple challah, as well as Sabbath challahs are found in their respective holiday chapters.**

Sponge-Starter Challah

Makes 2 medium-large loaves, or one very large loaf

A sponge-based bread is best described as the poor man's (or woman's) sourdough bread—very little planning (unlike real sourdough breads) or fiddling and feeding starters required. It does make use of a sponge leavener (a pudding-like mixture of flour, water, and yeast) to give the bread a kick-start, and produces the most moist and light-textured challah you have ever made or tasted. Sponge-based breads are not new, but they are regaining popularity among home bakers. In the unlikely event you have leftovers, you'll find this bread doesn't seem to get stale—a good thing if you are considering it for Yom Kippur. This is a large recipe—I often knead it by hand or in two half-batches in my KitchenAid fitted with the dough hook.

SPONGE STARTER
(30–90 minutes ahead—longer won't hurt)
1½ cups warm water
2 tablespoons dry yeast
Approximately 2 cups bread flour

DOUGH
All of the starter (above)
½ cup warm water
¾ cup sugar
3½ teaspoons salt
3 eggs, at room temperature, plus 1 egg yolk
½ cup vegetable oil
6–6½ cups bread flour

EGG WASH/TOPPING
1 egg plus 1 egg yolk
Pinch of salt
Pinch of sugar
Sesame or poppy seeds, for sprinkling

SPONGE: In a very large bowl, place the water and dry yeast and then mix together. Allow the mixture to stand for a couple of minutes to let the yeast swell or dissolve. Stir in the flour to make a soft, thick puddinglike batter. Cover the sponge with plastic wrap and leave it for 30 to 60 minutes. If you see the sponge is rising beyond the limits of the bowl during its fermentation period, stir it down.

DOUGH: Stir down the spongy mixture in the work bowl, then add the rest of the water, the sugar, salt, eggs, yolk, oil, and about 5 cups of the flour. (If you are using a mixer with a dough hook, stir down the sponge and put it into the work bowl.) Work with your hands, a large wooden spoon, or the mixing paddle of your mixer to make a soft dough. Mix until the dough is not smooth but a messy mass. Cover it with a damp tea towel and let it sit for 15 to 20 minutes (this allows the dough to relax; it changes its character by absorbing the flour better. It will be a lot easier to manage). After this rest period, knead the dough with the dough hook or by hand until it's smooth and elastic, 10 to 12 minutes, adding more flour as required to make a dough that is easy to handle (i.e., not too sticky or tacky).

Shape the dough into a ball and place it in a lightly greased bowl. Place the bowl in a large, clear garbage bag and seal it loosely. Let it rise in a draft-free, warm environment, until almost doubled, anywhere from 45 to 90 minutes. (You can also give it an overnight refrigerator rise if you are doing this a day in advance.) When the dough has risen, whisk together the ingredients for the egg wash.

Gently deflate the dough. Divide it in half for 2 loaves. Form the dough into loaves, braided or loaf style (this dough also makes good rolls). Place them on a parchment-lined baking sheet, and brush the bread thoroughly with egg wash. Sprinkle with sesame or poppy seeds. Insert the entire baking sheet in a large, plastic bag and loosely seal. Let the loaves rise until doubled, 45 to 90 minutes.

Preheat the oven to 375°F. Place the bread in the oven, *then reduce the heat to 350°F* and bake until the breads are medium brown in color, 30 to 35 minutes for 2 loaves; 40 to 45 minutes for 1 large loaf. Cool in the pan for 10 minutes, then remove to a rack. Slice a loaf when it's room temperature if you can wait.

NOTE: If the dough seems too massive or unmanageable for your mixer (depending on the weather and kitchen humidity and how much flour you add overall), you may remove half of it and allow the machine to knead one portion at a time for the allotted time. I have not found this necessary with my KitchenAid or Rival, but if you are concerned about straining your mixer's motor, just knead half at a time.

Friday Night Bread Machine Challah

Makes 1 large loaf or 2 medium loaves

*Bread machine–made dough, but regular-oven baking (do not bake this recipe in a
bread machine—it is too large), makes for superb and easy challah as well as other breads.
This recipe is for 1½-pound or larger-capacity machines.*

1¼ cups warm water
⅓ cup plus a pinch of sugar
4 teaspoons dry yeast
2 eggs plus 1 egg yolk
2 tablespoons honey
⅓ cup vegetable oil
Approximately 6 cups bread flour
2½ teaspoons salt

EGG WASH/TOPPING
1 egg plus 1 egg yolk
Sesame or poppy seeds, for sprinkling (optional)

In the bread machine pan, place the water and the pinch of sugar. Stir in the yeast. Let the mixture stand for a few minutes to swell or dissolve the yeast. Then add the ⅓ cup of sugar, eggs, yolk, honey, and oil. Add 1 cup of the flour, then the salt, and almost all of the remaining flour.

Put the machine on the Dough cycle. After a couple of minutes the dough should begin to form a mass. If not, use a rubber or plastic spatula to assist the dough in coming together. Dust in the remaining flour, a couple of tablespoons at a time, as the dough is kneaded. It should form a soft ball and clear the bottom of the pan. If the dough seems wet, even after it is well into the kneading cycle, add additional flour as required. (You will also notice on humid days, or just due to seasonal changes, that the recipe will absorb a larger amount of flour. This is normal.)

When the Dough cycle signals done (the dough will have one rise in the machine), remove the dough from the machine and gently deflate it. Whisk together the ingredients for the egg wash and set aside.

Divide the dough into 3 sections and roll or form into 3 strands. Braid the 3 strands and put the bread on a parchment-lined, doubled-up baking sheet or in a lightly greased 9 by 5-inch loaf pan. Alternatively, form each of the 3 portions into a ball. Lightly grease a 12 by 5-inch loaf pan (or two 9 by 5-inch loaf pans—in which case, make 4 balls). Place the balls of dough beside each other, almost touching, in the pan.

Generously brush the bread with the egg wash. Place the whole loaf pan or baking sheet in a large plastic bag and loosely seal the bag. Allow the bread to rise, 30 to 40 minutes, until it is almost doubled. Remove from the bag and brush again with the egg wash. Sprinkle on sesame or poppy seeds, if desired.

Preheat the oven to 375°F. Place the bread in the oven, and immediately reduce the heat to 350°. Bake for 30 to 35 minutes, until the crust is nicely browned.

VARIATION: For Bread Machine New Year's Challah

Increase the sugar to ½ cup and decrease the salt to 2 teaspoons. Halfway through the Dough cycle, add a cup of raisins to the dough. Form, using the instructions for New Year's Sweet Round Raisin Challah on page 120.

White Whole Wheat Honey Challah

Makes 1 large loaf

*Even those who reject whole wheat flour will take to this challah made with lighter-tasting,
new wave, "white whole wheat" flour. It's a slightly nutty and lightly sweet golden loaf. If you cannot find
white whole wheat flour in your supermarket, it can be ordered from Hodgson Mill or King Arthur. Regular
whole wheat flour is also fine, but the dough will be a trifle stickier and heavier. The resulting challah
will be hearty, rich, and flavorful no matter which type of whole wheat flour you use.*

1½ cups warm water
4 teaspoons dry yeast
¼ cup plus a pinch of sugar
¼ cup honey
1 tablespoon salt
⅓ cup vegetable oil
3 eggs
2 cups white whole wheat or regular whole
  wheat flour
4 cups bread flour

EGG WASH/TOPPING
1 egg, beaten
Sesame or poppy seeds, for sprinkling

In a large bowl, stir together the water, yeast, and pinch of sugar. Let the mixture stand for 3 to 5 minutes for the yeast to swell or dissolve. Then, stir in the honey, the remaining sugar, the salt, then the oil and eggs. Fold in the whole wheat flour, then most of the bread flour to make a soft, shaggy mass. Knead for 8 to 10 minutes, adding more flour as required to make a soft, elastic dough that does not stick to the mixing bowl. Doughs made with whole wheat flour are somewhat stickier, and profit from a longer kneading.

Shape the dough into a ball and place it in a lightly greased bowl. Place the bowl in a large plastic bag, sealing it loosely. Let the dough rise until almost doubled, 45 to 90 minutes. Then gently deflate it. Whisk together the eggs for the egg wash.

Divide the dough into equal parts and roll or form it into 3 strands. Braid the 3 strands and place the bread on a parchment-lined baking sheet. Let it rise until puffy and almost doubled in bulk, 35 to 45 minutes. Alternatively, divide the dough into 3 equal sections and shape each one into a slightly oval-shaped ball. Place the ovals, almost touching, side by side in a well-greased 12 by 5-inch loaf pan.

Brush the dough with egg wash and sprinkle with sesame or poppy seeds. Place the baking sheet or loaf pan with the dough in a large plastic bag to rise until the dough is almost flush with the top of the pan, 45 to 60 minutes.

Preheat the oven to 350°F. Remove the risen loaf from the plastic bag and place the bread in the oven. Bake until well-browned, 28 to 35 minutes in free-form style, or 45 to 50 minutes in a loaf pan.

Buttery Egg Bread

Makes 1 large loaf

Buttery challah seems almost to be a contradiction in terms—as challah is specifically a nondairy bread, making it appropriate for serving with a meat-based Sabbath meal. This is why vegetable oil is the usual fat in an authentic Sabbath challah. This bread, more appropriately called "egg bread," suitable for dairy meals, uses butter to emphasize the bread's rich, velvety texture. The result is a Jewish-style brioche. It is the perfect sandwich bread to accompany sliced fresh tomatoes or tuna salad, or as a lovely loaf offered after the Yom Kippur fast. This recipe also makes fabulous rolls or egg twists.

1¼ cups warm water
1 tablespoon dry yeast
⅓ cup plus a pinch of sugar
2½ teaspoons salt
½ cup unsalted butter, melted
4 eggs
6–7 cups bread flour

EGG WASH/TOPPING
1 egg, beaten
Sesame or poppy seeds, for sprinkling (optional)

In a large bowl, stir together the water, yeast, and pinch of sugar and let the mixture stand for 5 minutes, until the yeast swells or seems dissolved. Stir in the remaining sugar, the salt, melted butter, and eggs. Fold in the flour to make a soft, shaggy mass. Knead for 8 to 10 minutes, adding more flour as required to make a soft, elastic dough that does not stick to the mixing bowl.

Shape the dough into a ball and place it in a lightly greased bowl. Place the bowl in a plastic bag and seal loosely. Let the dough rise until almost doubled, 45 to 90 minutes. Then gently deflate it.

Divide the dough in 3 parts. Roll or form each part into a long strand and braid the 3 strands. Place the bread on a parchment-lined baking sheet. Brush the dough with egg wash and sprinkle with the poppy or sesame seeds, if desired. Insert the baking sheet into a large, clear, plastic bag and let the dough rise until puffy and almost doubled in bulk, 35 to 45 minutes. Alternatively, spray a 12 by 5-inch loaf pan with nonstick cooking spray. Divide the dough into 3 equal sections. Shape each into a smooth ball or slightly oval round. Place the dough balls, almost touching, side by side in the prepared loaf pan. Brush with egg wash and sprinkle with sesame seeds. Place the loaf pan in a large plastic bag to rise until the dough is almost flush with the top of the pan.

Preheat the oven to 350°F. When the dough has risen, remove it from the plastic bag and place the bread in the oven. Bake until well browned, 27 to 30 minutes; 35 to 40 minutes for a loaf-style bread.

RYE BREAD BASICS AND NICK THE BAKER

I have a baker friend named Nick Arcolakis who owns a wonderful wholesale bakery, the Elmont Bakery, in Montreal. When I first began wholesaling cakes years ago, I rented baking space from Nick—and made my carrot cakes and cheesecakes in a small nook in his bakery, not too far from where his bread production was going on.

From this experience, I learned a lot about baking. I always enjoyed seeing his crews of bakers at work, tending the vats of dough, nursing sourdough starters, rotating bagels, slicing fresh challahs, and scaling and molding countless varieties of rye breads and miniature rolls (intended for restaurant bread baskets), slashing French breads, dusting with flour those armies of country-style white breads that covered every bit of space available at each baker's table.

The air at Nick's always smelled warm and yeasty—it is one of the best, most comforting aromas in the whole world. The atmosphere was always busy and intense. On some days—before and after Yom Kippur in particular, or just before Rosh Hashanah, it was absolutely frantic. After Yom Kippur, there is a huge demand for more fresh bread with which to break the fast. Between times, it was just, as most good bakeries are, a very hectic, lively, passionate place.

I don't think anyone knows more about rye bread than Nick, and there are few delicatessens that serve up succulent slices of famous Montreal smoked meat—an extra spicy, tender pastrami—without Nick's rye bread underneath them. One day, long before I was doing the amount of yeast baking I now do, I saw Nick's rye bread in the making. A sponge or sourdough starter caught my eye. It was in a huge trough, filled to the brim with the seething, frothy, rye flour and water, all stewing away. It was almost alive! When I asked what was in the trough, Nick casually replied: "Oh, that's the starter for the rye bread. No yeast at all. It takes eight hours to make. Then more rye flour, white bread flour, and salt . . . caraway seeds are added to make the rye dough. Other bakers do not do that; they make a straight dough rye but I make a starter for the flavor." When I innocently (and erroneously) suggested to Nick that he "hurry up" the process by adding yeast to his starter, he became quite animated— almost frenzied. "No, no . . . never!" he exclaimed. "You cannot hurry up flavor, especially in rye bread." I had never seen Nick so excited. I had obviously touched a nerve. Rushing a rye bread was just craziness.

Actually, many Jewish bakers are the same way: the only way to get proper texture and flavor from a rye bread is with a starter, a sponge, or a sour . . . all varieties of a slurry that kick-starts superior rye breads. Of course, rye bread can be made without a starter, and many home bakers do that. However, they always notice that their breads do not taste at all like the bakery's rye.

The rye-based recipes in this book call for short or "quick" starters, rye sours, or sponges. But even a starter of one to two hours vastly improves the flavor and texture of the bread.

Nick always brushes his breads with a cornstarch glaze (see page 49) for shine. Home bakers can do the same, or if you prefer expediency over authenticity, simply brush your rye breads with a beaten egg white before baking.

The final thought on rye breads is rye flour. To test these recipes, I started with supermarket rye flour. The bags were marked "light" or "medium" rye. Occasionally I found a bag marked "dark." I even tried bulk ingredient stores, but it was really hard to tell what kind of rye flour occupied the scoop-it-yourself buckets. When I looked at all these rye flours I had purchased, I could hardly tell the difference between them. The breads that resulted from these flours were fine, but not outstanding, certainly not rife with rye fragrance—you know, that wafting, slightly sour aroma that advertises "Rye Bread!" loudly, before you've had a bite. The breads were also dull brown inside. They tasted all right, but these breads were still not what I had in mind. I called the people at King Arthur and immediately ordered light, medium, and pumpernickel rye flours. What a difference a bag makes! It was the same when I tested with Hodgson Mill rye flour. Exceptional rye breads start with exceptional rye flour.

Now, these were really rye flours—fresh, pungent, and each one different (in color, texture, performance). Now, I use a white rye flour for a very light, deli-style rye, and primarily a mixture of medium rye and pumpernickel rye flour for other rye breads. You can use medium or pumpernickel rye for any recipe here. The point is, all flour makes a difference. But supermarket rye flour, in particular, since it is often mislabeled (you just can't tell what you are using) and is not optimally fresh (because turnover is slow) is not a great option if you are fussy about rye bread. Actually, fussy or not, you are taking the time to make rye bread, it is worth every bit of effort to acquire proper rye flour. It is about freshness and character, which is what rye breads are all about.

Jewish Baker's Cornstarch Glaze

This is a typical mixture that professional bakers use to get that characteristic sheen on their rye breads. I have seen my friend Nick Arcolakis use this many times.

¹/₂ cup water
2 tablespoons cornstarch

In a small saucepan, with a small whisk, stir together the water and cornstarch. Heat the mixture to a gentle boil. Stir, lowering the heat, until the mixture thickens and is translucent. Cool. Brush on rye breads about 10 minutes before the baking is finished, and again 3 minutes before the bread is completely done.

Seeded Sour Rye

Makes 1 large loaf

*If you like rye bread, take the time to find good, fragrant, rye flour—preferably from a
flour company like Hodgson Mill or King Arthur. Supermarket rye flour has far less flavor. If it is all you
can find in a pinch and you are determined to make rye bread—give it a go. Specialists in rye use a well-
maintained rye starter sometimes called a rye "sour." The method described here is a good introduction for
home bakers looking to launch their first rye bread experience.*

Sponge Starter (2–8 hours ahead)
1 cup warm water
1 tablespoon dry yeast
¼ cup bread flour
1¼ cups dark rye or pumpernickel flour
2 tablespoons caraway seeds

Dough
All of the sponge starter (above)
¾ cup warm water
2 teaspoons sugar
2½ teaspoons salt
Approximately 3 cups bread flour

Cornmeal for dusting the pan
1 egg white, beaten, for glaze (optional)
Jewish Baker's Cornstarch Glaze (page 49—
    optional)

SPONGE: In a large bowl, whisk together the water
and the yeast. Let the mixture stand for a few minutes
to allow the yeast to swell or dissolve. Then stir in the
bread flour, rye flour, and caraway seeds to make a
very thick, puddinglike mixture. Add a bit of water if
it is too thick. Cover with plastic wrap and let the
starter sit from 2 hours to overnight.

DOUGH: Stir down the sponge with a spoon. Then
add the water, sugar, salt, and bread flour (reserving
about ½ cup to use as required). Knead for 10 to 12
minutes, by hand or with the dough hook of a
stand-up mixer. As the dough begins to form a soft
mass, add more flour as required to make a soft
dough.

Shape the dough into a ball and place it in a well-
greased bowl. Place the bowl in a plastic bag and seal
loosely. Let the dough rise until almost doubled, 45
to 60 minutes.

After the first rise, gently deflate the dough. Shape
it either into a large ball, squeezing it together at the
bottom to fuse the seam, or into an elongated bullet-
shaped loaf (for sandwich-style rye).

Line a baking sheet with parchment paper and
dust it with cornmeal. Gently place the bread on the

pan, seam side down. Brush it with a beaten egg white or, after baking, brush it with Jewish Baker's Cornstarch Glaze (page 49).

Place the whole baking sheet inside a large plastic bag, or lightly cover the bread with a large sheet of plastic. Let the dough rise a second time until it is puffy and 40 to 50 percent larger (from 45 to 60 minutes). Slash the bread with diagonal cuts about ¼ inch deep, or leave it plain. Brush again with a beaten egg white, covering any missed spots (when the bread rises this might happen), if you are not using the cornstarch glaze.

Preheat the oven to 375°F. Bake in the preheated oven until the bread sounds hollow when tapped, and is nicely browned on top (30 to 35 minutes).

VARIATIONS: For onion rye, add 2 tablespoons dehydrated onion flakes or fresh minced onions to the sponge starter.

For marble rye twist, use one batch of Seeded Rye and one batch of Russian Black Bread (recipe follows). Divide each batch in 2 (you will be making 2 loaves). Roll each portion into an 8-inch rope. Pinch the ends of one light rye and one dark rye bread together. Twist the 2 ropes. Place on a parchment-lined baking sheet. Repeat with the remaining 2 ropes. Proceed with the recipe as written.

Russian Black Bread (Dark Pumpernickel)

Makes 1 large bread

*One of my favorite breads—hard to tell it does not come straight from a
New York City Jewish bakery—fragrant, moist, full of character.*

SPONGE STARTER (2–8 HOURS AHEAD)
1 cup warm water
1 tablespoon dry yeast
1 cup dark rye or pumpernickel flour
1/4 cup bread flour
2 tablespoons caraway seeds

DOUGH
All of the sponge starter (above)
3/4 cup warm water
1 1/2 teaspoons dry yeast
4 teaspoons brown sugar
2 3/4 teaspoons salt
1/2 teaspoon malt powder or syrup (optional)
4–6 teaspoons baker's caramel
3 1/2–4 cups bread flour
Nonstick cooking spray
Cornmeal, for dusting the pan

GLAZE/TOPPING
1 egg white, beaten, or Jewish Baker's Cornstarch
   Glaze (page 49)
Cracked wheat, caraway seeds, or black cumin-
   seed

SPONGE: In a large bowl, whisk together the water and yeast; let the mixture stand a few minutes to allow the yeast to swell or dissolve. Add the rye and bread flours and the caraway seeds. Stir to make a thick, pudding-like mixture. Cover with plastic wrap and let the mixture sit from two hours to overnight.

DOUGH: Stir down the sponge with a spoon. Then add the water, yeast, brown sugar, salt, malt, baker's caramel, and bread flour (hold back about 1/2 cup to use as required). Knead for 10 to 12 minutes, by hand or with the dough hook of a stand-up mixer. As the dough begins to form a soft mass, add more flour as required to make a soft dough.

Shape the dough into a ball and place it in a lightly greased bowl. Place the bowl in a large plastic bag and seal it loosely. Let the dough rise until almost doubled (45 to 60 minutes).

Lightly grease a 5 by 12-inch loaf pan with non-stick cooking spray. Lightly sprinkle cornmeal on the bottom.

After the first rise, gently deflate the dough. Divide it into 3 equal parts. Shape into 3 balls, and place side by side in the pan. Alternatively, shape all the dough into 1 large ball and place it on a parchment-lined, cornmeal-dusted, doubled-up baking sheet.

Spray the bread with nonstick cooking spray and place either the loaf pan or the baking sheet in a large plastic bag. Let the dough rise a second time until puffy (40 to 60 minutes). Brush it with egg white and sprinkle with caraway seeds or cracked wheat. If you use the Jewish Baker's Cornstarch Glaze, still use the egg white to make the seeds adhere. Then use the glaze as instructed during baking.

Preheat the oven to 375°F. Put the bread in the oven and bake until the bread sounds hollow when tapped (35 to 40 minutes).

The New Bread

Makes 1 very large loaf

I was tempted to call this "Walla Bread"—for it is a hybrid of challah and white bread, less rich than challah, but richer than white bread. When I mentioned it to friends, I referred to it as "the new bread" and asked for their help in testing it. The name "the New Bread" stuck, and so did this great recipe. It is perfect for any holiday or informal occasion—it even makes fantastic hamburger buns—just ask tester Janet Goldstein, who makes this bread more than any other. I made this with fresh yeast in the bread machine, but it is wonderful with dry yeast as well. Deceptively simple, this bread is a winner. Bake it on the lowest rack of your oven—it tends to grow high enough to almost touch the roof of the oven's interior—even in my commercial Garland!

1¼ ounces fresh yeast, or 5 teaspoons dry yeast
1½ cups warm water
½ cup plus a pinch of sugar
⅓ cup vegetable oil
2½ teaspoons salt
¼ teaspoon malt powder or syrup (optional)
Approximately 6 cups bread flour, plus extra for dusting

Spray 12 by 5-inch loaf pan with nonstick cooking spray.

In a large bowl, stir together the fresh yeast (just crumble it up) or dry yeast, warm water, and pinch of sugar. Let the mixture stand to allow the yeast to swell or dissolve. Then stir in the oil, the remaining sugar, the salt, malt powder, and most of the flour. Knead for 6 to 8 minutes, to make a firm but soft, smooth dough. Shape the dough into a ball and place it in a well-greased bowl. Put the bowl in a plastic bag, seal loosely, and let the dough rise until doubled, about 45 minutes.

Gently deflate the dough. Divide it into 3 equal portions. Shape each piece into a large ball and place the 3 balls, side by side, in the prepared pan. Alternatively, place the 3 balls side by side (they will fuse as they rise) on a parchment paper–lined baking sheet. Spray the bread with nonstick cooking spray and generously dust it with flour. Place the pan in a large plastic bag, seal loosely, and let the dough rise until doubled in bulk (30 to 45 minutes).

Preheat the oven to 375°F. Remove the risen loaf from the bag and bake until well-browned (30 to 35 minutes).

Brothers, or a Baker's Best Friends

It is a myth among small children that their aunts and uncles are just that—born and bred as aunts and uncles. They cannot figure out, any more than we could at their age, that to be an aunt or uncle, one has to be first a sister or brother. The other thing young ones have a problem with is understanding that even adults, such as their moms and dads, can laugh and like and love their siblings, just as they do their own brothers and sisters.

If you are lucky, as I am, you start life as a sister to two older brothers. They baby-sit you as a toddler, entertain and protect as you grow, help you with homework, fabricate Halloween costumes and snow forts, and, between bouts of teasing, generally love you. Things change as you transform from daughter to sister to wife to mother. But the core of sibling love endures.

My boys see me as "Mom," but their uncles, my brothers, Lorne and Mark, still see their kid sister. When we get together, we still giggle and cavort, becoming absolutely giddy with silly memories. Between times, we help each other out.

My brother Mark, one of the few Renaissance men I know, is a media and marketing consultant, carpenter, photographer, musician, and cowboy. He is on hand for *everything!* When I fretted that my kitchen was not organized, he immediately designed and built a "baker's center" for me—a place to house all my different flours, topped with a butcher-block work surface. In return, I was supposed to bake up apple and raisin pies, but I never got around to it. I do make sure my chocolate chip cookie jar is always full, in case he shows up. Another treasure from Mark is a lovely maple challah board. It is a generous, elongated oval, made-to-measure in fact ("Marcy, just measure your next Friday night challah and fax me the length in inches!").

My brother Lorne, my fellow Taurean, is the family lawyer, patiently tolerating all my legal questions over the years, doing his utmost to help me navigate my culinary career. "Can I copyright a recipe?"; "Can I trademark my carrot cake?" are just some of the questions I badger him with. His advice and calm, reasonable tone, in the wake of my usual hysteria over something (which often turns out to be trivial, manageable, or academic), is always available. No fee, no strings, not even any "I told you so's."

As for me, I am always on hand as the family baking council. Both my brothers are excellent cooks and bakers themselves, but they do respect my skill and training. It is the only time when I get to be the "older" one. I keep them in recipes, flour, and yeast. When the phone rings, they may forget even to say hi and just launch into their latest bread adventure (I got them both into bread machines early on).

When I was younger, I recalled that my mother and her brother, my uncle Harry, called and yakked frequently. My father and his sister, my aunt Helen, as well as his brother, my uncle Ralph, throughout their adult lives, called each other every day. I could not fathom this. They had their own families and their own lives. What could they find to talk about each day? How much catching up can you do? Sometimes it seemed they were saying nothing new—just chatter about family and business. I didn't realize it was a generic conversation of connection. It was about that unique bond between siblings.

Often, when I am on the phone with my brother Mark, one or another son will try to interrupt. One of the others will hiss, "Shhhh, Mom's talking to her *brother*!" They understand by my tone that the conversation is special. And now I better understand about sibling bonds.

My Brothers Mark and Lorne's French Bread (*aka* My Favorite French Country Bread)

*I designed this recipe for my brother Mark, who, after buying a bread machine,
hounded me for a recipe for French bread. Every time I explained how it was not so simple and that
French bread was more the result of a technique than a recipe, he seemed to lose interest. Rather than lose
a good baker, I created a simple method, based on an old technique along with a new age bread machine,
to produce a French-style bread at home. Soon, my brother Lorne was making it too, using his own
adaptations, and the two were competing.*

*Easily made either in the bread machine set on the Dough cycle or traditionally (with a dough hook
or hand-kneaded), this recipe results in a real country French bread—hearty, rustic, and crusty. I
always offer this bread at holiday time. It usually sits beside a freshly baked challah
(which proudly rests on Mark's maple challah board).*

SPONGE STARTER (4–16 HOURS AHEAD)
1 cup warm water
½ teaspoon dry yeast
1¼ cups bread flour
3 tablespoons rye or whole-wheat flour

DOUGH
All of the starter (above)
1 cup warm water
½ teaspoon dry yeast
2½ teaspoons salt
2¾ teaspoons sugar
¼ teaspoon malt powder or syrup (optional)
Approximately 4 cups bread flour

SPONGE: In a small bowl, mix together the water and yeast. Allow a few minutes for the yeast to dissolve. Stir in the bread flour and the rye or whole-wheat flour. Stir to make a thick mixture. Cover and let stand, on a counter, 4 to 16 hours.

DOUGH: Stir down the sponge and put it into a large bowl or an electric mixing bowl. Add the water, dry yeast, salt, sugar, malt powder (if using), and most of the flour. Stir to make a soft mass, then knead for 8 minutes, by hand or using a dough hook on slow speed, adding more flour as required to make an elastic, supple dough.

Shape the dough into a ball and place it in a large, well-greased bowl. Place the bowl in a plastic bag and seal loosely. Allow the dough almost to double in bulk (45 to 90 minutes). (This dough can hang around for bit—you don't have to rush. If you are not going to be around during the day, place it in a

continued

lightly greased bowl, cover, and put it in the refrigerator for a long, slow, cool rise. Deflate the dough and allow to warm slightly before proceeding.)

Gently deflate the dough and form it into a ball. Place it, seam side down, on a doubled-up baking sheet (2 sheets stacked together). Place the entire baking sheet in a large plastic bag, seal loosely, and allow the dough to rise a second time until it is puffy and almost doubled in bulk.

Preheat the oven to 475°F. Slash or cross-hatch the loaf with ¼- to ½-inch incisions using a sharp knife. Spray the dough with water, dust it with flour, and place it in the oven. Spritz the oven interior every few minutes for the first 15 minutes (be careful not to spritz the oven light), then transfer the bread to the lowest rack, lower the heat to 425°F and continue to bake for another 10 to 20 minutes, until well-browned. Cool well on a rack, uncovered, before slicing.

BREAD MACHINE METHOD FOR MY FAVORITE FRENCH BREAD

Since I usually make My Favorite French Bread using the bread machine to prepare the dough, here are detailed instructions.

STARTER: Add all the starter ingredients to the bread machine pan and start the bread machine, on any cycle, just a few minutes to dissolve the yeast and make a thick mixture. Turn off the machine.

DOUGH: Add the remaining ingredients to the starter mixture in the bread machine. Set the machine on the Dough cycle. As the dough begins to mix, it should form first a soft mass, then eventually a ball that is not too stiff but not sticky either. Add flour as required to reach this consistency.

Remove the dough from the machine and proceed with the recipe as directed.

Bagels at the Holiday Table. The Circle of Life in a Ring of Dough

If chicken soup is "Jewish penicillin," bagels must be Jewish "soul food."

Az men est op dem baigel bleibt in keshene der lock. "If you eat a bagel, only the hole remains in your pocket."

Over the years, I have made a lot of bagels. When I did a whole feature on them for *Eating Well* magazine, I became even more obsessed. I make bagels, eat bagels, buy bagels, munch and assess, then get back to making and baking. It is a never-ending (but fun and satisfying) process.

As with pizza, bagels are an ethnic snack that has successfully crossed the food and culture line to achieve mainstream status. Good with anything, bagels are just everyone's favorite. Show me someone who doesn't like bagels, and I'll show you someone who has never had one. (All right, maybe they have, but I'll bet it wasn't a good one.) On the Jewish table, bagels are inevitable, comforting, and always appropriate. The most popular, accepted meaning of bagels, vis a vis the Jewish cultural calendar, is that they represent, through their round form, the ceaseless, never-ending continuity of the life cycle. We find bagels at *shiva* houses—served with eggs, as a reminder, even in a bleak moment of loss, that life does go on. We find them at life's most joyous event, the birth of a baby, or the joyful kiddish that follows a *brith*. A new baby, a renewed life cycle and, of course, break out the bagels. At Yom Kippur, we make many wonderful things to eat for the after-the-fast dairy meal, and bagels are the focal point. Again, the new year has begun, and bagels are a part of it. Bagels can be found at a Shavuot brunch, offered at a late Saturday breakfast, a Sunday brunch, as a midnight or mid-afternoon snack. For special times, for any time, bagels are just the right thing to serve. But, where did they come from?

A bagel, food historians explain, is a boiled, then baked yeast bun with a hole in its center. Bagels were brought to North America by European Jewish immigrants. Writer Leo Rosten mentions in his book, *The Joys of Yiddish,* that the first printed usage of the word *bagel* is in the "Community Regulations for Cracos," which stated that the item was given as a gift to women in childbirth. A nice gesture perhaps but probably grossly unappreciated by a laboring woman.

In *Deli,* Sue Kreitzman quotes a 1946 newspaper article describing bagels as a "doughnut with rigor mortis," a most unfortunate misconception although the point is well-taken. Oven-fresh bagels are worth a king's ransom, while stale contenders can be used as lethal weapons. In other words, freeze 'em or eat 'em, but don't let them hang around.

Hot! Hot! Hot! Authentic, From-Scratch Bagels at Home—the Hole Truth

As a professional baker and bakery consultant, I have seen many bakery treats become huge trends, peak, and eventually become classics. Carrot cakes, chocolate chunk cookies, and oversized muffins—to name a very few—come to mind. But bagels, those wonderful rings of boiled-then-baked dough, are not your average flash-in-the-pan success story. We can thank bagel maven Murray Lender's diligent marketing of this specialty product for ensuring national familiarity. But bagels have earned and retained their spot on the mainstream menu on their own merits, and it doesn't take a rocket scientist to figure why.

Bagels are innately low in fat, low in sugar, a diet-friendly complex carbohydrate, as easy on the budget as on the bulge, suitable with everything, and as comforting as an old friend. Not a roll, not a bread, but a unique hybrid, a bagel is at once crusty, amber-colored, and hearty looking. A hot bagel, along with its unrivaled aroma, fortunately, tastes as good as it looks: chewy yet crisp, honest, down-to-earth, wheaty in taste, satisfyingly simple. On their own, bagels are divine, but used as the foundation for a multitude of toppings, they become a meal in themselves.

Tricks of the Trade Yield Tasty Bagels

You don't have to live in a big city to enjoy the real bagels. But more than that, the unbelievable fact of the matter is that homemade bagels are both quick and easy to make, and are about the best bagels you will ever have. What's more, you can have them fresh as you demand, at the size you can indulge in. Thanks to dough hooks and bread machines, *and* the availability of superb bread flour, baker's malt, baking stones, and other ingredients previously denied to the average home baker, authentic homemade bagels are a reality. Someone once said that "good baking is just a series of little things done well," a philosophy that is the bagel creed. Assuming you have the best and most appropriate ingredients, making great bagels is a small matter of the right recipes and craftsmanship.

In essence, almost everything you have ever learned or read about traditional bread-making is *not* true of bagel-making. Bread is carefully balanced in order to produce a crumb structure that is somewhat light, perhaps riddled with some holes. Bagels you want dense, even slightly stodgy, but certainly not aerated or too developed. Bread dough should be as soft as the proverbial baby's bottom. Bagel dough should be stiff to the point of slickness (all the better

to hold its shape as the bagels are formed, kettled, and baked). Bread dough has a reasonable rise or fermentation period, punch down, a shaping, and then a final rise. Bagels are barely allowed to rest, let alone enjoy a leisurely rise. They inflate when they are kettled (the boiling bath) and have a final last gasp in the oven before the yeast finally dies and the bagel structure is set. If you allow bagels to rise too much before being shaped, the dough becomes slack and the hardy rings cannot hold their shape in the subsequent boiling water bath. Also, you lose that characteristic and appealing denseness. The finishing step is kettling again, or boiling the bagels, and is responsible for their shine. The water should be at a healthy simmer to allow for the proper gelatinization of the outer crust. Except for pretzels, bagels are the only bread that is boiled first, then baked.

Freeze fresh (but properly cooled) bagels pronto unless you are consuming them all that day.

THE RIGHT STUFF: AUTHENTIC INGREDIENTS FOR AUTHENTIC BAGELS

You can make bagels from ingredients sitting in your pantry and produce good results. But using dedicated bagel ingredients—strong bread flour; fragrant, mealy pumpernickel flour, baker's caramel; malt syrup or malt powder, to name a few, will render absolutely superlative results. Here's the run-down on some "bagel basics."

WATER

People love to think that New York bagels are special because of New York water. But the water in every city is different—as is the air, the climate, the humidity, etcetera. And all these things affect bagels—as they do sourdough bread, challah, whatever you are baking. But start with a good recipe and sound technique and you will come pretty close to replicating what you are after. Water will not make or break an otherwise superlative bagel (unless the water is foul and polluted or reeking with chlorine). Anyway, depending on where you live, you have two choices—buying bottled water or using tap water. If you are maniacal, you can always tote water back from New York City or from any other place you think has the best water for bagel-making.

After water, come some other basic ingredients:

MALT

Malt gives bagels their mystique and marvelous flavor and is a part of bagel history in America. Malt can be called "malt powder," "malt flour," "dry malt," or "malt syrup." No matter which malt you use, it will work for bagels (although dry malt is easier to work with than the syrup). Still, some professional bakers swear by it (others deny it has any business in their bagels) and it is an ingredient that home bakers often have to search for. Malt assists with browning, feeds the yeast, and adds authentic bagel flavor. You can find malt syrup—look for an unhopped, light variety—in any home beer brewing store or sometimes in the supermarket baking aisle (Premier Malt is one brand). Opt for malt powder or flour for ease of handling. If you want to get started right away and don't have malt on hand, use brown sugar instead. It's not malt, but better to substitute than not to make bagels at all.

BREAD FLOUR

This is the kind of flour I prefer for bagels—especially if you are using a bread machine or an electric mixer with a dough hook. This type of flour has enough gluten, the flour's protein, to give a finished bagel its chewiness and crustiness. If you can find unbleached bread flour in your supermarket, grab it, or order it from a mail order source. If you are hand-kneading, use unbleached all-purpose flour. All-purpose flour makes for slightly less chewy bagels but is good for helping attain that bland, dense stodginess, which is also a positive thing in a bagel. So, if it is a rainy day, you have no bread flour, and you want to start bagel-making, do give it a try. You will still have reasonable bagels.

DARK RYE, PUMPERNICKEL, LIGHT RYE, COARSE RYE (SEE PAGE 10)

YEAST

Bagels use comparatively less yeast than other bread recipes. These recipes work with either active dry yeast or instant or fast-rising yeast. If you want to adjust your bagels' texture, increasing or decreasing the yeast by small increments (a half teaspoon more or less) is one option. More yeast makes for airy, spongier bagels; less yeast results in denser, firmer bagels. Fresh yeast, of course, is ideal—most recipes would work with three quarters ounce of fresh yeast to replace the dry.

BAKER'S CARAMEL OR BLACKJACK (SEE PAGE 22)

OVEN BAKING STONES

Most retail bagels are hearth-baked—that is, directly on the oven floor or on pine or spruce boards that sit on the oven floor. Industrial or commercial bagel operations use special bagel rack ovens to accelerate and regulate production. At home, a good, easy compromise is to bake the bagels on a baking sheet and then turn them over once onto a preheated baking or pizza stone. The somewhat porous stone sucks any moisture out the bagel bottom and you wind up with a nice, crisp finish. The stone also radiates an intense heat, which helps replicate the hearth oven. I use doubled-up baking sheets for my bagels, starting them off on the lowest rack of the oven and, halfway through, switching them to the upper rack. Other times, I start in the middle of the oven, and place the bagels on a baking stone for the last few minutes. Homemade bagels have somewhat flatter bottoms than commercial bagels, but they still taste exceptional.

BAGEL TECHNIQUES

As with challah, bagel dough can be made almost any way you require, depending on your preference of kneading procedures or the equipment on hand.

By hand, kneading bagels is a rigorous task (it takes longer to activate the gluten in bread flour, which is a bagel-ingredient must) that only the dedicated are attracted to. If you are kneading by hand, it is best to use all-purpose flour (see page 8).

If you have a mixer with a dough hook, make sure you give the bagels a sufficient knead on low speed. Kneading too fast is not recommended—it overoxidizes the dough, causing it to whiten in color and, ultimately, to lose flavor and character. Better to knead nice and slow for best results.

Food processors also do a relatively good job on bagels. Place the ingredients in the work bowl, starting with the water and ending with the flour, but being careful not to let the yeast and salt come in direct contact with each other. Process until the dough forms a ball and continue for one or two minutes more. Processors will make for denser bagels, which is not undesirable.

Bread machines are one of your best bets for bagels, making superb bagel dough, as trouble free as you would want. The nonstick baking pan in bread machines enables a bagel dough to absorb more flour more readily. This yields an optimally stiff bagel dough. When using a bread machine, just dump the ingredients in the order given (avoid having salt touch yeast, however) and put the machine on the Dough cycle. As soon as the dough is mixed and has had its final knead, remove it from the machine and continue on with the recipe. Do not allow the dough to sit and rise in the machine, awaiting the cycle's customary completion. While most bread machines stipulate a three-cup capacity for bread-making, their dough-making capacity is greater, and most machines can easily manipulate four to almost six cups of flour, although sometimes you may have to assist the mixing process by manipulating the dough with a plastic spatula. I often make several batches of bagels—using my bread machines to make consecutive batches of dough. What's great is that since bagels must be hand shaped and then boiled and baked, my hands are free to do this work while the bread machine handles the dough-making task.

New York–Style Water Bagels

Makes 10 bagels

If the secret ingredient, as New Yorkers contend, to these classic bagels is indeed the water, out-of-town bakers are out of luck. However, these bagels are still a good replica of what many think is the definitive bagel.

1½ cups warm water
1 tablespoon dry yeast
1 tablespoon sugar
1 tablespoon vegetable oil
2 teaspoons malt powder or syrup (optional)
4½–5½ cups bread flour
2 teaspoons salt
Cornmeal, for sprinkling the pan (optional)
Toppings of choice of (optional—page 62)

KETTLE WATER
6 quarts water
2 tablespoons malt syrup
1 teaspoon salt

In a large bowl, whisk together the water, yeast, and sugar. Let the mixture stand for a couple of minutes to allow the yeast to swell and dissolve. Stir in the oil, malt (if using), and 1 cup of flour. Add the salt, then most of the remaining flour. Knead for 10 to 12 minutes to make a very stiff dough. Cover the dough with a tea towel and let it rest on a board for about 15 minutes.

Meanwhile, line 2 large baking sheets with baking parchment and sprinkle each generously with cornmeal. Fill a large soup pot or Dutch oven with the 6 quarts of water. Add the malt syrup and salt. Bring the water to a boil. Preheat the oven to 450°F.

Divide the dough in 10 sections and form each one into a 10-inch-long strip. Roll the ends together to seal and make a ring. Place the bagels on a very lightly floured surface near your stove and let them rest for 15 to 20 minutes. Bagels should have a half proof—that is, they should rise halfway or appear puffy.

Prepare 2 more baking sheets, lining one with a kitchen towel, the other with parchment paper sprinkled with cornmeal, if desired. Reduce the water to a simmer and add the bagels a few at a time. Allow them to come to the surface and simmer for 30 seconds. Turn them over and cook the other side for about 45 seconds more (a total of 1½ minutes). Place

continued

the boiled bagels on the towel-lined baking sheet. Leave plain or sprinkle on the topping of your choice.

Place in the oven, reduce the heat to 425°, and bake until done (17 to 22 minutes), turning the bagels once and switching the baking sheets once to ensure even browning. If you have a baking stone, finish the bagels directly on the stone (see page 59).

Topping Variations for New York–Style Water Bagels:

Sesame seeds
Poppy seeds
Dry or rehydrated garlic granules
Dry or rehydrated onion flakes
Minced fresh garlic
Minced fresh onions
Caraway seeds
Coarse salt
The "Everything" bagel: minced onion flakes, poppy seeds, granulated garlic, and coarse salt

Additions to Water Bagels:

Some are satisfied with classics, others can't resist gilding the lily. If you want to make your bagels more exotic, you can add (while you are mixing the dough):

Granola (1/4 cup)
Other extracts, such as maple (1 teaspoon)
Citrus zests (1 to 2 teaspoons)
Fresh herbs (1 to 3 teaspoons)
Replace some of the flour with oat bran, wheat bran, cornmeal, spelt, and so on.

Or, after the dough has been formed, gently knead in:
Frozen chopped or dried cranberries (1 cup)
Frozen or dried blueberries (3/4 cup)
Dried cherries (3/4 cup)
Nuts and seeds (1/4 cup)
Miniature chocolate chips (1/4 cup)
Shredded Cheddar cheese (about 1 cup)

MONTREAL BAGELS— A CANUCK LEGEND

Montreal may be the "Paris of the North" but just ask any American tourist who's ever been there (and all my Mendham, New Jersey, cousins who crave them!) about one of this city's specialty (the other being Montreal smoked meat). Montreal bagels are always made in a wood-fired bagel oven and are sweeter, enriched with honey, eggs, and oil, almost devoid of salt, and scaled smaller. The lack of salt allows the taste of the generous sesame seed coating to really shine through. Overall, these are less dense than traditional American bagels, unique as well as memorable.

Food trademarks: The best cities have them. Boston has its "chowdah" and baked beans, Chicago has deep-dish pizza sans rival, there's New York cheesecake, San Francisco sourdough, and you can count on a mean "bowl of red" as you make your way Southwest. But nowhere else can you get Montreal bagels—unless of course you make them yourself. Which bagelry makes the best in the city is a matter of some argument, but on the perfect, Montreal bagel profile there is rarely disagreement. Montreal bagels are divine fresh from the oven, without further enhancement, sublime when sliced cold and slathered with sweet butter, and exceptional toasted and treated to a decadent smear of snowy white cream cheese topped with slivers of Nova Scotia salmon. Forget about maple syrup and tourtière (that famed Quebec meat pie), *this* is the definitive Canadian culinary statement. How else to explain the countless New York and New Jersey visitors who make their way down Interstate 87, their cars packed with Montreal poppy and sesame seed bagels? Or what about the "Bagel Booth" at Montreal's International Airport, right beside the Duty Free Shop—surely it is obvious: Montreal bagels are special, a different breed. They are wonderfully chewy and tinged with a sweet and subtle "*je ne sais quoi*" (at least until the test recipe revealed otherwise). Authentic Montreal bagels are still baked in ever-stoked hard wood ovens, not gas or electric, to achieve their marvelous and irregularly charred outer surface. They shine too, with a gloss that only a short swim in a honey-sweetened water bath can give them.

How Montreal bagels came to be developed exactly in this fashion is difficult to determine. The recipe itself was no doubt modeled after one or two immigrant families' bagel know-how and preferences when the original family-run bagel stores came into existence. Over time, Montrealers enjoyed and expected bagels of this style and so the tradition continued. Some also argue that other cities do not allow for wood-burning commercial ovens as they are a fire hazard, giving Montreal the dubious distinction of having great bagels and a slightly more relaxed fire code.

In Montreal, the finest, legendary bagel shops are still located in the more colorful, earthy parts of town, (unlike the newer, spiffier bagel franchises) and are scrupulously without product marketing. Despite their location, and slightly less-than-health-board code of decor, these bagel shops have lines out the door all year long. An assortment of upscale, yuppie cars are double-parked alongside hordes of Italian racing bikes as bagel addicts get their fix. In Montreal winters, the bagel business booms as the temperature descends. The intense heat of the wood oven together with the frigid cold of winter coats the bagel shops' windows with condensation and the display front reveals only a blurry gloss of deep amber-colored bagels. A heady image for those who know what lies within.

Now the Good News: You Don't Have to Live in Montreal to Get Montreal Bagels

I spent years studying various Montreal bagel-makers and bakers. Then I would run home and, based on my observations and conversations, try batch after batch of homemade Montreal bagels. Finally, perfection! What distinguishes Montreal bagels from their American cousins is the use of oil, eggs, and malt in the dough (not all American bagels use malt—some do, some don't) and a significant lack of salt (often, there is none at all). Finally, these bagels are boiled in a honey-sweetened water bath for a special taste and shine. So you may lack the wood oven, and that surely is part of the charm, but this home recipe is pretty close to the city classic.

Montreal Bagels

Makes 12 bagels

*You can wait to visit Montreal or depend on Canadian relatives to ship down bagels
(not recommended) or try this absolutely authentic, good-enough-to-open-a-Montreal-bagel-franchise
bagel recipe. Although real Montreal bagels do not have any salt (or so they claim—I sometimes taste
some—depending on the bakery), this recipe has a modest amount, which serves to regulate the
fermentation. For really authentic bagels, you should try fresh yeast, but dry will
still give you outstanding results.*

1¾ cups water
2½ teaspoons dry yeast *or* ½ ounce fresh
5 tablespoons plus a pinch of sugar
2 tablespoons beaten egg
3 tablespoons vegetable oil
1 tablespoon malt powder
1½ teaspoons salt (optional)
4½–5 cups bread flour

KETTLE WATER
6 quarts water
⅓ cup honey

TOPPING
1½ cups sesame or poppy seeds (or half and
half)

In a large bowl, stir together the water, yeast, and pinch of sugar. Let the mixture stand for a couple of minutes, allowing the yeast to swell or dissolve. (If using fresh yeast, crumble it into the warm water along with the pinch of sugar.) Whisk in the remaining sugar, the beaten egg, vegetable oil, malt, and salt, if using it. Fold in most of the flour.

Knead for 10 to 12 minutes to form a stiff, smooth dough, adding additional flour as required. Cover with a tea towel or an inverted bowl and let the dough rest for 10 minutes.

Line a large baking sheet with a kitchen towel, and another with baking parchment. Fill a large soup pot or Dutch oven with 6 quarts water. Add the honey. Bring the water to a boil. Meanwhile, divide the dough in 12 sections and form each one into a 10-inch strip. Form these into bagel rings and place them on a cookie sheet. Let them rise for 12 to 16 minutes, until they are very slightly puffed up. Preheat the oven to 450°F.

Boil the bagels for about 1½ minutes, turning them once. Place them on the towel-lined sheet to dry out. Then sprinkle very generously with sesame or poppy seeds. (Montreal bagels are more seeded than regular bagels) and transfer them to the parchment-lined sheet.

Place in the oven, reduce the heat to 425°, and bake until done, 15 to 22 minutes, turning them once when they are just about done and switching baking sheets midway. Alternatively, you can start the bagels on the baking sheet and turn them onto a preheated baking stone to finish baking.

Pumpernickel, Onion, and Garlic Bagels

Makes 10 to 12 bagels

Chewy and dark, this bagel exudes a hearty, peasant-bread flavor. You don't have to boil these, but I do. Some bakeries simply glaze the bagels with egg white, then add the toppings and bake them as rolls. Outstanding. The dough can also be shaped into a round pumpernickel bread instead of a bagel.

1½ cups warm water
Pinch of granulated sugar
4 teaspoons dry yeast
2 tablespoons finely minced onion
1 small garlic clove, finely minced
3 tablespoons brown sugar
2 teaspoons malt powder or syrup
4 teaspoons baker's caramel
1¾ teaspoons salt
2 tablespoons cornmeal, plus extra for sprinkling
½ cup dark or coarse rye flour
1 tablespoon caraway seeds
3½–4½ cups bread flour

KETTLE WATER
About 6 quarts water
1 teaspoon salt
2 tablespoons brown sugar

TOPPING
Poppy seeds
Coarse sea salt
Caraway seeds
1 cup finely diced, lightly sautéed onion or rehydrated dry onion flakes (optional)

In a large bowl, stir together the warm water, granulated sugar, and yeast. Let the mixture stand for a couple of minutes to allow the yeast to swell or dissolve. Whisk in the onion, garlic, brown sugar, malt, baker's caramel, salt, the 2 tablespoons of cornmeal, the rye flour, and caraway seeds. Stir in most of the bread flour, until the dough is stiff enough to be kneaded. Knead for 10 to 12 minutes, adding flour as needed to make a very stiff but smooth dough. Remove the dough from the bowl, cover, and let the dough rest on a board for 10 minutes.

Meanwhile, line 2 large baking sheets with baking parchment and sprinkle one generously with cornmeal. Fill a large pot or Dutch oven with 6 quarts of water. Add the salt and brown sugar. Bring the water to a boil. Preheat the oven to 450°F, then reduce to 425°.

Divide the dough into 10 to 12 sections. Form each one into a 10-inch-long strip, and then form each strip into bagel rings and place them on the baking sheet. Let them rest for 18 to 22 minutes. Bagels should have a half proof—that is, rise halfway or appear puffy. Boil the bagels about 1½ minutes each, turning them once. Return them to the baking sheets, sprinkle with poppy seeds, coarse salt, caraway seeds, and additional onion, if desired. Bake until the bagels are medium- or golden-brown, 15 to 18 minutes.

Cinnamon Raisin Whole Wheat Bagels

Makes 8 to 12 bagels

*Try the new white whole wheat flour for these bagels (see page 9). You will get a lighter
texture but all the nutrition of regular whole wheat flour. I add the cinnamon when mixing the bagel dough.
Other bagel-makers, such as George Greenstein (Secrets of a Jewish Baker), add it when
hand kneading, to create a marbleized effect.*

1½ cups warm water
4 teaspoons dry yeast
Pinch of granulated sugar
2 tablespoons vegetable oil
2 tablespoons honey
¼ cup brown sugar
1¼ cups whole wheat flour
4 teaspoons ground cinnamon
1½ teaspoons salt
Approximately 3½ cups bread flour
1 cup dark raisins, plumped (see page 000)
1 egg, beaten (optional)

KETTLE WATER
6 quarts boiling water
2 tablespoons brown sugar or corn syrup

In a large bowl, stir together the warm water, yeast, and granulated sugar. Let the mixture stand for a couple of minutes to allow the yeast to swell and dissolve. Whisk in the oil, honey, and brown sugar, stirring to blend. Stir in the whole wheat flour, cinnamon, and salt and blend well. Add 3 cups of the bread flour and knead for 10 to 12 minutes, adding more flour as required to make a very firm but smooth dough. Let rest for 5 to 10 minutes, then knead or press in the raisins.

Place the dough on a work surface, cover it with a clean tea towel, and allow it to rest for 10 minutes. Then divide into 8, 10, or 12 portions (8 for large bagels, 10 for medium, or 12 for small). Form each portion into a rope about 10 inches long. Form the ropes into bagels by attaching the ends together and rolling them on a board to seal. Let the bagels rise for about 20 minutes, til they appear a little puffy. Preheat the oven to 450°F.

Meanwhile, bring the 6 quarts of water and brown sugar or corn syrup to a boil. Line a large baking sheet with parchment paper. Place a few bagels at a time in the boiling water. As they come to the surface, turn them over and cook on the other side for another minute. Remove them to the baking sheet and let them dry briefly. For extra shine, brush them with beaten egg white. Place them in the oven, reduce the heat to 425° and bake until the bagels are medium- or golden-brown, 18 to 22 minutes, turning them once midway.

THE BIALY—THE BAGEL'S FIRST COUSIN

Most cultures offer some variety of flatbread—Indian naan, Italian focaccia, and Armenian lavash to name only a few—and bialys seem to be the Eastern European Jewish version of these other ethnic breads. The origin of bialys is often attributed to Bialystock, Poland, where, apparently, and as their name would suggest, they made their debut. Since these are often featured alongside bagels, they seem most definitely to be a direct cousin to the bagel—perhaps thanks to the creativity of a baker who scratched his head one day and thought, "So, how about the same dough, but no hole and some onions?" Why not?

Bialys can be made with bagel dough, with or without malt, or even with Vienna or Kaiser role dough. Where I grew up, a flat, crisp, onion-topped bread-cum-roll was called an "onion pletzel" and resembled a large, flattened onion bun—no hole or indentation in its middle, although the top surface was somewhat puckered. A similar and better-known phenomenon, known as a bialy by New Yorkers, is also a flat round of dough, with a slight depression in its center, topped with diced onions and poppy seeds and finished with a brisk bake in a hot oven. Call it what you will, the result is an enticing flatbread that takes well to a copious spread of cream cheese. Bialys (or bialies) can be modest—three to four inches across—or the size of a small pizza. Thin, they are a good munch. A thicker, more risen bialy can be split and filled as a sandwich.

Cookbook author Joan Nathan (*Jewish Cooking in America*) muses that unlike the bagel, which enjoys absolute mainstream food acceptance, bialys have remained more of a New York specialty, although you will occasionally find them in other parts of the country. Most bialy-makers rely on bagel dough for the foundation, but permit the dough to rise, and, although the odd bialy expert may beg to differ, most agree that bialy dough is baked, *not* boiled.

Onion Bialy

Makes 12 bialys

*This recipe was inspired by George Greenstein's Secrets of a Jewish Baker.
Before reading Mr. Greenstein's book, I didn't give bialys much thought. Now I make them on a
regular basis. They are easy to make, taste wonderful, and freeze very well.*

BIALY DOUGH
1½ cups warm water
4½ teaspoons dry yeast
5 teaspoons sugar
Approximately 5½ cups bread flour
2½ teaspoons salt
Cornmeal for sprinkling (optional)

ONION TOPPING
½ cup finely minced fresh onion or dehydrated
  minced onion (see Note)
2 tablespoons vegetable oil
4 teaspoons poppy seeds
1 tablespoon coarse salt, for sprinkling

EGG WASH
1 egg, beaten
2 tablespoons water

NOTE: Dehydrated onion is easy to work with, sticks to the unbaked dough , and is similar to the topping used by professional bakers.

In a large bowl, whisk together the warm water, yeast, and sugar and allow the mixture to stand for a couple of minutes for the yeast to swell or appear dissolved. Stir in 1 cup of the flour and the salt. Add most of the remaining flour and stir with a wooden spoon to make a soft mass. Knead, by hand or using a dough hook, for 8 to 10 minutes. As with bagel dough, this should be a very stiff, slick dough. Shape it into a ball and place it in a well-greased bowl. Place the bowl in a plastic bag and seal loosely. Allow the dough to rise for about 45 minutes. Meanwhile, line 2 large baking sheets with baking parchment and lightly sprinkle with cornmeal, if using.

Preheat the oven to 425°F. Prepare the topping by covering the dehydrated onions with hot water and allowing them to soak for 15 minutes. Drain, and toss with the oil and poppy seeds. Set aside. If using fresh onions, mince, then toss with the oil and poppy seeds.

Gently deflate the dough and divide in 2 pieces. Then, divide each half into 6 equal pieces. Let the dough rest for 10 minutes. Then roll or stretch each portion into a 4- to 5-inch oval or round. (Be careful not to overwork the dough as it will begin to retract.) Place the bialys on the prepared baking sheets. Whisk together and set aside the ingredients for the egg wash.

Lightly glaze the perimeter of the bialys with egg wash. Spoon about 2 teaspoons of topping on each bialy and sprinkle with a very little bit of coarse salt. Cover the bialys with a floured tea towel and let them rise for 30 to 60 minutes or until puffy looking.

Bake until golden brown, 25 to 30 minutes. (If the bialys brown too fast, reduce the heat to 400°.) Devour all or freeze. For thicker bialys, allow a longer rise; for thin, crisp ones, reduce the rising time.

Butter Burches

Makes 16 rolls

So that it can be served with a meat-based meal, challah is traditionally made with a neutral fat, usually vegetable oil. This recipe for burches, also called "berches," is an old European formula that uses butter to emphasize the roll's rich, velvety texture. These traditional Yom Kippur rolls are a perfect foil for post-fast dairy dishes and spreads such as eggplant and tuna. Form them into rounds or mini-turbans— New Year's–shaped challah rolls. These can be made the day before, formed, and refrigerated. Remove them from the fridge about 2 hours before baking so the dough can warm and finish rising. A short bake means fresh, hot rolls with which to break the fast.

¼ cup warm water
¾ cup plus a pinch of sugar
5 teaspoons dry yeast
1 cup warm milk
2¾ teaspoons salt
½ cup (1 stick) unsalted butter, melted
4 eggs
Approximately 6 cups bread flour

EGG WASH/TOPPING
1 egg, beaten
Sesame or poppy seeds, for sprinkling

NOTE: If you want miniature butter burches, divide the dough into 20 to 24 pieces. This is good if offering rolls as part of a buffet meal. Bake until well browned (15 to 16 minutes).

In a large bowl, whisk together the water, pinch of sugar, and yeast. Let the mixture stand for about 5 minutes, until the yeast swells and dissolves. Stir in the warm milk, the remaining sugar, and the salt. Then blend in the melted butter and the eggs. Fold in the flour to make a soft, shaggy mass. Knead for 8 to 10 minutes, adding more flour as required to make a soft, elastic dough that does not stick to the mixing bowl.

Shape the dough into a ball and place it in a lightly greased bowl. Place the bowl in a large plastic bag and seal. Let the dough rise until almost doubled, 45 to 90 minutes.

Gently deflate the dough, then divide it in half. Divide each half into 8 pieces (see Note). Roll each, gently, into a length of about 8 inches, one end thicker than the other. Coil, starting with the thick end, into a round. Place the rolls on a parchment-lined baking sheet. Alternatively, form into round rolls as for a plain bun.

Brush the rolls well with the beaten egg and sprinkle them with sesame or poppy seeds. Place the entire baking sheet in a large plastic bag (or cover it with a large plastic sheet), and allow the rolls to rise until quite puffy, 30 to 45 minutes.

Preheat the oven to 350°F.

Place the rolls in the oven and bake until well browned (15 to 18 minutes) or until the rolls are a nice even brown all over.

Pumpernickel Cranberry Rolls

Makes 12 to 16 rolls

These are perfect with the light, dairy, breakfast-style foods for after the Yom Kippur fast. They can be made the day before, formed, and refrigerated. Remove them from the fridge about 2 hours before baking to allow the dough to warm up and finish rising. A short baking ensures fresh, hot rolls for before or after the fast. Also good if you substitute plumped dark raisins or currants for the cranberries.

QUICK SPONGE
1 cup warm water
1 tablespoon dry yeast
2 tablespoons caraway seeds
1 cup coarse or dark rye flour
¼ cup bread flour

DOUGH
½ cup warm water
2 teaspoons salt
¼ cup brown sugar
1 teaspoon instant coffee powder
1 teaspoon unsweetened cocoa powder
¼ teaspoon ground cinnamon
2 teaspoons malt powder or syrup
2–4 teaspoons baker's caramel
2½–3 cups bread flour
1¼ cups dried, plumped cranberries (see page 22)

GLAZE/TOPPING
1 egg white, beaten
Caraway seeds

SPONGE: An hour before making the dough, in a large bowl, mix together the water, yeast, caraway seeds, rye and bread flours. Stir to make a thick, gloppy mixture and let stand for 1 hour.

DOUGH: Stir down the spongy mixture and add the ½ cup water, salt, brown sugar, instant coffee, cocoa, cinnamon, malt powder, baker's caramel, and most of the bread flour. Stir until the dough can be kneaded (by hand or with a dough hook). Knead for 6 to 8 minutes, adding additional flour as required to make a soft, springy dough. Let the dough rest for a couple of minutes, then press in the cranberries. Shape the dough into a ball and place it in a well-greased bowl, cover with plastic wrap, and let the dough rise until almost doubled, about 45 minutes.

Divide the dough into 12 or 16 portions, depending on the size of the rolls you prefer. Form each portion into a ball. Place the dough balls on a parchment paper–lined, doubled-up baking sheet, spaced 3 inches apart. Brush each roll with the egg white and sprinkle on some caraway seeds. Let the rolls rise until quite puffy (30 to 45 minutes).

Preheat the oven to 375°F. Place the rolls in the oven and bake for 15 to 18 minutes, until the rolls are slightly firm when pressed with your fingertips. These can be made into other shapes as well. For a savory version, leave out the fruit and add ½ cup finely minced onion just before the flour when making the dough.

Whole Wheat Pita

Makes 16 pitas

Show me a bowl of eggplant or chick-pea dip on any Jewish holiday table, and chances are there will also be a basket of pita wedges nearby. These biblical dippers double as cutlery and are a must in the basic Jewish breads repertoire. Hodgson Mill mills and sells a white whole wheat flour that makes superb pita, and King Arthur also carries it. But you can use half regular whole wheat flour and half bread flour, if you prefer.

4 teaspoons dry yeast
2½ cups warm water
2 teaspoons sugar
2 tablespoons olive oil
2 cups white whole wheat flour (or regular
whole wheat flour)
3 cups bread flour
2½ teaspoons salt

In a large bowl, dissolve the yeast in the water and stir in the sugar. Let the mixture stand, allowing the yeast to dissolve, for 3 to 5 minutes.

Stir in the olive oil, and most of the flour (hold back 1 cup of the bread flour until you see how much more you will need) and the salt. Mix to form a soft dough, then knead for 8 to 10 minutes, adding the reserved flour as required to form an elastic, supple dough.

Shape the dough into a ball and place it in a large, well-greased bowl. Place the bowl in a large plastic bag and seal. Let the dough rise, until almost doubled, 45 to 90 minutes. Alternatively, put it in the refrigerator for several hours or overnight. Bring it to room temperature to warm up and finish rising.

Divide the dough into 16 pieces and form them into balls. Cover the dough balls with a damp kitchen towel and let them rest for a couple of minutes. Flatten each ball with a rolling pin into a disc about 6 to 9 inches in diameter and about ¼ inch thick. If the dough is resistant and springy, allow it to rest for a couple of minutes before rolling. Cover the pitas with a damp tea towel and let them rest and rise for 15 to 25 minutes, until slightly puffy.

Preheat the oven to 475°F.

Place several pitas on a parchment-lined baking sheet. Bake until the pitas puff up, 2 to 3 minutes. Turn and bake for 2 to 4 minutes on the other side. If the oven is too hot, the pitas will burn before they puff. Lower the heat if they seem to be browning too quickly.

Wrap the baked pitas in clean tea towels to keep them soft.

Freeze any leftovers in a Ziploc plastic bag.

2. Shabbat

The Day of Rest

Baruch ata Adonai, Eloheynu Melech ha'olam. Hamotzi lechem min ha'aretz.
"Blessed are You, O Lord our God, King of the universe,
who bringest forth bread from the earth."

—TRADITIONAL HEBREW BLESSING OVER BREAD, INCLUDING THE SABBATH CHALLAH

It may appear a minute matter to pronounce the Hebrew blessing over bread,
and to accustom one's children to do so. Yet if a Jew, at the time of partaking of food,
remembers the identical words used by his fellow-Jews since time immemorial
and the world over, he revives in himself, wherever he may be at
the moment, communion with his imperishable race.

—1916, W. M. HAFFKIN, A RUSSIAN-BRITISH BACTERIOLOGIST

THE SABBATH: SHABBAT

WHEN ✹ The seventh day of the Jewish week.

CORRESPONDING TO ✹ Commencing at sunset Friday and ending an hour after sunset, Saturday.

HOLIDAY CONTEXT ✹ No discussion of Sabbath ever excludes a reference to Genesis, which in turn mentions the "Day of Rest." According to Genesis, God spent six industrious days creating the world. On the seventh day, God rested. In recognition of this divine respite from work, we have *Shabbat*.

The maintenance and observance of the Sabbath is actually the fourth Commandment brought down by Moses from Sinai. The observance of the Jewish Sabbath, along with the laws of Kashruth, are probably two of the strongest cornerstones of Judaism.

Shabbat is a day of rest that revives both body and soul. Work ceases and in its place, family life and prayer take priority. The restrictions involved in appropriately observing Shabbat, are not there to limit the individual, but rather to make this day special, transforming it truly into a day of rest. It is an interlude that gives one pause.

ACTIVITIES/CUSTOMS ✹ Services are held Friday night, Saturday morning, and finish Saturday evening. On the domestic front, the day before the Sabbath arrives is typically a busy one, as the house is tidied, the chicken-soup-and-all-the-trimmings dinner is prepared, and challahs are set to bake.

Before the Sabbath meal begins, prayers are said over the candles, the wine, and the bread. It is customary to use two challahs on Shabbat. The meaning of this custom goes back to the Exodus. Two challahs remind us of that time when God provided the Jews with manna in the wilderness. Manna did not fall on the Sabbath, but a double portion of it fell the day *before* the Sabbath. This manna was wonderfully rich and fortifying, as challah is. The seeded tops of the challahs are said to represent the plentifulness of God's offering in the desert, where the double portion that rained down could be held for consumption the next day.

In antiquity, Jews cut off a portion of challah dough to give as an offering to the temple priests. Thus, a small piece of dough is removed from the batch of challah. As this is done, a blessing is recited, and soon after, the piece of dough is scorched. The custom is called "taking challah" or "separating challah."

Havdalah is the ceremony that marks the end of Shabbat. It occurs as Sabbath comes to an end, after sundown Saturday. Havdalah means "separation" in Hebrew. The ceremony of Havdalah represents closure for the Sabbath and delineates the work week from the Sabbath and the commencement of a new week. Havdalah customs include the lighting of a special, twisted Havdalah candle, drinking a Kiddush cup of wine, and inhaling spices from the *besamin* or spice box. Havdalah concludes with the candle being doused with drops of wine spilled from the Kiddush cup.

FOOD SYMBOLS ❋ Wine is served, as well as challah, as described above. Desserts are generally simple and traditional, such as strudel, marble cake, and mandelbrot or poppy-seed cookies. Usually, Shabbat desserts are pareve, since the Sabbath meal is often meat-based. If you are preparing for a Saturday dairy luncheon or brunch, or a vegetarian dinner, recipes from Yom Kippur, Sukkot, or Shavuot would also be appropriate. Sabbath sweets are offered with a leisurely generosity, as they are part of the relaxing, familial oasis that brings the week to an end. Depending on your taste and needs, anything from the Rosh Hashanah section is also appropriate.

Traditional Friday Night Challah

Makes 1 large loaf

Sabbath is often described as a bride or queen. Appropriately, one prepares for the arrival of the Sabbath with a special joy and lavishness, as is a bride's due. If the Sabbath is the bride, then challah must be her crown. It is traditional to place two challahs at the head of the table. This recipe is the definitive Friday-night-supper-double-duty-as-Saturday-morning-French-toast-challah. If you prefer a "bulka" challah, (a square-bottomed or loaf challah), see the instructions below. This recipe makes a light and velvety bread, richer than that from the corner bakery but a little less sweet than a Rosh Hashanah round challah. It is the most common formula for challah because it is so balanced—perfect sweetness, perfect amount of salt, not too large, not too small, not too rich, and not too lean. Perfect. Worth noting: I have seen challah recipes that use a touch of saffron to infuse the dough with an attractive yellow hue. Other recipes rely on an extra egg yolk (as does the Rosh Hashanah sweet challah).

1¾ cups warm water
2 tablespoons dry yeast
⅓ cup plus a pinch of sugar
Pinch of ground cinnamon (optional)
2¾ teaspoons salt
3 eggs
½ cup vegetable oil
6½–7½ cups bread flour

EGG WASH/TOPPING
1 egg plus 1 yolk
1 tablespoon water
Sesame seeds, for sprinkling

In a large mixing bowl, sprinkle the yeast, pinch of sugar, and the cinnamon over the water. Stir briefly and allow the mixture to stand for a couple of minutes to let the yeast swell or dissolve. Briskly stir in the remaining sugar and the salt, then the eggs and oil. Fold in most of the flour to make a soft, shaggy mass. Knead for 8 to 10 minutes by hand or with a dough hook, dusting in more flour as required to make a soft, elastic dough.

Shape the dough into a ball and place it in a lightly greased bowl. Place the bowl in a large plastic bag, seal, and let the dough rise until doubled, 45 to 60 minutes. Gently deflate the dough. Whisk together and set aside the ingredients for the egg wash. Line a baking sheet with parchment paper or, if using loaf pans, generously grease either one 12-by-5-inch pan or two 9-by-5-inch pans.

For a braided challah, divide the dough into 3 sections and form it into 3 ropes about 14 inches long. Make a traditional challah braid. Place the bread on the prepared baking sheet. For loaf-style challah, which I prefer, divide the dough in 3 portions. Shape each piece into a ball and place the balls side by side in the loaf pan. For two smaller loaves, divide the dough in 4, shape into 4 balls, and place 2 in each loaf pan. Mix the egg and yolk for the egg wash together. Brush the loaf (or loaves) with egg wash and sprinkle on the sesame or poppy seeds. Wait for about 10 minutes, then reglaze with another coating of egg wash. Insert the loaf pan or baking sheet in a large, clear plastic bag. Seal the bag, and allow the dough to rise until almost doubled, 45 to 60 minutes.

Lightly grease a 12 by 5-inch loaf pan. Divide the dough in 3 or 4 equal sections. Shape each section into a ball. Place the balls side by side in the prepared loaf pan. The bread can also be braided and baked free form, on a baking sheet. Glaze the bread with egg wash twice, sprinkle on the sesame seeds, and place the loaf pan in a large plastic bag. Let the dough rise until it is almost flush with the top of the pan (about 45 minutes).

Preheat the oven to 350°F. Place the bread in the oven and bake until evenly browned, about 30 minutes for a free-form braid; 35 to 45 minutes for a loaf-style bread. Cool on a rack before slicing.

"This Tastes Like Cake"
Fresh Yeast Sabbath Challah

Makes 1 large or 2 smaller loaves

Most breads do very well with active dry or instant yeast, but somehow challah made with fresh yeast is special. If you are wary of fresh yeast, put aside your trepidation and try this recipe. It may be the only bread for which you use fresh yeast, but the difference is indescribable. One tester noted: "Inside, the challah separates almost into strands of bread, rather than being cakey"; another tester's note read, "This makes amazing challah rolls, too! Disappeared very quickly!" This recipe makes a large, incredibly impressive challah, either as a loaf or as a traditional braid.

1¼ ounces fresh yeast
1½ cups warm water
⅔ cup plus a pinch of sugar
⅓ cup vegetable oil
1 egg yolk plus 3 eggs
2¾ teaspoons salt
6–7 cups bread flour

EGG WASH/TOPPING
1 egg plus 1 egg yolk
Sesame or poppy seeds, for sprinkling

This bread can be braided and baked on a large baking sheet or made in a 12 by 5-inch loaf pan or two 9 by 5-inch loaf pans.

In a large mixing bowl, crumble the fresh yeast into the water with the pinch of sugar. Let the mixture stand for 2 to 4 minutes. Once the yeast is dissolved, stir in the oil, the remaining sugar, the egg yolk, eggs, and salt, and blend well. Fold in most of the flour. When the dough can no longer be stirred by hand, cover and let it rest for 10 minutes. At this point, it should be a rough mass.

After the rest period, knead for 8 to 12 minutes, by hand or with a dough hook, adding more flour as required to make a smooth, satiny dough. Place the dough in a lightly oiled bowl and place the bowl in a large plastic bag. Seal and let the dough rest until doubled, about 1 hour. Gently deflate the dough. Line a baking sheet with parchment paper or, if using a loaf pan, generously grease either one 12 by 5-inch pan or two 9 by 5-inch pans.

For a braided challah, divide the dough into three sections and form it into three ropes about fourteen inches long.

Make a traditional challah bread. Place the bread on the prepared baking sheet. For loaf-style challah, which I prefer, divide the dough in three portions. Shape each into a ball and place the balls side by side in the loaf pan. For two smaller loaves, divide the dough in four, shape into four balls, and place two in each loaf pan.

Mix the egg and yolk for the egg wash together. Brush the loaf (or loaves) with egg wash and sprinkle on the sesame or poppy seeds.

Wait for about 10 minutes, then reglaze with another coating of egg wash. Insert the loaf pan or baking sheet in a large, clear plastic bag. Seal the bag, and allow the dough to rise until almost doubled, 45 to 60 minutes.

Lightly grease a 12 by 5-inch loaf pan. Divide the dough in three or four equal sections. Shape each section into a ball. Place the balls side by side in the prepared loaf pan. The bread can also be braided and baked free form, on a baking sheet. Glaze the bread with egg wash twice, sprinkle on the sesame seeds, and place the loaf pan in a large plastic bag. Let the dough rise until it is almost flush with the top of the pan (about 45 minutes).

Preheat the oven to 350° F. Place the bread in the oven and bake until evenly browned, about 30 minutes for a free-form braid; 35 to 45 minutes for a loaf-style bread. Cool on a rack before slicing.

VARIATION: **For Fresh Yeast Challah Rolls,** divide the dough into 8 or 10 portions. Roll each into a strip about 8 inches long. Tie gently in a knot. Place on a doubled-up baking sheet lined with parchment paper. Continue with the recipe as directed and bake at 375°F. for 20 minutes, until the rolls are browned.

Soul Food from the Jewish Spice Box—the Besamin Box

Many are familiar with how the Sabbath starts. But how it comes to an end is a comparatively lesser-known custom. The end of Shabbat is called *Havdalah* (meaning "separation" in Hebrew) and it occurs at sunset Saturday night, at synagogue services or at home.

It is during Havdalah that the besamin box comes into play. A besamin box is a special container, made of silver, wood, pottery, or other materials. Vintage, antique, silver besamin boxes are works of art. Some resemble miniature silver towers, like an exotic salt shaker, or birds, or windmills. Traditionally, the Jewish spice box contains whole cloves. At the end of Sabbath, the box is opened, and one partakes of the rich, highly perfumed scent. It is customary to pass the spice box around for all to share the aroma.

The interpretations of this custom are numerous and diverse. A common one is that on Shabbat one tries to reach a more exalted state and seeks an "added soul." It is suggested that the act of inhalation may in fact be akin to "inhaling" this extra soul. Others theorize that the extra soul leaves us as the Sabbath ends. The spicy fragrance of the besamin box "revives" us so we do not feel too depleted as we lose this extra soul.

The spice box cake recipe that follows would most appropriately be served for Havdalah, but it is also fine with a cup of lemony tea after an old-fashioned brisket and chicken supper.

Besamin Box or Spice Cake
aka That Ginger Ale Cake

Makes 10 to 12 servings

This moist cake is light and mouth-wateringly tender of crumb, topped with a tangy-sweet glaze.
Just as someone is saying, "I don't like spice cake," pop a forkful of this luscious cake into his or her mouth.
Try not to say "I told you so" as they finish a whole slice. My eldest son Jonathan says the trick
is not to call it "spice cake" but just call it "that ginger ale cake." Sounds more intriguing.
A good cake for Sukkot as well.

1 cup vegetable shortening or
  unsalted butter or margarine
1½ cups granulated sugar
1 cup brown sugar
4 eggs
2 teaspoons vanilla extract
1 teaspoon rum extract (optional)
1 cup ginger ale
½ teaspoon salt
2½ teaspoons baking powder
½ teaspoon baking soda
1 tablespoon ground cinnamon
¼ teaspoon ground ginger (see Note)
¼ teaspoon grated nutmeg
½ teaspoon ground cloves
½ teaspoon dried mace
½ teaspoon ground allspice
3 cups all-purpose flour

GINGER ALE–ORANGE GLAZE (OPTIONAL)
2 cups confectioners' sugar
2 tablespoons orange juice
2 tablespoons ginger ale

TOPPING
Finely chopped pecans and grated orange zest,
or confectioners' sugar

Preheat the oven to 350°F. Lightly grease a 9 by 13-inch rectangular pan or a 9- or 10-inch tube or angel cake pan.

In a large bowl, cream together the shortening, butter, or margarine with the granulated and brown sugars. Blend in the eggs and vanilla, then the rum extract, if using. Add the ginger ale. In another large bowl, whisk together the dry ingredients. Fold them into the wet ingredients and mix well. Spoon the batter into the prepared pan.

Bake until the cake springs back when lightly pressed (45 to 60 minutes—shorter for a sheet pan; longer for a tube pan). Cool for 5 minutes before removing from the pan. Cool thoroughly on a rack before glazing.

If using the glaze, in a bowl, stir together the confectioners' sugar, orange juice, and ginger ale. Blend well then drizzle slowly over the cake. Recover any excess and repeat. Top with the nuts and orange zest.

Alternatively, omit the glaze and dust the top of the cake with confectioners' sugar.

NOTE: You may substitute 1½ teaspoons pumpkin pie spice or pastry spice for the ground ginger, nutmeg, cloves, mace, and allspice.

Shirley and Anita's Ultra Thin and Crisp Mandelbrot

Makes 2 to 3 dozen slices

I thought a loaf-style mandelbrot was unique but have since seen similar approaches in other cookbooks and private recipe files. This recipe yields a crisp and decidedly refined mandelbrot—and is a good illustration of how versatile this cookie can be.

¾ cup sugar
⅓ cup vegetable oil
4 eggs
2 teaspoons vanilla extract
½ teaspoon almond extract
2 cups all-purpose flour
1¼ teaspoons baking powder
¼ teaspoon salt
1 cup whole almonds (or whole walnuts)

Preheat the oven to 350°F. Lightly grease a 9 by 5-inch loaf pan.

In a bowl, whisk together the sugar and oil. Stir in the eggs and beat well, then add the vanilla and almond extracts. Fold in the flour, baking powder, salt, and nuts.

Transfer the batter to the prepared pan and bake until the cake is puffed up, lightly golden, and appears set (it might be cracked on top), 40 to 45 minutes. Cool for 15 minutes, then remove the mandelbrot from the pan and wrap tightly in foil. Chill overnight in the refrigerator.

Slice the mandelbrot very thin (about ⅛ inch thick) and place the slices on a baking sheet in a single layer. Bake until golden, turning once, about 10 minutes total.

VARIATION: For Poppy Seed Ultra Thin and Crisp, omit the almonds and add ⅓ cup poppy seeds to the batter when adding the dry ingredients. Proceed as directed.

Shabbat Mandarin Marble Loaf

Makes 10 to 12 servings

*There is something so simple and satisfying about a marble cake.
No wonder it's a favorite in Jewish kitchens. Moister than a pound cake, richer than a quick bread,
this is the perfect sweet to have around over the weekend. For a vanilla marble cake,
substitute a cup of water for the orange juice and omit the orange zest.*

CHOCOLATE PASTE
4 tablespoons unsweetened cocoa powder
3 tablespoons warm vegetable oil

CAKE
1 cup vegetable oil
2¼ cups granulated sugar
5 eggs
4 teaspoons vanilla extract
¼ cup water
1 cup undiluted frozen orange juice, defrosted
  (see Variations)
Zest of 1 orange, finely minced
3¼ cups all-purpose flour
½ teaspoon baking soda
3½ teaspoons baking powder
½ teaspoon salt
½ cup finely grated semi-sweet chocolate or
  miniature chocolate chips (optional)

ORANGE GLAZE/TOPPING
1 cup confectioners' sugar
4–6 tablespoons orange juice
Long shreds of orange zest (optional)

Preheat the oven to 350°F. Generously grease a 10-inch tube or angel cake pan, a 12-cup bundt pan, or two 9 by 5-inch loaf pans. Line the bottom of the pan(s) with parchment paper.

Prepare the chocolate paste by placing the cocoa and oil in a small bowl and blending well. Add a drop or more of oil if the mixture appears too stiff or thick to stir or blend easily.

For the cake, in a large bowl, blend the oil with the sugar until light and fluffy, scraping the bowl often. Blend in the eggs and stir in the vanilla, water, orange juice, and zest.

In a separate bowl, whisk together the flour, baking soda, baking powder, and salt. Add to the wet ingredients.

Remove one third of the batter to a smaller bowl. Stir the chocolate paste into this to make a chocolate batter and add to this the grated chocolate or miniature chocolate chips. Spoon alternating portions of white and chocolate batter into the prepared pan. You can do this with a spatula or a soup spoon. It doesn't really matter how you place the batter in the pan—it works out in the baking.

Bake the large cake for 55 to 60 minutes, smaller cakes for 35 to 40 minutes. The cake should be

continued

lightly browned on top, perhaps slightly cracked, and spring back when lightly pressed. Cool in the pan for 15 to 20 minutes before inverting onto a wire rack. Then either dust with confectioners' sugar or glaze.

For the glaze, stir together the confectioners' sugar and orange juice to make a thick but pourable sauce. Drizzle this over the top of the cooled cake. Garnish with long shreds of orange zest, if desired.

VARIATIONS: For Vanilla Marble Cake, omit the orange zest. Substitute 2 to 4 tablespoons of water for the orange juice, and glaze with water combined with 1 teaspoon vanilla extract.

For Mild Mandarin Marble Cake, use 1 cup regular, reconstituted orange juice, or fresh rather than concentrated.

Marmalade 'n Spice Honey Cake

Makes 12 to 14 servings

*This high and moist cake is elegant and easy to make. It is well-suited to either a formal
or an informal Sabbath dinner or luncheon. The marmalade adds flavor, sweetness, and moistness.
The tea and spices give the cake its medium brown color.*

1 cup vegetable oil
¾ cup light honey
1 cup granulated sugar
⅓ cup brown sugar
½ cup orange marmalade
4 eggs
3 cups all-purpose flour
½ teaspoon salt
½ teaspoon baking soda
1 tablespoon baking powder
2 teaspoons ground cinnamon
1 teaspoon ground cloves
¼ teaspoon ground allspice
1 cup brewed tea, just warm (see Note)
⅓ cup slivered or sliced almonds

TOPPING
confectioners' sugar

**NOTE: For a darker cake, use brewed,
strong coffee to replace the tea.**

Preheat the oven to 350°F. Grease the *bottom only* of a 9- or 10-inch angel cake or tube pan. Cut out a circle of parchment paper and line the pan bottom.

In a medium bowl, combine the oil, honey, granulated sugar, brown sugar, and marmalade. Blend well, then add the eggs. In a larger bowl, whisk together the dry ingredients. Make a well in the center of the flour mixture and add the wet ingredients and the tea to moisten the batter. Blend well, by hand or with an electric mixer on slow speed, to make a smooth loose batter.

Pour the batter into the prepared pan. Sprinkle the top with slivered almonds, place the pan on doubled-up baking sheets (to prevent the bottom from browning too fast), and bake for 55 to 60 minutes, or until the cake springs back when pressed lightly with your fingertips.

Cool in the pan for 15 minutes, then remove and cool on a rack.

To finish the cake, dust it with confectioners' sugar and sprinkle on the shredded orange zest.

The Titanic Cafe's Chocolate Chestnut Torte

Makes 14 to 16 servings

Dense but light, this flourless torte is heaven. I adapted it from a recipe kindly provided by Montreal's trendy Titanic Cafe. Chef Rob Hack agrees this simple cake is a "killer" dessert. (For a Passover version, see the Mock Chestnut Torte on page 294.) One of the easiest and elegant cakes you will ever taste. I prefer this simply dusted with cocoa, but include a Ganache Glaze for a fancier presentation.

CHESTNUT TORTE
1 (15-ounce) can chestnut puree or chestnut cream (see Note)
4 ounces (1 stick) unsalted butter or unsalted margarine
1 teaspoon vanilla extract
6 eggs, separated
10 ounces semi-sweet chocolate (preferably imported), melted and cooled to room temperature
Pinch of salt
¼ cup granulated sugar

CHOCOLATE GANACHE GLAZE
6 ounces semi-sweet chocolate, coarsely chopped
½ cup whipping cream or brewed coffee

TOPPING (OPTIONAL)
Whipped cream *or* 1 (10-ounce) carton frozen raspberries pureed with 1 to 2 tablespoons sugar
Semi-sweet chocolate shavings
confectioners' sugar

Preheat the oven to 350°F. Line a 9- or 10-inch springform pan with a circle of baking parchment.

TORTE: In a large bowl, using a whisk, or an electric mixer, combine the chestnut puree or cream with the butter or margarine until well blended. Mix in the vanilla, the egg yolks, and the melted chocolate and blend well.

In another clean bowl, with clean, dry beaters, gently whip the egg whites with the salt, just to break up and foam the whites slightly. Then gradually increasing the mixer speed, dust in the sugar to form stiff, glossy (but not dry) peaks.

Fold one third of the egg whites into the chestnut mixture and work it in well to loosen. Then, gently fold in the remaining egg whites in 2 installments, blending well but taking care not to deflate the mixture.

Spoon the batter into the prepared pan and bake for 35 to 45 minutes. The cake will rise somewhat and look dry and slightly cracked on top when done. The middle should be soft but firm. Cool in the pan for 20 minutes, then remove to a wire rack. Freezes well.

GANACHE GLAZE: Bring the whipping cream (or coffee) to a boil and add the chopped chocolate all at once. Remove from the heat and stir briskly, using a wire whisk, until all the chocolate melts and you have a thick glaze or sauce-like topping.

Invert the cake (so that the smooth, flat bottom faces up) and put it on a wire cake rack set over a cookie sheet. Pour the glaze over the cake, using a metal spatula to even the glaze out and spread it along the sides. Serve with a dollop of whipped cream on the side or a pureed raspberry sauce. Or, garnish with chocolate shavings dusted with sifted confectioners' sugar.

NOTE: Chestnut puree, available in most supermarkets, ethnic stores and European grocers, is usually imported from France. Lightly sweetened chestnut cream or pureed chestnuts with a touch of salt (check the can label—it will indicate what is inside), will also work well.

Quick-and-Easy Cinnamon Apple Strudel

Makes 6 servings

An old-fashioned-tasting apple strudel, made quick and easy with prepared filo dough. This recipe makes 2 strudel rolls. Serve one warm and the other can be a gift or nibbled on during the week. In spring, I use some chopped rhubarb as well as apples.

6–8 cups peeled, cored, and thinly sliced apples
  tossed with 1 tablespoon fresh lemon juice
½ cup granulated sugar
2 teaspoons ground cinnamon
Pinch of pastry or pumpkin pie spice
2 tablespoons all-purpose flour
½ cup raisins, plumped and drained (see page
  22)
8–10 filo sheets
½ cup (1 stick) unsalted butter or unsalted
  margarine, melted
2 tablespoons unflavored bread crumbs
Confectioners' sugar, for dusting (optional)

Preheat the oven to 375°F. Line a large baking sheet with parchment paper.

To the apples, add the sugar, cinnamon, pastry spice, flour, and raisins. Set aside.

Use 4 or 5 filo leaves per strudel roll. Keep the remaining filo covered with a damp cloth to prevent it from drying out. Place one sheet down on your work surface and brush it with melted butter. Sprinkle on half the bread crumbs. Layer on 3 more filo leaves, brushing each with butter. Spread half the apple mixture across the lower third of the filo. Roll the bottom edge of the dough over the apples, just to cover. Turn the right and left edges in about 1 inch. Roll up jellyroll fashion to make the strudel roll and place on the prepared pan. Brush the top with melted butter. Repeat with the remaining filo leaves, bread crumbs, and apple filling.

Bake for 40 minutes, or until golden brown. Cool, and dust with confectioners' sugar, if desired. Cut, using a serrated knife, in diagonal slices.

Friday Night Banana Cake with Two Glazes *aka* Gotta-Do-Something-with-Those-Bananas-on-the-Counter Bundt Cake

Makes 12 to 14 servings

This is one of those split-seconds-to-make cakes. It is extra-moist and fine-grained. The glazes are optional.

2 cups granulated sugar
1 cup vegetable oil
4 eggs
2 teaspoons vanilla extract
2 tablespoons fresh lemon juice
1 1/2 cups mashed banana
3 cups all-purpose flour
2 teaspoons baking powder
1/2 teaspoon baking soda
1/4 teaspoon ground cinnamon
1/2 teaspoon salt
1/2 cup finely chopped walnuts (optional)

LEMON GLAZE
3/4 cup confectioners' sugar
2–4 tablespoons fresh lemon juice
1/2 teaspoon vanilla extract

CHOCOLATE GLAZE
1/2 cup confectioners' sugar
3 tablespoons unsweetened cocoa powder
4 tablespoons, or more, brewed coffee or water,
  as needed

Preheat the oven to 350°F. Generously grease and flour a 10-inch tube or a large Bundt pan. If using a Bundt, make sure the fluted sides are very well greased.

In a large bowl, whisk together the sugar, oil, eggs, vanilla, and lemon juice until smooth. Stir in the mashed banana. In a separate bowl, mix together the flour, baking powder, baking soda, cinnamon, salt, and walnuts. Fold the dry ingredients into the batter and blend well. Scrape the bottom of the bowl to ensure there are no unincorporated ingredients.

Pour the batter into the prepared pan and bake for 55 to 70 minutes (depending on the pan you've used), or until the cake springs back when gently pressed. Cool for 10 minutes, then invert onto a serving plate and cool to room temperature.

continued

LEMON OR CHOCOLATE GLAZE: In a bowl, stir the confectioners' sugar together with the other ingredients, adding water as required to achieve a thick but pourable glaze. Spoon or drizzle the glaze onto the cooled cake.

VARIATION: For Chocolate Chip Banana Cake, fold 1 cup chocolate chips into the batter, along with the dry ingredients. Proceed as directed.

Blitz Cherry Cake

Makes 8 to 10 servings

In German, the word blitz *refers to lightning, suggesting the speed with which this cake is put together. In fact, while researching old Jewish cookbooks, I came across quite a few "blitz cakes," most of which called for whipped egg whites and nuts. My impression was that they yielded somewhat elegant cakes and tortes in an expedient fashion. This Blitz Cherry Cake is mixed in under 5 minutes and when it emerges from the oven, you have a beautiful, golden treat, rippled with scarlet cherries. It impresses everyone.*

3 cups all-purpose flour
½ teaspoon baking soda
2½ teaspoons baking powder
½ teaspoon salt
1 cup vegetable oil
2 cups sugar
4 eggs
2 teaspoons vanilla extract
2 drops almond and/or lemon extract
1 cup fresh orange juice
1 (19-ounce) can cherry pie filling

Preheat the oven to 350°F. Lightly grease a 10-inch springform pan, a 9 by 13-inch rectangular pan, or two 9 by 5-inch loaf pans.

In a medium-sized bowl, using a large whisk, blend together the dry ingredients. Make a well in the center and blend in the oil, sugar, eggs, vanilla and almond extracts, and the orange juice. Stir to make a smooth batter.

Pour three quarters of the batter into the prepared pan, then the cherry filling, then half the remaining batter. Top with the remaining quarter of the batter dropped in dollops—it will be uneven but it does not matter.

Bake for 55 to 60 minutes, depending on the pan you've used. The cake will be set on top when baked and firm to the touch.

VARIATIONS: For Blitz Blueberry or Blitz Apple Cake, use 1 can blueberry pie or apple pie filling to replace the cherries. Proceed as directed.

THE MANDELBROT CONNECTION

Question: When is mandelbrot called "biscotti"?

Answer: When you call your grandmother "Nona," instead of "Bubbie."

Dry cookies, meant for dipping into coffee, wine, or tea, come in many guises. Italians call them biscotti and they are eaten as a dessert cookie, a wine accompaniment, or something to enjoy with morning coffee. Over the years, biscotti have become quite trendy.

Fashionable biscotti bear a pretty close relationship to another homey, similarly dry cookie, mandelbrot. Mandelbrot can also be found under its other Jewish alias, "kamishbrot" or simply, "kamish" or "comish." *Kamish* or *comish,* is Yiddish, and means either "odd" or "funny," as in comical. *Mandelbrot,* of Germanic origin, translates to "almond bread," but mandelbrot can be made with any nut or variety of nuts.

To a baker, biscotti, mandelbrot, and kamishbrot generally all refer to a variety of cookie that is distinct in that it is "double-baked," first while in a log or batter, then again at a lower temperature after being cut into cookies, which further crisps the cookie.

Both biscotti and mandelbrot are usually studded with nuts of some sort. Mandelbrot is generally oil-based—a concession to Jewish dietary laws— whereas biscotti can be fat-free or made with butter (or, in some cases, oil). While biscotti, especially Americanized biscotti, come in a staggering choice of flavors, mandelbrot is primarily walnut- or almond-filled and graced with a bit of cinnamon. Biscotti are quite crisp and crunchy, the result of a longer second bake; mandelbrot's second bake is a bit shorter, yielding a crisp, but slightly less resistant first bite. Call this cookie what you will—biscotti, mandelbrot, kamishbrot, or mandelbread—but consider these universal tips for making better ones.

MASTERING MANDELBROT

Although traditional mandelbrot is based on simple ingredients and simple formulas, contemporary versions know no limits when it comes to gilding the lily. Certainly, when something is homemade, it thrives on the personal touch.

The thick batter is very accommodating, an affable host to pretty well anything you care to throw in. Plainer mandelbrot can be slicked up with a coat of melted chocolate and dusting of chopped pistachios or a sprinkle of confectioners' sugar. ·

Mandelbrot, as biscotti, can, in fact, be made without added fat (the flour must be reduced somewhat), resulting in a crisper—destined for dunking—but still tasty cookie. Any mandelbrot recipe calling for butter can be made with canola or vegetable oil instead without too noticeable a difference in taste.

Place the mandelbrot in the upper third of your oven for even baking without risk of overbrowning the cookie bottoms. If you want to bake two sheets at once, double up the bottom baking sheet (one baking sheet sits inside another) to insulate further this bottom sheet from the direct heat of the oven's bottom element.

For very traditional mandelbrot, try the Traditional Chocolate Chip Mandelbrot (page 94), which also takes well to variations. For gourmet-style mandelbrot, there's the Gourmet Shop Double Almond recipe (page 138), Sugar-Crusted Wine Mandelbrot (page 197), Clementine-Cranberry Biscotti Loaf (page 143), or Shirley and Anita's Ultra Thin and Crisp Almond Mandelbrot (page 82), as well as the decadent Black and White Mandelbrot (page 168).

GLAZING—PLAIN, EGG WASH, OR CHOCOLATE DIPPING

Before the cookies are baked, you can paint or brush the top of the log of dough with a beaten egg white and sprinkle it with coarse or regular granulated sugar. When the cookies are cut and rebaked, they result in slices of mandelbrot that sport a slight sheen and glisten with a touch of sugar. You can also leave mandelbrot plain, or unglazed, for an equally elegant cookie. All mandelbrot can be further gilded by finishing with a chocolate glaze.

To glaze, melt four to eight ounces of semi-sweet dark or white chocolate in a double boiler or in the microwave. Using a small, flat icing knife, spread the melted chocolate on one side of each cookie. Cool on a cake rack until thoroughly dry or set. You can also freeze them but the gloss of the chocolate will dull. Alternatively, simply dip one end of each cookie in the melted chocolate, or even double dip (once into the dark chocolate and, when dry, a second, more "shallow" dip into the white chocolate—or vice versa.)

Traditional Chocolate Chip Mandelbrot

Makes 2 to 3 dozen

This is a classic mandelbrot. I use this basic recipe in a number of ways (see Mandelbrot Variations, page 95) and it is always a success. Make it by hand, in a mixer, or in the food processor. My youngest son Benjamin calls these "cookie sticks."

1½ cups sugar
1 cup vegetable oil
4 eggs
3 tablespoons fresh orange juice
2½ teaspoons vanilla extract
3½ cups all-purpose flour
½ teaspoon salt
2½ teaspoons baking powder
¼ teaspoon ground cinnamon
1½ cups chocolate chips
1 cup chopped walnuts (optional)

Preheat the oven to 350°F. Line a baking sheet with parchment paper.

In a large bowl, whisk together the sugar and oil. Stir in the eggs, then the orange juice and vanilla. Stir in the flour, salt, baking powder, and cinnamon to make a very thick batter. Fold in the chocolate chips. Add the walnuts, if you're using them.

Spread the batter out onto the prepared baking sheet in one large (3 to 5 inches wide by 10 to 14 inches long) or two smaller (3 to 5 inches wide by 6 to 8 inches long) logs. If you think this batter will crowd your baking sheet, put half on one sheet, the other half on another.

Bake until the top seems dry (30 to 40 minutes). Remove from the oven and cool for 10 minutes. Meanwhile, reduce the oven heat to 325°. Using a serrated knife, cut the log into ¾-inch-thick slices.

Place the mandelbrot on its baking sheet and into the oven. Bake to dry (10 minutes on each side) turning them once midway.

MANDELBROT VARIATIONS

Traditional Chocolate Chip Mandelbrot is the ideal "foundation" recipe to fiddle with.

FLAVORINGS

Instead of the vanilla:

Use ½ teaspoon lemon or orange oil/or extracts
  or almond extract

Increase the cinnamon to 1 teaspoon or toss in a
  bag with cinnamon sugar (½ cup sugar and
  1 teaspoon cinnamon) after baking.

Use brown sugar instead of granulated sugar.

Instead of orange juice:

Try brandy or whisky.

Instead of chocolate chips:

Try coarsely chopped semi-sweet chocolate.

Use milk or white chocolate or a combination of
  the two.

Add drained maraschino cherries.

Instead of walnuts:

Use almonds, hazelnuts, or pecans.

VARIATION Triple-Toned Mandelbrot

This is easy but results in a unique, zebra-like appearance.

Divide the dough into 3 parts: Remove 2 portions to separate bowls; leave one third in the original bowl.

CHOCOLATE BATTER
To one bowl, mix or knead in 2 tablespoons of unsweetened cocoa powder combined with 2 tablespoons vegetable oil.

CINNAMON BATTER
To second bowl, mix or knead in 1½ teaspoons ground cinnamon. Wet your hands or oil your palms slightly—this batter is sticky.

NOTE: Sometimes, I sprinkle a small handful of chocolate chips between the layers.

Other times I use espresso coffee powder to replace the cinnamon or cocoa in one of the batter portions.

First, spread a length of cinnamon batter on the baking sheet. Then, spread a layer of plain batter over it. Spread a layer of chocolate batter over this. The layers need not be exact or neat. If the mandelbrot is stiff (some days it turns out stiffer than others), you can even roll a length of dough in your hands and then flatten it onto the baking sheet.

If you want long mandelbrot sticks (baked, they are about 6 inches long), use all the dough. For smaller mandelbrot (baked, they are about 4 inches long), divide the dough in half and use 2 baking sheets.

Bake until the dough seems set and dry, 35 to 38 minutes. Remove from the oven and cool a little. Slice, on the diagonal, about ½ inch thick. Reduce the heat to 325°, and return the cookies to the cookie sheet, and bake for 15 to 18 minutes, turning once midway, to dry the cookies.

Bubbie-Style Yellow Cake

Makes 8 to 10 servings

Everyone who has tasted this cake agrees: It tastes like a "bubbie's" cake. Tester Janet Goldstein's husband called it "Very Shabbatish." It is the sort of cake you expect to see in a neighborhood deli or kosher bakery. Eggy and golden, and satisfying in a real comfort-food way. It tastes like a sponge cake, but is more like a moist chiffon cake in texture. Pareve or dairy, depending on which liquid you use, it is fine alone or covered with berries or fruit sorbet. For a more extravagant version of this cake, double the recipe and bake it in a 10-inch tube or angel cake pan.

¾ cup vegetable oil
1¼ cups granulated sugar
3 eggs
1½ teaspoons vanilla extract
2 cups all-purpose flour
¼ teaspoon salt
2½ teaspoons baking powder
½ cup milk or orange juice
Confectioners' sugar, for dusting (optional)

Preheat the oven to 350°F. Generously grease a 9 by 5-inch loaf pan.

Blend the oil and sugar very well. Add the eggs, one at a time, and blend thoroughly after each addition. Stir in the vanilla. Fold in the flour, salt, and baking powder. Mix, adding the milk or orange juice slowly to produce a smooth batter.

Pour the batter into the pan. Place the pan on 2 baking sheets stacked together (this ensures the bottom will not get too browned). Bake on the bottom rack of the oven until the top seems set and springs back when gently touched with a finger (the top of the cake may be cracked; this is fine), 50 to 55 minutes. Cool for 10 minutes in the pan before turning out to cool on a rack. Dust, if desired, with confectioners' sugar.

Incredible Cinnamon Chip Cake

Makes 10 to 12 servings

This is just about the best cake to come out of my test kitchen. It is rich and buttery tasting (although butter-free), moist, flavorful, and a good keeper.

CINNAMON CHIP PASTE
1/3 cup pecans or walnuts
1/2 cup brown sugar
1 tablespoon vegetable oil
1/2 teaspoon vanilla extract
1 teaspoon ground cinnamon
1/3 cup butterscotch chips

CAKE
3/4 cup vegetable oil
2 cups granulated sugar
3 eggs
1 cup water or fresh orange juice
1 tablespoon vanilla extract
2 3/4 cups all-purpose flour
1/2 teaspoon salt
1/2 teaspoon ground cinnamon
2 1/2 teaspoons baking powder
1 teaspoon baking soda

Preheat the oven to 350°F. Generously grease a 10-inch springform pan or a 9 by 13-inch cake pan. Line the pan bottom with parchment paper.

CINNAMON CHIP PASTE: Combine all the paste ingredients in a food processor and grind for about a minute or two, until the mixture is coarse. You can also put these ingredients in a plastic bag and chunk with a rolling pin. Set aside.

CAKE: Using a wire whisk (or an electric mixer), in a large bowl, blend together the oil, sugar, eggs, water or orange juice, and vanilla. In a separate bowl, combine the dry ingredients. Fold into the wet ingredients. This produces a wet, somewhat loose batter.

Spoon all but a couple of tablespoons of batter into the pan. Sprinkle the cinnamon chip paste all over the cake, taking care not to concentrate any topping in the center (this could cause the middle to sink during baking). Cover the topping with the remaining batter—it will not cover it all but it will bake into an interesting pattern.

Bake for 45 minutes in a cake pan, 60 to 70 minutes in a springform pan. The top will be just firm to the touch and will look slightly crusty, with bits of melted topping peaking through. The center may dip a bit—this is fine.

Let the cake cool in the pan for 15 minutes before removing it to a rack.

VARIATION: For Incredible Chocolate Streak Cake, substitute chocolate chips for the butterscotch and omit the cinnamon.

Polish Apple Tart

Makes 8 servings

More a pastry than a pie or a tart, this dessert impresses everyone and stays fresh-looking and -tasting for days. This fancy apple pie takes its inspiration from a dish served at Stash's Flea Market Restaurant in Montreal. If you prefer, you may use prepared pastry for a double-crust 9-inch pie.

PASTRY
2½ cups all-purpose flour
½ cup (1 stick) unsalted butter
½ cup vegetable shortening
Approximately ½ cup ice water
¾ teaspoon salt
1 tablespoon granulated sugar

APPLE FILLING
6–8 cups, peeled, grated or shredded sweet
  apples (such as McIntosh or Golden Delicious)
¾ cup granulated sugar
1 tablespoon fresh lemon juice
½ teaspoon ground cinnamon
2 tablespoons flour
1 tablespoon cornstarch
confectioners' sugar for dusting

Lightly grease a 9- or 10-inch quiche pan with a removable bottom. (Or use a large pie pan or tart pan—similar to a quiche pan but not as deep.)

PASTRY: Place the flour in a large bowl. Cut or rub in the butter and shortening until you have a somewhat even mixture of flour-covered fat resembling coarse meal. Make a well in the center and add most of the water, then the salt and sugar. Stir with a fork or your fingers to dissolve the salt and sugar. Stir the dough lightly with a fork to combine the dry and liquid ingredients. Use your hands when the dough gets too hard to mix, and combine to make a rough mass. If the dough seems too dry, add the remaining water. Knead very gently for a few seconds to smooth out the dough. Pat it into a flattened disc and wrap well in plastic. Chill for at least 1 hour or overnight before using.

FILLING: While the dough chills, in a large bowl, toss the apples with the other filling ingredients.

Remove the dough from the refrigerator and divide it in half. Wrap one of the portions and place it in the freezer. Roll the remaining pastry to fit the pan bottom and sides. Mound the apple filling into the prepared pie shell. Preheat the oven to 400°F.

Remove the reserved dough from the freezer and using a metal hand grater, shred it as you would cheese. If the dough is too cold to work with, allow it to warm for 10 to 15 minutes. Arrange the shredded dough over the apples. Place the pan on a baking sheet (this will catch the drippings) and bake for 15 minutes. Reduce the heat to 375° and continue to bake until the apple juices begin to come through the top and side surfaces and the dough on top is lightly browned (30 to 40 minutes). Remove from the oven and cool well.

Before serving, dust with a generous shower of confectioners' sugar.

Old-Fashioned Crumb Cake

Makes 12 to 16 servings

This crumb cake is based on a commercial Jewish bakery formula for "wine cake." Buttermilk makes it tender and rich but sour cream or yogurt could be substituted. It is even best a day or two later, and it freezes well. An absolute gem.

CAKE
2 cups granulated sugar
1 cup (2 sticks) unsalted butter
1/2 cup vegetable shortening
4 eggs
2 teaspoons vanilla extract
3 1/4 cups all-purpose flour
1/4 teaspoon salt
2 tablespoons cornstarch
1 teaspoon baking soda
2 teaspoons baking powder
1 1/2 cups buttermilk
1 1/2 cups frozen blueberries (optional)

CRUMB TOPPING
1/3 cup confectioners' sugar
1/3 cup all-purpose flour
1/2 teaspoon ground cinnamon
1/8 teaspoon grated nutmeg
2–4 tablespoons unsalted butter or margarine, melted

Preheat the oven to 350°F. Lightly grease a 9 by 13-inch rectangular pan, two 9 by 9-inch square pans, or two 9 by 5-inch loaf pans.

CAKE: In a large bowl, cream the sugar with the butter and shortening. Add the eggs, one at a time, until well-blended, then add the vanilla. Fold in the flour, salt, cornstarch, baking soda, and baking powder. As the batter is being mixed, slowly pour in the buttermilk. Gently fold in the blueberries by hand. Spoon the batter into the pan.

CRUMB TOPPING: In a small bowl, toss the confectioners' sugar, flour, cinnamon, and nutmeg with the melted butter to make a crumbly mixture. Distribute the topping evenly over the cake batter.

Bake until the cake seems just firm to the touch when pressed gently (about 50 minutes—60 minutes for loaf cakes). Cool completely, in or out of the pan, before serving.

THEY HAVE TO BE THIN!
THE MUN COOKIE DEBATE

Just say "mun cookie" and, as instantaneously and reliably as Pavlov's pooch, someone will inevitably respond with, "I like mun cookies, but they have to be the thin kind." How thin? As thin as strudel, thin enough to see through, thin enough to just about melt in your mouth, but . . . not so thin or so fragile that all you get is mun crumbs off the cookie tray. How do you get mun cookies that thin?

Step 1. Start with a perfect recipe that is innately balanced and suits your, and everyone else's, taste. It should be just sweet enough, with just enough oil, the proper amount of poppy seeds, a hint of vanilla, and a touch of salt. Once made, the dough has to be just the right texture. Too soft or too dry and it will be hard to work with. However, if your dough seems soft, this is easily remedied. Usually, once the dough is rolled on your floured board, it will naturally ingest additional flour and get to the right state. In other words, if you are in doubt when making the dough about how much flour to use, remember, *you can always add more.* Also, you can chill a slack dough to make it more manageable.

Step 2. Allow your freshly made dough a rest of ten minutes on the work surface, covered with a tea towel. Resting the dough, instead of immediately rolling it out, allows for a more complete flour absorption and also relaxes the gluten—that element which is great in breads but the enemy of tender cookies. A more relaxed dough rolls out much more easily.

Step 3. Use the heaviest rolling pin you have. A stainless steel one (see page 26) works wonders but a large, heavy-duty wood pin is also up to the task. Lightweight, ten-inch, wood pins just make the job that much harder. If you have a rolling pin stocking (I order mine through Sweet Celebrations, who sells them in packets of two), this works wonders. The stretch cotton sleeve is designed to surround the pin, stretching to fit snugly. Doughs release easily from the fabric-encased pin, and prevent you from adding too much flour, while enabling you to roll the dough very thin almost effortlessly.

Step 4. The best way to roll dough is between two pieces of floured parchment paper. You can apply quite a bit of pressure without tearing the dough, easily flattening it into optimal thinness. Then, just peel off the top parchment paper, cut the cookies directly on the bottom sheet, and transfer the paper that holds the cookies to the baking sheet (make sure the parchment paper is the same size as your baking sheet). Using a small metal spatula, remove the excess dough from around the sides of the cookies.

Step 5. If you are *not* using parchment paper, lift those very thin (possibly-sticking-to-the-work-surface) cookies off with a small metal icing spatula. A big help. Use a butter knife if you don't have one of these spatulas, although this inexpensive little tool is a treasure for this and a million other baking jobs.

Now, if people still complain that your cookies are good but they would "prefer them just a little thinner," hand out any one of the three outstanding mun cookie recipes in this book and tell them to bake their own.

Incidentally, if you love mun cookies but find cutting out all those circles too much of a chore, try the Mun Tiles/Lazy Person's Method (see page 102). Little effort, great results!

MUN TILES/
LAZY PERSON'S METHOD

As anyone who makes them can attest, mun cookies are just about the easiest cookies in the world to make. Except . . . sometimes, it would be nice to save a bit of time and do without the rolling part. It's also enlightening to see the unique effect of the same recipe sporting a different look. Lazy Person's Mun Cookies are perfect for mun-cookie-lovers who are time-constrained. For this easy approach to quantity mun cookies in a quarter of the time, you can use either the recipe for Melt-in-Your-Mouth Mun Cookies (page 103) or the one for Purím Mun Cookies (page 264). I usually make these two or three inches square but once in a while I make them as large as postcards and stack them on a pretty serving plate.

Preheat the oven to 350°F. Divide the dough in thirds and place one portion between two sheets of parchment paper and roll it out, turning and rolling in whatever direction is required to get an even thickness all around—making sure you do not extend past the parchment paper onto your work surface (leave a 1½-inch perimeter). Lift and place the dough and paper on a cookie sheet large enough to accommodate the parchment paper. Carefully peel off the top sheet. Repeat with the remaining dough. Bake for about 10 minutes, remove from the oven, and mark the sheet with a knife or small pastry or pizza wheel, into diamonds, squares, or rectangular cookies. Return the sheet to the oven to finish baking, 5 to 7 more minutes. Remove, recut the cookies, and make sure they are separated from each other. Cool well, then use a metal spatula to remove the cookies to a wire cooling rack. Makes 80 to 100, depending on the size.

Glistening Mun Sheets

For exceptionally dramatic-looking mun tiles, cut the cookies, using the method above, into postcard-sized shapes, about 3 by 5 inches (but take care to roll the dough very thin). Brush the top with a touch of vegetable oil and dust it lightly with granulated sugar before baking. These oversized mun cookies can be stacked upright in a basket for serving and always get a positive response. A good gift too.

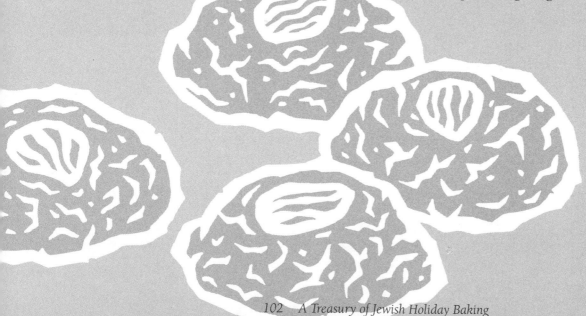

Melt-in-Your-Mouth Mun or Poppy Seed Cookies

Makes 6 to 7 dozen cookies

These light and thin, easy-to-roll cookies are a lovely way to break the fast.

¾ cup vegetable oil
1⅓ cups sugar
3 eggs
1 teaspoon vanilla extract
Approximately 3¼ cups all-purpose flour
2¼ teaspoons baking powder
¼ teaspoon salt
⅓ cup poppy seeds

Preheat the oven to 350°F. Line 2 large baking sheets with parchment paper.

In a medium-sized bowl, briskly whisk together the oil and sugar. Vigorously whisk in the eggs, and then the vanilla, mixing until well blended. Fold in the flour, baking powder, salt, and poppy seeds.

Cover the dough with a tea towel and let it rest 5 to 10 minutes. Working with a third of the dough at a time, on a very well-floured board, roll it out as thin as possible, between ⅟₁₆ and ⅛ inch thick. Make sure your rolling pin is well dusted with flour—a heavy pin covered with a rolling pin stocking is ideal. Rolling between 2 sheets of parchment, the bottom sheet lightly floured, makes this easier. Cut into 2-inch rounds, transfer to the baking sheets, and bake until the tops are lightly golden, 12 to 15 minutes.

VARIATION: Lightly brush each cookie with vegetable oil and sprinkle with sugar before baking.

Extra Zesty Lemon-Currant Loaf

Makes 12 to 16 servings

See the Cranberry, Poppy Seed, and Chocolate Chip variations for this selection. The citric acid, available in the kosher food section of most supermarkets or by mail order, is optional but gives this loaf a real jolt of tartness that lemon lovers enjoy. A lovely, tangy cake that is well received after a traditional Shabbat supper.

CAKE

1 cup currants
½ cup hot (about 100°F.) lemon juice
1 cup vegetable oil
2 cups sugar, plus 2 tablespoons for sprinkling
  (optional)
Zest of 1 lemon, finely minced
4 eggs
2 teaspoons vanilla extract
¾ cup water
3 cups all-purpose flour
½ teaspoon baking soda
2 teaspoons baking powder
½ teaspoon salt
½ teaspoon citric acid (optional)

LEMON SUGAR GLAZE

½ cup fresh lemon juice
½ cup sugar
Zest of 1 lemon, finely grated

Preheat the oven to 350°F. Generously grease one 10-inch tube pan or two 8 by 4½- or 9 by 5-inch loaf pans. Line the pan bottoms with parchment paper.

CAKE: Place the currants in a small bowl, cover them with the hot lemon juice, and allow them to plump for a couple of minutes. Drain, reserving ¼ cup of the juice.

In a large mixing bowl, blend the oil with the 2 cups of sugar and the lemon zest until light and fluffy, scraping the bowl often. Blend in the eggs, then stir in the vanilla, the reserved lemon juice, and the water.

In a separate bowl, whisk together the flour, baking soda, baking powder, salt, and citric acid. Add the flour mixture to the wet ingredients. Fold in the currants and spoon the batter into the prepared pan(s). Sprinkle the top with the 2 tablespoons of sugar if not using the glaze.

Bake large cakes for 60 to 75 minutes, smaller loaves for 45 to 50 minutes. The cakes should be lightly browned on top, perhaps slightly cracked, and should spring back when pressed gently. Cool for 15 to 20 minutes in the pan before inverting onto a wire rack to cool completely.

LEMON SUGAR GLAZE: Heat the lemon juice and sugar in a small saucepan to dissolve the sugar. Stir in the zest and cool well. When the cake is done and cooled, poke holes along the top with a cake tester or a fork. Drizzle the glaze over the cake. Recover the drippings and drizzle on the remaining glaze.

VARIATIONS: For Chocolate Chip Lemon Cake, omit the currants and fold 1 cup miniature semi-sweet chocolate chips or coarsely chopped regular chips into the batter.

For Lemon Poppy Seed Cake, omit the currants and fold ½ cup of poppy seeds into the batter.

For Lemon Cranberry Cake, omit the currants and fold 1 cup finely minced dried cranberries into the batter.

Everybody's Jewish Apple Cake

Makes 10 to 12 servings

*If this cake does not provide instant comfort, nothing will. It is probably the first apple cake
a new baker learns to make and one which seasoned bakers return to again and again.*

8 cups peeled and sliced apples, such as
  Cortland, McIntosh, or Golden Delicious
2 cups sugar
1½ teaspoons ground cinnamon
¾ cup vegetable oil
3 eggs
1 cup fresh orange juice
1 teaspoon vanilla extract
2½ cups all-purpose flour
¼ teaspoon salt
2 teaspoons baking powder

Preheat the oven to 350°F. Generously grease a 9 by 13-inch rectangular baking pan or a 10-inch spring-form pan.

In a large bowl, toss the apples with ½ cup of the sugar and the cinnamon. Blend the oil with the remaining sugar. Beat or whisk in the eggs, then the orange juice and vanilla. Fold in the flour, salt, and baking powder to make a smooth, soft batter.

Spoon half the batter into the prepared pan. Top with the apples, then the remaining batter.

Bake until the cake is crusty and set on top (about 45 minutes).

Caterer's Cookies

Makes 25 to 30 cookies, depending on size

A ubiquitous sort of cookie that turns up at catered affairs. Unassuming, but pleasant and satisfying when all you want is a little bite to go with a cup of coffee or tea. Kids like these with sprinkles. A pastry bag makes these cookies look very professional, but hand-formed dough is fine.

3 egg yolks, hard-cooked, crumbled
½ cup vegetable shortening
½ cup sugar
1 egg yolk
¾ teaspoon vanilla extract
2 cups all-purpose flour
Pinch of salt
2 teaspoons cornstarch
1–3 tablespoons water, as required
10–15 well-drained maraschino or
  candied cherries, halved

Preheat the oven to 350°F. Line 2 baking sheets with parchment paper.

In a medium-sized mixing bowl, combine the crumbled egg yolks with the shortening. Add the sugar, egg yolk, and vanilla and blend well. Fold in the flour, salt, and cornstarch to make a soft dough, adding a bit of water if necessary to make it hold together. Wrap the dough in plastic and chill it for about 10 minutes.

Break off about 2 teaspoonsful of dough, form into a ball, and place about 2 inches apart on the baking sheet. Repeat until all the dough has been used. Using the top of a soda bottle, make a depression in the middle of each dough ball and insert a cherry half.

Bake until lightly golden, 15 to 18 minutes. Remove to a wire rack and cool completely.

Grandma's Roly-Poly

Makes two 12-inch rolls, 10 to 15 slices each

If you were lucky enough to grow up with a Russian-born grandmother, you may be familiar with this unusual and delectable cookie-like strudel. Made with an orange-flavored dough, this strudel keeps for several weeks in the freezer.

ORANGE OIL DOUGH
2 eggs
²/₃ cup sugar
1 teaspoon vanilla extract
½ cup fresh orange juice
½ cup vegetable oil
Approximately 3 cups all-purpose flour
½ teaspoon salt
1 teaspoon baking powder

FILLING
1 cup raspberry or apricot jam
1 cup unsweetened shredded coconut
¾ cup plumped raisins (see page 22)
1 cup ground walnuts
2 teaspoons ground cinnamon
²/₃ cup glacé cherry halves, rinsed and dried
Approximately 1 cup Turkish delight, cut into small slivers

Preheat the oven to 350°F. Line a baking sheet with parchment paper.

DOUGH: In a large bowl, combine the eggs, sugar, vanilla, orange juice, and oil. Stir in the flour, salt, and baking powder to make a soft but rollable dough (you might need to add a extra few tablespoons of flour to achieve this). Knead the dough very briefly on a lightly floured board, cover it with a towel, and let it rest for a couple of minutes.

Divide the dough in half. Roll out each half about ¼ inch thick, to form two 12 by 8-inch rectangles.

FILLING: Spread half the jam on each rectangle. Sprinkle half the remaining ingredients in layers, onto each dough rectangle. Turn in the ends, and roll into a jelly-roll shape. Place the rolls on the cookie sheets and bake for 35 to 40 minutes, until golden brown.

Cool well. Slice on the diagonal, ¾ inch thick for serving. Wrapping and chilling the Roly-Poly for 1 hour makes slicing easier. To freeze, cut and wrap the individual pieces in freezer wrap.

Yeast Kichelah Sugar Twists

Makes 6 to 7 dozen cookies

The fanciest, most delightful pastrylike cookies. Coarse sugar, a key ingredient, is available at bulk food stores, cake decorating stores, by mail or from your neighborhood baker. When coarse sugar is used, the result is a slightly flaky cookie with a caramelized bottom.

¼ cup warm water
Pinch plus 3 tablespoons granulated sugar
½ cup warm orange juice
1 tablespoon dry yeast
2 eggs plus 2 egg yolks
½ cup vegetable oil
½ teaspoon salt
3 cups all-purpose flour
Approximately 1 cup coarse sugar

Preheat the oven to 350°F. Line 2 baking sheets with parchment paper.

In a medium-sized mixing bowl, stir together the water, a pinch of sugar, the orange juice, and the yeast just to combine. Let the mixture stand for a few moments to swell and dissolve the yeast.

Stir in the eggs, egg yolks, oil, the remaining sugar, the salt, and the flour to make a soft dough. Remove the dough to a floured work surface and knead for a few seconds to firm the dough up a little bit. Sprinkle the work surface generously with coarse sugar and roll out the dough ⅛ to ¼ inch thick. Cut in 3- by 1-inch strips, using either a pizza or pastry wheel or a sharp knife. Twist the strips in the middle, then pinch to seal (the cookies will look like little bowties).

Place them on the prepared sheet, about 1 inch apart and bake until golden brown (25 to 35 minutes). Remove from the oven and cool on the baking sheet. The twists will crisp further as they cool.

Double Fudge Chocolate Tube Cake

Makes 12 to 16 servings

A rich, moist cake that is milk-and-butter-free but absolutely flavorful. This cake takes literally seconds to put together. Sometimes I mix the dry ingredients the night before to save even more time.

CAKE
1¾ cups granulated sugar
1 cup brown sugar
1 cup vegetable oil
2 large eggs
2 teaspoons vanilla extract
¾ cup unsweetened cocoa powder, sifted
3 cups all-purpose flour
½ teaspoon salt
1½ teaspoons baking soda
2 teaspoons baking powder
2 cups brewed, just-warm coffee

CHOCOLATE TOPPING
¾ cup semi-sweet chocolate chips
confectioners' sugar, for dusting

CAKE: Preheat the oven to 350°F. Generously grease a large bundt or a 9- or 10-inch tube pan.

In a large bowl, combine the sugars, oil, eggs, and vanilla and beat with an electric mixer or a large hand whisk for 1 minute until smooth. Add the cocoa, flour, salt, baking soda, and baking powder. Stir briefly, then drizzle in the coffee, stirring, to make a smooth, somewhat loose batter.

Spoon the batter into the pan and bake for 60 to 72 minutes. Bundt cakes take longer to bake than those in a tube pan. The top should spring back to the touch when the cake is done.

CHOCOLATE TOPPING: Sprinkle the chocolate chips on top of the cake as soon as it comes out of the oven and allow them to melt. Use a butter knife to swirl the melted chocolate in a decorative fashion. As the cake reaches room temperature, give it a gentle shake to loosen it *but do not remove it from the pan.* Place the cake in the refrigerator to firm the chocolate. Once the chocolate is well set, place a plate on top of the pan and invert the cake onto the plate. Then turn it right side up again. If any of the melted chocolate stays on the plate when you do this, smear it back on the top of the cake with a butter knife or metal spatula. When the chocolate is set, dust it with confectioners' sugar.

This cake can also be topped with a combination of white chocolate and dark chocolate chips. When you spread the melted chocolate, you will get a marbled effect.

The Sisterhood's Cherry Squares

Makes 12 to 16 servings

Whenever I think of this recipe, I visualize a Pyrex baking dish filled with either a freshly baked apple cake or these cherry squares. A "kichel" dough or batter—an all-purpose egg-and-oil batter that is a theme in Jewish cuisine—with an abundance of cherry filling, makes a nice little bite at the end of a big dinner. A sisterhood cookbook classic.

1 cup sugar
¾ cup vegetable oil
½ cup fresh orange juice
2 eggs
2 teaspoons vanilla extract
¼ teaspoon lemon oil or extract (optional)
2 cups all-purpose flour
¼ teaspoon salt
1½ teaspoons baking powder
1 (19-ounce) can cherry pie filling (or another fruit filling of your choice)

Preheat the oven to 350°F. Lightly grease a 9 by 13-inch baking pan.

In a bowl, blend the sugar with the oil, then add the orange juice, eggs, vanilla and lemon extracts. Fold or mix in the flour, salt, and baking powder to make a smooth, thick batter.

Spread half the batter in the pan, then spread on the cherry filling. Cover with the remaining batter.

Bake until the top is lightly browned, 25 to 35 minutes.

Cool well in the pan, then cut into squares and serve.

Friday Night's Rich and Addictive Cocoa Fudge Brownies

Makes 12 to 16 squares

These are extravagant, truffle-like brownies—tender, crackly-topped, and slightly chewy.
I often double the recipe and always serve them directly from the fridge. How good are these? The gas man
who checks out my oven periodically had a couple to snack on. Next time he was by on a routine
range check, he asked for the recipe!

BROWNIES

1 cup vegetable oil or unsalted butter, melted and cooled
1 cup granulated sugar plus
1 cup firmly packed brown sugar (or use all granulated sugar)
3 eggs
2 teaspoons vanilla extract
¾ cup unsweetened cocoa powder, sifted
1 cup all-purpose flour
¼ teaspoon salt
¼ teaspoon baking soda
1 cup chopped pecans or walnuts (optional)

FROSTING

2–3 cups confectioners' sugar
1 cup unsweetened cocoa powder, sifted
½ cup (1 stick) unsalted butter or margarine
½ teaspoon vanilla extract
3–6 tablespoons warm water, as needed

NOTE: I sometimes use all granulated sugar, especially if I am making this with butter.

Preheat the oven to 350°F. Grease a 9 by 9-inch or an 8 by 10-inch baking pan.

BROWNIES: In a bowl, blend the oil or butter and the sugars together. Blend in the eggs, then the vanilla, cocoa powder, flour, salt, baking soda, and nuts to make a smooth batter. Spoon the batter into the prepared pan.

Bake for 25 to 28 minutes, or until the middle is just set and does not seem wet and jiggly when touched. Do not overbake. (Check the brownies during baking as the type of pan you use affects the length of baking time required.) Cool thoroughly in the pan.

FROSTING: In a bowl, combine the confectioners' sugar and cocoa. Add the butter or margarine and cream with the dry ingredients. Add the vanilla and water as required to make a fluffy, spreadable frosting. Add additional confectioners' sugar or water as needed to achieve the desired consistency. Frost the completely cooled brownies and refrigerate for 30 minutes before cutting and serving. Serve cold.

Nut Kipfel, or Viennese Nut Crescents

Makes 3 to 4 dozen crescents

A light, nutty treat.

1 cup (2 sticks) unsalted margarine or butter
¾ cup granulated sugar
2 cups all-purpose flour
1 cup walnuts or pecans, preferably toasted,
  finely ground
¼ teaspoon salt
½ teaspoon vanilla extract
Confectioners' sugar, for dusting

Preheat the oven to 350°F. Line a large baking sheet with parchment paper.

In a mixing bowl, cream the margarine or butter with the granulated sugar. Blend in the flour, nuts, salt, and vanilla until you have a stiff dough that can be handled or formed. Break off small pieces and shape or roll them into small crescents and place them 2 inches apart on the baking sheet. Bake for 15 to 20 minutes, until slightly golden. Cool, then toss liberally in confectioners' sugar.

VARIATION: For Cinnamon Kipfel add 1 teaspoon ground cinnamon with the flour.

Shabbat Chocolate Chip Cookies

Makes about 2 dozen cookies

These oil-based cookies are tender-crisp and bursting with melted chocolate chips. Perfect if you are looking for nondairy chocolate chip cookies for Friday night supper or any occasion.

½ cup vegetable oil
½ cup plus 2 tablespoons brown sugar
2 tablespoons granulated sugar
1 tablespoon honey
1 egg
1 teaspoon vanilla extract
1½ cups all-purpose flour
¼ teaspoon salt
½ teaspoon baking soda
1½ cups coarsely chopped semi-sweet chocolate

Preheat the oven to 350°F. Line 2 large baking sheets with baking parchment. Lightly grease the parchment paper or spray it with nonstick cooking spray.

In a mixing bowl, blend the oil, sugars, and honey together. Beat in the egg and vanilla. Fold in the flour, salt, and baking soda, then the chopped chocolate. You may have to knead in the chips by hand to incorporate them into this rather stiff dough.

Form into small balls, about 1¼ inches in diameter. Place 3 inches apart on the baking sheet and press to flatten slightly. Bake for 10 to 12 minutes, until they're dry on top and slightly colored.

3. Rosh Hashanah

The Jewish New Year

L'shanah tovah u'metuka.
"A good and sweet new year."

—TRADITIONAL HOLIDAY GREETING

"You will cast (tashlik) your sins into the depths of the sea."

—MICAH, 7:19

WHEN ❀ In the Hebrew calendar, the first two days of the month of Tishri.

CORRESPONDING TO ❀ Two days, occurring in September or early October.

HOLIDAY CONTEXT ❀ Each year, after the sun sets on the eve of Rosh Hashanah, our thoughts are on the year that has passed and the one that is about to unfold. It is a special, reflective, spiritual time and it marks the beginning of the High Holidays, also known as the Days of Awe. Yom Kippur, the most solemn, holy day on the Jewish calendar, marks the end of the Days of Awe.

ACTIVITIES/CUSTOMS ❀ More than for any other holiday, Jews—even those who do not consider themselves "religious"—celebrate the New Year at synagogue.

Congregants around the world join in the timeless New Year's songs, prayers, and seasonal rites and witness the blowing of the *shofar,* or ram's horn. The blowing of the shofar is more than ceremonial, it is a spiritual wake-up call, one that is supposed to evoke reflection and awareness.

Tashlik is another ritual of the Rosh Hashanah observance. A custom dating back to the Middle Ages, tashlik is performed wherever there is flowing water. Bits of bread or bread crumbs (I have seen people use bits of paper) are cast onto the water, to carry away one's sins.

FOOD SYMBOLS ❀ Festive meals are served the night before the first day of Rosh Hashanah, at luncheon the next day, after the morning services, and again the following evening. These are informal occasions, where family and friends can toast the New Year in their home with some sweet red wine and a slice of New Year's challah. At Rosh Hashanah, we also eat a "new fruit" or one that is not usually enjoyed. Pomegranates, exotic symbols of fertility (consider their numerous fleshy seeds) are often selected.

To symbolize the theme of "sweetness in the New Year," in addition to savory foods (roasted chickens, brisket, and other standbys) hosts are sure to offer a sweeter-than-usual raisin-studded, round challah, also known as a *faygala* or *faigele*. This bread is served with slices of apple and/or a dish of honey for dipping. Strudel, apple, and honey cakes are tempting traditions at this time as well.

ROSH HASHANAH'S
SHOWCASE CHALLAH

Discounting the inevitable bowls of honey and apples, the most universal food symbol of the Jewish New Year's table is the raisin-studded egg bread or *faigele,* also known as a New Year's "special challah." This enticing circular bread is a richer rendition of the regular Sabath challah. Its round form represents the continuity of life; its sweet additions of extra honey and raisins exemplify the holiday theme. According to Freda Reider in the now out-of-print *Hallah Book,* the *faigele's* ("little bird") roots go back as far as the eighteenth-century Ukraine.

In days long past, some Jewish bakers used to top the holiday challah with a bird's head made of additional dough, with two raisins for eyes. As Reider recounts, "The symbolism of the faigele 'little bird' is, may our sins be carried away by the bird, and may she fly with our prayers for salvation straight up to God." Eventually, the spiral challah divested itself of the quaint little bird of dough, but the name, faigele, remained and its "round bounteous form still symbolizes universal peace, harmony, and the full measure of prosperity for the new year."

STRATEGIES FOR MAKE-AHEAD,
HOT-FROM-THE-OVEN
NEW YEAR'S CHALLAH

There are many ways to ensure fresh challah for the New Year's table.

The dough for a New Year's challah can be made the day before you wish to serve it. Store the once-risen dough in a lightly oiled plastic bag or a large, sealed container. Allow the dough to come back to room temperature before forming it into its final shape and glazing it with egg wash. As it warms up, it will rise.

Alternatively, you can prepare the bread for baking by shaping and glazing and inserting the entire baking sheet inside a large plastic bag; then refrigerate it. The bread will rise slowly in the refrigerator overnight. When ready to bake, remove the bread from the fridge and allow it to have its final rise, warming up to room temperature as it does so.

Finally, you can form the bread after its initial rise, glaze it, and allow it to rise 20 to 30 percent. Then freeze the bread, wrapping it well once it is thoroughly frozen. When ready to bake, allow the bread to rise overnight in the refrigerator (freezer to room temperature is too big a shock to the bread). The following day, allow the bread to come to room temperature (it will rise more as it warms) and bake it a couple of hours before it is required. The only thing you want to avoid is taking chilled dough and popping it right into a hot oven. Let the bread adjust from fridge or freezer by allowing it all the time it needs to rise. You'll find that once it seems risen enough, coincidentally it will also be the right temperature for baking.

SO HOW DO YOU MAKE A
ROUND CHALLAH?

Making a round challah is not difficult, but it helps to know the technique. For years, I attempted to re-create the turban shape commercial bakeries produce in the thousands by coiling the entire length of challah dough in concentric circles, one on top of the other. The result, although tasty, was my annual, lopsided "roundish" faigele. The weight on the mounted coils either collapsed the bread into a vague round form or, more often, as the bread rose, the coils merged into one another and could not be distinguished after baking. A brief apprenticeship at a local Jewish bakery revealed the proper method. Form a length of eighteen to twenty-four inches, thicker at one end, tapered at the other. Take the rope of dough and, with one hand, lift the narrowed end and wind the entire length around the thicker end of the strand so that the thick part becomes the middle of the challah. Tuck the tip under the coil and press it down to seal it closed.

BRAIDED CHALLAHS: ELEGANT AND EASY

A very festive, alternate round challah can be formed simply by making the usual three-strand braid. Bring the ends of the braid around and pinch them together. Bake on a baking sheet or in a ten-inch springform pan (any high-sided, round pan will work). As the bread rises and bakes, the result is a spectacular round "crown" of challah.

If you are timid about braiding, you can also make a simple, but very pretty two-braid loaf by dividing the dough in two. Roll out two 15- to 18-inch strands and, locking one end, just twist or roll the two strands together, locking them at the other end once the whole length is twisted. Egg wash and seed this free-form loaf, allow a proper rising time, and you will be rewarded with an extravagant but easy challah twist.

New Year's Sweet Round Raisin Challah

Makes 2 medium loaves, or 1 very large loaf

The sound of the shofar, the ram's horn that trumpets in the New Year at synagogues the world over, is the sound that epitomizes Rosh Hashanah. A freshly cut wedge of this bread, liberally dipped in new autumn honey, is its most memorable taste. Update the raisin faigele with dried cranberries or sour cherries and make up a batch of miniatures to offer as a special Rosh Hashanah gift.

2 tablespoons dry yeast
1¾ cups warm water
⅓ cup plus a pinch of sugar
⅓ cup light honey
3½ teaspoons salt
½ cup vegetable oil
3 eggs plus 2 egg yolks
6½–7½ cups bread flour
1½ cups dark or yellow raisins, plumped
  (see page 22), or an equal amount of
  sour or sweet cherries

EGG WASH OR GLAZE/TOPPING
2 tablespoons water
2 teaspoons sugar
1 egg plus 1 egg yolk
Sesame seeds, for sprinkling (optional)

In a large mixing bowl, stir together the yeast, water, and pinch of sugar. Let the mixture stand for 5 minutes to allow the yeast to swell and dissolve.

Briskly stir in the remaining sugar, the honey, and the salt. Then add the oil, eggs, and yolks and about 5 cups of the flour. Stir into a shaggy mass. Then let the dough stand for 10 to 20 minutes to absorb the flour. Knead by hand or with a dough hook for about 10 to 12 minutes, adding the remaining flour as required to make a soft and elastic dough. The dough should leave the sides of the bowl. If it is sticky, add small amounts of flour until it is soft but no longer sticks. (If you find the dough too bulky for your mixer, divide it in two and knead one portion at a time.)

Let the dough rest on a lightly floured board for 10 minutes, then flatten it gently and press in the raisins (or cherries) as evenly as possible throughout the dough, folding the dough over the raisins to "tuck" them in. Place the dough in a greased bowl and either cover it with greased plastic wrap and a damp tea towel or cover it with a damp tea towel and place the entire bowl inside a large plastic bag. Seal the bag and let the dough rise until almost doubled and puffy (45 to 90 minutes).

(Alternatively, if you are doing an overnight, cool rise, place the dough in a large, lightly greased bowl, insert the bowl in a large plastic bag, and refrigerate overnight. If you see the bread rising too quickly in the fridge, open the bag, deflate the dough, and reseal the bag. Next day, allow the dough to warm up, then gently deflate it and proceed with the recipe.)

Divide the dough in two and shape as described on page 118. Place the shaped bread on a cornmeal-sprinkled baking sheet.

In a small bowl, whisk together the egg glaze ingredients. Brush the bread with egg wash and sprinkle on the sesame seeds. Let the dough rise until puffy (20 to 30 minutes).

Preheat the oven to 400°F. Bake the bread for 12 minutes, then reduce the heat to 350° and bake for another 25 minutes, or until the bread is evenly browned.

VARIATIONS ON NEW YEAR'S SWEET CHALLAH:
GIFT-SIZED "HONEY-GLAZED" NEW YEAR'S CHALLAH

This is a delectable, and different, presentation for a holiday challah and makes a great Rosh Hashanah gift. The overall effect is almost like a "honey-glazed" doughnut, only in a challah form. Much like store-bought "honey-glazed" doughnuts, this glaze does not contain any honey (although you can add a touch if you want to). The semi-translucent glaze coats the challah with just the right kiss of sweetness. This challah can be served as a dessert at a New Year's luncheon or dinner. You can also garnish the bread (before the glaze sets) with grated orange zest or sesame seeds. Another version of this pretty bread can be found on page 122.

1 recipe New Year's Sweet Round Raisin Challah (page 120)
1½ cups confectioners' sugar
2–4 tablespoons fresh orange juice
½ teaspoon orange oil or extract (optional)

Divide the dough into 2 to 3 smaller turbans. Combine the ingredients for the glaze. After the turbans are baked, glaze them with the confectioners' sugar glaze.

New Year's Apple Challah

Makes 1 large loaf or 2 smaller loaves

What could be more appealing than a rich challah studded with chunks of fresh autumn apples. This is the perfect cross between a bread and a cake—velvety slices of vanilla-scented challah highlighted by tangy sweet apples. The bottom of the baked bread becomes caramelized with sugar and apple juices. Serve it at an after-holiday-services luncheon, or to break the Yom Kippur fast. Leftovers make terrific "apple" French toast. If I entered a contest for a "trademark" recipe, this would be a major contender.

You can use almost any apple in this recipe—a combination of tart and sweet is best.

If apples are new and thin skinned, you can leave the peels on—the bright red bakes up very prettily in the finished loaf. Alternatively, I make this bread with a combination of apples and whole cranberries, or even add some plumped dried cherries. This recipe works equally well with either the oil or melted, unsalted butter for a slightly more danish-tasting loaf.

I have also tried this recipe by mounding up the chunks in a 10-inch springform pan. Leave it plain or drizzle on a vanilla fondant (see page 140).

DOUGH
1 cup warm water
½ cup plus a pinch of granulated sugar
2 tablespoons dry yeast
½ cup vegetable oil or unsalted butter, melted
2 eggs
2 teaspoons vanilla extract
2½ teaspoons salt
½ teaspoon ground cinnamon
5–6 cups bread flour

APPLE MIXTURE
3 cups coarsely chopped apples
½ cup granulated sugar
1 tablespoon fresh lemon juice
1 teaspoon ground cinnamon

EGG WASH/TOPPING
1 egg, beaten
1 teaspoon granulated sugar
1–2 tablespoons coarse sugar, for sprinkling

Generously spray one 5 by 12-inch loaf pan or two 9 by 5-inch loaf pans with nonstick cooking spray. You could also use a 10-inch springform pan.

DOUGH: In a large mixing bowl, briskly whisk together the water, pinch of sugar, and yeast. Let the mixture stand for 5 minutes to allow the yeast to swell or dissolve. Briskly stir in remaining sugar and the oil (or melted butter), the eggs, vanilla, salt, and cinnamon. Add most of the flour to form a smooth but resilient dough (this is a soft, but elastic bread dough). Add the remaining flour and knead for 8 to 10 minutes.

Shape the dough into a ball, place it in a lightly

greased bowl, place the bowl in a plastic bag, and seal loosely. Let the dough rise until doubled (45 to 60 minutes).

APPLES: Place the apples in a medium-sized bowl and toss them with the sugar, lemon juice, and cinnamon.

EGG WASH: Prepare the egg wash by whisking together the egg and granulated sugar.

Preheat the oven to 350°F.

Turn the dough out onto a lightly floured board and roll or pat it into a large round (about 10 inches across.) Press in half the chopped apples. Fold the edges of the dough over the apples (in any way you can). Roll to flatten with a heavy rolling pin (so as to offer more of a surface on which to place the remaining apples). Pat or press the remaining apples into the dough. Bring the edges of the dough over the apples, pressing in any that may pop out (just put them back on or stick them on top of the dough later on). This step will seem messy but it does not matter. The idea is to distribute the apples all over the dough in a random way. Let the dough rest for 5 minutes. Then, using a dough cutter or a sharp knife, cut into randomly shaped chunks— about 16 pieces in all. Lay the pieces of apple-filled dough in the prepared pan, lining the bottom first, then gently laying the remaining pieces on top. Sprinkle with any escaped apple pieces.

Alternatively, you can press the dough out to form a large oval or circle and press the apples into the dough. Roll it up, cut it in half and place each half in a 9 by 15-inch loaf pan that has been generously sprayed with nonstick cooking spray.

Dab on the egg wash as thoroughly and generously as possible. (Since the dough is not a smooth surface, you will have to drizzle and dab on the glaze rather than paint it on.) Sprinkle with coarse sugar if desired. Place the loaf pan(s) inside a large plastic bag, seal loosely, and let the dough rise until almost doubled or until it is puffy and has almost reached the top of the pan (45 to 90 minutes).

Bake for 40 to 45 minutes, until the bread is well browned all over. If the top of the bread starts browning too quickly (and its interior is not done), cover the loaf lightly with a sheet of foil to protect the top crust.

Cool in the pan for 10 minutes, then turn out and cool completely on a rack.

New Year's Sweet Challah Miniatures

Makes 3 to 4 dozen rolls, depending on size

Miniature New Year's round challahs, made from the same dough as the New Year's Sweet Round Raisin Challah, make a great gift. Just bundle up a bunch of them in a pretty basket, insert a jar of honey, some very red apples, and you have a beautiful New Year's present. These small breads also work well if you want to offer rolls at a New Year's luncheon table. Everyone gets their own—a big hit with children too! As a change of pace, miniature challahs can be made with sun-dried cherries, cranberries, apricots, or small pieces of diced apple replacing the raisins.

1 recipe New Year's Sweet Round Raisin Challah
(page 120)
Sesame seeds

Line several baking sheets with parchment paper.

Prepare the dough and allow it to rise once. Divide it into 36 to 48 pieces and roll them into 8-inch-long strips. Gently tie each strip in a knot. Place them on the baking sheets, brush them with the egg wash, and sprinkle with the sesame seeds, if desired. Cover lightly with a large sheet of plastic and let the rolls rise until puffy (15 to 20 minutes).

Preheat the oven to 375°F. Bake the rolls for 12 to 15 minutes, until lightly browned.

For gift-giving, line a basket with colored tissue paper. Place a wax paper liner on top of the tissue and fill the basket with 8 to 10 rolls. Tuck in a small jar of honey and some small red apples or dried fruit, a pomegranate or an *etrog* (a holiday citrus available at fruit stores for Jewish New Year). Cover with tinted cellophane paper (available at craft stores) or plastic wrap and tie with a ribbon.

HONEY CAKE—THE CROWN OF ROSH HASHANAH

Ask ten Jewish bakers for a honey cake recipe and chances are you'll be rewarded with a about ten-fold more than you asked for. Everyone has a favorite, and each honey cake, of course, has a special secret—a family tip, an unusual technique, a particular step. "I use coffee," swears one maven, while another woman maintains that fresh orange juice accounts for her cake's wonderful bouquet. One friend and recipe-tester maintains that a quarter cup of "rye" is the secret flavor-booster in her famed honey cake. Since I don't drink and I am always thinking in baking terms, I assumed she meant "a quarter cup of rye flour." While I said nothing at the time, I privately had my doubts. Then one day she explained and claimed the quarter cup of alcohol, although most baked out of the cake, gave it a special taste. "I thought you meant rye flour!" I said. "Who would ever put rye flour into a cake?" was the response. And then . . . a little while later, I happened on a commercial recipe for honey cake that called for rye flour exclusively! So, you never know.

The point is, honey cake, like most comfort foods, is a very personal thing, passed down from one generation to the next and shared among appreciative friends. People do try new honey cake recipes, always on the lookout for that extra one to add to their collection, but there is a particular loyalty surrounding honey cakes, rivaled only by the matzoh ball soup debate (hard ones versus soft and fluffy ones).

"A HONEY CAKE SHOULD BE MOIST" (OR HOW TO MAKE THE SAME CAKE A HUNDRED DIFFERENT WAYS—VARIATIONS ON THE HONEY CAKE THEME)

No matter how people argue over the merits of one honey cake or another, the point all can agree on is that "a good honey cake" must be *moist*. Yet, if you research *lekach,* honey cake, you might be surprised to learn that most of them started out relatively low in fat. Many recipes I found had only four tablespoons, a scant quarter cup, of oil. These cakes, while good, were drier. More contemporary Jewish community cookbooks reflect the newer era of honey cakes, and the fat, over the years, has increased accordingly.

Start with a moist batter as your foundation and you can easily make additions and adjustments (dark, light, spicy or not). In this book, I have included a wide selection of honey cakes. If you find you like the texture and crumb of a particular cake, feel free to play around with the spices: more spices for a darker, spicier cake; reduced spices for a more subtle cake. Try adding citrus zest and orange juice for a slight tang, or use ginger ale in a light honey cake. Substitute dark tea or cola to replace the coffee in another version. The possibilities are endless (just write down what you did so you remember it for next time!).

In general, dark honey cakes are the result of using a greater quantity and variety of spices and a dark, dominant honey such as buckwheat, as well as dark coffee or dark tea as the liquid, and dark brown rather than white sugar. Light honey cakes are the result of using orange juice or *light* tea, white or light brown sugar, and far fewer spices. Medium cakes can be half orange juice and half coffee, and incorporate only a couple of spices rather than the whole cinnamon-through-ginger-allspice-mace gamut. Honey cake, as you can see, is quite flexible.

BAKING WITH HONEY

Eat honey, my son, for it is good.

—PROVERBS

Honey has been used in Jewish baking since ancient times—it came long before white granular sugar was invented. At New Year's, honey-laced desserts go center stage. Honey makes a marvelous sweetener in baking, flavorful and distinct, and it is a very edible reminder of our wishes for sweetness in the new year. But baking with honey can be slightly tricky. Here is the low-down on sugar's alter ego.

There are many types of honey, depending on what flowers the bees have feasted on from spring through fall. Clover is a summer variety, and along with other honeys such as orange and apple blossom, golden rod, and wild raspberry, it is a light, delicate honey, well suited to a variety of baking needs. Buckwheat honey, which is quite popular, is a darker, more emphatic honey, best used in dark breads and spicy cakes, or on pancakes. There is one other way of classifying honey, and that is by its processing method: pasteurized or not, as in "natural honey." Pasteurization is a process whereby the honey is heated to a certain temperature, which prevents bacteria from forming or crystallization from occurring. While pasteurization is helpful in improving honey's conservation, it does take away much of its lovely flavor and bouquet. Pasteurized honey is also more likely to be blended in order to ensure a uniform product. It is also filtered more to remove impurities. All this handling results in a good-looking, consistent, but bland-tasting honey.

However, and this is an important however, pasteurized honey is more apt to be certified kosher. If you look hard enough, you may find unpasteurized honey that *is* certified kosher, but it takes some searching.

Generally, honey keeps for a very long time (unless, like Pooh bear, you eat it all first), although it might crystallize—and this is particularly true of once-filtered natural honey. Over time, all honeys will crystallize. If crystallization does occur in your honey supply, simply heat the honey on low heat and the crystals will dissolve. I often scoop honey that has crystallized into a one- or two-cup Pyrex measuring cup and microwave it for one or two minutes, stirring every so often. I am rewarded with warm, liquid, recipe-ready honey.

Warm honey makes for easier blending. Measure the oil in your recipe first (if the recipe calls for it) to make the honey slide out of the measuring cup. Then warm up the honey to ensure it is nice and liquid, as opposed to sludgy.

When you bake with honey, you'll find that cakes and loaves brown faster than sugar. To ensure that your honey cakes are fully baked and their bottoms do not brown too much or before the inside of the cake is baked, line the pans with parchment paper before baking and place them on doubled-up baking sheets. You will have fully baked, moist cakes without a dry or too-dark bottom.

Unlike granulated sugar, which is entirely neutral in taste, honey offers its special bouquet to whatever cake or pastry recipe it's used in. Hydroscopic or water-loving honey also helps in bakery conservation—goods baked with it have a tendency to stay fresh longer, which is why honey cakes seem to taste better as the days go by. Remember, honey is a bit sweeter than sugar—1 cup of honey is equal to about 1¼ cups granulated sugar. So, a reasonable substitution in a recipe calling for 2 cups of sugar would be to use ¾ cup of sugar and 1 cup honey and reduce the liquid by ¼ cup.

Even health food cookbooks agree that "sugar is sugar is sugar," or, essentially, that sugar, honey, molasses, brown, and raw sugar are not high-nutrition foods. However, natural honey is not a refined sugar and does contain some trace nutrients in the form of enzymes, minerals, and vitamins along with its distinct flavor.

To serve honey for Rosh Hashanah, I use a "skep," an acrylic, cylindrical honey server that resembles a beehive. Check the Source Guide on page 353 (Mann Lake supplies them) if you would like to order one (unless you can find it in your local housewares store).

Majestic and Moist New Year's Honey Cake

Makes 8–10.

I like a New Year's honey cake to be extra moist and sweet, as good on the day of baking as it is days later. This one is queen of the realm—rich, nicely spiced, in a word, majestic in taste and stature. I went through many variations and tasting sessions until I was satisfied with this definitive cake. One tester gave the ultimate compliment, saying, "This one is worth the price of the book." Like most honey cakes, it is a good keeper and can be made a couple of days ahead.

3½ cups all-purpose flour
1 tablespoon baking powder
1 teaspoon baking soda
½ teaspoon salt
4 teaspoons ground cinnamon
½ teaspoon ground cloves
½ teaspoon ground allspice
1 cup vegetable oil
1 cup honey
1½ cups granulated sugar
½ cup brown sugar
3 eggs
1 teaspoon vanilla extract
1 cup warm coffee or strong tea
½ cup fresh orange juice
¼ cup rye or whisky (see Note)
½ cup slivered or sliced almonds (optional)

I like this cake best baked in a 9-inch angel food cake pan, but you can also make it in a 10-inch tube or bundt cake pan, a 9 by 13-inch sheetpan, or three 8 by 4½-inch loaf pans.

Preheat the oven to 350°F. Lightly grease the pan(s). For tube and angel food pans, line the bottom with lightly greased parchment paper. For gift honey cakes, I use "cake collars" (available from Sweet Celebrations) designed to fit a specific loaf pan. These give the cakes an appealing, professional, look.

In a large bowl, whisk together the flour, baking powder, baking soda, salt, and spices. Make a well in the center and add the oil, honey, sugars, eggs, vanilla, coffee, orange juice, and rye or whisky.

Using a strong wire whisk or an electric mixer on slow speed, combine the ingredients well to make a thick batter, making sure that no ingredients are stuck to the bottom of the bowl.

Spoon the batter into the prepared pan(s) and sprinkle the top of the cake(s) evenly with the almonds. Place the cake pan(s) on 2 baking sheets stacked together and bake until the cake springs back when you touch it gently in the center. For angel and tube cake pans, bake for 60 to 70 minutes; loaf cakes, 45 to 55 minutes. For sheet-style cakes, the baking time is 40 to 45 minutes. This is a liquidy batter and, depending on your oven, it may need extra time. Cake should spring back when gently pressed.

Let the cake stand for 15 minutes before removing it from the pan. Then invert it onto a wire rack to cool completely.

NOTE: If you prefer not to use the whisky, replace it with orange juice or coffee.

Apple Cake, Marble Cake, Honey Cake, or Sponge: Which Is the Fairest Cake of Them All?

To my mind, even within the rich repertoire of Jewish holiday baking, apple cakes reign supreme. In fact, I mentally divide people into a few main dessert categories or types. These include: 1) "I'd do anything for something with chocolate in it"; 2) "It has to be moist because I hate anything dry"; and, finally 3) "If it has apples in it, it can't be bad."

This last category captures a lot of eaters. Truth to tell, I've never met anyone who refused something because it contained apples—the more the better. As soon as the new apples hit the farm stands, most of my baking friends and relatives begin thinking of apple cakes and where to slot one into their busy schedules, Rosh Hashanah or not. Invariably the recipe they turn to often is an oil-based, batter-topped apple kuchen—so popular I've even seen it in Junior League cookbooks under the name "Jewish Apple Cake." I suppose the oil is the give-away that it's "Jewish" (ensuring, as it does, that the dessert can be served with both meat and dairy meals). Apples are amenable, plentiful, and adaptable. They make for a variety of loaves, cakes, pies, and pastries to suit many occasions. Much as they quest for the "definitive" brownie, so do bakers hunt that "perfect" apple cake. The criterion is always the same: It should be easy, moist, contain a touch of cinnamon, and always have more apples than dough.

A Is for Apple or, When Rosh Hashanah Comes Early

A good baker gets to know the apples in his or her region and to appreciate them in the seasonal scheme of things. To assist, apple charts indicating which apple is good for which purpose appear in food magazines, and some are posted in fruit stores, given out by apple growers' associations—who should know, I suppose. But the *real* test is what works for you. Your own apple "truth" may be Granny Smith, Winesap, or a fresh Jonathan, but more importantly, it is *your* truth.

Some years, Rosh Hashanah comes very early—as early as the very beginning of September—and the new crop of apples has not yet been harvested. Apples for baking can be too young (bite into one—they turn green in minutes) or too old (storage apples from a previous crop). My solution is to try an apple-cake before the holidays set in and get to know what's going to work best.

There's nothing so disappointing as serving up a good-looking apple cake or tart, only to find that the apples are not juicy inside, or rock hard after prolonged baking, or have no flavor. Besides, who's going to refuse an extra apple cake in the house, just to snack on?

Most apples turn sweeter after a couple of nights of frost, so beware farmer market "specials" that boast of having August-ripe Cortland or Northern Spy for instance. It's just not likely. Some varieties *are* ready earlier, such as Paulared or Melba, local delights that are available for a short three weeks before vanishing. Check in your own region for similar early-maturing varieties. McIntosh apples, which abound in the Northeast, are often said to bake up mushy. Truth is, I like some "apple mush" to fill in the crevices and pockets of apple pies and strudels, and for that, McIntosh does a fine job. In baking, McIntosh has never disappointed. You can also cut larger wedges of softer-textured apples, ensuring that the apple wedges won't all "dissolve" during the baking. Ideally, combining apples, soft and firm, tart and sweet, makes for the best baking. You need some apples for structure, others for bulk, some mellow apple tones along with a touch of acidity. Granny Smith and Golden Delicious are two widely available, all-season apples that work well together. I know Granny Smith is a favorite among many bakers and colleagues, but I personally find it a bit too hard and crisp to succeed as the solo apple. For most baking, I use McIntosh, Cortland, Lobo, Melba, Paulared, Jonamac—each offering its own unique qualities. And I am always on the lookout for any new variety that seems promising.

Whatever apples are in your area, know and love them well, and feel free to experiment. You may prefer one or two varieties for pastries, others for muffin and quick bread batters. Try to take note of how an apple performed in a recipe so you can make a more informed choice the next time. When someone asks you the secret to your mouth-watering apple cake or pie, you can preen a bit, then say with pride, "Oh yes, well I always use ——— (insert favorite apple type) apples and they're the best."

HOW MUCH IS ENOUGH APPLES?

This is a question many bakers ponder as they select an apple recipe. Some apple cake eaters will quickly respond: "Never enough." But it still helps to have some idea of what you require for a specific recipe.

Many cookbooks call for apples by weight (two pounds of whole apples) or size (eight to ten medium), but everyone pares and cuts apples differently. So if you start with a weighed amount of whole, unpeeled apples, who knows exactly what you're going to wind up with after peeling, coring, and sectioning? Apples by amount—eight medium, five large—offer another ambiguity. One person's medium is another person's large.

For my recipes, I stipulate the amount of apples by cups. That way, no matter what size the apples are to begin with or what weight at the outset, we are all dealing with more or less the same quantity. In general, in the apple-baking business, more is better, so don't skimp. Also, beware of apple wedge thieves who roam unguarded kitchens. Always peel a couple more apples than necessary—no one seems able to keep their hands out of the pared apple bowl. So how much is enough apples? No one ever complains you have too much. If you are lucky, you have just enough.

My Mother's Fancy Apple Cake

Makes 12 to 16 servings

This cake is a part of all my best childhood memories and one of my mother's trademark recipes. Whenever we had a party, you could count on tasting my mother's three specialty cakes: a cherry cheesecake, a chocolate wafer–whipped cream "instant Black Forest" cake, and this one. I encountered it under another name, Gateau Rougement (Rougement Apple Cake), when I was in pastry school. It had a more sophisticated name but I remember thinking, "Call it whatever fancy name you like, this is my mom's apple cake, no matter how you slice it." Essentially, this is a pastry crust surrounding a filling that is almost solid apples. The vanilla sauce is really a tasty "glue" to hold it all together. You can also make this with pie pastry (instead of the cookie pastry crust suggested here). The cake needs an overnight stay in the fridge to get firm before serving.

CAKE CRUST
½ cup granulated sugar
½ cup (1 stick) unsalted butter or margarine, melted and cooled
1 egg
1 teaspoon vanilla extract
¼ teaspoon salt
1½ cups all-purpose flour
1½ teaspoons baking powder

APPLE FILLING
7–9 cups peeled and sliced apples (or enough to fill up your cake pan)
Juice of ½ lemon, to sprinkle on the apples
¼ cup granulated sugar

VANILLA SAUCE
3 tablespoons unsalted butter or margarine, melted
1 cup granulated sugar
2 large eggs
1 teaspoon vanilla extract
½ teaspoon ground cinnamon

TOPPING
Confectioners' sugar, for dusting

CRUST: In a large bowl, combine all the crust ingredients to make a soft but stiff dough. Add a bit more flour if needed to ensure that you have not a batter but a soft dough. Cover the dough with plastic wrap and chill it for 10 to 15 minutes.

FILLING: In a bowl, toss the apples with the lemon juice and sugar.

Brush the bottom and sides of a 10-inch spring-form pan with melted butter.

Preheat the oven to 350°F.

Pat the dough evenly over the bottom and sides of the pan (it should be between ⅛ and ¼ inch thick). Fill with the apple slices, pressing gently. Cover the pan with aluminum foil.

Bake the cake for 1 to 1½ hours, removing the foil after the first 15 minutes, or until the apples are soft. The top apples will seems dry; the interior apples should begin to feel a touch soft. You can put a cake tester in to give you an idea of how cooked the inner apples are.

VANILLA SAUCE: In a bowl, combine the ingredients for the sauce in the order given and pour the sauce over the hot cake, trying to get it to drip into all the crevices. Bake for another 20 minutes.

Refrigerate the cake for at least 4 to 6 hours or overnight. Dust it with confectioners' sugar before serving.

VARIATION ON MY MOTHER'S FANCY APPLE CAKE

Makes 12 to 14 servings

Made with pie crust, instead of the cookie-like dough in the preceding recipe, this cake takes on another personality. In this version, there are raisins added. It is quick and equally good made with a commercial pie crust dough.

FILLING
8–10 cups apples that have been cored, peeled, and cut into ¼ inch slices
¼ cup sugar
1 tablespoon cornstarch
1 teaspoon ground cinnamon
¾ cup raisins, plumped (page 22) and coarsely chopped (optional)

CRUST
Prepared pastry for a double crust 9-inch pie, or 1 recipe My Favorite Pie Pastry for a double crust 9-inch pie (page 135)

VANILLA SAUCE
½ cup (1 stick) unsalted butter or unsalted margarine, melted
1 cup sugar
1½ teaspoons vanilla extract
4 eggs
1½ teaspoons ground cinnamon
2 tablespoons all-purpose flour

Preheat the oven to 375°F. Generously grease a 10-inch springform pan.

continued

FILLING: In a bowl, toss the apples with the other filling ingredients. Set aside.

CRUST: Roll out the pastry dough to a little less than ¼ inch thick. Cut a bottom circle of pastry to line the pan bottom. Cut the remaining dough into a couple of strips or sections to line the pan's sides. The dough sometimes falls in, but persist—once the apples are in the pan, they will hold up the pastry. The pastry should be almost flush with the top of the pan.

Fill the crust with the apples, pressing them down lightly, and fill in any gaps with more apple slices. The top-most apple slices can be arranged in concentric circles for a more polished look. The apples should be flush with the top of the pan. If not, add more until the pan is filled. Cover the top lightly with foil.

Bake for 15 minutes, remove the foil, and continue baking for another 45 minutes or so, to allow the apples to soften.

VANILLA SAUCE: While the cake is baking, in a bowl, stir together the butter, sugar, vanilla, and eggs. Fold in the cinnamon and flour. When the cake comes out of the oven, pour the sauce directly into the hot cake. It will disperse itself into the crevices. Return the cake to the oven for 20 minutes.

When done, refrigerate the cake overnight, or for at least 4 to 6 hours to allow it to set.

My Favorite Pie Pastry

Makes enough dough for one 10-inch, two 9-inch, or three 8-inch double crust pies

If you want a dough that is a joy to work with, this pastry is a must. The recipe yields a large batch of flaky easy-to-work-with pie dough. Lemon juice tenderizes the dough a bit while the egg adds color, flavor, and assists with browning. You can use all vegetable shortening, but the 3/4 cup unsalted butter called for in the recipe gives the crust more flavor. This is a good pastry for almost any filling but it's especially useful for wetter ones.

4 cups all-purpose flour
3/4 cup shortening
3/4 cup unsalted butter (1½ sticks)*
1 egg
2½ teaspoons sugar
1¾ teaspoons salt
1 tablespoon fresh lemon juice
Approximately ½ cup ice water

Place the flour in a large mixing bowl. Cut in the shortening and butter until the mixture is crumbly—a random mixture of smaller and larger lumps of flour-covered fat.

In a separate bowl, stir together the egg, sugar, salt, and lemon juice. Make a well in the center of the flour mixture. Stir in the egg mixture and drizzle in most of the ice water. Using a fork or your fingers, toss the mixture together to moisten the flour. Stir to make a soft mass and pat into a dough. Add the remaining (or additional) ice water as required to make sure the dough holds together.

Turn the dough out onto a lightly floured work surface and knead it very briefly until smooth. Divide in two (for a 10-inch pie), wrap each section, and refrigerate for at least 1 hour (you can also freeze the extra section).

*Or use all shortening.

Almond Butter Cake

Makes 8 servings

This is one of those fine-grained, moist cakes that is bursting with flavor. Easy to make, this is a good company cake that would also go with a dairy Shabbat supper.

4 ounces almond paste or marzipan,
   cut into slivers
1 cup granulated sugar
½ cup (1 stick) unsalted butter or margarine
1 teaspoon vanilla extract
3 eggs
¾ cup milk
3 cups all-purpose flour
½ teaspoon salt
2½ teaspoons baking powder
1 tablespoon cornstarch
¼ cup sliced or slivered almonds

Topping/Amaretto Sugar Glaze
Confectioners' sugar (optional)
¼ cup water
¼ cup granulated sugar
¼ cup amaretto or almond liqueur (see Note)

NOTE: You can replace the liqueur with an additional ¼ cup water combined with ½ teaspoon almond extract.

Preheat the oven to 350°F. Generously grease a 9 by 5-inch loaf pan or a 9-inch springform pan. If you have a 9-inch bundt or kugelhupf cake mold, this also works well.

In a bowl, cream the almond paste with the sugar and butter. As the almond paste breaks up, add the vanilla, eggs, and milk. Blend well and fold in the flour, salt, baking powder, and cornstarch to make a thick but fluffy batter.

Spoon the batter into the prepared pan. Sprinkle the almonds on top. (Note: If you are serving the cake bottom side up, you can put the almonds on the pan bottom before adding the batter).

Bake for 50 to 55 minutes. The cake should be evenly golden brown and slightly cracked. When cool, dust with confectioners' sugar, if using, or alternatively, poke holes in the top of the cake and drizzle on Amaretto Sugar Glaze.

Glaze: Stir together the water and sugar in a small saucepan and set on low heat to dissolve the sugar. Stir in the amaretto liqueur and heat for 2 to 3 minutes more. Cool slightly.

Lemon, Vanilla, and Honey Baklava

Makes 30 pastries

A simple-to-make but exotic nut-and-honey pastry, this homemade baklava is more buttery and delicate than commercial versions. You could use a combination of ground almonds and walnuts. This also makes a big batch of soaking syrup for ultra-decadent baklava.

1 (1-pound) package filo pastry leaves (about 25 sheets)
1 cup (2 sticks) unsalted butter or margarine, melted
½ cup vegetable oil
4 cups finely ground walnuts
1 teaspoon ground cinnamon
2 tablespoons sugar

HONEY VANILLA SYRUP
2 cups water
2 cups sugar
1 cup honey
2 tablespoons fresh lemon juice
1 teaspoon vanilla extract
1 teaspoon ground cinnamon

Preheat the oven to 350°F. Trim the filo sheets to fit the pan you will be using—either a 9 by 13-inch or a rectangular pan with similar capacity, with 2½ inch sides. Do not use a nonstick pan as it will be ruined when you cut out pieces of baklava. Keep the filo sheets covered with a slightly damp towel.

In a bowl, stir together the butter or margarine and the oil. Drizzle a few tablespoons of the butter/oil mixture on the pan bottom. Center 1 sheet of filo on the bottom of the pan and brush it generously with the butter and oil. Continue layering filo sheets, brushing each very generously with melted butter/oil.

After 8 sheets, sprinkle one third of the ground nuts over the top surface. Continue layering filo leaves this way, sprinkling with nuts after another 8 sheets have been laid in place. Sprinkle on more nuts, then 4 more leaves, more nuts, and the remaining leaves, always brushing each sheet generously before you place the next one in the pan.

Brush the top layer with the butter/oil mixture. Using kitchen scissors or a very sharp knife, cut the pastry into diamond shapes, cutting only halfway through the pastry. (Diamond shapes are achieved by cutting 5 or 6 horizontal rows, then cutting diagonally across these rows to form diamonds.) Bake for 1 hour, or until the pastry is golden brown. Meanwhile, make the syrup.

HONEY VANILLA SYRUP: In a saucepan, combine the syrup ingredients and heat until the sugar dissolves. Bring to a boil and simmer for about 5 minutes. Cool to room temperature before pouring evenly over the pastry. Let the baklava sit for 1 hour or overnight before serving.

Gourmet Shop Double Almond Mandelbrot

Makes 24 to 30 cookies, depending on size

This wonderful dessert relies on almond paste or store-bought marzipan, along with whole and chopped almonds for an elegant mandelbrot-cum-biscotti with a unique candylike surface. I like all mandelbrot, but this one, modeled on a typical biscotti da Prado, is still one of my favorites—and yes, it's worth going out to get the almond paste, which is available in most supermarkets.

1 (7-ounce/200-gram) package almond paste
  or marzipan
1¾ cups sugar
½ cup (1 stick) unsalted butter
½ cup finely chopped almonds
½ cup ground hazelnuts
4 eggs, lightly beaten
2 teaspoons vanilla extract
2 teaspoons almond extract
3 cups all-purpose flour
½ teaspoon salt
¼ teaspoon ground cinnamon
½ teaspoon baking soda
1 teaspoon baking powder
1 cup whole blanched almonds (see Note)

Preheat the oven to 350°F. Line 2 baking sheets with parchment paper.

Using a grater or food processor, grate or shred the almond paste.

In a mixing bowl, cream the almond paste and sugar together (the sugar helps break up the almond paste), then add the butter and cream it into the sugar/almond paste mixture until smooth. Stir in the chopped almonds and ground hazelnuts. Blend in the eggs, vanilla, and almond extract.

In a separate bowl, stir together the flour, salt, cinnamon, baking soda, and baking powder. Fold the flour mixture into the batter and blend well. Fold in the whole almonds.

Spoon half the batter onto one of the prepared baking sheets. Repeat with the remaining batter and the second baking sheet. The batter will be thick but should be spread roughly into a 9 by 4-inch rectangle.

Bake for approximately 40 minutes, until the dough is richly golden and seems dry to the touch. If the dough browns too quickly, reduce the temperature to 325° and bake a little longer.

Remove from the oven and cool for about 15 minutes. Transfer the pastry to a board and, using a long, sharp knife, cut the pastry into slices, slightly on the diagonal, ½ to ¾ inch thick. (Sometimes the whole almonds make cutting the biscotti difficult. You can freeze the whole biscotti in its pan for 1 hour, then cut as required—the nuts should not interfere with clean slices.)

Reduce the oven heat to 300° and return the cut cookies to the baking sheets. Bake for another 35 to 45 minutes or longer, depending on how long it takes for the biscotti to brown and crisp. Turn them once, to bake evenly, and cool on wire racks.

NOTE: You may use walnuts in this recipe with excellent results.

Sour Cream Yeast Coffee Cake

Makes 1 large or 2 medium babkas

Half bread and half all-purpose flour is the ideal combination, but you can use one or the other. This recipe makes a rich coffee crescent that is moist yet light and tastes very much like a danish. I use a food processor to cut the butter into the flour, then I turn the mixture into a large bowl and continue the recipe by hand or use a dough hook on my mixer. The dough should be refrigerated for a couple of hours or overnight.

DOUGH
½ cup warm water
1 cup plus a pinch of granulated sugar
2 tablespoons dry yeast
1½ cups (3 sticks) unsalted butter, very cold, cut into chunks
Approximately 3 cups bread flour and 3 cups all-purpose flour (or 6 cups of either one)
1¾ teaspoons salt
2 eggs plus 2 yolks
½ cup warm (100°F.) milk
1 teaspoon vanilla extract
1 cup sour cream

CINNAMON AND RAISIN-NUT FILLING
Approximately 1 cup brown sugar
1–2 tablespoons ground cinnamon
1 cup finely ground walnuts
1 cup raisins, plumped (see page 22) and dried
½ cup (1 stick) unsalted butter, in small bits

EGG WASH/TOPPING
1 egg, beaten
Coarse sugar

VANILLA FONDANT (OPTIONAL)
1½ cups confectioners' sugar
2–4 tablespoons water or milk, as needed
1 teaspoon vanilla extract

DOUGH: In a small bowl, stir together the water, pinch of sugar, and yeast. Whisk briefly and allow the mixture to stand for a couple of minutes until the yeast swells or looks dissolved.

Meanwhile, in a large bowl, cut the butter into the flour until it is coarse and dispersed (it does not have to be perfectly even). Stir in the salt and the remaining sugar. Make a well in the center of the flour/butter mixture. Stir in the yeast mixture and the eggs, egg yolks, milk, vanilla, and sour cream. Stir to make a soft dough. When the dough can no longer be stirred, begin kneading.

Knead for 8 to 10 minutes, adding additional flour as required (you may need up to another cup) to make a soft, smooth dough. This dough is very rich and will be smooth, but not as bouncy and elastic as other bread doughs.

Place the dough in a lightly greased bowl, insert the bowl in a plastic bag, seal, and refrigerate it for 4 to 6 hours or overnight. If you see the dough rising substantially during this period, gently deflate it to encourage a *slow* rise.

Remove from the refrigerator and gently deflate the dough. (For 1 large coffee cake, leave as is; for 2, divide it in 2 and divide the filling ingredients between them.)

FILLING: If making 1 large babka, roll the dough out to a 24 by 20-inch rectangle. If making 2 babkas, roll each piece of dough to a rectangle about 12 by 14 inches. Sprinkle with the brown sugar, cinnamon, nuts, and raisins. Dot with the butter. Roll up into a snug jelly roll. Place the large babka on a baking sheet. If making two, place them in 2 lightly greased 10-inch springform pans or two 10-inch tube pans. For the springforms, shape the jelly rolls into crescents; for the tube pans, overlap and seal the ends of the jelly rolls.

Brush thoroughly with the beaten egg and sprinkle on the coarse sugar, if using it. Place the pan(s) in a plastic bag and allow the dough to rise until almost doubled (45 to 60 minutes).

Meanwhile, preheat the oven to 350°F. Bake until evenly browned all over, with the filling beginning to ooze out (45 minutes for smaller babkas; 55 to 60 minutes for the larger one).

FONDANT: In a bowl, mix all the ingredients together, blending them to make a glaze. Drizzle the fondant over the baked, cooled coffee cake in a random design.

> **NOTE:** For more on babkas, and alternative ways of preparing the dough, see Babka Basics, page 327.

Apple Strudel in the Round

Makes 10 to 12 servings

If you're a fan of apple desserts, but strudel intimidates you, this is the apple dessert for you—a strudel in the round, so to speak. It's extra-easy to assemble with store-bought filo sheets and has the support of a springform pan. Once baked, it makes for convenient cutting as the rounded shape yields attractive wedges, stuffed with apple slices. This cake could make you famous!

8–10 cups peeled and sliced apples (use a semi-soft, sweet variety such as McIntosh, Cortland, or Golden Delicious, and cut them into ⅛–¼-inch wedges)
½ cup granulated sugar
Juice of 1 lemon
1 teaspoon ground cinnamon
2 tablespoons cornstarch
¼ cup yellow raisins, plumped (see page 22) and dried
½ cup (1 stick) unsalted butter or margarine, melted
16 sheets filo dough
confectioners' sugar, for dusting

In a large bowl, toss the apples with the sugar, lemon juice, cinnamon, cornstarch, and raisins. Set aside.

Preheat the oven to 375°F. Lightly brush the bottom of a 10-inch springform pan with butter. Lay 1 sheet of filo on your work surface and generously brush it with melted butter. Top it with a second filo leaf, brush it with butter, and keep layering until you've used 9 sheets of filo. Gently press the sheets into the pan, allowing them to drape over the sides.

Brush the top sheet of filo with butter and spoon the apples into the pie shell pressing gently. You should have enough apples to mound nicely, reaching slightly above the top of the pan. Fold the overlapped ends of filo over the apples (in any old fashion—it all works out in the end).

Lay 3 more buttered filo leaves on top of the apples. Brush the top with butter. Fold the filo in, overlapping it in any fashion over the apples. With the remaining filo leaves, cut 4 circles the size of the springform pan. Discard scraps or trimmings. Brush each with butter, including the top, and gently place on top of the apples. Make small knife marks in the pastry through to the apples in order to allow steam to escape.

Place the springform pan on a foil- or parchment paper–lined baking sheet to catch the drippings. Set the cake on the lowest rack of the oven, and immediately reduce the heat to 350°. Bake until the pastry puffs up and the apples begin to ooze juice (40 to 50 minutes). Cool very well before unmolding (20 to 30 minutes). Loosen the sides with a flat knife before pushing up the bottom. Just before serving, dust the strudel lightly with confectioners' sugar.

Clementine-Cranberry Biscotti Loaf

Makes 20 to 28 biscotti, depending on size

A basket of these, along with some miniature holiday oranges, makes a great gift. These biscotti look quite unusual and are a hit with anyone who likes things sweet and tart.

1 clementine or seedless orange
$\frac{1}{2}$ cup vegetable oil
$1\frac{3}{4}$ cup sugar
2 eggs
1 teaspoon vanilla extract
$2\frac{3}{4}$ cups all-purpose flour
$\frac{1}{2}$ teaspoon salt
2 teaspoons baking powder
$\frac{1}{4}$ teaspoon ground cinnamon
$1\frac{1}{2}$ cups coarsely chopped frozen cranberries

Preheat the oven to 350°F. Spray a 9 by 5-inch loaf pan generously with nonstick cooking spray.

Wash the orange well and cut it into quarters. Puree the orange in a food processor or coffee grinder until it is smooth ($\frac{1}{2}$ cup of orange puree is required—if missing a tablespoon or so, add enough orange juice to reach the $\frac{1}{2}$-cup mark on a measuring cup).

In a mixing bowl, blend the oil, sugar, and eggs. Stir in the orange puree, then the vanilla, and mix well. In a separate bowl, stir together the flour, salt, baking powder, and cinnamon. Fold in the wet batter to combine. Fold in the cranberries.

Transfer the batter into the prepared pan and bake until the top seems set and dry (45 to 55 minutes). If the loaf is browning too quickly, reduce the heat to 325° and lengthen the baking time. Allow the loaf to cool completely before removing it from the pan. Wrap the loaf well in foil and freeze for about 2 hours, or refrigerate overnight.

Preheat the oven to 325°F. Line 2 baking sheets with parchment paper. Cut the loaf into very thin slices (about $\frac{1}{8}$ inch thick). Place the slices on the baking sheets and bake, turning once, for 20 to 30 minutes, allowing the cookies to brown only lightly. Store them in an airtight container.

Chocolate Honey Cake

Makes 14 to 16 servings

A variation on the holiday classic, this moist and delicious chocolate honey cake is satisfying for traditionalists and chocoholics alike.

1 cup vegetable oil
1 cup granulated sugar
⅔ cup brown sugar
1 cup light honey
1 teaspoon vanilla extract
4 eggs
½ cup unsweetened cocoa powder, sifted
2¾ cups all-purpose flour
½ teaspoon baking soda
1 tablespoon baking powder
½ teaspoon salt
¼ teaspoon ground cinnamon
1 cup flat cola or brewed coffee, at
   room temperature
⅓ cup slivered or sliced almonds

TOPPING
½ cup coarsely chopped semi-sweet chocolate
Confectioners' sugar and/or unsweetened cocoa
   powder, for dusting

Preheat the oven to 350°F. Grease the bottom only of a 9- or 10-inch angel food cake or tube pan. Cut out a circle of parchment or baking paper and line the bottom.

In a medium-sized bowl, blend the oil with the sugars, honey, and vanilla. Blend in the eggs and mix well. In a separate larger bowl, mix together the dry ingredients. Make a well in the center of the dry ingredients and stir in the wet ingredients, slowly adding the cola (or coffee). Blend well to make a smooth batter.

Spoon the batter into the pan and sprinkle the top with slivered almonds.

Bake the cake for 15 minutes, then reduce the heat to 325° and bake for another hour, or until the cake springs back when touched. Remove the cake from the oven.

TOPPING: Sprinkle on the chopped chocolate. Shake the pan to loosen the cake from the bottom but do not remove it. Refrigerate the cake to set the chocolate. Once the chocolate is set, invert and remove the cake from the pan. To serve, dust the top with cocoa and/or confectioners' sugar.

Golden Shofar Cake

Makes 14 to 16 servings

*This golden cake, laced with lemon zest and apricot nectar, is light in color and moist of crumb.
A refreshing option amidst all the honey and apple treats.*

CAKE
¾ cup vegetable oil
1½ cups granulated sugar
4 eggs
1 teaspoon vanilla extract
½ teaspoon lemon oil or extract
1 tablespoon finely minced lemon zest
2½ cups all-purpose flour
¼ teaspoon salt
1 tablespoon baking powder
¾ cup apricot juice or nectar
½ cup chopped dried apricots or chopped frozen
  mango pieces
¼ cup chopped golden raisins

LEMON GLAZE/TOPPING
1½ cups confectioners' sugar
⅓ cup fresh lemon juice
Shredded lemon zest, for topping

Preheat the oven to 325°F. Generously grease and flour a 9-inch tube pan or a 12-cup bundt pan.

CAKE: In a large mixing bowl, blend together the oil and sugar. Blend in the eggs, vanilla, lemon oil, and the zest. Stir in the flour, salt, and baking powder, alternately with the apricot juice. Blend until smooth. Fold in the apricots or chopped mango and the raisins.

Spoon the batter into the pan and bake until the cake is lightly golden and springs back when pressed gently (45 to 55 minutes). Cool for 10 minutes before inverting onto a serving plate.

LEMON GLAZE: In a bowl, whisk together the confectioners' sugar and lemon juice. Using a cake tester, make holes in the still-warm cake. Drizzle the glaze over the cake and garnish it with shreds of lemon zest. Cool well before serving.

Cuisine d'Or Classic Carrot Cake with Cream Cheese Icing

Makes 12 to 14 servings

I have probably made this version of carrot cake thousands of times. It was once the flagship recipe of my own specialty bakery, Cuisine d'Or. Kind of faddish years ago, carrot cake still holds it own. At Rosh Hashanah carrots are traditionally served in a tzimmes, a braised carrot, honey, and dried fruit casserole. Carrots are thematically correct but showcasing them in a cake instead of a casserole is a way of sneaking them onto the holiday coffee and tea table. The cream cheese icing makes this suitable for Shavuot as well. When I sold this cake commercially, I finished it off with a cinnamon-tinted icing, piped on with a star tip and pastry bag to give an American cake a little "Je ne sais quoi." I sold thousands of these cakes, so something must have worked!

CAKE
2 cups granulated sugar
1¼ cups vegetable oil
1 tablespoon finely minced orange zest
4 eggs
2 teaspoons vanilla extract
2 tablespoons fresh lemon juice
2 cups all-purpose flour
½ teaspoon salt
2 teaspoons ground cinnamon
1 teaspoon baking soda
2 teaspoons baking powder
3 generous cups grated carrots
¾ cup golden raisins
¼ cup well-drained crushed pineapple
½ cup coarsely chopped walnuts

CREAM CHEESE ICING/TOPPING
8 ounces cream cheese
½ cup (1 stick) unsalted butter or unsalted margarine, softened
1 teaspoon vanilla extract

2 teaspoons fresh lemon juice
3–4 cups confectioners' sugar
Ground cinnamon, ground walnuts, grated carrots, for dusting

Preheat the oven to 350°F. Lightly grease a 10-inch springform pan or a 9 by 13-inch rectangular pan.

CAKE: In a large mixing bowl, blend together the sugar, oil, and orange zest. Whisk in the eggs, vanilla, and lemon juice. In a medium bowl, stir together the dry ingredients. Fold them into the batter and stir in the carrots, raisins, pineapple, and nuts. The batter will be thick.

Spoon the batter into the prepared pan and bake for 55 to 60 minutes, or until the cake springs back when gently pressed. Cool for 10 to 15 minutes in the pan, then turn out onto a rack to cool completely. Wrap the cake well, and place in the freezer to chill even more to make icing it easier.

CREAM CHEESE ICING: In a bowl, cream the cheese with the butter. Add the vanilla and lemon juice. Blend in the confectioners' sugar until the icing reaches a spreading consistency. After icing, decorate the top of the cake with a dusting of cinnamon, ground walnuts, and some additional grated carrots in the center. You can also split the cake in half horizontally and ice the interior to make a 2 layer cake.

NOTE: For a pareve icing, omit the cream cheese and butter and use 1 cup (total) of unsalted margarine.

Holiday Teiglach

Makes 4 to 6 servings

This unusual but traditional confection is made with little knots of dough that bake up into small puffs. The knots are coated with a honey and ginger syrup, then sprinkled with coconut and cut into bite-sized pieces or stacked in a small mound. Also suitable for Chanukah.

DOUGH
3 eggs
1 teaspoon vegetable oil
1 teaspoon sugar
1/4 teaspoon salt
Approximately 1 1/2 cups all-purpose flour

HONEY SYRUP
3/4 cup light honey
1/3 cup sugar
1 teaspoon ground ginger
1 cup chopped walnuts
3/4 cup shredded coconut

Preheat the oven to 375°F. Line a cookie sheet with parchment paper and lightly smear with vegetable oil.

DOUGH: In a bowl, whisk together the eggs, oil, sugar, and salt. Blend in the flour to make a very soft dough. Turn the dough out onto a lightly floured board, adding just enough flour, if necessary, to make it easy to roll. With your hands, roll the dough into long ropes or snakes, about 1/2 inch wide. Pinch or cut off 1/2-inch pieces. Place all these little pieces on the cookie sheet.

Bake, shaking the sheet occasionally, until the dough pieces puff and are golden brown, (15 to 20 minutes).

SYRUP: In a saucepan, heat the honey and sugar together and boil very gently for 3–5 minutes until just amber-colored. Lower the heat, then stir in the ginger, the nuts, and the baked puffs or teiglach, tossing to coat them. Spread the mixture out onto a lightly greased baking sheet, (using wet hands). Sprinkle it with coconut and allow it to harden (or place it in the freezer on the baking sheet for about 30 minutes), and then cut it into bite-size pieces. Alternatively, mound the mixture in the center of a serving platter and allow it to cool and harden. Take pieces or sections as required, with 2 spoons, or simply pull off a piece—this is a sticky dessert.

Honey Butter Squares

Makes about 3 dozen small squares

This recipe, origin unknown, was taken directly from a nursery school bulletin my son Ben brought home during Rosh Hashanah, along with some sample cookie-like squares. Tinged with honey, rich with butter, these are a fitting end to a Rosh Hashanah luncheon.

½ cup (1 stick) unsalted butter or margarine
¼ cup granulated sugar
2 tablespoons honey
Pinch of salt
¼ teaspoon baking powder
1¼ cups all-purpose flour
Confectioners' sugar, for tossing

Preheat the oven to 350°F.

In a bowl, cream the butter with the sugar and honey. Stir in the salt and baking powder. Work in the flour to make a stiff dough. Press the dough evenly into a 9-inch square pan, patting it all around.

Bake until lightly golden, 18 to 22 minutes, reducing the heat if the squares start to brown too quickly.

Cool, then cut into 1½-inch squares and toss lightly in the confectioners' sugar.

Free-Form Apple or Plum Tart

Makes 6 servings

Free-form puff pastry tarts, also known as open-faced flans or as galettes, are increasingly popular. They are easy to make, light, and pretty as a picture. There are never any leftovers!

¾–1 pound commercial puff pastry dough or Sour Cream Mock Puff Dough (page 188)
4–5 cups peeled and thinly sliced apples (see Note)
1 tablespoon fresh lemon juice or brandy
3–8 tablespoons granulated sugar
2 tablespoons unsalted butter or margarine, in small bits
Confectioners' sugar, for sprinkling (optional)

NOTE: You may also use plums or peaches, ripe but firm, sliced very thinly.

Preheat the oven to 400°F. Line a large baking sheet with parchment paper.

Roll out the dough into a 14-inch circle. You can roll out a large section of dough about ½ inch thick and use an inverted bowl to trace, then cut out the circle.

Arrange the fruit on the dough in concentric circles, leaving a 1-inch border. Sprinkle the apples with the lemon juice or brandy, then some of the granulated sugar (use 2 to 6 tablespoons, depending on your taste and how tart the apples are). Dot with the bits of butter. Sprinkle with 1–2 tablespoons of the remaining sugar.

Bake until the pastry is golden brown and the fruit is softened, 25 to 35 minutes. (Reduce the heat to 375° if the pastry seems to be browning too quickly.)

Cool slightly before serving. (This can be served warm or at room temperature.)

Dust, if desired, with confectioners' sugar.

CLASSIC, OR STRETCH STRUDEL DOUGH

The strudel we are best acquainted with and most intimidated by, the one that inspires the Strudel Legend, is a good many years old. Based on the Turkish baklava recipe (which uses filo dough) and dating back to the sixteenth century, it was subsequently "borrowed" and ultimately perfected by several generations of talented Hungarian and Viennese cooks. This ultra-thin, stretched dough is one of the classic European pastries and is prepared, albeit somewhat differently in each country, with loving dedication and a strict adherence to timeless methods.

Classic strudel isn't really that hard to make but does get better with practice. To make it properly, one must first start with a bread or hard flour-based dough and develop (knead or otherwise manipulate) the gluten content within the dough. That done, the dough is allowed to rest and then it is gently stretched until it is supple, elastic, and as thin as possible. Once this is achieved the dough can be brushed with the melted butter and filled with a substantial choice of fillings. During baking, the moisture in the butter turns to steam, and thus causes the thinly coiled dough to puff up into flaky strata of pastry.

To make life easier, opt for stretch strudel dough made in your food processor or bread machine. The first makes great strudel dough in about ninety (!) seconds. Your bread machine Dough cycle provides perfectly fashioned dough in about fifteen minutes—without your even touching the dough (don't worry—you will touch it plenty once you start stretching). Either method works well, is quick and easy and trouble free. Either method or machine will give you superb dough. Pheww . . . half the battle. Now, to quell your fears about the stretching part. Ready? Okay, here goes: You don't have to stretch your very first batch of dough to kingdom come. A dough stretched to about eighteen by twelve inches is sufficient for starters. You will still get *phenomenal* strudel. Each time you stretch this dough, you will get *even better.* Along the way, you will be eating outstanding strudel. The point is, your *worst* effort will still make great strudel. You simply cannot go wrong. Plus, you will have a wonderful time. You can do this alone or invite friends over for a strudel bee (the best way to get strudel stretched out evenly all over the place).

If you are not making your own stretch strudel dough but like that style of dough to roll around your apples, try out the Quick-and-Easy Cinnamon Apple Strudel (page 88), which uses reliable store-bought filo sheets. Another strudel shortcut is to use commercial French puff pastry dough (*pâte feuilletée*), bought from the freezer case or from an indulgent neighborhood pastry shop.

Before baking, strudels must be glazed to achieve that appealing, golden brown color. You can brush the pastry with additional melted butter and then sprinkle on decorative sugar and cinnamon or poppy seeds. Alternatively, you can make a light egg wash glaze and gently "paint" the strudel before baking. Be sure to glaze all pastries evenly—leaving no puddles of egg wash or crevices filled with melted butter. These little glaze excesses will burn or brown unevenly during baking, or will dribble and stick on the baking sheet.

Strudel is best served warm or at room temperature. Strudels made with wet fillings, such as apple, are not as suitable for freezing because they lose much of their original flaky texture.

Traditional Stretch Strudel Dough—
Four Methods

Makes enough dough for three medium or two large strudels

This dough is foolproof. Just choose a method and away you go.

3 1/2 cups all-purpose flour
3/4 cup warm water
1 teaspoon fresh lemon juice
1 teaspoon salt
1 tablespoon sugar
1/3 cup vegetable oil
2 eggs

HAND METHOD: Place the flour in a large mixing bowl. Make a well in the center and add the water, lemon juice, salt, and sugar, then the oil. Stir in the eggs. Blend well to make a soft dough. Knead 8 to 12 minutes, until the dough is smooth, elastic, and satiny. Wrap the dough in a Ziploc bag and let it rest one hour. Alternatively, refrigerate it for up to 1 or 2 days. Allow it to warm up before stretching.

BREAD MACHINE METHOD: Place the flour, water, lemon juice, salt, sugar, oil, and eggs in the bread machine. Put the machine on the dough cycle. After the first knead, remove the dough (you do not have to let it sit there for the complete cycle), wrap it in a Ziploc bag and let it rest one hour. Alternatively, refrigerate it for up to 1 or 2 days. Allow it to warm up before stretching.

ELECTRIC MIXER METHOD: Use both the mixer paddle and the dough hook. Using the paddle, mix the water, lemon juice, salt, and sugar, oil, and eggs to blend. Add the flour and mix until the dough forms a mass. Attach the dough hook and knead 8 minutes, until smooth and elastic. Remove the dough from the work bowl, cover it with a damp tea towel, and let it rest one hour before using. Alternatively, place it in a Ziploc bag and refrigerate for up to 1 or 2 days. Allow it to warm up before stretching.

FOOD PROCESSOR METHOD: Place the water, lemon juice, salt, sugar, oil, and eggs in the processor and whiz everything around to combine. Add the flour and process until a smooth mass forms. The dough should be smooth and elastic and slack. Add a touch more flour, if needed, to achieve this. Remove the dough from the work bowl, cover it with a damp tea towel, and let it rest one hour before using. Alternatively, place it in a Ziploc bag and refrigerate it for up to 1 or 2 days. Allow it to warm up before stretching.

HANDLING STRETCH STRUDEL DOUGH:

Divide your dough into two or three portions.

You will need a work surface of at least 12 by 18 inches covered with a clean linen tablecloth. Gently roll the dough with a rolling pin to flatten it. Let the dough rest 5 minutes, then begin stretching the strudel. Use your fists to do this (and make sure you are not wearing watches or rings that would tear the dough or make holes). Stretch from the center out, much like someone making a pizza. Stretch, moving your hands around the edges of the dough, lifting and stretching each new section. Every 3 to 5 minutes, rest (you and the dough). Cover the dough with a damp tea towel or a clean, damp tablecloth. Use your fingertips to stretch the dough when it is too thin and fragile for your fists (the dough sheet may be too large at some point to get from the sides into the center). Always allow the dough a chance to rest so that it will not resist your efforts. Once you get a rectangle of 12 by 18 inches, discounting thicker overlap, you can fill dough. Bigger than this is great, but this is fine for a first effort. Trim the thick edges and discard the trimmings.

Brush the surface of the dough generously with melted butter. Sprinkle on 3 to 6 tablespoons of bread crumbs or crushed graham crackers or plain cookies.

On the edge closest to you, spread out about six cups of filling. Using the tablecloth to lever the dough up, start rolling the strudel into a log. Do this until the loaf is about 3 inches thick. Trim and gently lift the log onto a prepared baking sheet. Brush the top with melted butter and make small air slits. Repeat with the remaining dough and filling.

Bake at 375 F. on a doubled-up, parchment-lined baking sheet until the top of the strudel is golden and juices begin to ooze out, about 35 to 40 minutes. Dust with confectioners' sugar and cut on the diagonal into single portions.

Traditional Apple Strudel

Enough for two 18 to 24-inch strudels, 6 to 8 servings each.

Be brave—you can do this. Even your first effort will still result in outstanding, mouthwatering strudel. The so-called test of a quintessentially thin strudel dough is being able to read a newspaper through it, preferably the Yiddish Times. *For your first effort, the dough should be thin enough to read the thick, black "E" on the doctor's eye chart.*

1 recipe Stretch Strudel Dough (page 152)

APPLE CINNAMON STRUDEL FILLING
10 cups peeled, cored, and thinly sliced apples
1 tablespoon fresh lemon juice
3/4 cup sugar
2 teaspoons cinnamon
Pinch of pastry spice (optional)
3 tablespoons cornstarch or all-purpose flour
1/2 cup plumped (see page 22), well-drained
    raisins, optional
1/3 cup very well-drained pitted red cherries
    (optional)
3/4 cup unsalted butter or unsalted margarine,
    melted

TOPPING
Bread or plain cookie crumbs for sprinkling
Confectioners' sugar for dusting

Toss the apples with the lemon juice. Combine the sugar, cinnamon, pastry spice, and flour. Toss the apples, raisins, and cherries. Paint the strudel generously with the butter or margarine, and sprinkle it with the crumbs and confectioners' sugar.

Follow the instructions for "Handling Stretch Strudel Dough" (page 153).

4. Yom Kippur

The Day of Atonement

Der vos hot nit farzucht bittereh, vaist nit voz zies iz.
"He who has not tasted the bitter, does not understand the sweet."

—YIDDISH PROVERB

L'shanah tovah tikatevu!
"May you be inscribed for a good year!"

G'mar hatimah tovah!
"May you end this day with a good signature!"

—TRADITIONAL HOLIDAY GREETINGS

YOM KIPPUR—BEFORE THE FAST, BREAKING THE FAST

Known most commonly as the Day of Atonement, but also as the Day of Judgment, this is the most solemn day on the Jewish calendar.

WHEN ✸ Tenth day of Tishri.

CORRESPONDING TO ✸ Mid-September to mid-October.

HOLIDAY CONTEXT ✸ Yom Kippur, as Rosh Hashanah, is a holiday of reflection and reassessment. As we reflect on our lives, our deeds, and the year that is coming to a close, we also think of our hopes for the New Year. God will judge, as He prepares the book of life for the coming year "who will live and who will die, who will prosper. . . ."

ACTIVITIES ✸ No work or labor is performed on Yom Kippur. As with Rosh Hashanah, much of the day is spent at synagogue. At home, Yom Kippur is a quiet day. Activities, even for children, are low-key and revolve around resting at home between services. Kol Nidre services usher in the fasting ritual of the holiday. The fast allows one to concentrate on spiritual thoughts and not be distracted by concerns such as meals.

The twenty-five-hour Yom Kippur fast concludes with services the following evening. As Yom Kippur finishes, the shofar, or ram's horn, is sounded once again—the New Year's holiday is over. Families observing the fast break or end it, usually at home, with family and friends.

FOOD SYMBOLS ✸ It seems almost odd to discuss food in conjunction with a holiday which involves a day-long fast, but food is still a part of it. At least, planning the food *before* and *after* the fast is a major part of it. For the evening before the fast begins, *erev* of Yom Kippur, a hearty, usually meat-based meal (although not spicy or too salty) is traditional, so as to fortify the fasters for the next day. At sundown the next day, as services end, so does the fast. Needless to say, there are going to be some very hungry people at your table. If you are hosting a break-the-fast meal for a large group, you must plan ahead.

In respect for those empty tummies, "break-the-fast" foods are simple, usually dairy dishes, and include such items as cream cheese and bagels, comforting soups like mushroom and barley, and any assortment of appetizers, as well as traditional cookies, such as mun or mandelbrot, along with a centerpiece cake or two.

Since one is away all day at Yom Kippur services and will be returning home with little time to prepare a big meal, the dishes for this holiday are those that can be made ahead, eaten cold, or take well to rewarming. Slow-rising sweet buns, such as Overnight Cinnamon Schnecken (page 176), can bake in the oven as you eat the main meal.

You can also look to the Shavuot chapter for some other choices in dairy-based cakes and pastries. If you are serving a meat meal before the fast, you will find additional nondairy recipes in the Shabbat and Rosh Hashanah chapters.

Quiche in a Loaf

Makes 8 to 12 servings, depending on portion size. Can be served in small squares as an hors d'oeuvre

One of the few savory dishes in this book, this crustless, loaf-style quiche is elegant, easy to make, and unique. It is ideal make-ahead, break-the-fast fare. Loosely inspired by Linda Dannenberg's recipe for Cake aux Olives in Paris Boulangerie Patisserie, this dish is good hot, warm, or cold, as a main course with a salad, or cut into small appetizer squares. A good choice for Shavuot as well. Make this once, and it will become a part of your standing repertoire.

1³/₄ cups all-purpose flour
1³/₄ teaspoons baking powder
³/₄ cup water or vegetable bouillon or white wine
¹/₂ cup vegetable oil
¹/₂ cup half and half or light cream
6 eggs, lightly beaten
¹/₂ cup minced scallions
¹/₂ cup minced black or green olives
¹/₂ cup finely minced sun-dried tomatoes or roasted red peppers
1¹/₂ teaspoons salt*
1 teaspoon garlic powder
2 tablespoons minced fresh flat-leaf parsley
2 teaspoons minced fresh dill
¹/₄ teaspoon pepper
2 cups shredded white Cheddar cheese
1 cup shredded Swiss or mozzarella cheese

GARNISH, OPTIONAL
2 tablespoons grated Parmesan cheese
Paprika, for sprinkling

Preheat the oven to 350°F. Lightly grease a 9 by 5-inch loaf pan (You can also use a 9-inch springform pan for a different presentation and wedge-shaped servings).

In a large bowl, blend the flour and baking powder. Into the center of the dry ingredients, stir the water or vegetable bouillon, the oil, half-and-half, and eggs. Fold in the remaining ingredients. Pour or spoon the mixture into the prepared pan. Sprinkle the top with Parmesan cheese and dust with some paprika.

Bake for 40 to 45 minutes, until set. Allow the quiche to cool a little before cutting and serving it. Or, refrigerate it for serving later. Offer thin slices with a side salad, salsa, or yogurt. Or serve it plain, or cut into 2-inch squares as an appetizer. It can be served cold if made ahead, or reheated in a microwave.

*If the cheese you are using is salty, use 1¹/₄ teaspoons salt.

Vanilla and Cinnamon Challah Bread Pudding

Makes 12 to 14 servings

Here it is, pure challah ambrosia: chunks of challah bread pulled together in a creamy batter of eggs, evaporated milk, and vanilla, studded with tender morsels of apples, and kissed with a hint of cinnamon. French toast is the common way for leftover challah to meet its end, but this bread pudding—terrific fresh and hot from the oven—will start a new tradition. Served cold from the fridge and cut into generous squares, this dessert or snack is reminiscent of a firm cheesecake in texture and taste. Bread puddings hail from a generation of Jewish bakers and homemakers who wouldn't think of wasting anything— certainly nothing as fine as a leftover loaf of challah. Great as a New Year's holiday company side dish as well. This recipe can be made 1 or 2 days ahead and refrigerated until needed. It can be reheated in a 325°F oven for 30 minutes or in a microwave on medium-high for 6 to 10 minutes.

10 cups challah chunks or cubes
1½ cups (one 12-ounce can) evaporated milk
1 cup whole milk
1 cup half and half
8 eggs, lightly beaten
1 cup granulated sugar
½ cup (1 stick) unsalted butter, melted and
    cooled
2 teaspoons vanilla extract
1 teaspoon ground cinnamon
2 teaspoons baking powder
Pinch of salt
2 cups peeled and coarsely chopped apples
    (optional)
½ cup raisins (optional)
confectioners' sugar and ground cinnamon, for
    sprinkling

Preheat the oven to 350°F. Lightly grease a 9 by 13-inch baking dish.

Place the bread cubes in a large mixing bowl. In a separate bowl, mix together the evaporated milk, whole milk, half and half, eggs, sugar, butter, vanilla, cinnamon, baking powder, and salt. Pour this mixture over the bread cubes and let stand for 10 minutes. Fold in the apples and the raisins, if using. Spoon the mixture into the prepared pan and dust the top with a little confectioners' sugar and cinnamon.

Bake until lightly golden (35 to 45 minutes). Cool about 5 minutes before serving. This can be served warm or cold.

Layered Apple Cinnamon Cake

Makes 14 to 16 servings

I have been using this recipe for years and see variations of it everywhere—under many different names—true proof of its popularity. It takes only minutes to prepare—even by hand with a whisk. If I were trapped on a desert island, I would want to have this recipe with me. It can be made 2 or 3 days ahead and will still be fresh and tasty.

APPLE FILLING
5–6 cups sliced, peeled apples
2 tablespoons fresh lemon juice
¼ cup sugar
1 tablespoon ground cinnamon

CAKE
2 cups sugar
1 cup vegetable oil
1 tablespoon vanilla extract
½ cup fresh orange juice
4 eggs
3 cups all-purpose flour
1 tablespoon baking powder
½ teaspoon salt
Small pinch of nutmeg

TOPPING
Ground cinnamon and granulated sugar, for
  sprinkling

Preheat the oven to 350°F. Generously grease a 10-inch tube pan, a 12-cup Bundt pan, or two 8- by 4-inch foil loaf pans.

FILLING: In a bowl, toss the apples with the lemon juice, sugar, and cinnamon.

CAKE: Place the sugar, oil, vanilla, orange juice, and eggs in a large bowl and whisk until smooth. Fold in the flour, baking powder, salt, and nutmeg and blend to make a smooth batter.

Spoon a little more than one third of the batter into the prepared pan(s). Cover with half the apple mixture, then repeat with the remaining batter and filling. Sprinkle the top lightly with additional sugar and cinnamon. Place the cake on doubled-up baking sheets and bake for 60 to 70 minutes, until the top is slightly crusted and richly golden in color, and a cake tester inserted in the center comes out clean.

Let the cake rest in its pan for 20 minutes before removing it.

NETTIE'S BABKA

The recipe for the very first yeast coffee cake I ever made was given to me by Nettie Ross. Nettie was and is, first and foremost, one of the most generous people I know. Generous with smiles, friendly warmth, compliments, approval, and recipes. She also happens to be an outstanding baker. There is nothing she cannot bake and that does not taste wonderful, and wonderfully *haimish,* be it rolypoly, hamantaschen, apple cake, or this babka. Long after other women of her generation have hung up their baker's aprons, Nettie continues to find the time to make her special things and give them to the lucky people in her life.

One day, when I was still a new bride, my mother-in-law brought home a sample of Nettie's babka—a yeasted, cinnamon-laced round cake, higher than anything a bakery ever sold, more professional than any homemade cake I'd ever seen. Aside from the fact that this cake tasted incredibly good, it was also made with yeast. Up until then, any cake I had ever made was leavened with baking powder. Frankly, no one I knew had the knowledge (or courage!) to make a yeast coffee cake. Of course, nothing tastes as sublime as a babka. Not a regular cake, more than a piece of danish, babka is a category unto itself. It is good hot, warm, cold, toasted—any way you slice it. It can be modest or extra-rich with sour cream and butter. Fill it with nuts, cinnamon, raisins, poppy-seed paste, chocolate bits, almond paste, or just some brown sugar. Babka can be high or low, dense or airy—it is absolutely versatile, a hybrid that seems to cross the elements of a good cake with those of a danish. But I digress. . . .

Well, Nettie passed on her recipe and I found it strange, primarily because I had never attempted such a cake, and second, because I was not sure I would have any sort of success. But I did. *Her recipe is that good.* The results were spectacular. I have made it for years now, altering my method from time to time, and I'm always amazed that it works superlatively, no matter what.

Babka, regardless of its sophisticated European reputation, should not intimidate. You'll find several more babkas, primarily in the Shavuot section, since they are rich with dairy ingredients. They are all easy yet exceptional, but I suggest Nettie's to get you started. I am convinced that part of its charm and sure-fire results come from the warm-hearted spirit of Nettie herself.

NOTE: For more on babkas, and alternative ways of preparing dough, see "Babka Basics," page 327.

Almost-Nettie's Cinnamon Meringue–Walnut Babka

Makes 12 to 14 servings

A babka for beginners that can be made in the food processor, by hand, in an electric mixer, or in a bread machine. Wonderful fresh or toasted, you can use dried cranberries or cherries to replace the raisins; or cocoa powder to replace the cinnamon. My biggest time-saver in this recipe is to omit the beaten egg whites and replace them with cut up regular or miniature marshmallows. Testers were so thrilled with this tip, they almost convinced me to leave out the original method altogether. To find out how to substitute, read on.

BABKA DOUGH
1/4 cup warm water
4 1/2 teaspoons dry yeast
2/3 cup plus a pinch of granulated sugar
1 teaspoon salt
2 cups all-purpose flour
Approximately 2 cups bread flour (see Notes)
1 cup (2 sticks) unsalted butter
1 cup warm milk
3 egg yolks (reserve whites)
1 1/2 teaspoons vanilla extract
1 tablespoon fresh lemon juice

CINNAMON MERINGUE FILLING (SEE NOTES)
3 egg whites, reserved from above
1/4 teaspoon salt
1 cup granulated sugar
1 cup ground walnuts
2 tablespoons ground cinnamon
1 cup raisins, plumped (see page 22)

TOPPING
1 egg, beaten
Coarse sugar, for sprinkling
Confectioners' sugar, for dusting (optional)

DOUGH: In a small bowl, stir together the water, yeast, and the pinch of sugar. Allow the mixture to stand for a couple of minutes to dissolve the yeast.

Meanwhile, in a large bowl, stir together the remaining sugar, the salt, and the flour. Cut the butter into the flour until it is evenly dispersed. Stir together the milk, egg yolks, vanilla, lemon juice, and yeast mixture and stir this into the flour-butter mixture. Blend into a soft batter. Turn the batter out onto a lightly floured board and knead it 3 to 5 minutes, just enough to make the dough smooth, adding additional flour as required.

Place the dough in a plastic bag and refrigerate it for 4 hours or overnight. Alternatively, place it in a lightly greased bowl, cover the bowl with plastic wrap and a damp tea towel, and let the dough rest an hour or two.

When ready to make the babka, remove the dough from the fridge and divide it into 2 or 3 portions. (Nettie uses 3 but 2 is fine for a first effort.) Set aside. Generously grease a 10-inch tube pan.

FILLING: With an electric mixer set on slow speed, beat the egg whites and salt until foamy. Increase the speed, and, dusting in the sugar gradually, beat until stiff and glossy but not dry. Fold in the nuts and cinnamon. (If using marshmallows, sprinkle these on the dough when the meringue is called for, along with the cinnamon, raisins, and walnuts.)

On a lightly floured surface, roll out each portion of dough into a rectangle about 10 by 14 inches. Spread each section with one third of the filling. Sprinkle one third of the raisins on each. Starting from the wider end, roll each piece up into a long log or jelly roll.

Stack the rolls, in any fashion, slightly overlapping, in the prepared tube pan (once they rise, they will merge). Brush well with the beaten egg, cover with a damp tea towel, and let the dough rise until doubled in size—(45 to 90 minutes). This can also be done overnight in the fridge. An hour or two before baking, remove the babka from the fridge and let stand to warm up and rise some more before baking.

Preheat the oven to 350°F. Before baking, brush the babka again with the beaten egg, and sprinkle it with coarse sugar. Bake until medium brown, 60 to 70 minutes, covering it lightly with foil if the top browns too quickly. Cool in the pan for about 15 minutes before removing. Sift with confectioners' sugar, if desired. Serve warm or at room temperature, or sliced and toasted.

NOTES: You can also use 4 cups all-purpose flour instead of using bread flour.

Instead of meringue filling, you can substitute 3 cups of miniature marshmallows or chopped regular marshmallows with the cinnamon and walnuts.

Hungarian Walnut or Poppy Seed Strudel (Macoush or Makos)

Makes two 10-inch strudel rolls, each with about 1 cup of filling

Hungarian friends call this "makos," others refer to it as "potica," and I have also seen similar cakes called walnut or poppy seed kindel cake. Make this by the creaming method or, if you have a large food processor, by cutting the butter into the flour. Although it is usually filled with nuts or poppy seeds, you could also try other fillings such cheese. (See Judith's Cheese Pastries, page 234), or use a commercial filling instead of making your own. On the first day, this strudel seems quite light and yeasty, but as it matures, it becomes delightfully dense and moist. It lasts a week or so, well-wrapped.

DOUGH
2½ teaspoons dry yeast
¼ cup warm water
¾ cup plus a pinch of sugar
½ cup warm milk
1 teaspoon vanilla extract
2 eggs
4 tablespoons sour cream
1 tablespoon fresh lemon juice
1 cup (2 sticks) unsalted butter, softened
½ teaspoon salt
¼ teaspoon ground cinnamon
¼ teaspoon baking powder
Approximately 4¼ cups all-purpose flour

EGG GLAZE
1 egg yolk
2–3 tablespoons half and half or milk

FILLINGS
1 generous cup Poppy Seed Filling (page 254) or Walnut Paste Filling (recipe follows)

DOUGH: In a small bowl, whisk together the yeast, water, and pinch of sugar. Allow the yeast to swell for a couple of minutes, then stir in the milk, vanilla, eggs, sour cream, and lemon juice.

Meanwhile, in another larger bowl, cream the butter with the remaining sugar. Blend in the yeast/milk mixture. Then fold in the salt, cinnamon, baking powder, and flour to make a soft dough. Add more flour as needed to make a kneadable dough, and knead for about 5 minutes. It's not necessary to really work this dough—you want it smooth but not as elastic as a bread dough. Place the dough in a well-greased bowl and cover it with plastic. Let the dough rest until almost doubled (about 45 minutes).

GLAZE: In a bowl, whisk together and set aside the ingredients for the glaze.

Gently deflate the dough and divide it in half. Roll each section into a rectangle about 10 by 10 inches and about ¼ inch thick. Spread half the filling on each section. The filling should be about ⅜ inch thick—fill quite generously. Roll up jelly-roll fashion and place, seam side down, on a baking sheet. Press the rolls down gently to flatten them slightly. Brush each roll with the glaze and, using a sharp knife, make several diagonal slashes on the top. Cover with a damp tea towel and let rise briefly, about 20 minutes. Meanwhile, preheat the oven to 350°F.

Bake until nicely browned (25 to 35 minutes). Cool well, before cutting into serving pieces. Cover very well with plastic wrap to store.

NOTE: Although not as traditional, pecans can be substituted for the walnuts for a slightly sweeter nut filling.

FOOD PROCESSOR METHOD: When using this method, make sure the butter is cold (not softened). In a small bowl, whisk together the yeast, warm water, and pinch of sugar. In the work bowl of a processor, place the flour, baking powder, cinnamon, remaining sugar, and salt and process to blend. Then add the butter to the dry mixture and pulse to break up the butter into the flour. Process, pulsing all the while, until you have a grainy, mealy mixture. Turn out into a large bowl. Make a well in the center and stir in the vanilla, eggs, sour cream, lemon juice, and the yeast mixture. Stir to make a soft dough, then knead (about 5 minutes), adding more flour as required, to make a smooth dough. Let rest for 10 minutes, then continue as above.

WALNUT PASTE FILLING

Makes about ¾ cup

This filling can also be used in rugelach, yeast coffee cakes, hamantaschen, or other filled cookies and pastries such as ma'amoul. Double or triple the recipe and freeze the leftovers to have prepared filling on hand.

¼–½ cup half and half, evaporated milk, or water
2 cups finely chopped walnuts
½ cup sugar
2 tablespoons corn syrup or honey
1 teaspoon ground cinnamon
Pinch of salt
2 tablespoons unsalted butter or margarine
1 tablespoon fresh lemon juice
½ teaspoon vanilla extract

Blend all the ingredients in a food processor until the mixture becomes a thick paste. If too thick, loosen it with more half and half. If not using right away, refrigerate. Warm up (at room temperature, stirring to loosen) to a spreadable consistency before using. You may have to add additional half and half or a touch of warm water at this point.

Double Raspberry, Very Decadent, Sour Cream Rugelach

Makes about 4 dozen pastries

You could fill this versatile, rich rugelach dough with just about anything—apricot jam, almond paste, coconut, chopped chocolate, raisins—whatever. This is a classic. If you want crisp rugelach, bake as soon as the pastries are assembled. For a more danish-like rugelach, refrigerate the dough overnight. The next day, make up the pastries but allow them to rise for 20 minutes before baking. For Yom Kippur, these can be made well ahead and frozen. Just toss them on a cookie sheet and bake them without defrosting. This is my favorite rugelach—as close to miniature French croissant pastry as you'll ever make (but as easy as can be). Also suitable for Chanukah. Incidentally, the 1 pound of butter is correct. It's what makes these so special. You may use ³/₄ pound of butter but the pastries will not be as good. For a more modest recipe see the Traditional Rugelach on page 349. For all rugelach, the use of parchment paper is essential.

DOUGH

3 tablespoons warm water
1 tablespoon dry yeast
¹/₃ cup plus a pinch of sugar
3 egg yolks (reserve whites)
¹/₄ cup sour cream (optional)
¹/₂ teaspoon vanilla extract
3 cups all-purpose flour
¹/₂ teaspoon salt
2 cups (4 sticks) very cold unsalted butter, cut into 16–20 chunks

EGG WASH/TOPPING

3 egg whites, reserved from above, whisked to blend
Sugar, coarse or regular, for sprinkling

FILLING

2 teaspoons raspberry extract
2 cups raspberry jam
8–16 tablespoons sugar
1 cup ground walnuts
4 teaspoons ground cinnamon

DOUGH: In a very small bowl, combine the water, yeast, and pinch of sugar. Let the mixture stand for a few minutes to allow the yeast to swell and dissolve. In another small bowl, stir together the egg yolks, sour cream (if using), and vanilla. Place the flour, remaining sugar, and salt in a large bowl and cut in the butter until it is more or less evenly dispersed in the flour. Make a well in the center of the butter/flour mixture. Stir in the dissolved yeast and the yolk mixtures. Work with a fork or your hands, squeezing slightly to combine, to make a soft dough. Place the dough on a lightly floured work surface. Gently shape it into a flattened mound, using additional flour as required. Cut the dough into 4 portions. Wrap each separately and refrigerate for at least 45 minutes to 1 hour before using. (At this point, the dough can also be wrapped well in plastic and frozen.)

FOOD PROCESSOR METHOD: This recipe can also be done partially in a large food processor (or do half the flour and butter at a time). Put the flour in the processor and place the butter chunks on top. Pulse to cut the butter into the flour until you have an uneven, grainy mixture.

Turn out the flour/butter mixture into a large mixing bowl and proceed as above, making a well in the center and adding the remaining ingredients.

TO ASSEMBLE PASTRIES: Roll a section of dough out into a 10- to 12-inch circle. Stir the raspberry extract into the raspberry jam and spread about ½ cup onto the dough, then sprinkle on 2 to 4 tablespoons of sugar, ¼ cup of ground nuts, and 1 teaspoon of cinnamon. Using a pastry or pizza wheel, cut into wedges (12 to 16). Roll up each wedge into a miniature crescent. Brush the pastries with the egg wash and sprinkle additional sugar on top. Repeat with the remaining dough and filling. Bake at 350°F for 25 to 30 minutes.

These pastries will ooze a little butter and sugar as they bake but will crisp and brown nicely.

Black and White Mandelbrot

Makes 28 to 32, depending on size

½ cup (1 stick) unsalted butter, melted, still
  warm
½ cup unsweetened cocoa powder, sifted
¾ cup granulated sugar
½ cup brown sugar
3 eggs
2 teaspoons vanilla extract
2 tablespoons brewed coffee
2¼ cups all-purpose flour
¼ teaspoon salt
¼ teaspoon baking soda
1½ teaspoons baking powder
1½ cups white chocolate, in coarse chunks
½ cup semi-sweet chocolate, in coarse chunks
1 cup coarsely chopped macadamia or pecans
  (optional)

TOPPING (OPTIONAL)
4 ounces white chocolate, melted and cooled

Preheat the oven to 350°F. Line 2 baking sheets with parchment paper.

In a large mixing bowl, stir the warm, melted butter with the cocoa. Blend in the sugars, then the eggs, vanilla, and coffee.

In a separate bowl, blend together the flour, salt, baking soda, and baking powder. Stir the solids into the wet batter, then fold in the white and semi-sweet chocolates and the nuts, if using.

Divide the batter into 4 equal parts. Form 2 logs on each prepared baking sheet, approximately 8 inches long by 3 or 4 inches wide. (You can use a wet, metal spatula to do this.)

Bake one sheet at a time if the oven cannot fit two, or both sheets, but rotate the sheets halfway through to ensure even baking. Bake until the top seems set, 25 to 35 minutes. Cool for 20 minutes.

Transfer the logs to a board and cut them on a diagonal, into ½- to ¾-inch-thick wedges. Reduce the oven heat to 325°. Transfer the cookies to the baking sheets and return them to the oven.

Bake for 15 to 20 minutes to dry out, turning them once midway to brown both sides evenly. Since the cookies are dark, it is difficult to see when they are done. They should seem almost dry to the touch when ready.

You can spread melted white chocolate on one side of these baked cookies, if you like, or drizzle on white chocolate for a more gourmet look. Using a spatula, you can also combine this batter with the Traditional Chocolate Chip Mandelbrot batter (page 94) to create a marbleized cookie.

Lemon Dairy Cheesecake

Makes 10 servings

A small but tasty little cheesecake.

BOTTOM CRUST
1¼ cups vanilla wafer or graham cracker crumbs
¼ cup (½ stick) unsalted butter, melted
1 tablespoon brown sugar
¼ teaspoon ground cinnamon

CHEESECAKE FILLING
1 pound dry cottage cheese (see page 18)
8 ounces cream cheese, softened
1 cup granulated sugar
¼ cup all-purpose flour
½ cup plain yogurt or sour cream
4 eggs plus 1 egg yolk
2 tablespoons fresh lemon juice
1 tablespoon finely minced lemon zest

Preheat the oven to 425°F.

BOTTOM CRUST: In a medium-sized bowl, mix together the crust ingredients with a fork until evenly moistened. Press them into the bottom of a 9-inch springform pan.

FILLING: In a large mixing bowl, cream the cheeses until smooth, then add the sugar and flour. Blend in the yogurt, and then add the eggs, yolk, lemon juice, and zest, combining until smooth and thoroughly incorporated. Pour the batter into the prepared pan and bake for 15 minutes. Reduce the heat to 225° and bake for another 40 minutes. The cake will be set in middle and slightly golden in color.

Cover the top of the cake with plastic wrap and chill it overnight.

Shredded Dough Plum Tart

Makes 8 to 10 servings

This pie, which looks like a fancy tart or fruit torte, was inspired by a recipe that once appeared in the Montreal Gazette *in response to a request for "Stash's Flea Market Polish Apple Squares." While this no longer resembles the original recipe for apple squares, the unique element of shredded dough remains. Semi-frozen tart dough is shredded (like cheese) and showered on top of the filling. Baked and dusted with confectioners' sugar, this tart is a stunning sensation of curls of golden pastry nesting on top of a fresh fruit filling. It also works well with a combination of diced apples and rhubarb or fresh peaches. If you like this concept, try the Polish Apple Tart on page 98. I make this very often using regular pie dough for an equally tasty tart.*

TART DOUGH
3 cups all-purpose flour
1/3 cup granulated sugar
1/2 teaspoon salt
3/4 cup unsalted butter
2 tablespoons vegetable shortening
1 egg yolk
1/2–3/4 cup half and half or light cream

FILLING
6–8 cups quartered ripe plums
3 tablespoons fresh lemon juice
1 1/3 cups granulated sugar
3 tablespoons cornstarch
1/2 teaspoon ground cinnamon

TOPPING
1/2 cup confectioners' sugar

Lightly grease a 9- or 10-inch quiche pan.

DOUGH: Place the flour, sugar, and salt in the work bowl of a food processor. Process to combine these ingredients. Add the butter and shortening and pulse to cut the fat into the dry mixture. Stop the machine and add the egg yolk and half and half. Process, pulsing intermittently, until the mixture comes together in a mass or forms a dough (20 to 40 seconds), adding additional half and half if necessary. Wrap the dough in plastic and chill for 20 minutes. Freeze one third of the dough (this is the section that will be shredded).

On a well-floured board, roll the dough out to fit the pan. If any tears occur, simply patch them into the pan and press to fit.

FILLING: In a bowl, toss the plums with the lemon juice, sugar, cornstarch, and cinnamon. Preheat the oven to 375°F.

Mound the plum filling into the dough-lined pan. Remove the frozen dough from the freezer. Shred it on the large holes of a hand grater. Arrange the shredded dough over the top of the pie.

Place the pan on a parchment paper–lined cookie sheet and place it in the bottom third of the oven. Bake for 20 minutes, then reduce the heat to 350° and bake until the top of the tart is golden brown and you can see some juices bubbling through (45 to 55 minutes). Remove from the oven and cool for about 20 minutes, then sift confectioners' sugar over the top.

NOTE: If you are in a hurry, you may use prepared pie dough for this pie.

Crisp and Rich Mun Cookies

Makes 5 to 6 dozen cookies

Another great poppy-seed cookie. Just-rich-enough, with a touch of orange juice, these mun cookies have many fans. Perfect with a steaming pot of tea.

¾ cup vegetable oil
1½ cups sugar
¼ cup fresh orange juice
1 teaspoon vanilla extract
2 eggs
⅓ cup poppy seeds
Approximately, 3¼ cups all-purpose flour
¼ teaspoon salt
2½ teaspoons baking powder

Preheat the oven to 350°F. Line 2 baking sheets with parchment paper.

In a mixer or using a hand whisk in a mixing bowl, blend the oil, sugar, orange juice, and vanilla. Stir in the eggs. Fold in the poppy seeds, flour, salt, and baking powder to make a stiff batter. Cover the dough with a tea towel and let it rest for 5 to 10 minutes before rolling.

Working with a third of the dough at a time, roll it out on a well-floured work surface. Dust more flour, as required, on both the dough and the rolling pin, to ensure there is no sticking. Roll to a thickness of between ¼ and ⅛ inch. Using a 2½-inch cookie cutter, cut out as many cookies as possible. Place them on the baking sheets and bake until lightly golden or the edges start to brown (12 to 14 minutes).

Lekach, or Spirited Honey Cake

Makes 12 to 14 servings

In my mother-in-law's recipe files (in her mother's handwriting) I found a recipe that simply said, "Honey Cake, Yetta." I fiddled with it, added a bit of this and that, and came up with this mild, moist, traditional-tasting honey cake. I suppose it is no longer "Yetta's" cake, but I give her credit, whoever she was. A touch of whisky (hence the "spirited") makes this special, but if you prefer, just use coffee as your liquid.

2¾ cups all-purpose flour
½ teaspoon salt
2½ teaspoons baking powder
½ teaspoon baking soda
2 teaspoons ground cinnamon
½ teaspoon ground cloves
½ teaspoon ground allspice
1 cup vegetable oil
1 cup honey
1½ cups sugar
3 eggs
1 teaspoon vanilla extract
⅔ cup warm, strong coffee
⅓ cup whisky
½ cup slivered almonds (optional)

Preheat the oven to 350°F. Lightly grease a 9 by 13-inch baking pan or two 8 by 4½-inch loaf pans or a 9-inch angel food cake pan.

In a large bowl, whisk or stir together the flour, salt, baking powder, baking soda, and spices. Make a well in the center, and add the oil, honey, sugar, eggs, vanilla, coffee, and whisky. Using a strong wire whisk, stir the ingredients well to make a thick, well-blended batter, making sure that no ingredients are stuck on the bottom. This can also be done in an electric mixer, using the beating paddle on low speed.

Spoon into the prepared pan(s). Top by evenly sprinkling with almonds if desired, and bake for 40 to 45 minutes for sheet style cakes, or for 45 to 55 minutes for loaves and angel food pans, until the cake springs back when gently pressed.

Cherry Kirsch Gugelhupf

Makes 10 to 14 servings

Also known as kugelhoph, this yeast-raised sweet coffee bread has a Viennese heritage.
Because gugelhupf is less rich than most babkas, the use of a sponge to kick-start the dough makes for a
better-keeping cake. Dried cherries are added for a contemporary touch. This would also work well with
dried cranberries or dried apricots, or a mix of raisins and currants. It's good fresh or toasted. The French
bakeware company, Matfer, makes a variety of gugelhupf molds, available from
several mail order sources (see Source Guide).

MARINATED FRUIT AND NUTS
1/3 cup raisins
1/3 cup sweet or sour dried cherries
1/4 cup kirsch or rum
1/2 cup slivered almonds
1/4 cup citron (optional)

SPONGE
3/4 cup warm water
4 teaspoons dry yeast
Pinch of granulated sugar
1 cup all-purpose flour

DOUGH
Sponge from above
1/2 cup warm milk
2/3 cup granulated sugar
2 eggs plus 1 egg yolk
1 teaspoon vanilla extract
2 tablespoons rum or kirsch (from marinade,
   above)
1 teaspoon finely minced lemon zest
1 1/4 teaspoons salt
1/2 cup (1 stick) unsalted butter, cut into bits
Approximately 3 1/2 cups bread flour
Raisins and cherries (fruit from above, drained)

TOPPING
Melted butter or nonstick cooking spray
Confectioners' sugar

FRUIT AND NUTS: About 1 to 3 hours ahead, plump the raisins (page 22) and dried cherries in very hot water. Drain and cover with the kirsch or rum. Set aside.

Generously grease a 9-inch Turk's head or gugelhupf mold with butter and scatter the slivered almonds over the pan. You can also use a large Bundt pan.

SPONGE: In a large bowl, stir the water with the yeast and sugar. Let the mixture stand for a couple of minutes to allow the yeast to swell and dissolve. Stir in the flour and beat well, about 3 minutes. Cover with plastic wrap and let stand for 1 hour.

DOUGH: Stir down the sponge and add the milk, sugar, eggs, yolk, vanilla, rum or kirsch, the lemon zest, salt, and butter. Stir briefly, then fold in most of the bread flour. Mix, then knead (in a large bowl, not on a work surface) to make a soft dough. Let the dough rest for a few minutes and then press in the raisins, cherries, and zest. (Adding the fruit may require a bit more flour to ensure that the dough does not get wet.)

Place the dough in a well-greased bowl, insert the bowl in a plastic bag, and let the dough rise for 30 minutes. Gently deflate the dough, then arrange it around the center tube or post of the prepared pan. You can do this by forming the dough into an 8- to 10-inch roll and coiling it around the mold. If the dough is very slack, just arrange it in the mold. Brush the top of the cake very lightly with melted butter or spray with nonstick cooking spray.

Place the entire cake pan in a plastic bag and let the dough rise on the counter until almost doubled (30 to 40 minutes) or refrigerate it to bake the next day.

Preheat the oven to 375°F. Bake until the cake is golden brown on top (about 50 minutes). If the cake is browning too quickly, cover the top with a sheet of aluminum foil.

Let the cake cool for 15 minutes before removing it from the pan. Dust with confectioners' sugar before serving.

Overnight Cinnamon Schnecken

Makes 2 dozen schnecken

These can be made a day ahead and left to rise slowly in the refrigerator. Bake, as required, for fresh hot schnecken or "snails"—a lavish cinnamon sticky bun pastry that is a Yom Kippur tradition. Larger versions, baked in a rectangular baking pan and decorated with quick fondant, make sublime Pecan Cinnamon Sticky Buns (page 176).

SCHNECKEN DOUGH
1/3 cup warm water
5 teaspoons dry yeast
3/4 cup plus a pinch of granulated sugar
3/4 cup warm milk
1/2 cup (1 stick) unsalted butter, in small chunks
1 teaspoon salt
1 teaspoon vanilla extract
1/4 teaspoon lemon extract
1 cup sour cream or thick, plain yogurt
1/4 teaspoon ground cinnamon
5–6 cups all-purpose flour

CINNAMON GLAZE
1/2 cup (1 stick) unsalted butter
1 1/2 cups brown sugar
2 1/2 teaspoons ground cinnamon

CINNAMON SUGAR FILLING
1/3 cup unsalted butter, melted
2 cups brown sugar
2 teaspoons ground cinnamon
1 cup coarsely chopped walnuts
1 cup raisins, plumped (page 22) and dried

DOUGH: In a large bowl, whisk together the water, yeast, and pinch of sugar. Let the mixture stand for a couple of minutes, until the yeast swells or dissolves. Stir in the milk, butter, remaining sugar, salt, vanilla and lemon extracts, sour cream or yogurt, and cinnamon. As the ingredients blend, fold in most of the flour. Mix to make a soft but kneadable dough. Knead for 6 to 8 minutes, until the dough is smooth and elastic. Place it in a greased bowl, place the bowl in a plastic bag, and seal loosely. Let the dough rise until doubled, 45 to 60 minutes.

CINNAMON GLAZE: Melt the butter and stir in the brown sugar and cinnamon.

Very generously grease two (preferably nonstick) 12-cup muffin tins.

Gently deflate the dough. Let it rest for about 10 minutes, then roll it out to an 18-inch square between 1/8 and 1/4 inch thick.

CINNAMON SUGAR FILLING: Brush the dough with the melted butter. Sprinkle it with the brown sugar, cinnamon, nuts, and raisins. Roll it up, starting with the edge closest to you, into a snug roll. Cut it in 1 1/2-inch slices—you should have about 24 slices.

Drizzle a little of the cinnamon glaze into each prepared muffin cup and then place a schnecken inside each cup. Place the muffin tins in plastic bags and put them in the fridge. Allow the dough to rise overnight.

To bake, remove the muffin tins from the refrigerator and allow the dough to warm up for about 30 minutes. The dough will rise a bit more as it warms to room temperature. Preheat the oven to 350°F. and bake for 25 to 30 minutes, until the schnecken are medium-brown. Invert them onto a serving tray. Drizzle the syrup remaining in the muffin tins over the tops of the schnecken.

Pecan Cinnamon Sticky Buns

Makes about 2 dozen buns

My middle son, Gideon, is not a big "sweets" eater, but he does have some favorites, like apple challah and these cinnamon buns..

1 batch of dough, Overnight Cinnamon
  Schnecken (page 176)
1 batch of Cinnamon Sugar filling made with
  pecans instead of walnuts (raisins optional),
  Overnight Cinnamon Schnecken

STICKY PECAN CINNAMON GLAZE
1½ cups brown sugar
½ cup (1 stick) unsalted butter, softened
2½ teaspoons ground cinnamon
1 cup whole pecans

MOCK FONDANT
2 cups confectioners' sugar
4–6 tablespoons water
1 teaspoon vanilla extract

Generously grease a 9 by 13-inch baking pan. Roll out the dough, fill it with the cinnamon sugar filling, and roll it up as described on page 176.

GLAZE: In a bowl, combine the brown sugar with the softened butter and cinnamon. Spread the glaze on the bottom of the pan. Distribute the whole pecans evenly over the glaze. Cut the roll of dough into twenty to twenty-four 1-inch slices. Place the slices flat (almost next to each other) in the prepared pan. Spray the top of the dough with nonstick cooking spray. Place the whole pan in a plastic bag and seal it. Refrigerate overnight or, if you are making these right away, let the dough rise at room temperature until almost doubled (30 to 60 minutes). If refrigerated, allow to warm to room temperature, 30 to 45 minutes, and then rise till almost doubled.

To bake, preheat the oven to 350°F. Bake until the sticky buns are lightly golden (25 to 35 minutes). Remove from the oven and invert onto a large tray.

MOCK FONDANT: In a bowl, whisk together the ingredients to make a spreadable glaze. Pour or spread the glaze over the warm cinnamon buns. Serve warm or at room temperature.

Sour Cream Marble Cake

Makes 14 to 16 servings

A simple, rich, delicate, moist cake, similar to a bakery-style marble cake (but much, much better).
This cake needs nothing more than a hot cup of coffee or tall glass of milk.

1 cup (2 sticks) unsalted butter
2¼ cups granulated sugar
1½ teaspoons vanilla extract
4 eggs
⅓ cup milk
1 cup sour cream
3¼ cups all-purpose flour
½ teaspoon salt
1 tablespoon baking powder
½ teaspoon baking soda
3 ounces semi-sweet chocolate, melted and
  cooled
confectioners' sugar, for dusting

Preheat the oven to 350°F. Generously grease a 10-inch springform pan, or a 10-inch tube or angel food pan, and line it with a circle of baking parchment.

In a bowl, cream the butter until softened and blend in the sugar until the mixture is light and fluffy. Stir in the vanilla, and add the eggs, one at a time, blending after each addition (if the batter seems curdled, stir in a little of the flour).

In a small bowl, stir the milk and sour cream together. In another small bowl, stir together the flour, salt, baking powder, and baking soda.

Fold the dry ingredients into the batter and slowly pour or spoon in the milk/sour cream mixture. Mix on low speed until the batter is smooth and well-blended. Be sure to scrape down the bottom and sides of the mixing bowl to incorporate all the ingredients and make sure no pieces of butter or sugar get stuck at the bottom.

Remove one third of the batter to a bowl. Stir a couple of tablespoons of batter into the melted chocolate. Add the chocolate mixture back into the reserved portion and blend well.

Pour the vanilla batter into the prepared pan and, using a spatula, gently fold and swirl in the chocolate batter. You are simply introducing the batters. After baking, the cake will be sufficiently marbleized. Place the pan on doubled-up baking sheets (this prevents the bottom from baking faster than the top) and bake until the cake springs back when gently pressed (50 to 65 minutes; 60 to 65 minutes is for the springform pan). If the cake appears to be browning too quickly and does not seem done, reduce the heat to 325° to finish baking.

Yom Tov Shortbread

Makes about 18 cookies

*A superb cookie, made in minutes in a food processor, a good keeper, and the ideal little
nosh to enjoy with a pot of tea or coffee after the fast. This is not an occasion to substitute margarine for
butter—the butter makes all the difference. You can, however, use brown sugar, packed firmly,
to replace the white sugar for a rich, shortbread taste.*

1 cup (2 sticks) unsalted butter
²/₃ cup sugar
¹/₄ teaspoon salt
2¹/₂ cups all-purpose flour

BY HAND: In a large mixing bowl, cream the butter until softened. Add the sugar and cream until well blended. Stir in the salt, then fold in the flour to make a firm dough. Use your hands if necessary to knead and incorporate all the flour—this is a stiff dough.

FOOD PROCESSOR METHOD: Have the butter a little colder than room temperature. Using the blade attachment, pulse the butter and sugar to blend into a creamed mixture. Add the salt and flour and pulse to make a stiff, slightly crumbly-looking dough. Remove from the machine and knead on a lightly floured board to make the dough hold together.

Preheat the oven to 350°F. Line a baking sheet with parchment paper.

Turn the dough out onto a lightly floured board. Roll it out to between ³/₈ and ¹/₂ inch thick. Cut it into ³/₄ inch by 3-inch rectangles. Press the scraps together and cut out additional rectangles. Mark the top of each cookie with the tines of a fork.

Place the cookies about 2 inches apart on the baking sheet, place in the oven, and immediately reduce the heat to 325°. Bake until just lightly browned around the edges (25 to 30 minutes). Reduce the heat if the cookies are browning too fast. If the cookies are baking too slowly, you may raise the oven temperature to 350°, but watch carefully. Cool the cookies on a rack.

Egg Kichel

Makes 5 dozen cookies

*A classic. A glass of wine or schnapps and a kichel cookie is a traditional treat for holidays,
a birth, a wedding, or after Sabbath services.*

3 eggs
½ cup vegetable oil
½ cup granulated sugar
2½ cups all-purpose flour
¼ teaspoon salt
1 tablespoon baking powder

Preheat the oven to 350°F. Line a baking sheet with parchment paper.

In a mixer, beat the eggs, oil, and sugar until very light and voluminous, about 5 minutes. Fold in the flour, salt, and baking powder.

Adding as little extra flour as possible, roll the dough to between ⅛ and ¼ inch thick. Cut it into circles, squares, or diamond shapes 2 inches in diameter. Transfer to the prepared baking sheet and bake until lightly browned (25 to 30 minutes).

VARIATION: **For Cinnamon Sugar Kichel** sprinkle the cookies with ½ cup sugar mixed with 1 teaspoon ground cinnamon before baking.

5. Sukkot

Festival of Booths

And ye shall take you on the first day of the fruit of goodly trees, branches of palm-trees, and boughs of thick trees, and willows of the brook, and ye shall rejoice before the Lord your God seven days.

You shall live in huts seven days, all citizens of Israel shall live in huts, in order that future generations may know that I made the Israelite people live in huts when I brought them out of the land of Egypt, I the Lord your God.

—LEVITICUS, IN REFERENCE TO COMMAND OF SUKKOT

SUKKOT

Sukkot is known as the Holiday or Festival of Booths, a reference to the small huts (in Hebrew, *sukkot* or *succot)* the wandering Israelites occupied.

WHEN ✸ On the Hebrew calendar, the 15th to 21st of Tishri.

CORRESPONDING TO ✸ End of September through October.

HOLIDAY CONTEXT ✸ Sukkot is part of a holiday cycle based on a trio of events. The cycle starts with Exodus (Passover), followed by the wandering of the freed Jewish slaves in the desert (Sukkot), and reaches closure with the giving of the Torah at Sinai (Shavuot). In contrast to the more somber Days of Awe, Sukkot is marked by joy and celebration. Occurring as it does so soon after the High Holidays, Sukkot keeps us busy with activities from September through October. In his book, *The Jewish Holidays,* Michael Strassfeld remarks that Sukkot is an occasion of new beginnings. We have experienced forgiveness at Yom Kippur and now are ready to go forward, with a fresh slate, into the new year. It is fitting to celebrate this against the backdrop of the harvest.

Sukkot recalls the wandering of the Jews following the exodus from Egypt. As the children of Israel continued on their nomadic trek, searching for the promised land, they made do with temporary huts or booths as shelter, and our contemporary sukkots are a nod to this period in Jewish history.

Others suggest that Sukkot bears a more simplistic connection to agricultural symbolism. Our ancestors, as other ancient peoples, depended on the seasons and the land. Sukkot occurs during harvest time (its other name is the Holiday of Ingathering) and the sukkah replicates the makeshift huts that were erected in the fields where workers could rest or pass their nights until the crop-gathering was complete. In any case, this unique holiday serves as a reminder of these early days when the harvest, and God's generous bounty, were celebrated.

ACTIVITIES ✸ In honor of Sukkot, building a sukkah is a holiday *mitzvah*. It is especially important to "live" in the sukkah (primarily for meals, and if weather permits, to sleep).

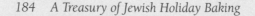

Symbols decorate the sukkah: the etrog or citron fruit, the lulav or palm branches, as well as branches from the willow, and sprigs from the fragrant myrtle bush. These natural items represent the variety of growing things.

FOOD SYMBOLS ✹ Any food that is "harvest-oriented" is appropriate for Sukkot. A jelly or marmalade made with the thick-skinned etrog is one option, but there are more familiar choices. Foods made with fruits and nuts, particularly if they are native to your region, symbolize the harvest and are appropriate. In addition to the recipes in this chapter, almost any recipe from Rosh Hashanah is suitable. Modest finger foods, such as strudel miniatures; cookies; old-fashioned, multilayered fluden; and quick breads such as the Harvest Zucchini Loaf (page 200) all work. Remember, if you are serving foods in a sukkah, they should be informal.

ETROGS FOR DECOR, ETROG ZEST FOR BAKING

Just before Sukkot, local synagogues arrange for members to obtain imported etrogs as well as palm branches with which to decorate their sukkots. An etrog is also known as a "citron," which we more commonly find as a prepared ingredient in the form of candied citron, a staple for holiday fruit cakes. Candied citron can be found in the baking section of most supermarkets along with dried fruits such as raisins and dates, or candied orange peel.

A fresh etrog looks like an enlarged lemon. Scrape away a bit of the zest and you'll find a heady citrus bouquet, reminiscent of lemons and limes blended together in a tropical, citrusy perfume. At Sukkot, the etrog is displayed in a special "etrog box" or container in the sukkah. This can be the modest wooden box (lined with straw) the etrog often comes in or as ornate as a silver "egg" with intricate filigree and a hinged lid.

A particularly thick-skinned fruit used primarily as a symbol on the Sukkot table, the etrog is not particularly juicy nor filled with usable pulp. However, the outer zest is exceptionally flavorful and plentiful. If you are ambitious, you can make etrog marmalade from a standard marmalade recipe, substituting a couple of etrogs for the Seville oranges usually called for.

An appropriate cake for Sukkot that incorporates the zest of an etrog, is the Sukkot Lemon Lime Cake (page 187). Lemons and limes, or etrog if you have one to spare for baking (or wish to use it after the holiday), invoke the flavor, fragrance, and feeling of this harvest festival, offering a pleasant tart sweetness in every bite. If you are saving your etrog for a Sukkot centerpiece, don't throw it out after the holiday. Remove the zest, and freeze it. Later on, when you have the urge to make a lemon or lime loaf, or add zing to any tangy cake, you can use the fragrant zest you have frozen away for rainy-day baking. Whatever you do, don't waste it!

Etrog or Lemon Lime Sukkot Cake

Makes 8 to 10 servings

Moist and fragrant, this cake puts an etrog to use—but lemons and limes work well. You can garnish the cake plate with citrus or myrtle leaves, as well as palm branches. Creaming the zest with the butter and sugar is a technique which ensures the flavors will disperse well.

½ cup (1 stick) unsalted butter or margarine
1 cup sugar
2 tablespoons finely minced etrog or lime zest
  (or lemon/lime combination)
2 eggs
¼ cup milk
½ teaspoon vanilla extract
2 tablespoons fresh lemon juice
2 tablespoons fresh lime juice
½ teaspoon lime oil or extract
1½ cups all-purpose flour
¼ teaspoon salt
2 teaspoons baking soda
¼ teaspoon baking powder

LEMON LIME GLAZE
2 tablespoons fresh lemon juice
2 tablespoons fresh lime juice
¼ cup sugar

Preheat the oven to 350°F. Generously grease an 8 by 4-inch loaf pan or an 8-inch layer pan or an 8-inch springform pan.

In a mixing bowl, cream the butter, sugar, and zest together until well blended. Stir in the eggs, then the milk, vanilla, lemon and lime juices, and lime oil to combine well. Fold in the remaining dry ingredients to make a smooth batter.

Spoon the batter into the prepared pan and bake until the cake is evenly browned and slightly cracked on top (30 to 35 minutes). Cool well before removing it from the pan.

LEMON LIME GLAZE: In a small saucepan, heat the lemon and lime juices. Stir in the sugar until dissolved. Cool well.

Using a cake tester, poke holes all over the cake and drizzle the glaze on top.

Romanian Dried Fruit Strudelettes

Makes 15 to 20 pastries, depending on size
(These can also be made into smaller or miniature strudels, for a sweet table tray.)

Sometimes referred to as "haimish strudel" or dried fruit strudel, this delicacy is a cross
between a confection and a pastry. You can use stretch strudel dough (see page 151) for this recipe, or
store-bought kosher puff dough, but this easy sour cream mock puff dough is tops in flavor and texture.
This is a good keeper and a wonderful gift.

SOUR CREAM MOCK PUFF DOUGH
2 cups flour
½ teaspoon salt
1 cup (2 sticks) unsalted butter or margarine,
  cut into 12 chunks
1 cup sour cream
Unsalted butter, melted, for brushing pastry

MIXED DRIED FRUIT AND TURKISH DELIGHT
FILLING
(FOR EACH ½ BATCH OF DOUGH)
⅔ cup jam (apricot, strawberry, or
  seedless raspberry)
1 cup finely chopped nuts
2–4 tablespoons sugar
½ teaspoon ground cinnamon
½ cup shredded coconut
⅓ cup chopped Turkish delight or any
  gummylike, chewy candy (see Note)
½ cup plumped (page 22) raisins
⅓ cup cut-up candied cherries
⅓ cup canned pineapple, well-dried and diced

TOPPING
Confectioners' sugar, for dusting

DOUGH: In the bowl of a food processor, place the flour and salt. With the machine on, drop in the butter and pulse to create a grainy mixture. Add the sour cream and process only until a ball forms. If a ball doesn't form in 1 to 2 minutes, remove the dough from the processor and work it on a lightly floured board for a couple of seconds. Do not overwork the dough. Pat it into a smooth disc and chill.

Preheat the oven to 375°F. Line a large baking sheet with parchment paper.

FILLING AND ASSEMBLING: Divide the dough in half. Roll out one half on a lightly floured board to a rectangle of about 14 by 14 inches. Brush the dough lightly with the melted butter. Spread on the jam, then evenly sprinkle on the nuts, sugar, cinnamon, coconut, Turkish delight, raisins, cherries, and pineapple. Roll up the dough half way (to the middle). Cut away the remaining dough. Cut the rolled dough into 3-inch lengths (each individual pastry should be about the size of an egg roll—perhaps slightly wider) and transfer the strudels to the prepared pan. Continue rolling and cutting with the remaining dough, then transfer those pastries to the baking sheet.

Bake until the top of the pastry is golden or almost medium brown, and the fruit filling is beginning to ooze out, about 35 minutes. Cool well. Dust with confectioners' sugar.

ALTERNATE FILLING: For Chocolate Hazelnut Filling (for each ½ batch of dough), layer ½ cup hazelnut chocolate spread, ½ cup coarsely chopped semi-sweet chocolate, ¼ cup sugar, ¼ teaspoon ground cinnamon, and ⅓ cup chopped pecans or macadamia nuts onto the dough and roll up. Proceed as above.

NOTE: Instead of the Turkish delight, I often use gummy bears, Swedish berries (cut) or any other sort of jelly-like candy.

Sukkot Fluden with Horn-of-Plenty Filling

Makes 25 to 35 squares, depending on size

*Fluden is a hybrid of strudel, baklava, and cake. It is layered as
is baklava, filled with fruit like strudel, but in texture, it is like cake. A very old, East European confection,
fluden or fladen is most commonly served at Sukkot. You do not often see it in cookbooks these days,
unless the name has been changed. Some cookbooks I came across refer to any layered fruit-and-nut
cakes as "zserbo" cake. Some of these were rolled; others are made in square or rectangular
tins. Older recipes call for prune, date, or poppy-seed filling, or even alternating levels of
different fillings such as jam, nuts, and coconut. Fluden doughs can be rich yeast doughs,
strudel or filo doughs, or, most often, a cookie-like sweet tart dough like this one. If you wish,
you can substitute any of the fillings in the Purim chapter (such as apricot or prune)
for the one suggested here.*

FLUDEN PASTRY
1/4 cup vegetable shortening
3/4 cup (1 1/2 sticks) unsalted butter
1 cup sugar
3 eggs
1/4 cup milk
1 1/2 teaspoons vanilla extract
Approximately 3 1/4 cups all-purpose flour
1/2 teaspoon salt
2 1/4 teaspoons baking powder

HORN-OF-PLENTY MIXED FRUIT FILLING
6 cups peeled and shredded or finely chopped
  apples
1 1/2 cups cranberries, coarsely chopped
1/3 cup dried cherries, plumped (page 22) and
  dried
1 cup raisins, plumped (page 22) and dried
1/3 cup diced Turkish delight (optional)
1/3 cup ground walnuts (optional)
1/3 cup apricot or peach jam
3/4 cup sugar

2 tablespoons fresh lemon juice
1/2 teaspoon ground cinnamon
2 tablespoons flour

DOUGH: In a medium-sized bowl, cream the shortening and butter with the sugar. Blend in the eggs, milk, and vanilla. Fold in the flour, salt, and baking powder and stir to make a stiff dough. On a lightly floured surface, pat the dough into a round disc, wrap it in plastic, and chill it for about 1 hour.

FLUDEN FILLING: In a large bowl, combine the apples, cranberries, cherries, raisins; Turkish delight and walnuts if using; and jam. Stir or toss briefly to combine. Fold in the remaining ingredients. Using a large spoon, mix well. Set aside.

Preheat the oven to 350°F. Generously grease a 9 by 13-inch pan.

Divide the dough into 3 portions. Roll out one portion, or simply pat and trim the dough to fit the pan bottom. Spoon on half the filling. Roll or pat another portion of dough on top of the fruit. Cover with the remaining fruit mixture, then the last portion of dough. Press lightly. Bake for 20 minutes, then reduce the heat to 325° and bake for an additional 30 to 40 minutes, until the top of the pastry is lightly golden.

Cool and cut into squares to serve. Cover the pastry well to store.

Almond Pastry Croissants

Makes about 10 pastries

Use Traditional Rugelach Dough or the extra-rich dough from the Double Raspberry Rugelach or Sour Cream Mock Puff Dough for these melt-in-your-mouth gems. The almond paste melts during baking and the result is a crisp and sweet pastry croissant.

⅓ recipe Sour Cream Mock Puff dough,
  Traditional Rugelach dough, or
  Double Raspberry Rugelach dough
  (pages 188, 349, or 166)
¼ cup (½ stick) unsalted butter, melted
½ cup apricot jam
½ cup almond paste, cut into small chunks
1 egg white, lightly beaten
Sugar, for sprinkling

Preheat the oven to 375°F. Line a baking sheet with parchment paper.

Roll the dough out into a circle about ⅛ inch thick and 10 to 12 inches in diameter. Brush with the melted butter. Spread on the apricot jam as evenly as possible and disperse the chunks of almond paste over the jam. Cut the circle into 10 wedges and roll up each one into a crescent. Curve the crescents slightly and place them on the baking sheet. Brush with the beaten egg white and sprinkle with the sugar.

Bake until golden brown, 20 to 22 minutes. Cool on a rack.

Pomegranate and Sour Cherry Mandelbrot

Makes 2 to 3 dozen slices, depending on size

Cookbook author Paula Wolfert gets the credit for introducing me to pomegranate molasses—an extraordinary tangy sweet syrup. Mahogany colored and dotted with zesty cherries, these cookies are a nice, sweet bite.

½ cup vegetable oil
¼ cup pomegranate molasses (see Note)
3 tablespoons honey
1 cup granulated sugar, plus extra for sprinkling
1 teaspoon vanilla extract
3 eggs, lightly beaten; plus 1 egg white, beaten, for glaze
3 cups all-purpose flour
1¾ teaspoons baking powder
¼ teaspoon salt
¼ teaspoon ground cinnamon
1 cup whole walnut halves
¾ cup dried sour cherries, plumped (page 22) and dried

NOTE: Pomegranate molasses (usually Cortas brand) is available in Middle Eastern food stores or from one of the Middle Eastern mail order houses in the Source Guide. If you cannot find it, substitute 2 tablespoons honey with 2 tablespoons balsamic vinegar.

In a medium-sized mixing bowl, stir together the oil, pomegranate molasses, honey, sugar, and vanilla. Blend in the beaten whole eggs. Stir in the flour, baking powder, salt, cinnamon, walnut halves, and dried cherries to make a thick batterlike dough.

Preheat the oven to 325°F. Line a large cookie sheet with parchment paper.

Spoon out 2 rows of mandelbrot dough about 8 inches by 3 or 4 inches wide (or one large length of 10 to 12 inches). Brush the top with the beaten egg white and sprinkle with a little sugar.

Bake until the top of the dough seems firm and dry, 25 to 35 minutes. Remove from the oven and reduce the heat to 300°. Slice the mandelbrot about ¾ inch thick. Replace the baking sheet in the oven for 20 to 30 minutes to dry the cookies, turning them once after 10 to 15 minutes.

Grandma Goldman's
Sour Cream Chocolate Cake

Makes 8 to 10 servings

This is a delicate sour cream–based chocolate layer cake that, for years, my mother attributed to my dad's mother, Annie Goldman. "The best cake I ever had," my mom often claimed, "was Grandma Goldman's sour cream chocolate cake." Once she even mentioned that my grandmother made this weekly for my father when he was a young man. Later on, she confided that she thought the recipe was from the back of the Swan's Down cake flour box. (Five Roses flour in Canada has a similar recipe.)

CAKE
3 squares unsweetened chocolate, melted and cooded
$\frac{1}{2}$ cup (1 stick) unsalted butter, softened
2$\frac{1}{4}$ cups brown sugar
3 eggs
1$\frac{1}{2}$ teaspoons vanilla extract
2$\frac{1}{4}$ cups all-purpose flour
1 tablespoon cornstarch
2 teaspoons baking soda
$\frac{1}{4}$ teaspoon salt
1 cup sour cream
1 cup boiling water

DOUBLE CHOCOLATE ICING
$\frac{1}{4}$ cup vegetable shortening
$\frac{3}{4}$ cup (1$\frac{1}{4}$ sticks) unsalted butter or unsalted margarine
3–4 cups confectioners' sugar, sifted
$\frac{1}{3}$ cup unsweetened cocoa powder, sifted
1 cup semi-sweet chocolate chips, melted and cooled
$\frac{1}{2}$ cup brewed coffee or half and half

Preheat the oven to 350°F. Lightly grease two 9-inch layer pans or a 9 by 13-inch rectangular pan and line the pan(s) with parchment paper.

CAKE: In a large bowl, cream the melted, cooled chocolate with the butter. Mix in the sugar until fluffy and well blended. Add the eggs, one at a time, until the mixture is smooth. Stir in the vanilla. In a separate bowl, whisk the dry ingredients to blend. Mixing on low speed and scraping the bowl often, add the dry ingredients, along with the sour cream, to the batter, alternating dry ingredients and sour cream until the batter is smooth. Add the boiling water. The batter will be thin. Pour it into the prepared pans.

Bake for 35 to 40 minutes, until the cake springs back when gently pressed with your fingertips. Cool it in the pan for 10 minutes, then turn it out onto a cake rack to cool completely.

CHOCOLATE ICING: In a mixing bowl, cream the shortening and butter or margarine together with 1 cup of the confectioners' sugar. Add the remaining confectioners' sugar, the cocoa, and the melted chocolate. Whip on high speed, adding a bit of coffee or half and half to get a light, fluffy consistency. If not using the icing right away, rewhip before using, adding milk or cream to get the correct consistency (a tablespoon at a time). Assemble and ice as you would any other double layer cake.

Hazelnut-Walnut Linzertorte

Makes 8 to 10 servings

A torte in name only. This classic jam tart is a breeze to whip up.

¾ cup (1½ sticks) unsalted butter
¾ cup granulated sugar
¼ teaspoon salt
1 teaspoon ground cinnamon
¼ teaspoon grated nutmeg
Pinch of ground cloves
1½ cups all-purpose flour
½ cup skinless hazelnuts, ground
½ cup walnuts, ground
2 egg yolks
1 teaspoon vanilla extract
1 tablespoon half and half or light cream
1 cup preserves (raspberry, apricot, plum, or peach)
1 cup lightly packed grated apples

EGG WASH TOPPING
1 egg, lightly beaten
Confectioners' sugar, for dusting

In a large bowl, cream the butter with the sugar until well blended. Blend in the salt, cinnamon, nutmeg, cloves, flour, and nuts. Stir in the egg yolks, vanilla, and half and half. Chill for 30 minutes.

Divide the dough into 2 sections, one slightly larger than the other (more dough for the bottom; smaller piece for the top). Using floured parchment or wax paper, roll the larger piece of dough into a circle about ½-inch thick and large enough to fit a 9- or 10-inch tart or quiche pan. Transfer the dough to the pan, pressing in or patching up any areas that tear. Chill for 10 minutes.

Meanwhile, roll the remaining dough, again on floured parchment paper or wax paper, to a thickness of ¼ inch. Cut it into ½-inch strips with a serrated pastry wheel or a sharp paring knife. Leave the strips intact on the paper. Transfer the paper to a small baking sheet and chill or freeze the dough for about 20 minutes to firm up (this makes it easier to transfer the strips to the tart).

Mix the preserves with the grated apples. Cover the bottom of the tart with the preserve/apple mixture. Paint the edges of the tart with the egg wash. Using a long metal spatula, arrange the chilled pastry strips in a lattice design on top of the tart, pressing them into the edges to seal. Brush the top of the strips with the egg wash. Chill the tart for 20 minutes.

Preheat the oven to 350°F. Bake the chilled tart until it is light to medium golden in color (40 to 50 minutes). Let it cool, then dust it with confectioners' sugar.

VARIATION: Use the dough to make small, fancy nut cookies. Dust them with confectioners' sugar. Bake for 15 to 17 minutes.

Sugar-Crusted Wine Mandelbrot

Makes 2 to 3 dozen cookies, depending on size

Inspired by the recipe for Rhode Island Wine Biscuits in La Dolce Vita,
*by Michele Scicòlone. Savory dry biscuits made with marsala or another red wine
are an Italian-American tradition. These look extraordinary and have a taste to match.
Bundle up a bunch of these in tinted cellophane for a unique gourmet gift. I nicknamed
these "fruit-of-the-vine" mandelbrot, since they use a good portion of Manischewitz or
Carmel ceremonial sweet kosher wine.*

3 cups all-purpose flour
1/4 teaspoon salt
1 teaspoon baking powder
1/2 teaspoon baking soda
1/2 cup vegetable oil
1 cup sugar
1 teaspoon vanilla extract
3 eggs
1/2 cup sweet red kosher wine
1 cup coarsely chopped walnuts
3/4 cup coarsely chopped cranberries

DIPPING MIXTURE
1/2 cup sweet red kosher wine
3/4 cup sugar

Preheat the oven to 350°F. Line 2 baking sheets with parchment paper.

In a medium-sized bowl, whisk together the flour, salt, baking powder, and baking soda. In a large mixing bowl, blend the oil, sugar, and vanilla. Blend in the eggs, then add the wine. Fold in the dry ingredients to make a smooth batter, then stir in the nuts and cranberries. The batter will be loose and sticky.

Spread or spoon the batter onto the prepared baking sheets in strips approximately 9 inches long by 4 to 5 inches across.

Bake until set and golden, 28 to 35 minutes. Cool for 15 minutes.

DIPPING MIXTURE: Set out 2 plates, fill one with the wine, and the other with the sugar.

Cut the baked cookies on the diagonal about 1/2 inch thick. Using a pastry brush or spoon, generously drizzle some wine onto one side of each cookie, then dip it into the sugar. Alternatively, you can just dip one side of the cookies in wine, then in sugar. If you do this, the cookies will be outstanding, but you might find they will need a longer second bake to dry out properly. Lay the cookies sugar side down on the parchment-lined baking sheets.

For the second bake, return the mandelbrot to the oven until they appear crisp and dry (30 to 35 minutes), turning them once after 20 minutes.

Mamaliga (Corn) and Cherry Cake

Makes 10 to 12 servings

*A crunchy exterior and an airy, moist interior, make this an all-time
favorite coffee cake. Blueberries would make it classic, but sour cherries make it intriguing.
(You can even leave the fruit out.) A baker's trick, is to use 3½-ounce tuna cans for molds. Spray the
interiors very generously with nonstick cooking spray, then insert muffin liners. The result is
oversized, flush-topped "muffin-cakes" that look as unique and delicious as they taste.*

¾ cup vegetable oil
1½ cups sugar
3 eggs
1 cup water
1 teaspoon vanilla extract
¼ teaspoon lemon oil or extract
1¼ cups all-purpose flour
1 teaspoon salt
2½ teaspoons baking soda
½ teaspoon baking powder
1 cup cornmeal, preferably stone-ground
1 cup well-drained and dried sour cherries

Preheat the oven to 375°F. Spray or generously grease 10 miniature loaf pans (1½ by 3 or 4 inches) or 12 muffin cups. (Alternatively, you can use a 10-inch springform pan.) Line the mold bottoms with muffin liner cups (widened to line the loaf molds).

In a large mixing bowl, blend the oil and sugar. Mix in the eggs, then the water, vanilla, and lemon oil. Fold in the flour, salt, baking soda, baking powder, and cornmeal. The batter will be loose and pourable. Stir in the cherries.

Pour the batter into the prepared pan(s). Bake for 20 minutes, then reduce the heat to 350° and bake for 25 to 30 minutes more, until the edges are lightly browned and the tops are just firm (the cake may crack down the center) and spring back when touched.

Miami Beach Coffee Cake

Makes 12 to 16 servings

Why the name "Miami Beach"? Two reasons: the many Miami Beach delicatessens which are renowned for the coffee cakes (sometimes called "Russian" or "Hungarian" coffee cake) with which they bolster their coffee and tea sales. Second—the title is my unofficial salute to Miami dessert queen, Maida Heatter, whose recipes, writing, and teaching style have inspired a generation of bakers. You may substitute a regular streusel filling here. The cake is smooth, moist, and buttery. Great for Sukkot.

FILLING
⅓ cup firmly packed brown sugar
2 teaspoons unsweetened cocoa powder
⅓ cup coarsely chopped semi-sweet chocolate
1 teaspoon ground cinnamon
⅓ cup dark raisins, plumped (page 22) and dried, coarsely chopped
⅓ cup yellow raisins, plumped, dried, and coarsely chopped
½ cup chopped walnuts (preferably toasted)

CAKE
¾ cup (1½ sticks) unsalted butter
1 cup very firmly packed brown sugar
⅓ cup granulated sugar
4 ounces cream cheese, softened
5 eggs
1½ teaspoons vanilla extract
1 cup plain yogurt or sour cream
3¼ cups all-purpose flour
¼ teaspoon salt
1 tablespoon baking powder
½ teaspoon baking soda

Preheat the oven to 350°F. Grease a 9- or 10-inch tube or angel food cake pan.

FILLING: In a bowl, mix all the ingredients and set aside. You also may chunk the filling ingredients in a food processor for a different texture.

CAKE: In a large mixing bowl, cream the butter with the sugars until fluffy. Add the cream cheese and cream until blended. Add the eggs and vanilla and mix thoroughly, then blend in the yogurt or sour cream. Fold in the dry ingredients, scraping down the sides and bottom of the bowl occasionally. Mix well on low speed. Spread one third of the batter over the bottom of the prepared pan. Top with some of the filling mixture. Layer in this fashion until filling and batter are used up. Bake until golden (50 to 60 minutes). Cool in the pan for 10 minutes before removing, and continue to cool on a rack.

Harvest Zucchini Loaf

Makes 8 to 12 servings

What better way to use up those extra garden or market squash than inside a Sukkot zucchini loaf? Shredded carrots can stand in for the zucchini, or use half carrots, and half zucchini. Sometimes I use ½ teaspoon minced fresh or jarred ginger to replace the ground ginger. These loaves freeze well and the batter can also be made into mini-loaves or muffins.

2 cups sugar
1 cup vegetable oil
3 eggs
1½ teaspoons vanilla extract
3¼ cups all-purpose flour
½ teaspoon salt
2 teaspoons baking powder
1 teaspoon baking soda
1 tablespoon ground cinnamon
½ teaspoon ground ginger
1 tablespoon finely minced lemon zest
3 cups shredded zucchini
1 cup yellow raisins, plumped (page 22) and
  well-dried
1 cup coarsely chopped walnuts

NOTE: To make one loaf, halve all the ingredients except the eggs—use 2 eggs.

Preheat the oven to 350°F. Generously grease two 9 by 5-inch loaf pans, one 10-inch tube pan, or a large Bundt pan.

In a large bowl, combine the sugar, oil, eggs, and vanilla until well-blended. Fold in the dry ingredients, and lemon zest. Stir well, then add the remaining ingredients.

Spoon the batter into the prepared pan(s). Bake for 50 to 60 minutes in the loaf pan or 60 to 70 minutes in the tube or Bundt pan. The loaf is done when it springs back to the touch and a toothpick inserted in the center comes out clean. Cool in the pan.

Building Your Own Sukkah

People often joke that so many Jewish holiday traditions revolve around food. But building your own sukkah is another sort of tradition—a tradition that requires some muscle, ingenuity, and cooperation. You will get to eat in your sukkah eventually, of course, but first you have to use some elbow grease to get there.

For the longest time, I never even considered building my own sukkah. It seemed something reserved for only the most observant in the community or, realistically, something the local synagogue did for "all of us" to come and enjoy. One year, a friend who was very active in the shul called and asked if our family would be part of the synagogue's annual "Sukkot Hop." Apparently, synagogue members rallied together to build the communal sukkah, and then departed to assist members with their own individual or family sukkahs (sukkot), much like a roving Jewish barn raising. How could I say no?

My family gathered old bits of wood, branches, and some nails and started hammering away. Fortunately, in our neighborhood fall is the time when the municipal locality trims the trees. The sidewalks are filled with piles of maple and spruce branches, almost a gift on a platter for sukkah builders. Although palm branches (lulav) are considered the "real thing," any sort or organic materials will do. With my three boys giving their varied assistance(?) and advice(!) our first sukkah was mounted. The roof was topped with a thick coat of pungent pine and spruce branches as well as trimmings from scarlet-colored maple trees, emerald-green cedar branches, as well as some reed-like bush trimmings from a field near our house. Through the crevices left in this thatched roof the stars were, at night, clearly visible, in keeping with one of the basic customs of a sukkah. Inside, the boys tacked up fruit and vegetable pictures they had made themselves, we hung fruits such as apples and bananas and strung cranberries. A fold-up table with a colorful tablecloth went in the center of the sukkah. An old camp blanket was partially tacked over the entrance to form our "door." It didn't take long and it was a really special family time.

Apple Strudel Miniatures

Makes 1½ to 2 dozen pastries, depending on size

You could use any dough for these—the Cottage Cheese Dough or Sour Cream Mock Puff Dough work especially well. Because the apples are unpeeled, and shredded instead of pared, this little apple pastry takes barely minutes to prepare.

FILLING
Approximately 4 cups shredded (unpeeled, cored) apples
¾ cup granulated sugar
1 teaspoon ground cinnamon
3 tablespoons flour
1 tablespoon fresh lemon juice
½ recipe Sour Cream Mock Puff Dough or Cottage Cheese Dough (page 188 or 234)
Approximately ⅓ cup unsalted butter, melted
Confectioners' sugar, for dusting

Preheat the oven to 400°F. Line 2 baking sheets with parchment paper.

FILLING: In a bowl, toss the apples with the other ingredients.

Roll the dough out as thinly as possible (about 18 by 20 inches) and brush it generously with melted butter. Spread the apple mixture all over the dough. Roll it up, starting from the edge closest to you, until you have a roll about 1½ inches thick. Cut the roll off the remaining dough. Repeat this procedure with the remaining dough. Cut this roll into mini strudels, each about 1½ inches long. Place the rolls on the baking sheets, brush the tops with additional melted butter, and bake, until they are golden brown and the apple juices start to leak out the sides, 18 to 25 minutes. Cool well and dust generously with confectioners' sugar.

Hungarian Plum Kuchen

Makes 6 to 8 servings

There are many versions of this cake, some made with a sweet, not-too-rich yeast batter and others, like this one, with a soft, buttery batter leavened with baking powder and laced with a dollop of sour cream. The common thread is the use of rows of plums, dotted all over the top of the cake, making it perfect Sukkot fare. In the fall, a good choice are freestone, blue-skinned Italian plums. You could also make this cake with apricots. Best consumed the first day or two after baking.

KUCHEN
½ cup (1 stick) unsalted butter, softened
½ cup sugar
2 eggs
¼ cup sour cream
1 teaspoon vanilla extract
½ teaspoon almond extract
Zest of 1 lemon, finely minced
1½ cups all-purpose flour
¼ teaspoon salt
1 teaspoon baking powder

TOPPING
6 cups pitted, quartered plums
Juice of 1 lemon
3 tablespoons sugar
½ teaspoon ground cinnamon
Pinch of grated nutmeg
1 tablespoon unsalted butter, in bits

Preheat the oven to 350°F. Grease a 10-inch springform or quiche pan.

KUCHEN: In a large bowl, cream the butter and sugar until smooth. Add the eggs, one at a time, then the sour cream, vanilla, almond extract, and lemon zest. Fold in the flour, salt, and baking powder.

TOPPING: If the plums are very large, cut them into eighths. Spoon the batter into the prepared pan. Arrange the plums on top, cut side up, in concentric rows, spiraling out from the center to fill the surface of the pan. Drizzle the lemon juice and sugar, then dust with the cinnamon and nutmeg. Dot with the butter bits.

Bake until the fruit releases its juices and the pastry is browned on top (about 35 minutes). Cool well before removing from the pan.

Bubbie Esther's Sweet Cherry Buns

Makes about 20 buns

*My children's great grandmother, Esther Carpman, was a sprightly, ash-blond, kitchen dynamo
who was famous for her hearty potato "kugelins," served with old-fashioned sweet and sour cabbage
borscht, as well as these gems. Yeasty sweet bun dough is stuffed with cherry filling, then folded into odd
shapes. A version of this appeared in a feature I wrote for* Bon Appetit *on quick yeast breads.
Bubbie Carpman used sweet cherries and often cherry pie filling if she was pressed for time,
but I am partial to Hungarian sour cherries. Any one of these works well, as do blueberry or apple filling.
As a friend of mine said, "These are pure memory food."*

SWEET DOUGH
¼ cup warm water
2 tablespoons dry yeast
⅔ cup plus a pinch of sugar
1 cup warm milk
2 teaspoons vanilla extract
2 teaspoons salt
3 large eggs
½ cup vegetable oil or unsalted butter, melted
  and cooled
5½ cups unbleached all-purpose flour

CHERRY FILLING (or use a 19-ounce can of cherry
  pie filling)

1 (28-ounce) can or jar of sour cherries in juice
½ cup sugar
¼ cup cornstarch

GLAZE/TOPPING
1 egg mixed with 2 tablespoons milk or water
Sugar, for sprinkling

SWEET DOUGH: In a large mixing bowl, stir together the water, yeast, and pinch of sugar. Let the mixture stand for a couple of minutes, until the yeast swells or seems dissolved. Whisk in the milk, remaining sugar, vanilla, salt, eggs, and oil or butter. Stir in most of flour. Using a dough hook, knead on slow speed for 6 to 8 minutes to form a soft dough, or knead by hand for 8 minutes. Dust in more flour, as required, to get a soft dough.

Shape the dough into a ball, place it in a lightly greased bowl, and cover it with greased plastic wrap. Let the dough rest until doubled (about 45 minutes).

FILLING: Drain the cherries, reserving the juice. Measure and set aside ¼ cup of the juice. In a medium saucepan, heat the remaining cherry juice with the sugar. Mix the ¼ cup cherry juice with the corn starch. When the mixture on the stove comes to a gentle boil, stir in the cornstarch mixture. Stir, reducing the heat to low until the mixture thickens (1 to 2 minutes). Stir in the cherries. Cool well in the refrigerator (it should thicken further) until needed.

Preheat the oven to 350°F. Line a baking sheet with parchment paper.

Gently deflate the dough and divide it into 20 pieces. Roll each piece into an oval or rectangle about 4 by 6 inches and a little less than ¼ inch thick. Brush the egg glaze around the edges. Place a tablespoon of cherry filling in the center. Fold the right and left sides over each other, then fold the top and bottom toward the center to seal. Place the buns on the baking sheet, brush them with the egg glaze, and sprinkle them lightly with sugar.

Alternatively, you can prepare circles of dough. Place some cherry filling in the center. Glaze the edges of the dough before folding the ends toward the middle. This will result in a rectangular pastry with 2 open ends, exposing the filling.

Let the buns rise for 15 to 20 minutes. They should look puffy but not be doubled in size.

Bake the buns for 25 minutes, or until evenly browned. Cool in the pan.

Aunt Helen's Chinese Chews

Makes 14 to 20 chews, depending on size

A wonderful recipe from an exceptional baker, one of my special role models—my aunt Helen. As Aunt Helen says, these taste rich (but aren't), taste buttery (but are pareve), and seem fancy (but are easy to make). You can make these squares entirely in the food processor.

³/₄ cup all-purpose flour
1 teaspoon baking powder
¹/₄ teaspoon salt
1 cup granulated sugar
1 cup coarsely chopped walnuts
1 cup coarsely chopped dates
2 eggs, beaten
Confectioners' sugar, for topping

Preheat the oven to 325°F. Lightly grease an 8-inch square pan. In a mixing bowl, stir together the flour, baking powder, and salt. Stir in the sugar, walnuts, and dates. Mix well, then add the beaten eggs to bind the mixture.

Spread the batter in the pan. Bake for about 25 minutes, or until the batter is set and dry-looking. Cool very slightly, then cut into squares and dip the tops in confectioners' sugar.

Bar Mitzvah Sweet Table Apricot Squares

Makes about 2 dozen

*I always associate these with bar mitzvahs because when I was growing up, there was rarely
a bar mitzvah sweet table that didn't feature them. Unassuming but addictive, especially if you are
an apricot fan, these are a "sisterhood" classic and are appropriate for any holiday.*

½ cup (1 stick) unsalted butter or margarine
1 cup sugar
2 teaspoons fresh lemon juice
¼ teaspoon vanilla extract
2 eggs, separated
1 cup all-purpose flour
¼ teaspoon plus a pinch of salt
¼ teaspoon baking powder
1½ cups apricot filling or butter (see page
  257–258 or store-bought)
Pinch of ground cinnamon
½ cup walnuts, ground very fine

Preheat the oven to 350°F. Lightly grease an 8 by 12-inch rectangular pan or a 9-inch square pan.

In a bowl, cream the butter with ½ cup of the sugar until light and fluffy. Add the lemon juice, vanilla, and egg yolks and blend well. Fold in the flour, ¼ teaspoon of salt, and the baking powder and stir to make a stiff batter. Chill the dough for about 20 minutes for easier handling.

Pat the dough into the pan, flouring your hands if necessary to prevent the dough from sticking to them. Spread the apricot filling or butter evenly on top with a knife or a small, metal spatula.

In a clean mixing bowl with dry beaters, whip the egg whites, cinnamon, and pinch of salt on slow speed just to get the whites to foam a bit. Increase the speed and dust in the remaining ½ cup of sugar. When the whites hold soft peaks, fold in the ground nuts. Spread this nut meringue over the the apricot filling.

Bake for 35 to 40 minutes—the top of the meringue should seem dry and crisp. Cool very well before cutting into squares.

Fresh Fruit–Topped Baby Cheesecakes

Makes a dozen miniature cheesecakes

Most of the time a large cheesecake is for a large occasion. These miniature cheesecakes are perfect for the "little times." This recipe can also be made in one 8-inch springform pan.

CRUST
1½ cups graham cracker crumbs
¼ cup (½ stick) unsalted butter, melted
3 tablespoons brown sugar
¾ teaspoon ground cinnamon

FILLING
2 (8-ounce) packages cream cheese, softened
¾ cup granulated sugar
1 tablespoon all-purpose flour
3 eggs
1½ teaspoons vanilla extract
¼ teaspoon lemon extract
¼ cup half and half or unsweetened evaporated milk

TOPPING OPTIONS
Confectioners' sugar, for dusting
Canned pie topping
Fresh fruit
Apricot preserves
Melted chocolate

Preheat the oven to 350°F. Line the cups of a 12-cup muffin tin with paper muffin cups.

CRUST: In a small bowl, toss together the graham cracker crumbs, butter, brown sugar, and cinnamon. Sprinkle equal amounts of the crumb mixture into the muffin cups.

FILLING: In a bowl, cream the cheese with the sugar and flour. Blend in the remaining ingredients. Pour the batter evenly into the prepared muffin cups. Bake just until set (20 to 24 minutes).

Chill for a couple of hours. These can also be frozen. Defrost for 30 to 60 minutes before serving.

TOPPING: Dust the tops with confectioners' sugar, *or* garnish with a dollop of canned pie topping *or* a slice of fresh fruit glazed with warmed apricot jam, or drizzle with melted chocolate.

Baker Boulanger, The OnLine Magazine for Bakers Who Cook (www.betterbaking.com) was a web site I launched with a colleague, Yvan Huneault, while this book was in its final testing and editing stages. I first met Yvan when I was invited to a popular Montreal AM Radio station, CJAD, as a culinary guest for his popular show, "What's Cooking?" Ironically, I was so busy writing this cookbook that I initially refused to appear on the show—fretting that "I had this cookbook" to finish! However, soon after the broadcast, we spoke of creating a web site that would feature my recipes and food articles along with his talents in web design. Not long after, we quietly launched our fledgling site.

For the web site, I contribute content; that is, I supply culinary features and recipes, and Yvan, along with editing and a myriad of other associated tasks with this endeavor, is the capable web master. One of the most popular sections on the web site has been Excerpts From *A Treasury of Jewish Holiday Baking* where, via an electronic medium, visitors to the site could have a taste of recipes from a soon-to-be published cookbook. Surprising and fortunately, the site seemed to grab a lot of attention in a very short time. Indeed, our Baker Boulanger web site continues to be a rather big success for a modest site—and we receive email from around the world: a Scottish father of three makes my Friday Night Chocolate Cake; a bagel entrepreneur in Cadiz, Spain, is relying on my Montreal and New York–style bagels for his new business, and apparently, my Passover Matzoh Buttercrunch is famous in Boston. It is very exciting.

In the beginning, setting up the Baker Boulanger web site was a whirling dervish of activities. I was testing recipes around the clock. However, whenever I have a free moment, I also enjoy indulging the tastes of others. Like most bakers, it is always a challenge to see if I can produce some whim for someone else: a dream of a brownie, an incredible cheesecake, or a knock-out marble cake. At any rate, around the time I was creating this web site, in appreciation of those early days of Baker Boulanger's launch on the international web, I created what became one of our web site's most requested recipes, Web Master Oatmeal Cranberry Raisin Walnut Cookies. It really was my "electronic nod" of thanks to the Baker Boulanger's toiling web master who professed, when asked, to a special hankering for oatmeal cookies.

Yvan likes nutty, fruity things—the denser and heartier, the better. I worked on this recipe many times—about seven to eight test batches in all! I also make them with Hodgson Mill white whole wheat flour for extra nutrition. They are always terrific. Yvan, as well as my brother Mark, other colleagues and friends, likes these cookies any time—but they are especially good, and appropriate, at Sukkot. Studded with dried as well as fresh cranberries, raisins, and chunks of walnuts, these oatmeal cookies break the mold. Originally billed as Webmaster's Oatmeal Cookies, in my mind, I renamed them Yvan's Oatmeal Cookies—less catchy but accurate nonetheless.

Web Master's Oatmeal Cranberry Raisin Walnut Cookies

Makes about 2½ dozen cookies

If you can find a better oatmeal cookie, let me know. I make these very autumnal cookies in miniature form for Sukkot. Often, I make a double batch and freeze the dough. Once in a while, I add some Saco Chocolate Chunks to the batch. These are a favorite in my home and for my web master, Yvan Huneault, who inspired them.

1 cup unsalted butter, room temperature
1¼ cups brown sugar
¾ cup granulated sugar
1 teaspoon honey
2 teaspoons vanilla extract
2 tablespoons milk
2 eggs
2 cups all-purpose flour
½ teaspoon salt
1 teaspoon baking powder
1 teaspoon baking soda
1 teaspoon cinnamon
2½ cups oatmeal*
1½ cup raisins
¾ cup dried cranberries
½ fresh cranberries
1 cup chopped walnuts
1 cup coarsely chopped semi-sweet chocolate**

Nonstick cooking spray

Preheat oven to 350°F. Line two baking sheets with parchment paper and spray very generously with nonstick cooking spray.

Cream the butter with the brown sugar, granulated sugar, and honey. Stir in vanilla extract, milk, and eggs and blend well. Fold in flour, salt, baking powder, baking soda, cinnamon, and then oatmeal, raisins, dried and fresh cranberries, nuts, and chocolate. Stir to ensure everything is incorporated.

Scoop batter into generous balls—large marble-size for modest cookies, or golf ball–size for hefty, impressive cookies.

Bake on the upper third of the oven for 12 to 15 minutes—just let them color on the edges. If you allow them to get too brown, they will be crisp rather than chewy and dense-centered.

*I use a combination of quick and old-fashioned oatmeal.

**I prefer Saco Chocolate Chunks.

Buttery Walnut Squares

Makes about 3 dozen squares

Simple but buttery and rich. A classic brown sugar and nut square.

BOTTOM LAYER
1 cup all-purpose flour
2 tablespoons brown sugar
¼ teaspoon salt
½ cup (1 stick) unsalted butter

TOP LAYER
1 cup walnuts, coarsely chopped
1 cup unsweetened shredded coconut
2 cups brown sugar
2 eggs
2 tablespoons all-purpose flour

Preheat the oven to 350°F. Lightly grease the bottom and sides of an 8-inch square pan.

BOTTOM LAYER: In a bowl, combine the flour, sugar, and salt. Cut in the butter until the mixture is fine and grainy. Press this crumbly mixture into the prepared pan. Bake for 10 minutes. Remove from the oven and increase the temperature to 375°.

TOP LAYER: In a bowl, combine all the ingredients well, using a wooden spoon to blend. Spread this mixture over the baked bottom layer. Bake for another 20 minutes. Remove and cool well before cutting into 1½-inch squares. (Slightly chilled or semi-frozen squares cut more easily.)

Ma'Maouls
Middle Eastern
Filled Date Cookies

Makes 2¹/₂ to 3¹/₂ dozen ma'maouls

These popular Middle Eastern–style cookies are delicate and easy to make. It is a typical Purim basket item as well as an appropriate Sukkot finger food. Orange extract or oil stands in for the more commonly used orange-blossom water, which is available in ethnic supermarkets or gourmet stores. You can form these cookies by hand into cigar-shaped pastries or use a ma'maoul mold (available in Middle Eastern food stores or from mail order sources such as Sultan's Delight) to make the traditional decorative shape. A ma'maoul mold looks like a paddle with a handle. The wide part of the paddle has an indentation into which one molds the shaped cookies. Traditionally, larger-sized molds are used for date-filled ma'maoul, smaller or shallower molds are used for walnuts. I like smaller cookies, so I always use the smaller mold. For children, I make these with the mold but do not use the filling. I use either this dough or substitute a shortbread cookie dough for a more decorative butter cookie. To make the traditional Walnut Paste Filling see page 165. You can also use traditional date filling, or any of the fillings, such as cranberry or apricot, from the Purim chapter.

COOKIE DOUGH
3 cups all-purpose flour
¹/₂ teaspoon salt
1 tablespoon sugar
1 cup (2 sticks) unsalted butter
¹/₂ teaspoon orange extract or oil
6–8 tablespoons ice water

DATE FILLING
¹/₂ cup fresh orange juice
2 cups dried, pitted dates
¹/₂ cup raisins
¹/₂ cup dried apricots
¹/₂ teaspoon ground cinnamon
1 tablespoon finely minced lemon zest
¹/₂ cup walnuts, ground

TOPPING
Confectioners' sugar, for sprinkling

Preheat the oven to 325°F. Line a large baking sheet with parchment paper.

DOUGH: In a large bowl, stir together the flour, salt, and sugar. Cut or rub the butter into the flour mixture until crumbly and mealy looking. Drizzle on the orange extract and enough ice water to form a stiff dough. Set the dough aside while making the filling.

FOOD PROCESSOR METHOD: Place the flour, salt, and sugar in the work bowl. Add the butter, in chunks, pulsing to cut it into the flour. Add the orange extract and most of the water to make a stiff dough.

FILLING: In a medium saucepan, heat the orange juice with the dates, raisins, and apricots for 5 to 8 minutes to soften the fruit. Add the cinnamon and lemon zest. Cook over low heat until the mixture is pasty. Cool well, then place in a food processor, along with the walnuts, and process 1 to 2 minutes to produce smooth filling.

If using a ma'maoul mold, put a generous tablespoon of dough into the mold and press slightly to fill it out. Insert a teaspoonful of filling, then cover with an additional scant tablespoon of dough. Press with your hands to compress the cookie. Invert the mold onto a work surface and briskly slap it out. Place on the prepared cookie sheet and repeat this process with the remaining dough and filling. To form by hand, break off a walnut-sized piece of dough and make an indenture in the middle. Fill it with a generous teaspoonful of filling. Mold or wrap the dough around the filling and seal it with your hands to make a round, slightly cylindrical shape. Roll it lightly on a board to further shape and seal. Transfer to the prepared baking sheet, sprinkle with confectioners' sugar, and bake 22 to 28 minutes until lightly browned. Cool on the baking sheet.

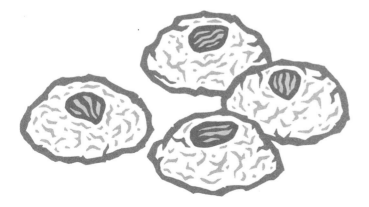

Pie Dough Roly-Poly

Makes 2 to 3 dozen slices

*A brilliant idea from my aunt Helen. My consulting her on this cookbook reminded her
of how much her son-in-law, my cousin Lenny, likes this traditional treat made with pie dough,
rather than the usual oil-based, sweeter roly-poly dough. Make this with your own
or purchased pie dough—great for getting rid of scraps. This dough makes flaky,
pastrylike roly-poly. Unsalted margarine is used for this pastry but you can substitute
half unsalted butter and half shortening.*

ROLY-POLY
¾ cup (1½ sticks) unsalted margarine or
  vegetable shortening
2 cups all-purpose flour
1 tablespoon fresh lemon juice
¾ teaspoon salt
2 tablespoons sugar
1 egg
2–4 tablespoons ice water

FILLING
⅔ cup jam of your choice
¼ cup sugar
1 teaspoon ground cinnamon
½ cup ground walnuts
½ cup chopped Turkish delight (optional)
½ cup chopped candied cherries
½ cup grated coconut

GLAZE/TOPPING
1 egg
2 tablespoons water
Sugar, for sprinkling

ROLY-POLY: In a large bowl, cut the margarine or shortening into the flour until it is a crumbly, mealy mixture. Make a well in the center and add the lemon juice, salt, sugar, egg, and half the water. Mix to combine the wet and dry ingredients, adding more ice water as needed to make a soft but not too wet dough.

Wrap the dough and chill it for 1 hour before using.

Preheat the oven to 350°F. Line a baking sheet with parchment paper.

FILLING: Roll out the dough on a well-floured surface to a rectangle of about 12 by 8 inches. Spread on the jam, then the sugar, cinnamon, nuts, Turkish delight (if using), cherries, and coconut.

Turn in the ends, and roll up into a jelly-roll shape. Place on the prepared baking sheet.

GLAZE: Whisk together the egg and water and brush it on the pastry, sprinkle with sugar and bake for 30 to 35 minutes, or until the top is golden brown and the filling has begun to leak. Slice the roly-poly into ¾-inch portions for serving.

Bakery-Style Jam Tartlets

Makes 25 to 30 cookies, depending on size

These are light and crisp and the dough is good for making plain sugar cookies. A favorite with adults and children alike, they look like store-bought pastries. To make them for a Sabbath supper, use 1½ cups of margarine and eliminate the butter.

1 cup (2 sticks) unsalted butter
½ cup (1 stick) unsalted margarine or vegetable shortening
1¼ cups confectioners' sugar
1 egg yolk
2 teaspoons vanilla extract
¼ teaspoon almond extract
2–4 drops orange extract
3 cups all-purpose flour
¼ teaspoon salt
1 teaspoon baking powder
1–2 cups jam of your choice
Confectioners' sugar, for dusting

In a large mixing bowl, cream the butter and margarine until blended. Add the confectioners' sugar, egg yolk, vanilla, almond, and orange extracts. Fold in the flour, salt, and baking powder.

Turn the dough out onto a lightly floured surface and smooth it into a disc. Wrap well in plastic and refrigerate for about 30 minutes.

Preheat the oven to 350°F. Line 2 baking sheets with parchment paper.

On a generously floured board, roll the dough out to a thickness of about ⅛ inch. Cut it into 2- to 3-inch rounds using a miniature cookie cutter. With a sewing thimble or soda bottle twist cap, cut out the centers of half the cookies.

Place all the cookies on the baking sheets and bake until lightly browned, 12 to 18 minutes.

Cool well. Spread a little jam on the bottom cookies (no holes). Top with a cut-out cookie and press down very lightly. Dust with confectioners' sugar.

6. Chanukah

Festival of Light

They were ready either to live or to die nobly.

—I MACCABEES 4.35

*The Maccabees boldly faced overwhelming odds, not for their own selfish ends,
but in a spirit of self-sacrificing fidelity to the holiest of all causes . . . they did it not for
gain or glory, but solely for conscience sake. They felt that God was calling to them,
and they could not hold back. . . .*

*The little Maccabean band was like a rock in a midst of a surging sea.
[The Maccabees] kept a corner of the world sweet in an impure age. They held aloft the
torch . . . at a time when thick darkness was covering the nations.*

—MORRIS JOSEPH, 1903, IN *A BOOK OF JEWISH THOUGHTS*, LONDON,
OFFICE OF THE CHIEF RABBI, 1941

WHEN ❋ In the Hebrew calendar, eight days beginning the 25th of Kislev

CORRESPONDING TO ❋ Late November until mid to late December

HOLIDAY CONTEXT ❋ Chanukah, or the Festival of Light, commemorates a battle for freedom fought over two thousand years ago, in the year 165 B.C.E. by a small but tenacious band of men, led by the five Maccabee brothers Judah, John, Simon, Eleazar, and Jonathan, the sons of the Mattathias, of Modin. In an incident which later becomes a turning point, the Maccabees' father, Mattathias of Modin, defies the empowered Hellenic authorities. Rather than surrender their convictions, the five brothers, following their father's lead, chose resistance to the ways and beliefs of their oppressor, Antiochus. Determined to be true to their faith and resistant to assimilation, the Maccabees were soon joined by others with the same strong sentiment. The original Maccabees swelled into a cluster of warriors—ill-equipped, small in number, but determined to defend their ways.

Zealous freedom fighters on a divine mission, the Maccabees were renowned for striking fiercely. The Maccabees not only managed to resist domination; they eventually won back their sacred temple.

With the temple back in their possession, the Maccabees went about the task of purifying and rededicating their sanctuary. Religious ritual required that oil be lit and burned continually. Only one small vial of undesecrated oil was found in the temple, but the sacred candelabrum was lit just the same—the oil lasted for a full eight days.

Although Chanukah does, in fact, mean, "dedication" and the historical event that is at its foundation is about rededication, the holiday has come to be called the Festival of Light.

The obvious reason is because of the tradition of lighting the menorah each night for eight nights, recalling the occasion when the Maccabees' lit their candelabrum so long ago. The second reason is that the "light" of Chanukah is brought forth to "light up" the darkness of ignorance and evil.

The triumph of the Maccabees, coupled with their enduring, relentless faith in their convictions, is an eternal symbol of strength and hope.

CUSTOMS/ACTIVITIES ❋ Though it is not considered a high holiday, this celebration of freedom is nonetheless important, and especially anticipated by children eager to know about Jewish heroes.

Youngsters celebrate Chanukah with traditional foods, *dreidel* or spinning top games, small gifts, and gold-covered chocolate coins or Chanukah *gelt*.

Jewish families all over the world light the *menorah*, the eight-branched candelabrum, with either colorful candles or oil, for the duration of the holiday. The top candle, known as the shamash, is responsible for lighting the others, one for each night. The shamash's role is to act as a "leader" or "server" to the others.

FOODS SYMBOLS ❋ The two foods most commonly served during the eight-day celebration are both fried in oil—presumably a symbolic association with the miracle oil in the rededicated temple.

Most familiar are potato pancakes, or *latkes*, prepared in great batches. Tangy apple sauce or fresh sour cream are usually offered as accompaniments.

In Israel, and increasingly in North America, plain doughnuts, as well as jelly doughnuts (in Hebrew, *soufganiot*) are a typical holiday treat. Yeast-raised dough is fried briefly in oil, the puffy pastries are filled with jam or jelly, and then tossed lightly with granulated or sifted confectioners' sugar. The result is a plump, sweet doughnut that delights children and adults alike.

Cheese dishes, although less commonly served, are also appropriate at Chanukah. According to some historical sources, a Jewish widow who was a contemporary of the Maccabees dined with the enemy, Holofernes. Plying him with her charm as well as a cheese dish (presumably a salty dish) that made him thirsty. After he consumed many goblets of wine, Judith waited for her moment, and then slayed the drunken general. In recognition of Judith's courage and ingenuity, cheese latkes, as well as cheese rugelach, and sometimes cheese blintzes, are served. (See more cheese recipes in the Shavuot chapter.)

Oil-based teiglach, found in the Rosh Hashanah chapter, is also a Chanukah treat.

Oil-based desserts are symbolic and pareve (if you are serving a meat-based meal).

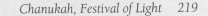

Chanukah Jelly Doughnuts (Soufganiot)

Makes 2 to 2½ dozen doughnuts, depending on size

Easy to prepare in advance (the dough can be refrigerated the day before frying), these plain or jelly-filled doughnuts are a favorite treat in Israel and a sweet alternative to the traditional Chanukah latkes, or potato pancakes. I discovered soufganiot a while back when an Israeli friend, Micha Avni, commented that latkes were not the only festive Chanukah food. As a mom, a baker, and a food writer, I was thrilled to find something new to engage readers and my own three sons during the 8-day holiday. No one ever says no to doughnuts, and this two-biteful variety fits any appetite perfectly. I generally make a double batch of dough, refrigerate it, and pinch off portions as needed for fresh treats or for taking along to a Chanukah party. I usually make this dough in the bread machine (on the Dough cycle). You can sprinkle fine sugar over the doughnuts or fill them with jelly, as is more traditional. I make both filled and unfilled doughnuts.

DOUGH

½ cup warm water
5 teaspoons dry yeast
⅓ cup plus a pinch of granulated sugar
1 cup warm milk or water
1 teaspoon vanilla extract
2 eggs
⅓ cup vegetable oil or melted vegetable shortening
1½ teaspoons salt
4¼–5 cups all-purpose flour
Vegetable oil, for frying

FILLING

2 cups jam or jelly of your choice, at room temperature (optional)
Granulated or confectioners' sugar, for dusting (optional)

DOUGH: In a large mixing bowl, stir together the warm water, yeast, and pinch of sugar. Allow the mixture to stand for a couple of minutes to allow the yeast to swell or dissolve. Stir in the remaining sugar, the milk, vanilla, eggs, oil, salt, and most of the flour to make a soft dough. Knead for 5 to 8 minutes, by hand or with a dough hook, adding more flour as needed to form a firmer dough that is smooth and elastic. Place the dough in a greased bowl, place the bowl in a plastic bag, and seal. (If not using right away, you can refrigerate the dough at this point.) Let the dough rise for about 1 hour. Gently deflate it. (If the dough is coming out of the fridge, allow it to warm up for about 40 minutes before proceeding.)

Pinch off pieces of dough and form them into small balls, a little larger than a golf ball. Alternatively, roll the dough out to about ¾ inch thick. Using a 2½- or 3-inch biscuit cutter, cut out rounds.

Cover the doughnuts with a clean tea towel and let them sit for 20 to 30 minutes. Heat about 4 inches of oil in a deep fryer or a heavy Dutch oven to about 385°F. (see Note).

Add the doughnuts, 3 or 4 at a time, to the hot oil and fry until the undersides are deep brown. Turn over once and finish frying the other side. The total frying time will be no more than 1½ to 3 minutes. Lift the doughnuts out with a slotted spoon and drain them well on paper towels.

To fill, make a small opening and spoon in jam or jelly *or* shake the doughnuts lightly in a paper bag with regular or confectioners' sugar.

NOTE: To test oil temperature, it is a good idea to try frying one doughnut to start with. Once the doughnut seems done, take it out and cut it open to see if the inside is cooked. Then proceed with the rest. Try to fry at a temperature at which the oil bubbles but is not so hot that you brown the doughnut before the center is cooked.

Chanukah Beignet Squares

Makes 20 to 28 beignets, depending on size

Easy to prepare, these puffy, dairy-enriched doughnut squares are a variation on the usual Chanukah fare and based on a recipe for New Orleans French market beignets. Serve them simply dusted in sugar or drizzled with vanilla doughnut glaze.

BEIGNET DOUGH
1/4 cup warm water
4 teaspoons dry yeast
1/3 cup plus a pinch of granulated sugar
1 1/4 cups warm plain evaporated milk or half and half
2 1/2 teaspoons vanilla extract
2 eggs
1/4 cup (1/2 stick) unsalted butter, melted
1 1/2 teaspoons salt
4 1/4–5 cups all-purpose flour (see Note)
Vegetable oil, for frying

DOUGHNUT GLAZE
2 cups confectioners' sugar
4–6 tablespoons water
1 teaspoon vanilla extract (or use rum, maple, or coffee extract, or any flavor you prefer)
Superfine granulated or confectioners' sugar, for dusting

NOTE: This recipe can also be made in a bread machine, set on the Dough cycle.

DOUGH: In a large mixing bowl, stir together the warm water, yeast, and pinch of sugar. Allow the mixture to stand for a couple of minutes to allow the yeast to swell or dissolve. Stir in the evaporated milk or half and half, the remaining sugar, the vanilla, eggs, melted butter, salt, and most of the flour to make a soft dough. Knead for 5 to 8 minutes, by hand or using a dough hook, adding more flour as needed to form a firmer, smooth and elastic dough. Place the dough in a greased bowl, place the bowl in a large plastic bag, and seal. (If not using right away, you can refrigerate the dough at this point.) Let the dough rise for 45 to 60 minutes. If the dough has been refrigerated, allow it to warm up for 30 to 45 minutes before proceeding. Gently deflate it, then roll it out to a rectangle, about 15 by 18 inches. If the dough is too elastic (i.e., if it retracts every time you work with it), allow it to relax for a few minutes before stretching or rolling it further. Cut it into 3 by 5-inch rectangles, cover, and let sit for 15 minutes while heating the oil.

In a deep fryer or heavy Dutch oven (a wok also works well), heat 4 inches of oil to 385°F. Stretch the doughnuts slightly before adding them to the oil and fry until the undersides are deep brown and the doughnuts have puffed up noticeably, about 1 to 1 1/2 minutes. Turn once and finish frying for 1 to 1 1/2 minutes on the other side. Lift the beignets out with a slotted spoon or tongs and drain them well on paper towels. Dust lightly with sifted confectioners' sugar, superfine granulated sugar (or even cinnamon mixed with sugar), or drizzle with the Doughnut Glaze.

NOTE: Half bread flour, half all-purpose flour is ideal.

DOUGHNUT GLAZE: While the doughnuts are cooling, in a bowl, whisk together the confectioners' sugar, water, and vanilla or other extract of your choice. Stir or whisk to achieve a very thick glaze. Add water as needed to achieve this.

VARIATIONS: For Apple Stuffed Beignets, prepare the doughnuts as for Chanukah Beignet Squares. After frying, make a small slit in each square either across the top surface or on the side. Using 1 can of apple filling, spoon some filling into each. Toss lightly in cinnamon sugar.

For Beaver Tails, a Canadian fried dough specialty, you can also use the above beignet recipe. It is perfect for Chanukah and a favorite winter treat of my son Jonathan's hockey team. Easier to make than regular doughnuts. I always use a wok to make these, and have a pair of stainless-steel tongs handy to remove the doughnuts as they are done.

Cut off portions of the beignet dough about the size of a mandarin orange. Stretch or roll the dough into long, thin "tails" (oblong shapes) and place them on a parchment or wax paper–lined baking sheet. Prepare all the dough this way, layering paper between the stretched pieces of dough. When the oil is hot enough (385°F.) fry the beaver tails, one or two at a time, turning them over as soon as they puff up to fry on the other side. This takes well under a minute to complete.

Drain on paper towels. Prepare a bowl with a cup or two of sugar and toss in one beaver tail at a time to coat well with sugar, shaking the excess back into the bowl. You can also serve these with pie toppings or a dollop of strawberry or raspberry jam on top. I like them just with sugar.

Chocolate-Glazed Ring Doughnuts

Makes 10 to 14 doughnuts

Made with an extra-moist potato and yeast dough, these doughnuts have the texture of commercial-style chocolate-glazed doughnuts but with a wonderful homemade taste. After your kids tire of latkes (anything is possible), surprise them with these during Chanukah week. I use a wok to fry these and a large, slotted spoon to pluck them out.

1½ cups warm water
4½ teaspoons dry yeast
¼ cup plus a pinch of sugar
2 tablespoons vegetable shortening
1 medium potato, boiled and mashed to make a
 generous ½ cup
1 egg
½ teaspoon salt
Approximately 4 cups all-purpose flour
Chocolate Glaze (recipe follows)

Mix ¼ cup of the water with the yeast and pinch of sugar, and let the mixture stand for 5 to 10 minutes, to allow the yeast to swell or dissolve. Add the remaining warm water along with the shortening, potato, egg, remaining sugar, salt, and flour. Blend, and when the mixture can no longer be stirred, knead to form a soft, smooth, elastic dough (it may be necessary to add a little more flour). Place in a greased bowl, place the bowl in a large plastic bag, and seal.

Let the dough rise until doubled in size (45 to 90 minutes). Gently deflate it and roll it out to between ¼ and ½ inch thick. Cut out with a doughnut cutter (or use a large cookie cutter for circles and a smaller one to cut out the centers). Cover the doughnuts with a clean tea towel and let them rise until puffy looking (20 to 30 minutes).

In a wok or Dutch oven, heat about 4 inches of oil to 385°F. Fry the doughnuts, turning once, until golden brown (45 to 60 seconds on each side). Cool, then glaze.

CHOCOLATE GLAZE

2 ounces semi-sweet chocolate, melted
1 tablespoon unsalted butter, melted
1½ cups confectioners' sugar
½ teaspoon vanilla extract
¼ cup hot water

In a bowl, stir the chocolate with the butter. Blend in the confectioners' sugar and vanilla and stir until smooth. Add just enough water to make a thin glaze. Cool for 1 minute, then drizzle over the doughnuts or dip the top surfaces of the doughnuts into the glaze. If the glaze gets too stiff, add more hot water to make it workable again. Allow the glaze to set on the doughnuts before serving.

Colored Sugar, Tinted Icing, Specialty Cookie Molds Make Chanukah Cookies Festive

There are a number of ways to decorate Chanukah cookies. First, I keep doubles of inexpensive metal cookie cutters such as dreidels, Maccabee soldiers, menorahs, and Stars of David. I'm rarely by myself when I make Chanukah cookies, and there is no sense in fighting over whose turn it is to use that certain dreidel cookie cutter. Sweet Celebrations baking supply company stocks wonderful nested Star of David cookie cutter sets ranging in size from the tiniest little star—for miniature Chanukah cookies—to a larger one of some five inches that is suitable for decorating. You can obtain Sweet Celebrations icing pens, suitable for creating designs directly on an iced cookie.

After the cookies are cut, they can be wiped with beaten egg white and sprinkled with regular or colored, coarse or table sugar. Colorful sprinkles are also available from cake-decorating supply stores.

To color coarse sugar, place a cup or two of sugar in your food processor along with a few drops of liquid food coloring or about ¼ teaspoon food coloring paste. Pulse to combine the sugar and food coloring evenly. For granulated sugar or to do this by hand, place the sugar in a bowl along with a few drops of liquid food coloring or about ¼ teaspoon food coloring paste. Insert your hand in a small plastic sandwich bag and knead or toss until the sugar and food coloring are well blended.

Alternatively, you can also ice the cookies *after* they are baked with a simple frosting of water, vanilla, confectioners' sugar, and food coloring. I prepare a few small stainless-steel bowls, each filled with 1 or 2 cups of confectioners' sugar and enough water (usually 2 to 4 tablespoons) to make a spreadable icing. Add about ¼ teaspoon vanilla extract, or any other extract, along with some food coloring to make a nicely tinted icing. Food colorings come in either liquid (commonly found in the supermarket baking supplies aisle) or paste form. Pastes are more vibrant and can be found in decorating stores or via mail order. Once the icing is made, spread it on a baked cookie with a small metal spatula or butter knife. It will set quickly. Before it sets, you can dust on sprinkles. Another pretty finish involves filling 8-inch pastry bags with a second color icing and then drizzling on a design. Simply outline the cookie with the contrasting icing, or inscribe a dreidel letter such as *gimmel* or *shin*.

If you have leftover icing, do not throw it out. Cover it well with plastic wrap and keep it at room temperature. When you require it again, add a few more drops of warm water and blend it with a small wire whisk or a fork to make it smooth and pliable once again. These icings keep for a couple of days.

Iced cookies are a particularly nice Chanukah project for children, but it helps to prepare before hand. A good schedule is as follows:

DAY BEFORE: Make a few batches of cookie dough, wrap, and refrigerate. Assemble the cutters.

DAY OF BAKING: Roll, cut, and bake the cookies. Prepare bowls of frosting and sprinkles.

Pack in cellophane or small bakery boxes or tins with the recipe, a Chanukah cutter, some chocolate Chanukah gelt, and a dreidel or two. These packages make unique gifts.

Kids' Chanukah Cookies

Makes 3 to 4 dozen cookies

What's holiday baking without kids around? Why not provide them a big batch of their own cookie dough and cutters? An all-butter dough can get too much of a workout when juvenile bakers take over. This buttery-tasting dough is "kid-proof"—strong but tender of crumb. It's the dough I prepare for my own crew of young bakers and their friends. If you require a dairy-free cookie, use all vegetable shortening and orange juice or water instead of the milk. You can also use the dough for Delicate Purim Butter Cookies if you want upscale Chanukah cookies. Rycraft Ceramic Cookie Stamps company makes a Star of David cutter suitable for Chanukah shortbread cookies (use the Yom Tov Shortbread recipe).

³/₄ cup (1¹/₂ sticks) unsalted butter, softened
¹/₄ cup vegetable shortening
1¹/₂ cups sugar
2 eggs
1 tablespoon vanilla extract
2 drops *each* lemon, orange, and almond extract
4 cups all-purpose flour
¹/₂ teaspoon salt
1 tablespoon baking powder
¹/₄ cup half and half, milk, or water

TOPPING
1–2 egg whites, lightly beaten
Sugar or colored sprinkles

In a large mixing bowl, cream the butter and shortening with the sugar. Blend in the eggs, vanilla, and extracts. Fold in the flour, salt, and baking powder and mix, adding the half and half gradually, to make a firm but rollable dough. Chill the dough for 10 minutes.

Preheat the oven to 350°F. Line 2 large cookie sheets with parchment paper.

Roll the dough out about ¹/₄ inch thick and cut it into rounds or, if you have them, use Chanukah cookie cutters to make holiday shapes.

Brush the cookies with the beaten egg white and sprinkle with sugar (regular or coarse, plain or colored) or colored sprinkles. Leave the cookies plain if you will be icing them after baking.

Bake on the prepared sheets until golden brown, 15 to 18 minutes.

Decorative Icing for Chanukah Cookies

This simple icing sets to a light luster within minutes of being applied. Spread it with a small, flat icing spatula. Paint designs with new paintbrushes or, before the icing sets, decorate with colored sprinkles.

FOR EACH COLOR, PREPARE A SEPARATE BOWL
WITH:

1 cup confectioners' sugar
1–2 tablespoons water, to make a spreadable
  glaze
Food color, to taste
Flavor extracts—almond and/or white vanilla
  (see Note)

NOTE: White, or clear, vanilla (usually artificial) can be ordered from Wilton Co. Brown vanilla will work, too, but it will discolor the icing a bit.

In a small bowl, whisk together the confectioners' sugar and water to make a smooth glaze. Stir in the food coloring for the desired tint, and add a few drops of either almond extract or clear vanilla (or both) to flavor the glaze. Cover with plastic wrap if not using right away and store at room temperature. Stir again before using. This will keep for 3 or 4 days.

Chocolate Cream Cheese Rugelach

Makes 2 dozen pastries; the recipe doubles well

Chocolate makes this recipe unique; a cream cheese dough makes it easy. For chocolate addicts, use chocolate hazelnut filling; for a "Black Forest" rugelach, use raspberry or cherry preserves as filling.

DOUGH
1/3 cup granulated sugar
1/2 cup (1 stick) unsalted butter or margarine
1/2 cup cream cheese, softened
1 cup all-purpose flour
2 tablespoons unsweetened cocoa powder
1/4 teaspoon salt
1/2 teaspoon vanilla extract

FILLING
1 cup chocolate hazelnut paste (see Note)
2 tablespoons granulated sugar
1/4 teaspoon ground cinnamon
1/2 cup finely chopped pecans (optional)

TOPPING
1 egg white, beaten
Confectioners' sugar, for dusting (optional)

DOUGH: In a large bowl, cream the sugar with the butter or margarine and the cream cheese. Blend in the remaining dough ingredients. Stir to make a soft dough, adding a little more flour as necessary if the dough is too sticky. Turn the dough out onto a lightly floured board and pat it into a flattened disc. Wrap it in plastic and chill for 30 to 60 minutes or overnight.

FOOD PROCESSOR METHOD: Use the steel blade and place the flour, cocoa, sugar, salt, and vanilla in the work bowl. Drop in the butter and cream cheese in chunks. Process until the ingredients blend and the dough forms a mass or ball (this may take a good minute or two). Remove from the processor and sprinkle on a little flour to keep the dough from being too sticky. Wrap it in plastic and chill for 30 to 60 minutes or overnight.

Preheat the oven to 350°F. Line a baking sheet with parchment paper.

Divide the dough in two. Roll each portion into a 10-inch circle on a well-floured board. Be careful not to exert too much pressure on the rolling pin because the dough is delicate. Spread the chocolate paste on the dough, then sprinkle on the sugar, cinnamon, and nuts, if using. Cut the circle into 12 wedges and roll up each wedge into a miniature crescent. (Or, if using jam, spread on the jam, then sprinkle on the sugar, cinnamon, and nuts, and roll up.)

Transfer the rugelach to the prepared baking sheet, brush with the beaten egg white and bake until done, about 25 minutes. Cool thoroughly on a wire rack, then dust with confectioners' sugar, if desired.

NOTE: Chocolate hazelnut paste can be found in gourmet stores, or in the supermarket near the peanut butter. It is made of chocolate and ground hazelnuts and comes in many brands, such as Nutella, usually imported from Italy. Kosher brands are available.

EASY CHANUKAH DREIDEL CAKE

A quickly assembled holiday cake can be made with a cake mix and decorated with some simple craft items. Although a homemade vanilla or chocolate cake recipe would do, this decorative cake consumes an awful lot of batter and a mix makes it a little more feasible. This is one of those cakes whose main function is to thrill and entertain, although making it taste good is still important. To make things even easier, ask a neighborhood bakery to sell you some white icing you can color yourself.

The Dreidel Cake makes an instant centerpiece for your holiday table or can be a school treat. It is always a hit with youngsters and something they will always remember—even if you only make it once!

Aside from a couple of boxes of cake mix, you will require a cardboard dowel from a paper towel roll, foil or metallic wrapping paper, some decorative sprinkles, and Chanukah gelt. Chocolate-covered Chanukah gelt is available at Judaica stores at this time of year. Gold and blue glitter, or one-color sprinkles, can be found in cake-decorating stores or through the Source Guide in the back of this book.

Essentially, two rectangular cakes are sandwiched together with icing. Two corners are trimmed, the cake is iced and decorated in a holiday design. If you are inclined, able, or adventurous, use a pastry bag fitted with a large star tip to make a professional cake border or a nice, decorative edge, and add a holiday greeting (Happy Chanukah), or the symbols, *"Shin," "Nun,"* etcetera. If you shy away from pastry bags, you will still have that wonderful dreidel shape to work with. Just sprinkle on gold chocolate gelt and colorful sprinkles. In minutes, you have a professional-looking, festive cake. Complete construction details follow.

Chanukah Gelt Double Fudge Chocolate Layer Cake None Better!

Makes 12 to 16 servings

A boastful title to be sure, but absolutely true. You just don't get cakes like this every day:
easy to make, moist, almost half a foot high, nondairy but very flavorful, stays fresh for days,
can be frozen for months. When you think of a classic chocolate layer cake in an old-fashioned diner,
this is it. My youngest son, Benjamin, expects this cake at least once a month (daily when it is Chanukah).
When I tested this cake, someone left a chocolate crumb-covered napkin nearby with the words
(all in capitals) "THIS CAKE IS UNBELIEVABLE!" scrawled in that "midnight snack" scribble.
This cake thrills my three boys—it's just a matter of hiding the gold-covered coins so they
make it to this cake! For a bakery store look, garnish the sides with chocolate sprinkles and plant
one solitary glacé cherry in the center. If you don't have cola on hand, you can substitute warm mild coffee.

CAKE
2 cups granulated sugar
1¼ cups vegetable oil
3 eggs
2 teaspoons vanilla extract
2½ cups all-purpose flour
½ teaspoon salt
1½ teaspoons baking soda
1½ teaspoons baking powder
¼ teaspoon ground cinnamon
1 cup unsweetened cocoa powder, sifted
1½ cups warm, flat cola soda

CHOCOLATE ICING
½ cup chocolate chips, melted and cooled
2 tablespoons vegetable shortening
¾ cup (1½ sticks) unsalted butter or unsalted margarine
1 teaspoon vanilla extract
¾ cup unsweetened cocoa powder, sifted
3–4 cups confectioners' sugar, sifted
½ cup water, cola, or half and half

TOPPING
Colored sprinkles
20–30 gold-colored chocolate coins
Miniature decorative plastic dreidels

Preheat the oven to 350°F. Lightly grease two 9-inch layer pans and line them with parchment paper circles.

In a large mixing bowl, blend the sugar and oil. Add the eggs and vanilla and combine until the mixture is well blended. In a separate bowl, stir together the dry ingredients. Fold them into the wet, and mix, drizzling in the cola as the mixture blends. If using an electric mixer, use the slow speed and mix for about 3 minutes, scraping the sides and bottom once to incorporate all the ingredients. This is a thin batter.

Bake on the middle rack of the preheated oven for 35 to 40 minutes, until the cakes spring back when lightly touched.

CHOCOLATE ICING: In a bowl, cream together the melted chocolate, shortening, butter, and vanilla with the cocoa and 1 cup of the confectioners' sugar. Add the remaining confectioners' sugar and whip on high speed, adding a bit of water, cola, or half and half to get a light, fluffy consistency. If you're not frosting the cake right away, rewhip before using, adding additional warm water, a tablespoon at a time, to achieve the right consistency.

TO DECORATE: Place one layer on a cardboard circle. Ice it with about ½ inch of frosting. Cover with the second layer and ice the sides first, then the top. Coat the sides with colored sprinkles. Garnish the bottom edge with gold-covered coins. Garnish the top with gold-colored coins, making any arrangement you want, placing the coins either flat on top of the cake or standing up, sticking them in the icing to hold. (You may cut some of the coins in half to garnish the border of the top layer.) Place a couple of miniature dreidels in the center if you wish, or Chanukah candles. (They can be lit when the menorah is lit.)

Dreidel Cake

Makes 16 to 24 servings

Preheat the oven to 350°F. Line two 15 by 11-inch jelly-roll pans with parchment paper. Prepare the cake mix according to package directions. Divide the batter equally between the 2 prepared pans.

Bake until the cake springs back when touched lightly with your fingertips (about 35 minutes). Cool well, then wrap with foil (still in the pan) and place in the freezer (a semi-frozen cake is easier to decorate).

TO CONSTRUCT AND DECORATE THE CAKE: Place both cake layers on a work surface with the shorter ends facing you. Trim off 2 corners on each cake to make a **V** point at the bottom. Ice one layer with any color icing. Gently press the second layer on top, making sure the edges match up.

Ice the sides and tops of the cake. Insert the decorated cardboard tube into the edge (you can dig out a bit of the cake to insert the tube) opposite the **V** to make the "handle" of the dreidel.

Finish the cake by using a pastry bag to create an icing border in a contrasting color. Inscribe a holiday greeting. Alternatively, dust the cake with sprinkles and/or add gold-covered Chanukah gelt or miniature dreidels.

DECORATIVE ICING FOR DREIDEL CAKE

1 cup (2 sticks) unsalted butter
½ cup vegetable shortening
6 cups confectioners' sugar, sifted
Pinch of salt
1 tablespoon vanilla extract
¼ teaspoon almond extract
Yellow and blue food coloring, as desired

In an electric mixer, cream the butter with the shortening, confectioners' sugar and the salt on low speed. Add the vanilla and increase the speed to high, adding in a bit of water as necessary to make a light, spreadable frosting. Leave some icing white (about 1½ cups) and divide the remaining icing into 2 bowls. Stir or whip blue food coloring into one bowl and yellow or gold food coloring into the other. (If not using the icing right away, freeze or refrigerate it. *Rewhip* before using.)

Halvah Filo Cheesecake

Makes 14 to 16 servings

This is for those who enjoy very smooth cheesecakes with a Middle Eastern accent.
This recipe is part of a collection of cheesecakes that first appeared in Bon Appetit *magazine*
in a feature called "Fabulous Cheesecakes," my debut as a food writer.
This would also be suitable for Shavuot.

FILO CRUST
12 filo pastry leaves
½ cup (1 stick) unsalted butter, melted

FILLING
1½ pounds cream cheese, at room temperature
4 eggs plus 1 egg yolk
1 teaspoon vanilla extract
½ teaspoon sesame seed oil
2 tablespoons plain yogurt
¼ cup honey
¼ cup sugar
¼ cup flour
⅓ cup coarsely chopped pistachio nuts
   (optional)
¾ cup coarsely chopped vanilla halvah

TOPPING
2–3 tablespoons honey
¼ cup lightly toasted sesame seeds
½ cup ground or finely chopped pistachio nuts

Preheat the oven to 350°F. Use a 9- or 10-inch springform pan.

FILO CRUST: Spread 1 sheet of filo lightly with melted butter. Line the pan with the filo, allowing the excess to overhang. Repeat this process with another 4 leaves of filo, pressing each one into the pan, starting at the center and allowing the excess to drape over the sides. (If your brand of filo is smaller, overlap the leaves to achieve the same overhang.) Reserve the remaining leaves for garnishing the top after baking.

FILLING: In a bowl, cream the cheese with the eggs, yolk, vanilla, sesame oil, yogurt, honey, sugar, and flour until smooth. Stir in the nuts and halvah. Pour into the prepared shell. Trim the filo overhang to rest just on the rim of the pan. Bake until the cake is set (about 45 minutes).

Meanwhile, cut the remaining filo leaves in quarters and brush them with butter.

Remove the cake from the oven and increase the temperature to 400°. Arrange the buttered filo leaves on top of the cake in an irregular patchwork. The cake surface should be covered. Return the pan to the oven to brown the top filo (8 to 10 minutes). Remove and chill the cake until set (or overnight).

To serve, warm the honey and drizzle it over the cake, then top with toasted sesame seeds and additional ground or chopped pistachios.

Judith's Cheese Pastries

Makes 2 to 2½ dozen pastries

According to Chanukah legend, Judith served cheese pastries to the Syrian general whose troops had besieged Judith's city. The cheese pastries and wine with which Judith plied the general made him sleepy. Once he was asleep, Judith beheaded him. Upon discovering this, the general's troops fled the city in terror. In honor of Chanukah's heroine, cheese dishes are traditional. This dough makes a delicate, lemon-scented pastry suitable for a variety of fillings. The recipe does double duty as a blintzlike appetizer for Shavuot.

COTTAGE CHEESE PASTRY DOUGH
2½ cups all-purpose flour
½ teaspoon salt
¼ cup sugar
2 teaspoons baking powder
1 cup (2 sticks) unsalted butter, very cold, cut into 16 pieces
1 cup small curd ricotta or dry cottage cheese
2 teaspoons finely minced lemon zest
1 teaspoon vanilla extract
1 teaspoon fresh lemon juice

FILLING
½ pound cream cheese
½ pound dry cottage cheese
½ cup sugar
1 teaspoon finely minced lemon zest
1 egg
Pinch of salt
½ teaspoon vanilla extract
1 tablespoon all-purpose flour

TOPPING
Melted butter
Confectioners' sugar

DOUGH: In a large bowl, sift the dry ingredients together. Cut the butter into them until the mixture resembles small crumbs. Blend or knead in the ricotta or cottage cheese until a soft dough forms. Blend in the lemon zest, vanilla, and lemon juice. Wrap the dough in plastic and refrigerate for 1 to 3 hours or overnight.

FOOD PROCESSOR METHOD: Place the dry ingredients in the work bowl fitted with the steel blade. Pulse briefly. Add the butter pieces through the feed tube and process until the mixture resembles small crumbs. Add the remaining ingredients and process only until a ragged mass forms (20 to 40 seconds). Turn out onto a lightly floured board and knead briefly to form a smooth ball. Wrap in plastic and refrigerate for 1 to 3 hours or overnight.

FILLING: In a bowl, cream the cream cheese, cottage cheese, and sugar together until blended. Stir in the remaining ingredients to make a thick filling. Refrigerate the filling if not using it right away. It will keep overnight.

Preheat the oven to 350°F. Line 2 large baking sheets with parchment paper.

Divide the chilled dough in half and roll each half into a rectangle 12 by 8 or 10 inches. Brush each rectangle lightly with melted butter. (If the dough is too cold to work with, pound it a few times with your rolling pin to soften it a bit.) Spread half the cheese filling on each rectangle, leaving a 1-inch plain border all around. Turn in the ends, then roll up each piece half way (each portion of dough will make 2 narrow jelly rolls or logs) into a jelly roll or strudel-like roll. Cut off the remaining half of each piece and repeat the rolling process. You will have 4 strudel rolls in all.

Brush the top of the rolls with melted butter. Chill for 10 to 15 minutes, then remove from the fridge, and cut the rolls into 2-inch pastries. Place the pastries on the baking sheets.

Bake for 25 to 30 minutes, until the pastries are golden brown. Cool slightly and dust with sifted confectioners' sugar before serving. Serve warm (with sour cream, yogurt, or plain) or at room temperature as an accompaniment to coffee and tea.

Frozen Cheesecake with Brandied Cherries

Makes 12 to 14 servings

This is the easiest cheesecake ever, and it's made with 2 main ingredients—ice cream and cream cheese. Allow time for this cake to thaw slightly before serving. A nice finale for a festive Chanukah gathering. For best results, make sure you use premium-quality ice cream.

CRUST
1 store-bought round sponge cake

CHEESECAKE FILLING
1 (28-ounce) can pitted sour cherries, drained, syrup reserved
½ cup cherry brandy
½ pound cream cheese, softened
6 tablespoons sweetened condensed milk
2 teaspoons pure vanilla extract
1 quart vanilla ice cream

CHERRY BRANDY SAUCE
Reserved syrup from drained cherries
Reserved cherry brandy from soaking cherries
⅓ cup sugar
1 tablespoon cornstarch
2 tablespoons water
1 teaspoon unsalted butter

Place the cherries in a small glass bowl. Cover them with the cherry brandy and allow them to marinate at least 4 hours or overnight. Drain the cherries, adding the brandy to the reserved cherry syrup. Stir in the sugar and set the sauce aside.

CRUST: Prepare a 9-inch springform pan by lining the bottom with a circle of parchment paper. Split the sponge cake into 2 layers and line the bottom of the pan as evenly as possible with one of the layers, using pieces of the remaining layer to fill any gaps.

FILLING: In a mixer, blend the cream cheese until smooth. Add the condensed milk and vanilla and blend well. Then, with the mixer running on medium speed, blend in chunks of ice cream. Mix just until combined since the ice cream will begin to melt. Pour half the batter into the prepared pan. On top of this, place the brandied cherries, as evenly as possible. (Make sure to have cherries around the perimeter—these will show through when the cake is unmolded later.) Cover with the remaining batter. Cover the top of the springform mold with plastic wrap. Freeze overnight.

CHERRY BRANDY SAUCE: Heat the reserved brandy/syrup/sugar mixture in a small saucepan to a gentle boil. In a small bowl, stir the cornstarch with the water. Add the cornstarch mixture to the boiling syrup. Stir over medium heat until the mixture thickens. Cool, then stir in the butter. The sauce can be offered separately or poured over the cake. It may be served slightly warmed or at room temperature. Before serving, allow the cake to thaw for 30 to 45 minutes (depending on how cold your freezer is), then cut it into small wedges.

Honey Bear Roly-Poly

Makes 3 to 4 dozen slices, depending on size

Roly-poly, a filled cookie-like pastry, is one of the more old-fashioned sweets to come out of the Euro-Jewish kitchen. Most roly-polys used to be made with oil-of-Bergamot-scented Turkish delight. While the jellylike candy melted into an appealing, chewy texture, many were not enamored with its somewhat flowery taste. This updated version uses gummy bears (you may also use chopped gumdrops) to achieve the chewiness and color with a fresher, more natural fruit taste. (For traditional roly-poly, or Romanian strudel, see pages 108 and 188).

DOUGH

2 eggs
¾ cup sugar
2 tablespoons honey
¾ cup vegetable oil
½ cup orange juice
Zest of 1 orange, finely minced
1 teaspoon vanilla extract
½ teaspoon salt
2 teaspoons baking powder
Approximately 4 cups all-purpose flour

FILLING

6 tablespoons sugar
3 teaspoons ground cinnamon
1½ cups strawberry or apricot jam, warmed
1 cup raisins, plumped (page 22) and well dried
1 cup chocolate chips
1½ cups gummy bears or minced Turkish delight
1 cup shredded coconut
1½ cups finely chopped walnuts or pecans

GLAZE

1 egg, beaten
Coarse or regular sugar

Line 2 baking sheets with parchment paper (using parchment paper is imperative since the pastry will leak a sticky syrup).

DOUGH: In a large mixing bowl, stir together the eggs, sugar, and honey. Stir in the oil, orange juice, orange zest, vanilla, and salt. Fold in the baking powder and flour to make a soft dough. Let the dough sit, covered with a tea towel, for 5 to 10 minutes.

Preheat the oven to 350°F. Divide the dough into 3 equal pieces. On a well-floured board or, for even easier handling, on parchment paper or wax paper, roll one piece at a time into a 10 inch by 12-inch rectangle.

FILLING: On each piece of dough spread one third of the ingredients in the order listed.

Starting at the long end nearest you, gently roll up the pastry into a jelly-roll-style log, using the parchment or wax paper as an aid. The dough might tear a bit—this is fine—just gently squeeze it back together and continue rolling. Paint the log with beaten egg and sprinkle with sugar. Repeat this process with the 2 remaining pieces of dough and the rest of the filling ingredients.

Place the 3 logs on the prepared cookie sheet and bake until nicely browned (25 to 28 minutes). Remove from the oven, cool on the baking sheet, then remove to a board. Cut into ½-inch slices.

7. Purim

Feast of Lots

. . . the king held out toward Esther the golden sceptre; and Esther arose, and stood up before the king; And she said, If it be pleasing to the king, and if I have found grace before him, and the thing seem proper before the king, and I be pleasing in his eyes, let it be written to recall the letters, the device of Haman, the son of Hammeda the Agagite, which he hath written to exterminate the Jews who are in all the provinces of the king. For how could I endure to look on evil that is to befall my people?

And in every province, and in every city, whithersoever the king's command reached with his law, there were joy and gladness for the Jews, entertainments and a feast-day . . . and of sending portions to each other.

. . . they did call these days Purim, after the name of Pur . . . and these days are remembered and celebrated throughout each and every generation, every family, every province, and every city; and these days of Purim will not pass away from the midst of the Jews. . . .

—*THE BOOK OF ESTHER*, EXCERPTS, TRANSLATED AND REVISED BY RABBI SIMON GLAZER

ESTHER'S COURAGE, ESTHER'S TRIUMPH: THE PURIM CELEBRATION

WHEN ❀ In the Hebrew Calendar, the 14th day of Adar.

CORRESPONDING TO ❀ Some time in March.

HOLIDAY CONTEXT ❀ Also known as the "Festival of Lots," the story of Purim is based on events found in the Book of Esther, that occurred around the fifth century B.C. Although scholars often dispute and debate the authenticity and historical merits of the Story of Esther, her legend continues. It goes as follows:

Esther, purportedly as wise as she was beautiful, was the Queen of the Persian ruler, King Ahasuerus. It is said that King Ahasuerus was unaware that his queen was Jewish. In his kingdom, the Jewish people lived under threat from the King's advisor, Haman.

Unbeknownst to the King, Haman was planning a mass murder of all the Jews in the kingdom.

Esther was warned of the plan by her uncle Mordecai (some sources refer to Mordecai as her uncle, others as her older cousin), who implored his niece to inform her husband of these sinister maneuverings and appeal to him to prevent the mass murder of her people.

As the Queen of Persia, even though she was Jewish, Esther would have been entitled to preferred status and treatment, but risking her own safety and position, she courageously complied with her uncle's urgent request. She presented her case in such a convincing fashion that her husband was moved (either by love for his wife or, it is hoped, a sense of morality) to intercede. Esther's intervention saved the Persian Jews.

ACTIVITIES ❀ Much like New Orleans' famed Mardi Gras, the Jewish holiday of Purim is a rambunctious celebration punctuated by colorful costumes and music. The holiday celebrates the Purim story's happy ending. Local synagogues host Purim carnivals or parties. Platters of fruit-filled hamantaschen are served with sweet kosher wine, which one is encouraged to consume in copious amounts, and there are games to occupy the younger congregants. The the-

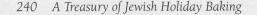

matic "music" of Purim is provided by Purim "greggers," colorful, metallic noise-making gadgets that are cranked up by children with alarming regularity.

Another important Purim custom is making small donations of money to the needy, such as a community charity.

FOOD SYMBOLS ✤ We send small gift baskets of baked goodies to friends and family—a tradition known as *mishloach manot*. A typical Purim basket should contain at least two varieties of treats—hamantaschen, of course, as well as nuts, some dried fruits perhaps, gaily wrapped candies or chocolates, and maybe a gregger.

The quintessential Purim sweet is the "Haman" taschen. Some sources suggest that the original name for these pastries was "mohntaschen," (*mohn* or *mon* translates to poppy), simply meaning poppy pockets or small pockets of pastry with poppy-seed filling. Over time, the Haman reference was added, perhaps because the three-cornered cookies resemble Haman's hat. However, the direct translation of the Hebrew is "Haman's Ears" (*oznei Haman*). But no matter how they are defined linguistically, the theme sweet of Purim is most delectable.

Purim Carnival Twist

Makes 3 small breads

*This makes 3 pretty "little" breakfast or tea-time sweet challah-cum-coffee cakes.
Just the right size for one meal with family, and the perfect challah to include in a Purim gift basket.
A citrus glaze makes it unique and the sprinkling of multicolored sprinkles (available in supermarkets
or cake-decorating stores) redefines challah, giving it a Mardi Gras or carnival accent
that is made for this fun-filled holiday.*

¾ cup warm water
1 tablespoon active dry yeast
Pinch plus ⅔ cup granulated sugar
1¼ teaspoons salt
⅓ cup unsalted butter or margarine, melted and
   cooled, or vegetable oil
1 egg plus 1 egg yolk (reserve white for egg
   wash)
½ teaspoon vanilla extract
Approximately 3 cups bread flour

EGG WASH
1 egg white, beaten with a pinch of granulated
   sugar

CITRUS GLAZE/TOPPING
1½ cups confectioners' sugar
2–4 tablespoons orange juice
½ teaspoon orange extract (optional)
Colored sprinkles

In a mixing bowl, briskly stir together the water, yeast, and pinch of sugar. Let stand for 5 minutes to dissolve and swell the yeast. Stir in the remaining sugar, the salt, melted butter or oil, the egg, egg yolk, and vanilla. Stir in most of the flour and mix until you have a kneadable dough. Knead for 5 to 8 min-utes, or until the dough is smooth and elastic. Place it in a lightly greased bowl and place the bowl in a large plastic bag. Let the dough rise until puffy (30 to 45 minutes). Gently deflate and divide the dough into 3 equal pieces. Either make each portion into a small, braided, 3-strand challah or roll each portion into a 10-inch strip and coil it into a turban shape.

Line a baking sheet with parchment paper. Place the breads on the baking sheet and brush each one with the egg wash. Cover lightly with greased plastic wrap or a large plastic bag, and let rise until puffy (30 to 45 minutes).

Preheat the oven to 350°F. Bake the challahs until golden all over (25 to 30 minutes).

While the challahs bake, stir the glaze ingredients together, adding more confectioners' sugar or orange juice as required to achieve a pourable consistency.

While the loaves are cooling, drizzle or spread on the glaze. Before it sets, sprinkle each loaf with colored sprinkles. Allow the glaze to set. For gift-giving, wrap the bread in a sheet of colored cellophane paper. Twist the ends and/or tie them with ribbon. Place in a gift basket along with 2 other treats.

THE PURIM HAMANTASCHEN PRODUCTION LINE

In my more zealous days, referred to in some parts as the Era of the Super Baker, I would make bushels and bushels of hamantaschen every few days in and around Purim to be sure I had enough pastries for family, friends, and relatives. It was an impressive ritual that lasted several years but eventually took its toll. Unwilling to admit to hamantaschen burn-out, I then made hamantaschen well ahead, and froze them unbaked—eight to twelve dozen of them— until I required them, baking off a few dozen every few days. I ran the "Purim Assembly Line" like a commercial enterprise, and while some of the whimsy of the holiday went by the wayside, things were organized, and there were certainly plenty of hamantaschen available at any given time. This system worked well for another couple of years but also got the best of me. *Purchased* hamantaschen were out of the question, but since I wanted to survive the holiday, I necessarily became more relaxed in my approach and developed the Modified Hamantaschen Assembly Line. Here's what I do now.

First, I make a couple of batches of dough and freeze it in packets. Next, I make a variety of fillings, which I freeze or refrigerate (it doesn't matter which). Then, Purim arrives and baking begins. Every day or two, I bake up only one or two dozen pastries (usually the days just preceding and then for a few days following the holiday itself). This is pretty easy because the dough and fillings are all premade. The only thing left is to turn on the oven and whip up a batch of egg wash or glaze. The house smells wonderful, the pastries are absolutely, right-from-the-oven fresh, and I don't feel taxed. Also, it truly feels like a holiday occasion because the baking continues—not

just in a gargantuan burst for one day, but for several days. It's a treat for family and friends, reminding them, as they walk into my fragrant, warm kitchen, that Purim is special and traditions are worth keeping. "Oh, you sweet dear," they exclaim. "You made fresh hamantaschen! That's so nice!" Then they sit down, pluck up a tender apricot, prune, or cherry triangle, and wax lyrical about its old-fashioned taste, comparing it to this Bubbie's, or that grandmother's or so-and-so's aunt's. Fortunately, the comparisons are usually equally complimentary to both of us. Extra hamantaschen are packed up as a gift to take home.

It's nothing to bake up two dozen pastries, but far too formidable to make five to six dozen at one shot. So take it easy. Bake less but more often, and prepare in advance.

GOOD, BETTER, BEST—A GUIDE TO SUBLIME HAMANTASCHEN

As far as hamantaschen evolution goes, yeasted hamantaschen doughs probably predate oil-based doughs. Vegetable shortening–based doughs are farther along the evolutionary ladder, as vegetable shortening itself is a relatively modern invention. Once it was introduced to the marketplace, Jewish bakers were quick to use the neutral fat in their baking for much of their pastry and cakes. The most recent innovation has to be cream cheese hamantaschen dough, and this rich dairy dough, delicate and tender, is one that upscale bakeries use for a variety of goods. For great hamantaschen, regardless of the dough, there are some pointers you should consider.

When making any hamantaschen, dough recipe, allow it to stand for a couple of minutes. This allows the flour to absorb the liquid more thoroughly.

The rest period makes a soft dough suddenly manageable (i.e., easy to roll) and prevents you from being tempted to add extra, unnecessary flour.

Use parchment paper on your baking sheets—this eliminates cleanup but, more important, ensures that the bottoms of these pastries don't get too brown before their tops are done. An added protection against burnt bottoms is to double-stack your baking sheets. Fit one baking sheet onto another one. This extra insulation allows you to brown the tops of the pastries properly while keeping the bottoms from getting too brown.

Bake your pastries on the upper third of the oven—usually the bottom part of the oven is too hot and may also cause premature bottom-browning.

Paint the whole bottom interior (the part on which the filling goes) of the pastry with water or, preferably, egg wash. This is quicker than just trying to moisten the outer perimeter and makes for a great seal when you form the rounds into hamantaschen triangles.

Roll the dough once and set the scraps aside. Roll the scraps only once—hopefully you will not have too much excess—because a lean dough like hamantaschen dough can only be rolled a couple of times before becoming really tough and baking into dry pastries.

Some bakers like to leave a little space where the three sides of the pastry meet, exposing some of the fruit filling. It looks pretty and you know at a glance which filling is in that particular pastry. On the other hand, this leaves the filling exposed during baking which may cause it to dry out some. I seal my pastries completely and sprinkle additional poppy seeds on top of the poppy-seed hamantaschen, sprinkle some coarse sugar on the prune, and leave other varieties plain. However, you can decide what is best for you.

The dough can be frozen for about two months (if you want to get a head start) or refrigerated (wrapped well in plastic) for one to three days. Just allow the dough to warm up a bit before rolling it out.

Prune, poppy, and apricot are standard fillings, but nut, chocolate hazelnut paste, cheese, and especially dried sour cherries and cranberries are outstanding alternatives. Do experiment with different doughs and fillings, mixed in with your traditional favorites.

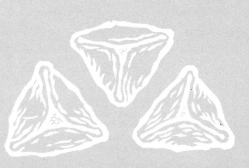

Two Glazes for Hamantaschen

Makes enough for 2 to 3 hamantaschen

If you want a golden-colored finish on your pastries, use the Golden Egg Wash. For a more delicate, slightly shiny glaze, use the Egg White Glaze. After glazing, you can also sprinkle the hamantaschen with sugar or colored or chocolate sprinkles (depending on the dough and filling used). Both recipes can be doubled or tripled, according to your requirements.

GOLDEN EGG WASH

This all-purpose glaze brings a golden glow to most pastries and acts as a "glue" when sealing pastries

1 egg plus 1 egg yolk
1–2 tablespoons milk or water
Pinch of sugar

In a small bowl, whisk together all the ingredients. Use a pastry brush to glaze or brush on prepared, unbaked hamantaschen.

EGG WHITE GLAZE

2 egg whites
1 teaspoon sugar

In a small bowl, thoroughly whisk together the egg whites and sugar. Use a pastry brush to apply to unbaked hamantaschen.

Almost-Like-a-Bakery Traditional Hamantaschen

Makes 4 to 6 dozen pastries

*This dough, made with vegetable shortening and butter, produces a cookie-like texture
and is similar to the hamantaschen you might find in a commercial bakery. It is my favorite
hamantaschen dough. If you require a dairy-free version, simply use all shortening or nondairy margarine
(instead of butter and shortening). You can also use this dough to make cookie triangles—"mock"
hamantaschen—for children who prefer unfilled cookies. Brush the dough with egg wash and sprinkle it
with plain sugar or colored sprinkles.*
This recipe doubles well.

½ cup vegetable shortening
½ cup (1 stick) unsalted butter or unsalted
  margarine
1¼ cups sugar
3 eggs
¼ cup orange juice or milk
1½ teaspoons vanilla extract
Approximately 4 cups all-purpose flour
½ teaspoon salt
2½ teaspoons baking powder
Golden egg wash (page 245)
Fillings: chocolate hazelnut paste, cherry, apricot,
  prune, or poppy (pages 254–261)
Regular or coarse sugar (optional)

In a mixing bowl, cream the shortening, butter, and sugar together. Add the eggs and blend until smooth. (If the mixture is hard to blend or seems curdled, add a bit of the flour to bind it.)

Stir in the orange juice or milk and the vanilla. Fold in the flour, salt, and baking powder and mix to make a firm but soft dough. Transfer the dough to a lightly floured work surface and pat the dough into a smooth mass. Cover and let it rest for 10 minutes.

Preheat the oven to 350°F. Line 2 large baking sheets with parchment paper.

Divide the dough into 2 or 3 flattened discs and work with one portion at a time.

Roll out the dough on a lightly floured board to a thickness of ⅛ inch. Use a 3-inch cookie cutter and cut as many rounds as you can. Brush the rounds with egg wash. Fill with a generous teaspoonful of the desired filling. Draw 3 sides together into the center. You should now have a 3-cornered or triangular pastry. Repeat this process with the remaining dough and filling. Brush the pastries with additional egg wash. If desired, sprinkle with regular or coarse sugar, and bake in the center of the preheated oven until golden brown (18 to 25 minutes). Cool on the baking sheets.

If you prefer, this dough can be made ahead and refrigerated, wrapped in plastic, for up to 2 days, or frozen (either as a disc of dough or as already formed and filled pastries, for a couple of months). If refrigerating, allow the dough to warm up before rolling out. For frozen pastries, bake without defrosting.

Giant Hamantaschen, or the Hamantaschen That Ate Brooklyn

A couple of years ago, exhausted from having made far too many hamantaschen, I found myself staring at the remaining dough. "Roll me," it cried. "Too tired," I replied. And then, the light bulb flashed on—as it does when you are giddy and overtired and are blessed with either fascinating but unusable ideas or true inspirations. Why not make one giant hamantaschen? I thought, and take it as a special Purim Party Show-and-Tell for my middle son's nursery school class. A huge success on all levels, the Giant Hamantaschen was presented on a gold metallic cake board and toddlers broke off chunks of it, giggling and munching. What was great about it was that, aside from being visually riveting, the kids were able to feast on lots of the cookie-like pastry. The very center, stuffed with prune filling, was left for the teachers, moms, dads, and visiting grandparents.

You can make this giant hamantaschen filled or not filled. If *not*, roll up a large wad of foil and stick it in the center of the unbaked hamantaschen to support the middle a bit while the pastry bakes. Once baked, remove the foil and fill the center with colored, crumbled tissue paper, some other, similarly decorative, colorful paper, or metallic streamers, or whatever strikes your fancy. You can even plant a couple of Purim groggers or noisemakers in the center. If it is to be filled, first spread the whole circle of pastry with a thin layer of filling, then mound a good cupful in the center.

Present the Giant Hamantaschen on a large tray or cake board. It makes a great Purim party centerpiece. The big secret is that it also represents about four dozen hamantaschen in one giant pastry!

1 Batch Almost-Like-A-Bakery Hamantaschen
  Dough (page 244)
1–2 cups any flavor filling (optional)

Egg Wash
1 egg, beaten
2 tablespoons cream or milk

Colored sprinkles

Bubbie's Orange-and-Oil Hamantaschen

Makes 4 to 6 dozen pastries, depending on size

This orange-scented dough made with oil is delicious and easy to make. The cornstarch is optional but helps to tenderize the dough just a bit for a gentle crispness. This recipe doubles well.

1 cup sugar
1 cup vegetable oil
½ cup orange juice
Zest of 1 orange, minced very fine
1 teaspoon vanilla extract
3 eggs
Approximately 4 cups all-purpose flour
1 tablespoon cornstarch (optional)
½ teaspoon salt
1½ teaspoons baking powder
¼ teaspoon baking soda

Golden egg wash (page 245)
Fillings: Prune, poppy, cherry, apricot, etc. (pages 254–261)
Sugar, for sprinkling

In a large bowl, using a wooden spoon or a wire whisk, blend together the sugar and oil. Mix in the orange juice, zest, vanilla, and eggs. Fold in the flour, cornstarch (if using), salt, baking powder, and baking soda to make a soft but firm dough. Cover the dough with a clean tea towel and let it rest for 15 to 20 minutes. (It can also be refrigerated for 2 to 3 days; let it warm up before rolling it out.)

Preheat the oven to 350°F. Line a couple of baking sheets with parchment paper.

Work with half the dough at a time (cover the remaining dough with a clean, dry tea towel). Roll it out on a lightly floured board to a thickness of about ⅛ inch. Using the top of a tuna or soup can, or a cookie cutter, cut out as many 3-inch circles as you can. Brush one side of each circle with egg wash. Fill the hamantaschen with a generous teaspoonful of the desired filling. Bring the 3 sides or flaps together to form a triangle.

Brush the pastries with additional egg wash and, if desired, sprinkle them with granulated sugar. Bake until lightly golden (18 to 25 minutes). Cool in the pan.

Cream Cheese Hamantaschen

Makes about 1 dozen pastries

*Although less traditional, many bakers find that this all-purpose dough
yields a very delicate and flaky pastry. Also suitable for Chanukah rugelach.
This recipe doubles well.*

¼ cup sugar
½ cup (1 stick) unsalted butter or margarine
½ cup cream cheese, softened
½ teaspoon vanilla extract
1 cup unbleached all-purpose flour
¼ teaspoon salt

Golden egg wash (page 245)
Fillings: poppy, prune, apricot, dried cherry, etc.
  (pages 254–261)

In a bowl, cream the sugar with the butter or margarine and the cream cheese. Blend in the vanilla, flour, and salt to make a soft dough, adding a little more flour as necessary if the dough is too sticky.

FOOD PROCESSOR METHOD: Use the steel blade and place the flour in the bottom of the work bowl. Drop in the butter and cream cheese in chunks, then the remaining ingredients. Process until the dough forms a ball (25 to 50 seconds). Remove from the processor and sprinkle on a little flour to keep the dough from being too sticky.

Wrap the dough in plastic and chill it for 30 minutes, or use it the next day.

Preheat the oven to 350°F. Line a baking sheet with parchment paper.

Roll the dough out on a well-floured board to about ¼ inch thick, being careful not to press too hard on the rolling pin because the dough is fragile. Cut out 3-inch circles with a cookie cutter, brush them with egg wash, and fill them with a very generous teaspoonful of your preferred filling. Fold in 3 edges of the circles to form triangles. Brush the triangles with additional egg wash.

Place on the prepared sheets and bake for 25 to 28 minutes, or until golden. Cool on the baking sheet.

Old-Fashioned Yeast Hamantaschen

Makes 2 to 2½ dozen pastries

This is probably the oldest way of making hamantaschen. These puffy, yeast triangles resemble a not-too-rich danish. Using a sponge starter not only gives these hamantaschen a leavening boost, it also makes them tender. These are just as good the next day, or even two days later. Some bakers make Oznei Haman ("Haman's ears"), fried rounds of dough sprinkled with sugar, from this same recipe. This recipe doubles well.

20-Minute Sponge Starter
½ cup scalded milk, cooled to warm
½ cup warm water
5 teaspoons dry yeast
Pinch of sugar
1 cup all-purpose flour

Dough
½ cup sugar
½ cup (1 stick) unsalted butter, melted, or vegetable oil
¼ teaspoon lemon oil or extract
½ teaspoon vanilla extract
3 eggs, at room temperature, lightly beaten
1½ teaspoons salt
4–5 cups all-purpose flour

Golden egg wash (page 245)
Fillings: prune, cherry, or poppy (pages 254–260)
Sugar, for sprinkling

SPONGE: Place the milk in a large mixing bowl and mix it with the water, yeast, sugar, and flour. Stir to make a gloppy batter. Cover and let stand for 20 to 30 minutes.

DOUGH: Stir down the sponge, and add to it the sugar, melted butter, lemon oil, vanilla, eggs, salt, and enough flour to make a soft, kneadable dough. Knead for 5 to 8 minutes until smooth. Cover well with greased plastic wrap and let rise until doubled. (You can also refrigerate the dough until the next day. If you do, allow the dough to reach room temperature before proceeding.)

Divide the dough in half. Work with one piece, leaving the remaining dough covered with a tea towel. Roll the dough out to a thickness of about ¼ inch. Cut out 3-inch circles with a cookie cutter. Brush the circles with egg wash. Fill each with a tablespoon of filling. Bring 3 edges together to form triangles. Brush the filled hamantaschen with additional egg wash and, if desired, sprinkle lightly with granulated sugar. Repeat with the remaining dough.

Fifteen minutes before baking, preheat the oven to 350°F. Line 1 or 2 baking sheets with parchment paper.

Place the hamantaschen on the baking sheets. Cover them lightly with a tea towel and let them rise until puffy (15 to 25 minutes).

Bake the pastries until medium golden in color (18 to 20 minutes). Cool on the baking sheets.

The Quest for Homemade Poppy Seed Filling a Culinary Saga and Adventure

Poppy seed as well as prune fillings may be purchased in a ready-to-use state. It is time consuming and quite an effort to prepare the poppy seed filling. The steamed poppy seeds must be ground to eliminate the coarse, granular feeling. Pastry chefs will often improve the quality of the prepared and purchased poppy filling by adding honey, chopped nuts, jam, and cake crumbs to extend the filling. The degree of "stretching" the filling in this manner depends upon the pastry chef and price concerns.

—WILLIAM J. SULTAN, *THE PASTRY CHEF*

Hamantaschen devotees usually fall into two categories: prune lovers or poppy seed lovers and rarely do the twain meet. It's sort of like coffee and tea drinkers—sure, some people like both, but mostly they have a marked preference. For years, I attempted to satisfy the poppy seed lovers in my circle by making fresh poppy seed, or mun, filling. The taste was always fine, but no kitchen tool I own—food processor, mortar and pestle, or coffee grinder—seemed up to the task of properly grinding the small black seeds. Soaking them overnight in warm water, then boiling them in a honey-milk mixture *helped* (this method is covered in the recipe for Poppy Seed Filling When You Don't Have Ground Seeds, page 255), but doesn't quite pulverize them. In eras gone by, most Jewish homemakers had, or inherited, a special grinder that, on its finest setting, *would* properly grind the poppy seeds. In my secret heart of hearts, I suspected factory-made poppy seed filling was produced by placing tons of poppy seeds in a giant industrial strength plastic bag. Then, about four, maybe six steamrollers drove back and forth over this bag of poppy seeds until they were crushed into a black sticky paste. Machines scraped out the poppy seed paste, and sugar or honey, cinnamon, nuts, and a touch of lemon juice were all added to make it sweet and tasty. Then of course, it was packed into the jars and cans we see in the supermarket. Maybe it wasn't four steamrollers, it could be only one, but the thing I was absolutely sure about is that poppy-seed paste is a secret art form known only to our European ancestors, or is the result of specialized machine grinders, designed to deal with poppy seeds.

At one point, I wrote about all my trials and tribulations in a hamantaschen feature for the *Washington Post*. No other feature I ever had published touched a nerve with so many people. Many, many readers wrote back (their letters relayed to me by the *Post*'s food department), each with their secret trick, along with family recipes, for poppy seed paste. Most of the surnames on the envelopes were, predictably, European-sounding. But finally, one reader, who agreed that poppy seeds could not be pulverized in either a blender or a coffee mill, advised me to sleuth out a European poppy seed grinder. So I began looking around but had no luck.

One day, however, I received yet another letter from a *Washington Post* reader. In it, the writer kindly offered me her mother's vintage poppy seed and nut grinder. I gladly accepted. Here was more than good advice, a true gift. The grinder arrived shortly thereafter, and with it, the reader had generously enclosed her mother's recipes for poppy seed strudel and walnut rolls (the recipes bore a close resemblance to the recipes for Hungarian Walnut Strudels, page 164, and Nettie's Cinnamon Meringue-Walnut Babka, page 162, although the methods are

I will never forget this lovely act, and I will always treasure this grinder.

I put the grinder to work at once and was thrilled to find it easy to work with. The result? Perfectly ground poppy seeds, just ready to be cooked into even more perfect poppy seed filling.

When poppy seeds are not thoroughly pulverized, you are left with a tasty but seedy, gritty filling that gets worse after baking. Some claim they have had luck with a coffee mill. I did this both with a blade grinder (it just vigorously whirled the seeds around) and with a burr-style grinder (messy, ineffective, a big mistake). Others counsel using a blender or the food processor. Done it, tried it, been there. I also tried boiling, poaching, and stewing the seeds in milk first, then grinding (or attempting to grind) them. I have soaked them overnight in milk or in water, placed them in a plastic bag and run a rolling pin over them. I have added lots of honey and nuts to hide their gritty texture. In short, I have done it all, and I cannot with any conviction say that the resultant poppy seed paste or filling was up to my standards.

Poppy seeds really have to be thoroughly crushed in order to extract their starchy interiors. For a while, I bought and recommended Solo or Simon Fisher brands of poppy seed filling. Of course, my hamantaschen dough was homemade, and adding a touch of lemon juice, cinnamon, and chopped raisins to the purchased filling helped immensely.

But . . . if you insist on or are intrigued with the notion of homemade filling, as I have become, you must have a proper poppy seed grinder. Since I received my gift grinder, I have found two sources for poppy-seed grinders—La Cuisine, Ares Equipment, and King Arthur (see Source Guide, page 353) both offer good ones. I use both the grinder my reader sent to me and one called a Porkert poppy seed grinder, made in Czechoslovakia. I strongly recommend you invest in one—homemade poppy seed filling is sublime. It takes so little effort, and a grinder easily pays for itself in two Purims. If you are still debating buying a grinder, you can buy already-ground poppy seed filling through Penzeys—a spice mail order company that furnishes wonderful, ground poppy seeds that can also be used in the following recipe.

Poppy Seed Filling

Makes about 1½ cups, enough for 2 dozen hamantaschen

This is a recipe many families have tucked in their files. It is similar to the one found in The Settlement Cookbook (1991 Edition, Simon and Schuster). This is a piece of American culinary history, originally published in 1901. Compiled by a group of community-oriented Jewish matrons in turn-of-the-century Milwaukee, The Settlement Cookbook offers a host of mainstream American recipes, with some European Jewish standbys. For the best flavor and texture, you must use ground poppy seeds. The fragrance of ground seeds is a slightly sweet, almost "Earl Grey" scent. Ground seeds also ensure that your filling is smooth, not dry and gritty. Ground poppy seeds are available by mail order from Penzeys (see Source Guide). Alternatively, purchase good poppy seeds and grind them yourself with a poppy seed grinder such as the Porkert Grinder (see Source Guide, page 353). Use this filling with hamantaschen, as well as strudels, yeast coffee cakes and babkas, or any other variety of European pastry calling for poppy seed or "mun" filling.

1½ cups (approximately 4 ounces) ground poppy seeds
½ cup water
1 cup milk
3 tablespoons unsalted butter or margarine
2 tablespoons honey
1 tablespoon finely minced lemon zest
⅓ cup raisins, coarsely chopped
½ cup sugar
Pinch of salt
¼ teaspoon ground cinnamon
½ cup chopped almonds (optional)
4 tablespoons seedless raspberry jam or jelly
1 small tart apple, peeled and grated

In a 3-quart saucepan, place the poppy seeds, water, and milk. Bring to a gentle boil and simmer for a couple of minutes. Add the butter, honey, lemon zest, raisins, sugar, salt, and cinnamon and stir well, reducing the heat so that the mixture cooks but does not burn or stick. You want the ingredients to meld slowly and the liquid (milk and water) to be absorbed by the seeds. The final mixture should be a paste. This should take from 10 to 15 minutes. Stir occasionally to ensure the mixture does not scorch—the lower the heat the better.

Remove from the stove and stir in the almonds, if using, and either the jam or the apple (or both). Cool completely before using. The filling will thicken further as it cools.

Keep the filling refrigerated until needed. If the mixture seems too thick when it comes out of the refrigerator, allow it to warm up a bit. You can also loosen the filling by adding a touch of warm water.

VARIATION: For Poppy Seed Filling When You Don't Have Ground Seeds, read on. An overnight soaking softens the seeds. Rolling over them with a pin helps extract the "pulp". A coffee grinder (blade grinder style) makes them pasty. It sounds like a lot of bother, but it makes a substantial amount of long-keeping, great-tasting filling. Incidentally, this filling also works well when you blend it with store-bought (from a bakery) or canned filling. The store-bought variety gives it a pastier texture and your own filling boosts the flavor. One tester added a couple of scraps of diced apricot leather to her filling and the results were excellent.

The night before, place the poppy seeds in a bowl and cover them with very warm water. Cover the bowl with plastic wrap and let the seeds soak overnight. The next day, drain the seeds well. Place about half of them in a plastic Ziploc bag. With a very heavy rolling pin, roll over the seeds to press and flatten them as best you can. Do this for a couple of minutes. Repeat with the remaining seeds. Place the seeds in small amounts in a very clean blade coffee grinder, food processor (the mini-bowl of a KitchenAid processor works very well), or a good blender. Process for a few moments. Proceed with the recipe.

Prune or Lekvar Filling

Makes approximately 3 cups, enough for 4 dozen pastries

Store-bought filling works fine, but this homemade version is much more flavorful and appealingly tart/sweet. Even people who shun prunes seem to like this filling. This recipe doubles well.

¾ cup water or orange juice
⅓ cup fresh lemon juice
2 cups pitted prunes
1 cup dark raisins
⅓ cup sugar
¼ teaspoon ground cinnamon
½ cup chopped walnuts (optional)

In a small saucepan over low heat, combine the water or orange juice, lemon juice, prunes, raisins, sugar and cinnamon. Toss and stir the fruit to soften the prunes and plump the raisins (about 8 to 10 minutes). Make sure the bottom doesn't stick, and lower the heat if the mixture starts to boil. Remove the mixture from the heat and place it in the bowl of a food processor. Let cool for about 5 minutes.

Add the cinnamon and walnuts, if using, and process well to form a thick puree, adding more water or orange juice, a bit at a time, to thin the filling, if necessary. Taste the filling and add extra sugar (a tablespoon at a time) at this point if required. The filling should be thick and moist.

Chill the mixture slightly before using. It will keep in the refrigerator for up to 2 weeks or in the freezer for up to 6 months. If the chilled filling seems too stiff to spread, loosen it with a bit of warm water or juice.

VARIATION: For Mixed Dried Fruit Filling, you can use almost any combination of dried fruits. Try the prune recipe, but use 2 cups of dried fruit made up of any combination of the following: ½ cup *each* dates, raisins, dried pears or peaches, dried cherries or figs. Procedure is the same.

Apricot Filling I

Makes 2 cups, enough for 2½ dozen hamantaschen

When I was small, finding apricot hamantaschen in the local bakery was a rare treat. They sold out very quickly! Even when we did scrounge up a couple, I had to squabble with my brother Lorne to get at them! This is a classic apricot filling that makes for superb hamantaschen. Use California apricots for best results, but Turkish apricots will also work nicely. If you want an even more intensely flavored filling, try Apricot Filling II. This recipe doubles well.

¾ cup water or orange juice
¼ cup fresh lemon juice
½ to ¾ pound (2 to 3 cups) dried apricot halves
  (preferably from California)
⅓ cup sugar
1 cup golden raisins
1 cup walnuts (optional)

In a small saucepan, combine the water or orange juice, lemon juice, apricots, sugar, and raisins. Heat the fruit over low heat, tossing and stirring to soften it (8 to 12 minutes). Add additional water if the mixture seems to require it, or if the water in the pot is evaporating more quickly than the fruit seems to be cooking down.

Remove the pot from the stove and let the mixture cool for about 5 minutes. Place it in a food processor and add the walnuts, if using. Process the fruit to a thick puree, adding additional water or orange juice if the mixture requires thinning. Taste, and add additional sugar (a tablespoon at a time) if required. Refrigerate the filling for up to 2 weeks or freeze it for up to 6 months. If the chilled filling seems too stiff to spread, loosen it with a little warm water or juice.

Apricot Filling II

Makes 2 cups, enough for 2½ dozen pastries

The use of Middle Eastern rolled apricot sheets adds an intense, full-bodied taste.
If you can't find them, use Apricot Filling I (preceding recipe) which calls for regular dried apricots.
This recipe doubles well.

1 (1-pound) package rolled apricot sheets or
   pressed apricot paste (see Note)
¾ cup water
¼ cup fresh lemon juice
¼ cup orange juice
2 tablespoons finely minced orange zest
1½ cups golden raisins
¼–½ cup sugar
1 cup walnuts (optional)

NOTE: The apricot sheets or paste can be found in Middle Eastern or ethnic markets.

Cut or tear the apricot sheet into pieces and place them in a small saucepan. Add the water, lemon and orange juices, orange zest, raisins, and ¼ cup of the sugar. Over very low heat, toss and stir gently to soften (10 to 15 minutes). Make sure the fruit does not scorch. Add a little more water if necessary. When the apricot pieces are softened (they will begin to get mushy), remove the pan from the heat and cool the mixture for about 5 minutes.

Place the cooled mixture in a food processor and add the walnuts, if using. Process to a puree, adding a bit more water if required to loosen the mixture. Taste, and add more sugar (about a tablespoon at a time) if required. Use immediately, refrigerate for up to 2 weeks, or freeze for up to 6 months. If the chilled filling seems too stiff to spread, loosen it with a bit of warm water or juice.

Dried Sour Cherry and Cranberry Hamantaschen Filling

Makes about 3 cups, or enough for 4 dozen hamantaschen

The combination of cranberries and cherries offers a sweet but tangy taste. The sweetness of the cherries is balanced by the tartness of the cranberries. This recipe doubles well.

½ cup orange juice
¼ cup water
Zest of 1 orange, minced
Pinch of ground cinnamon
⅓ cup sugar
1 cup dried sour cherries (see Note)
1 cup dried cranberries
1 cup golden raisins
½ cup finely chopped walnuts (optional)

NOTE: You can omit the cherries and use 2 cups of dried cranberries.

In a medium-sized saucepan over low heat, combine the orange juice, water, zest, cinnamon, sugar, cherries, cranberries, and raisins. Stir and toss gently to soften the fruit (5 to 10 minutes). If the fruit sticks, add a bit more water to help it simmer along. Remove the pan from the stove and place the mixture in a food processor. Let it cool for about 5 minutes. Add the walnuts, if using, and process well to form a thick puree. If the mixture seems too thick, add a bit of water to loosen it.

Use the filling right away, refrigerate it for up to 2 weeks, or freeze it for up to 6 months. If the chilled filling seems too stiff to spread, loosen it with a bit of warm water or juice.

Sour Cherry Hamantaschen Filling

Makes about 3 cups, enough for 4 dozen hamantaschen

*If you want the deep, pure flavor of dried sour cherries alone, try this terrific filling.
This recipe doubles well.*

¼ cup fresh lemon juice
½ cup orange juice
¼ cup water
Zest of 1 orange, minced
¼ teaspoon almond extract
Pinch of ground cinnamon
⅓ cup sugar
2 cups dried sour cherries
1 cup golden raisins
½ cup finely chopped walnuts (optional)

In a medium-sized saucepan over low heat, combine the lemon and orange juices, water, zest, almond extract, cinnamon, sugar, cherries, and raisins. Stir and toss to soften the fruit (5 to 10 minutes). If the mixture sticks, add a bit more water to help it simmer along. Remove the pan from the stove and place the mixture in a food processor. Let it cool for about 5 minutes. Add the walnuts, if using, and process well, to a puree. If the mixture seems too thick, add a bit more water to loosen it.

Use the filling right away, refrigerate it for up to 2 weeks, or freeze it for up to 6 months. Let the dough warm up a bit before using, if it has been chilled.

Chocolate Hamantaschen

Makes 4 to 5 dozen pastries

Sometimes young children like the dough of the hamantaschen but they carefully eat around the filling. You can try Hamantaschen Flats (page 262) or these chocolate hamantaschen. Chocolate hazelnut paste is recommended. Cherry or apricot filling also work well, and this dough makes great Hamantaschen Flats. You may, if it is required, substitute ½ cup vegetable shortening or nondairy margarine for the ½ cup butter in this dough. Try these once and you will have a new "classic" on your hands.

DOUGH
¼ cup vegetable shortening
¾ cup (1½ sticks) unsalted butter or unsalted margarine
1½ cups sugar
2 eggs
½ cup milk or water
2 teaspoons vanilla extract
½ cup unsweetened cocoa powder
Approximately 4 cups all-purpose flour
½ teaspoon salt
2½ teaspoons baking powder

FILLING
1 jar chocolate hazelnut paste

TOPPING
Beaten egg white
Regular or coarse sugar (optional)
Chocolate sprinkles (optional)

DOUGH: In a large bowl, cream together the shortening, butter or margarine, and sugar. Add the eggs and blend until smooth. Add the milk or water and the vanilla. (If the mixture seems curdled, add a bit of flour to bind it.) Fold in the dry ingredients. Mix to make a firm but soft dough. Transfer the dough to a lightly floured work surface and knead gently to form a large, smooth ball. Divide the dough in half, wrap each piece in plastic. Chill for 10 to 20 minutes.

Preheat the oven to 350°F. Line 2 baking sheets with parchment paper.

Roll out one piece of dough on a lightly floured board to a thickness of between ¼ and ⅛ inch. Cut 3½-inch rounds with a cookie cutter and brush the rounds with the beaten egg white. Fill each round with a generous teaspoonful of chocolate hazelnut paste or another filling (apricot or cherry work well). Fold in the edges of the circle to form a triangle of pastry encasing the filling. Brush the pastries again with the glaze and, if desired, sprinkle them with regular or coarse sugar and/or chocolate sprinkles. Repeat with the remaining dough and filling. Bake until golden brown (18 to 22 minutes). If you prefer, this dough can be made ahead and refrigerated for up to 2 days or frozen for a couple of months. Allow the dough to warm up before rolling it out.

Hamantaschen Flats or Mock Hamantaschen

Makes 5 to 6 dozen flats

After watching one kid after another nibble around hamantaschen filling, I decided to give them what they like best—the crust! The usual hamantaschen dough is rolled out as for cookies, cut in triangles, and garnished with some very festive Purim sprinkles. No left-over middles, tradition is preserved, everybody wins. Decorate these with a group of young helpers and in no time you will have scads of mock hamantaschen or hamantaschen flats to pack into Purim baskets or share with friends.

1 batch of Almost-Like-a-Bakery Traditional
    Hamantaschen dough (page 246) or Chocolate
    Hamantaschen dough (page 261)
Beaten egg white
Coarse sugar
Colored sprinkles
Chocolate sprinkles
Colored sugar

Preheat the oven to 350°F. Line 2 baking sheets with parchment paper.

Work with one portion of dough at a time. Roll it out on a lightly floured board to ¼ inch thick. Using a sharp paring knife, cut triangles 2 to 2½ inches on each side. Place the cookies on the baking sheets. Brush with beaten egg white and sprinkle on coarse sugar or colored sprinkles, chocolate sprinkles, or colored crystals.

Bake until lightly golden around the edges, 12 to 15 minutes. Cool on the baking sheets.

Delicate Purim Tea Cookies

Makes 2¹/₂ to 3¹/₂ dozen cookies

These cookies are perfect plain with coffee or tea or decorated for kids.
You can also use a ma'maoul mold (see page 212) for a different looking cookie. Check the Source Guide to
find out where to purchase one of these pretty wooden cookie molds.

1¹/₂ cups flour
¹/₄ teaspoon salt
1¹/₂ teaspoons baking powder
¹/₂ cup (1 stick) unsalted butter, at room
   temperature
¹/₂ cup sugar
1 egg yolk
3 tablespoons half and half or light cream
¹/₂ teaspoon vanilla or almond extract (see Note)

TOPPING
1 egg white, lightly beaten
Colored sprinkles (optional)
Colored or white granulated sugar (optional)

NOTE: You can use other extracts as well, such as orange, lemon, or maple.

OPTIONAL: You can add food coloring to the dough, and garnish with colored sprinkles.

Preheat the oven to 350°F. Line a large baking sheet with parchment paper.

In a small bowl, combine the flour, salt, and baking powder. In a separate bowl, cream the butter and add the sugar until fluffy. Stir in the egg yolk, half and half or cream, and the vanilla or almond extract. Fold in the dry ingredients. Chill the dough for 15 minutes.

On a very well-floured board, roll out the dough to ¹/₄ inch thick and cut it into whatever shapes you desire. If you don't have fancy cutters, plain circles will do—the sugar and sprinkles will fancy them up.

Place the cookies on the baking sheet, brush them with beaten egg white, and sprinkle them with colored sprinkles or colored or white sugar, if desired. Bake for 15 to 17 minutes, or until the edges are brown and the tops of the cookies are beginning just to become golden. Cool on a rack.

Purim Mun Cookies

Makes 3 to 4 dozen cookies

*A combination of oil and vegetable shortening makes these poppy-seed cookies especially light,
slightly reminiscent of a bakery-style mun cookie, but with homemade taste. You can substitute ⅓ cup
miniature chocolate chips for the poppy seeds to make different, but equally good cookies. These cookies are
good rolled micro thin or thicker—from ¼ to ⅜ inch thick.*

½ cup vegetable shortening
½ cup vegetable oil
1¼ cups sugar
2 eggs
1 teaspoon vanilla extract
¼ teaspoon orange oil or extract
⅓ cup poppy seeds
2¾ cups flour
¼ teaspoon salt
1 tablespoon baking powder

Preheat the oven to 350°F. Line 2 baking sheets with parchment paper.

In a bowl, cream together the shortening, oil, and sugar. Blend in the eggs, vanilla, and orange oil or extract. Fold in the poppy seeds, flour, salt, and baking powder. The dough should be stiff but rollable. Cover it with a tea towel and let it rest for 10 to 15 minutes. (Alternatively, you can always refrigerate the dough and roll it out several hours or up to 2 days later. Allow the dough to warm slightly before rolling.)

Roll the dough—very gently—to between ⅛ and ¼ inch thick and cut it into 3-inch rounds. Bake the cookies on the prepared sheets until golden brown (15 to 18 minutes). Cool on a rack.

Mun Kichel

Makes 5 to 6 dozen kichel, depending on size

3 eggs
½ cup vegetable oil
¾ cup sugar
½ teaspoon vanilla extract
2½ cups all-purpose flour
¼ teaspoon salt
1 tablespoon baking powder
¼ cup poppy seeds

Preheat the oven to 350°F. Line a baking sheet with parchment paper.

Beat the eggs, oil, sugar, and vanilla with an electric mixer until very light and voluminous (about 5 minutes). Fold in the flour, salt, baking powder, and poppy seeds.

Adding as little extra flour as possible, roll the dough to between ⅛ and ¼ inch thick. Cut it into circles, squares, or diamond shapes. Bake the cookies on the prepared baking sheet until lightly browned (25 to 30 minutes). Cool on the baking sheet.

White Chocolate, Cherry, and Macadamia Nut Mandelbrot

Makes 28 to 32 mandelbrot, depending on size

Chock full of good things, this is a great mandelbrot to tuck into Purim baskets or just to have on hand for Purim week.

½ cup (1 stick) unsalted butter, melted, or vegetable oil
½ cup unsweetened cocoa, sifted
1 cup granulated sugar
¼ cup brown sugar
3 eggs
2 teaspoons vanilla extract
2¼ cups all-purpose flour
¼ teaspoon salt
1½ teaspoons baking powder
¼ teaspoon baking soda
1½ cups white chocolate, in coarse chunks
½ cup semi-sweet chocolate, in coarse chunks
1 cup coarsely chopped macadamia nuts
1 cup sour cherries, plumped and dried

Preheat the oven to 350°F. Line 2 baking sheets with parchment paper.

In a large mixing bowl, stir the butter or oil with the cocoa. Blend in the granulated and brown sugars, then the eggs and vanilla.

In a separate bowl, blend the flour, salt, baking powder, and baking soda. Stir the dry ingredients into the wet batter, then fold in the white and semi-sweet chocolates, the nuts, and the cherries.

Spread the batter onto the prepared baking sheets in an oblong 8 inches long by 3 or 4 inches wide.

Bake until the top seems set (25 to 35 minutes). Cool for 15 minutes, then transfer to a board and cut, on the diagonal, into wedges ½ to ¾ inch thick. Reduce the oven heat to 325°F. Transfer the cookies back to the baking sheets and return them to the oven for 15 to 20 minutes to dry out, turning them once midway to brown both sides evenly. Since the cookies are dark, it is difficult to see when they are done. They should seem almost dry to the touch when ready.

OPTIONAL: Spread or drizzle melted white chocolate on one side of the finished cookies.

Chocolate Hazelnut Filo Roll

Makes 6 to 8 servings

Flaky, buttery pastry wrapped around barely melted chocolate and toasted hazelnuts.

4 sheets filo dough
⅓ cup ground hazelnuts
1 teaspoon ground cinnamon
2 teaspoons granulated sugar
½ cup (1 stick) unsalted butter or margarine,
  melted and cooled

CHOCOLATE HAZELNUT FILLING
8 ounces semi-sweet chocolate, coarsely chopped
¾ cup hazelnuts, toasted and chopped
Confectioners' sugar, for dusting (optional)

Preheat the oven to 375°F. Lightly grease a baking sheet and line with parchment paper.

Unroll the filo sheets and cover them with a slightly damp cloth. In a bowl, mix together the ground hazelnuts, cinnamon, and sugar.

FILLING: In a small bowl, combine the chopped chocolate and toasted hazelnuts. Lay out 1 sheet of filo. Brush it generously with melted butter. Sprinkle on half of the ground hazelnut mixture. Lay another filo sheet on top. Brush with butter and proceed as with the first sheet. Brush the top layer with butter. Place the chocolate-hazelnut mixture on the lower third of the stacked filo sheets. Lift the pastry gently over the chocolate to cover it. Fold in the left and right edges of the filo about 2 inches toward the center. Then, roll from the bottom jelly-roll fashion. Place seam side down on the prepared baking sheet. Bake for 35 to 40 minutes, until lightly browned.

Let cool before slicing. Use a serrated knife to cut. Dust with confectioners' sugar before serving, if desired. Be very careful to cool the pieces completely. The melted chocolate inside is very hot.

Queen Esther's Jaffa Poppy Seed Tea Cake with Orange Brandy Sugar Glaze

Makes 12 to 14 servings

For Purim, make this cake in miniature loaf pans (usually 12 mini loaves per baking tray) and pack 2 or 3 of them in each Purim basket. This is an especially moist, fragrant cake. You can substitute half and half or orange juice (for a pareve cake) for the evaporated milk, but the milk makes for a fine-textured, delicately crumbed loaf.

CAKE
1½ cups sugar
⅔ cup vegetable oil
3 eggs
1½ cups unsweetened evaporated milk or orange juice or half and half
1 teaspoon vanilla extract
1 tablespoon undiluted frozen orange juice or orange liqueur
2 tablespoons finely minced orange zest
⅓ cup poppy seeds
3 cups all-purpose flour
½ teaspoon salt
4 teaspoons baking powder

ORANGE BRANDY SUGAR GLAZE
½ cup orange juice
¼ cup brandy (or ginger ale)
Zest of 1 orange, finely minced
½ cup sugar

Preheat the oven to 350°F. Grease two 8½ by 4½-inch loaf pans, one large 12-cup bundt pan, or a 12-portion mini-loaf pan. (If using miniature loaves for a Purim basket, first spray the loaf pan generously with nonstick cooking spray, then line each mold with a paper baking cup widened to fit the loaf molds. This will make the loaves easy to remove and lend them that professional look.)

CAKE: Using a whisk or in an electric mixer, blend the sugar and oil. Beat in the eggs. Stir in the evaporated milk, vanilla, frozen orange juice, zest, and poppy seeds and beat well. Add the flour, salt, and baking powder, and blend until smooth. Pour the batter into the prepared pan(s). Bake for 50 to 60 minutes, depending on the pan(s) used. When a toothpick inserted in the center comes out clean, the cake is done. Cool in the pan for 10 minutes, then invert onto a cake rack.

GLAZE: In a small saucepan, mix together the glaze ingredients. Stir over low heat until the sugar is dissolved (about 5 minutes). Let cool, then drizzle over the cooled cake(s). Gather together the drippings and drizzle on the remaining glaze again.

Brenda and Lee's Sugared Cinnamon Nuts

Makes about 1³/₄ pounds

*This easy recipe is adapted from one I received from my neighbor and dear friend,
Brenda Bernamoff, and her mother, Lee Troster. Usually Brenda makes them at Passover or Rosh Hashanah
as holiday gifts, but they are perfect for Purim baskets as well. I have seen many people avoid a seven-
course meal just to snack on these.*

1½ cups sugar
¼ cup water
2–3 teaspoons ground cinnamon
4 cups (about 1 pound) almonds, with or
   without skins
1 cup pecan halves
2 cups walnut halves

Preheat the oven to 350°F. Line 1 large or 2 medium baking sheets with parchment paper.

To toast the nuts, place them all on the baking sheet(s). Bake until evenly browned, checking often and shuffling them around for 20 to 25 minutes. Taste to verify doneness. The nuts will be a touch more crunchy and fragrant.

In a medium saucepan over medium heat, stir together the sugar, water, and cinnamon. Cook, stirring to dissolve the sugar, for 5 to 6 minutes.

Fold the nuts into the sugar-cinnamon mixture and stir to coat.

Spread the nuts out evenly again in a shallow layer on the baking sheet(s). Bake for 15 to 20 minutes, tossing every once in a while to coat and bake the nuts evenly. The sugar will bubble up and ooze out of the nuts and eventually become crusty looking. Be careful not to overbrown the nuts—test one at the 15-minute mark to see if it is done. As they cool, the nuts will become crunchy, although they may not seem crunchy right away. Underbaked nuts may be soft *even* after cooling.

Remove from the oven and place the nuts on a large, cool baking sheet.

8. Passover

Feast of Freedom, the Exodus

*We were slaves of Pharaoh in Egypt and the Eternal our God
brought us out from there with a strong hand and an outstretched arm. Now if God
had not brought out our forefathers from Egypt, then even we, our children, and our
children's children might still be enslaved to Pharaoh in Egypt. Therefore,
even if we were all old and learned in the Torah, it would still be our duty
to tell the story of the departure from Egypt. And the more one tells
of the departure from Egypt, the more is he to be praised.*

—THE PASSOVER HAGGADAH, RABBI NATHAN GOLDBERG, 1949

*And I am come down to deliver them out of the hand of the Egyptians, and to bring
them up out of that land unto a land flowing with milk and honey.*

—EXODUS

PASSOVER (PESACH)

WHEN ❈ In the Hebrew calendar, the 15th day of Nisan, for seven days, commencing with two Seder meals, on the first and second nights.

CORRESPONDING TO ❈ Early spring, from March through April.

HOLIDAY CONTEXT ❈ Passover or *Pesach* is the Feast of Freedom and commemorates God's freeing of the Jews, once slaves of the Pharaoh, and their flight from Egypt to the Promised Land. Led by Moses, the Jews fled Egypt in such great haste that they had no time to pack properly, or to allow their bread to rise. The unrisen bread was baked up hard and flat—we call it "matzoh"—and that is what nourished them on their journey.

As they fled, the former slaves were horrified to see the Pharaoh's army gaining on them. Via a miracle, the parting of the Red Sea, the Jews were able to elude their would-be captors, who perished as the water of the Red Sea washed over them. At Passover, as on Rosh Hashanah, there is a sense of anticipation that builds as the holiday approaches. Passover is not associated with an exceptional synagogue attendance (at least, compared to Rosh Hashanah and Yom Kippur), but it is nonetheless perceived as being an important home-and-table celebration.

HOLIDAY ACTIVITIES/CUSTOMS ❈ Before the holiday arrives, preparations are made to ensure that a home is made *Pesadigah* (kosher for Passover). It is in keeping with the holiday custom to ensure that *hamaetz* (products and foods deemed to be unsuitable for Passover) is not present. Symbolic "sales" of *hamaetz,* complete with certificates of authentication, are arranged by a community rabbi.

At Passover, we initiate the Feast of Freedom with two lavish Seder meals. In Hebrew, Passover simply means "order." On the Seder nights, before the meal is served, it is the obligation of the host to ensure that the story of Passover is read.

Family customs and menus vary, but the recitation of the Passover tale; the Passover plate with its five symbolic foods (a scorched or roasted egg, a shank bone, bitter herbs, *haroseth,* a mixture of crushed nuts, wine and grated apple and parsley); the serving of the four cups of sweet kosher wine; hiding of the matzoh (*afikoman*), are usually included. In addition, we offer the prophet Elijah his own cup of wine in the hope that he will visit during the Seder.

FOODS/SYMBOLS ✿ To recall the flat, crackerlike bread the Jews ate in their hasty departure from Egypt, matzoh replaces bread for the eight-day holiday. Leavened baked goods of any kind—cakes, cookies, as well as any items made with flour, are not permitted during Pesach. Leavened refers to leavening by fermentation—something that occurs naturally over time with any flour and water mixture and certainly when flour, water, and yeast are mixed together (see Stocking the Passover Pantry, page 274). Matzoh for Passover is made within eighteen minutes, too short a time to produce any significant leavening by natural means.

Matzoh meal and matzoh cake meal replace flour for Passover baking. In addition to wheat flour, other grain and grain products, such as spelt, corn, barley, and oats, are also avoided. Pasta products are forbidden as well as fermented substances such as beer, whisky, and alcohol-based baking extracts. Special kosher for Passover wines are permitted.

"Kosher for Passover"— Stocking the Passover Baking Pantry

When I see "Kosher for Pesach" white sliced bread, then I will know the messiah has arrived.

—RABBI LIONEL MOSES, MONTREAL

A couple of weeks before Passover, stores that feature kosher products will usually dedicate whole displays, in some cases whole aisles to products that are "kosher for Passover." I have even seen "Passover" warehouses, chock full of interesting *Pesach* specialty products, manufactured for this unique holiday.

At one time, Passover products meant simply a couple of brands of regular and egg matzoh, matzoh meal, cake meal, and the odd sponge cake mix. These days, there is very little you cannot obtain. One of the nicest evolutions in this market are the many new baking products, such as brown sugar, cocoa, Passover vanilla sugar, chocolate chips, and Passover unsalted margarine that have made baking for Passover so much easier. For an annual update on what products are available at Passover, contact the Haddar company in the Source Guide or the Union of Orthodox Jewish Congregations of America, which provides a current list of permissible Passover products each year (Orthodox Union, Dept. K, 45 West 36 Street, New York, NY 10018).

Before you begin baking for Passover, it is wise to stock up on "foundation" ingredients. Here is a list of "must haves" for the holidays. Some of these items may seem obvious (such as nuts and chocolate), but others are equally important and helpful.

PASSOVER BAKING POWDER; PASSOVER BAKING SODA

Passover baking powder and Passover baking soda? My grandmothers would have had kittens! Of course, they would also have had a problem with products like "turkey bacon." However, technically, it is leavened goods resulting from fermentation (as with yeast baking) that are forbidden on Passover. Baking soda and baking powder are *chemical* leaveners so they are not in the regular category of "leavened" goods, if one is going to abide by technicalities. Also, Passover baking powder is made without cornstarch, so there is no dispute there. *However* . . . my personal feeling is that I can appreciate whipped egg whites to aerate my Passover cakes, but somehow once baking soda and baking powder, even okay-for-Passover ones, are introduced, the spirit of the holiday is compromised (never mind that all the big kosher packaged goods companies include these leaveners in their cookies and cakes—just check the ingredient lists). Passover cakes that use these products, even though they have no wheat flour, approach regular baking—at least in style. Incidentally, if you have always wondered why these packaged items "taste almost normal," it is because they are using these leaveners. In any case, I have not included these more modern baking concessions in my recipes.

BROWN SUGAR

A relatively recent addition to the Passover line, brown sugar adds flavor to Passover cakes. It's great in Passover Spice Sponge Cakes, cookies, and squares. Domino Sugar Company offers kosher for Passover brown sugar—*but* you may have to ask your grocer to stock or order it. It is *available* but not always brought in.

CAKE MEAL (MATZOH CAKE MEAL)

A more finely ground version of matzoh meal, this fine, sandy powder is used in most cakes. It works best when combined with matzoh meal and potato starch for optimal balance (all things considered) between body and tenderness in the finished cake. Many brands are available, but some are more finely ground than others. A medium grind works better as it tends to dry out a cake *less* than a fine grind.

COCOA AND CHOCOLATE

Another prime ingredient in Passover cakes, although semi-sweet is usually what is called for as it contains no dairy solids. Look for kosher, quality chocolate. You will be using it in every form—shredded, melted, shaved, and chopped. Also, chocolate chips are readily available and very helpful when adding a bit more decadence to Passover cookies and brownies (or for plain snacking!). Cocoa too is a boon at Passover as it is flavor-rich and very convenient, easily converting a vanilla sponge into a chocolate one.

PASSOVER CONFECTIONERS' SUGAR

Another, relatively new product in the Passover pantry, this confectioners' sugar is made with sugar and potato starch and replicates regular confectioners' or icing sugar. It can be used to dust a sponge cake or to make frosting. Since it is a relatively recent addition and is not yet widely available, it is not included in these recipes. However, if you wish to use it, you might find it locally at Passover, or contact Jewish food product companies such as Haddar for a source near you.

EGGS

At Passover, you might as well buy a hen house. Passover cakes rely on eggs for their leavening, which is why sponge cakes are synonymous with Passover. Honestly, buy *lots and lots* of eggs. They last for a couple of weeks, so, instead of buying two dozen, look for a good egg sale and come home with a lot.

FRUIT

Fruits lighten up the modest treats of Passover. They are fresh, flavorful, and colorful. Orange and lemon zest perk up many recipes, and slices of citrus, strawberries, raspberries, or mandarin orange boost taste and eye appeal. Fruit salads, an afterthought at many other occasions, do a lot to revive a tired, after-the-Seder-meal palate. Also, not everyone can eat an egg-rich cake, or chocolate, or a nut-laden square, so fruit is a wonderful and appropriate alternative.

UNSALTED OR PAREVE PASSOVER MARGARINE

When it is not Passover, neutral or pareve fat can be either regular pareve margarine or good old Crisco, or any other brand of nondairy fat or all-vegetable shortening you may prefer. If you do not require a neutral or dairy-free fat, you can use an unsalted margarine that may have traces of dairy solids in it. However, in deference to the unique laws of Kashruth that occur at Passover, the rules change somewhat. At Passover, look for an *unsalted, sweet,* or *pareve* margarine that is specially marked "For Passover." I tested and use Migdal's brand because it has the most neutral taste in baked goods. Depending on what you are serving or what your needs are, you may not require a nondairy fat in your Passover baking, that is, if your Seder meal is dairy-based or vegetarian. In this case, feel free to substitute unsalted butter for the unsalted Passover margarine. This is particularly good advice for Passover between-meal treats such as cookies and brownies. Whatever you do, do not use a whipped, salted margarine to bake with. The results will not be good.

MATZOH MEAL

A ground-up matzoh product used in Passover cake baking. There are many equally good and reliable brands to choose from.

NUTS

Ground nuts are used in many Passover cakes to replace the flour and to give the cake flavor. They are often the *starring* flavor and character of the cake, so stock up on all your favorites: walnuts, almonds, hazelnuts. Most important, make sure they are fresh, fresh, fresh. Rancid nuts will destroy a cake (and never assume they are fresh—taste, taste, taste). Toasted nuts (toast first in a 325°F. oven, then grind, making sure you do not pulverize the nuts into a paste or nut butter) lend the most flavor. Store toasted, ground nuts in the freezer.

POTATO STARCH

When it is not Passover, a more typical starch would be cornstarch. But corn and corn products (i.e., cornstarch, corn syrup) are on the "no-no" list; potato starch is what Passover recipes rely on to add a bit of tenderness to baked goods.

PASSOVER VANILLA AND OTHER EXTRACTS

Vanilla, since it is an extract made with alcohol, a fermented substance, is generally not recommended on Passover. Artificial vanilla powder mixed with sugar is now widely available. It comes in packets or envelopes or better yet, twelve-ounce tubs that have a little measuring spoon inside. "Kosher for Passover" vanilla powder or vanilla sugar does not compare at all to real, pure vanilla *but* . . . it is an approved and oh-so-helpful ingredient for Passover. Look for brands such as Haddar, Lieber's, Rokeach, or Itkowitz (check the Source Guide in back of the book). If you have any vanilla sugar left over after Passover, you can add it to your regular sugar jar. Serve the vanilla-scented sugar with that special mug of coffee.

I have seen almond and rum extract for Passover. You can add these wherever you like. However, they are less widely available and are not used extensively in these recipes. If you are interested in them, contact companies such as Haddar (see the Source Guide). If you want to use any of these recipes when it is *not* Passover, a substitution of one teaspoon regular pure vanilla extract would replace the one to two tablespoons Passover vanilla powder called for in the Passover recipes.

REFLECTIONS OF A BAKER AT PASSOVER

A couple of weeks before Passover, I take a look at my kitchen and get ready for the big Passover clean-up. It's more than the regular spring clean-up. It's time to put away all the tools of my trade and passion—the tools of traditional baking.

In essence, Passover means that flour and yeast as well as other leaveners and grains, take a hike, and matzoh moves in. No mean feat, in my case. At any given time, I store some six to seven hundred pounds of flour (creamy all-purpose, velvety unbleached pastry flour, hard bread flour, sandy, gray rye, golden semolina) in all the crevices of my home. Jars and bricks of yeast can be found in every fridge and freezer. Wild yeast spores, like elusive mustangs, fly invisibly, in the air. Two bread machines sit on the counter, their very presence a silent statement. This is a baker's place, my kitchen. If rolling pins sported odometers, mine would boast a most impressive mileage—on highways and byways fashioned of pie, cookie, bread, and danish doughs. But as this wonderful, historical festival of freedom draws near, the activity that defines me and my life must pause. Passover is a good time for me to take a breath as a baker. Given the choice, I would never have my hands out of the flour barrel too long. Flour is irresistible, as necessary to a baker's soul as air is to lungs. So I am happy for the Passover respite. It is a gentle, enforced sabbatical that provides perspective. It reminds me as a person to recall my history and imagine Moses' trek. It reminds me as a baker to respect my craft and to appreciate the luxury of abundance in its simple ingredients.

"My Trademark" Caramel Matzoh Crunch

About fifteen years ago, I was in a Passover "rut." I made scores of cakes and labored over all sorts of interesting Passover tortes and pastries. All tasty—but I noticed, as the Seder concluded, everyone was too full to do these desserts justice. I also noticed that people have a tendency just to nibble at sweets after a big meal. Small items had a real appeal. I wanted to make something modest but sweet and, for a change, nut-free (since so many Passover treats have nuts). I was also looking for something that was egg-free to offer family and Seder guests.

Then I had it! For years, I had made a confection-like recipe that called for nothing but soda crackers, butter, and brown sugar. I believe I got the recipe from an old *Farm Journal* cookbook, but I noticed that others seemed to make the same recipe. Some people make a similar recipe using graham crackers. Now, I thought, what could I use to replace those soda crackers? And then it came to me—matzoh! How logical, how appropriate. I wondered at first if the matzoh would absorb the sugar and butter as well as the soda crackers, and, happily, I found it did. When I discovered unsalted Passover margarine and kosher for Passover brown sugar, I knew I was in business.

Well, the resultant Caramel Matzoh Crunch, aka Matzoh Buttercrunch, was an instant hit. It had the perfect one-two punch—ease of preparation and dynamite taste. I printed out copies and copies of it

each year for friends in my community. (I did, by the way, credit *Farm Journal* with the soda cracker concept.) Many times readers would write and inform me that the soda cracker version was *their* special family recipe—goes to show you that a good recipe does make the rounds. Each Passover feature I ever contributed to the many papers I wrote for, from one coast to another, included my Caramel Matzoh Crunch. Once a neighbor gave me a copy of the recipe (printed out on my own printer and photocopied umpteen times!) unaware that I was the source. I chuckled and told her the recipe had come from my Passover feature etcetera. "Sure," she said, humoring me. "That's what they all say!" I have been flattered to see it in other people's cookbooks as well as on the Internet. I am thrilled to know I have been part of a new tradition. And I thank whoever it was who stumbled on the soda cracker idea. If I knew who you were, I would credit you by name. I would also share with you my version—who knows, maybe you also could use an easy Passover recipe.

This recipe is sublime made with unsalted butter (and that is what I use when it is not being served at the Seder meals) but still wonderful made with unsalted Passover margarine. If you choose, it can also be made with white chocolate and added chopped toasted nuts, such as almonds. It is pure confectionary delight, but you do not need any special techniques or even a candy thermometer to make it. In fact, if you are terrified of Passover baking, just make this. It is a winner .

My Trademark, Most Requested, Absolutely Magnificent Caramel Matzoh Crunch

An outstanding, unique, and easy confection. If you make only one *thing at Passover, make this.*

4–6 unsalted matzohs
1 cup (2 sticks) unsalted butter or unsalted
  Passover margarine
1 cup firmly packed brown sugar
¾ cup coarsely chopped chocolate chips or
  semi-sweet chocolate

Preheat the oven to 375°F. Line a large (or two smaller) cookie sheet completely with foil. Cover the bottom of the sheet with baking parchment—on top of the foil. This is very important since the mixture becomes sticky during baking.

Line the bottom of the cookie sheet evenly with the matzohs, cutting extra pieces, as required, to fit any spaces.

In a 3-quart, heavy-bottomed saucepan, combine the butter or margarine and the brown sugar. Cook over medium heat, stirring constantly, until the mixture comes to a boil (about 2 to 4 minutes). Boil for 3 minutes, stirring constantly. Remove from the heat and pour over the matzoh, covering completely.

Place the baking sheet in the oven and immediately reduce the heat to 350°. Bake for 15 minutes, checking every few minutes to make sure the mixture is not burning (if it seems to be browning too quickly, remove the pan from the oven, lower the heat to 325°, and replace the pan).

Remove from the oven and sprinkle immediately with the chopped chocolate or chips. Let stand for 5 minutes, then spread the melted chocolate over the matzoh. While still warm, break into squares or odd shapes. Chill, still in the pan, in the freezer until set.

This makes a good gift.

VARIATION: You can also use coarsely chopped white chocolate (or a combination of white and dark), and chopped or slivered toasted almonds (sprinkled on top as the chocolate sets). You can also omit the chocolate for a caramel-alone buttercrunch.

SPONGE CAKES MADE SUBLIME

Whether you are a big fan of sponge cake or not, Passover is just not Passover without at least one sponge cake. Sponge cakes are quite adaptable and a mouthful of a fresh one says "Happy Passover" in a sweeter way than any batch of gefilte fish could hope to. With this in mind, it pays to pick up some sponge cake pointers.

For optimal sponge cakes, use a strong, stationary mixer such as a KitchenAid or Rival. Other mixers are adequate but the top-of-the-line ones really do an exemplary job of beating egg whites. Also, while some of the newer, more powerful hand mixers are great, for Passover you might get tired standing and beating egg whites so frequently. Some people like a hand mixer, and reserve it expressly for Passover, but when you consider all the baking you do for this holiday, investing in a heavy-duty standing mixer makes sense. These mixers have something that KitchenAid calls "planetary action." This means that they fully beat a larger surface in their work bowls instead of going over the same ground again and again. One tester who upgraded her equipment was astounded by the added height of her cakes. True, your grandmother probably made exceptional sponge cakes with a vintage Sunbeam or her own hands, but even Bubbie wouldn't have minded a little extra, electrically driven elbow grease.

Always use clean, dry beaters. A touch of water, fat (even a spot of egg yolk) will inhibit the whites from being properly mounted. If you do not have two bowls for your mixer, use a very large hand whisk to mix the egg yolks and sugar (and any other ingredients to be combined with the yolks). Use the clean mixing bowl to mount the egg whites.

Do not use the empty egg shell half to remove bits of shell from egg whites. You might spread bacteria that way (bacteria could be lurking on the outer shell). Use a clean spoon or butter knife to remove any bits of shell.

Use the size eggs (usually large) called for in a recipe and make sure your eggs are fresh. Stale whites will not whip up well. Since sponge cakes depend on their balance and eggs are an inherent part of that balance, do not substitute a different size egg. The results will differ.

Separate your eggs when they are cold, *but* whip the whites at room temperature. You can use a touch of salt to stabilize them (the usual pinch of cream of tartar is not permitted at Passover because cream of tartar is derived from fermented grapes), but using sugar, to create a meringue, is more stabilizing and is the tactic I have used in most of these recipes.

Do not overbeat your whites to the point where they are dry. Make them thick, stiff, and glossy. Even if you are unsure about how whipped is whipped enough, your cake will still come out. Chances are, slightly underbeaten whites will render a less statuesque, but still good cake. Overbeaten whites dry out a cake.

Some old sponge cake recipes call for dairy-free mousses as fillings. These are usually flavored starch and sugar mousse mixes that are then bulked up with beaten egg whites and chilled. Since those recipes were created long ago, and we now know that raw egg whites can harbor salmonella bacteria—harmful to all, but especially to those with compromised immune systems, children, and pregnant women—I do not recommend these mousse mixes as fillings. They are not safe.

Traditional Passover Sponge Cake

Makes 8 to 10 servings

*This should really be called "1001 Sponge Cakes" because it is a basic recipe that takes well
to almost any variation. Instead of changing recipes each time you want a different sponge cake,
it is easier to use one as a foundation. There are bigger sponge cake recipes circulating,
but a 9-egg sponge, for me, is just right.*

9 eggs, separated
1/3 cup matzoh cake meal
1/2 cup potato starch, plus extra for the pan
1 cup sugar
1 tablespoon Passover vanilla sugar
2 teaspoons finely minced lemon zest
2 teaspoons finely minced orange zest
2 tablespoons lemon or orange juice
1/4 teaspoon, plus a pinch salt

Preheat the oven to 350°F. Lightly grease an angel food or 10-inch tube pan and dust it with potato starch.

Place the egg whites over a bowl of warm water and allow them to stand for a couple of minutes to warm (or leave them at room temperature for 20 to 30 minutes).

Meanwhile, sift together the cake meal, potato starch, and 1/4 teaspoon salt. Set aside.

In one bowl, briskly whisk together the egg yolks, 1/2 cup of the sugar, the vanilla sugar, orange and lemon zest, and lemon or orange juice. Stir in the cake meal and potato starch and combine well.

In a mixing bowl, with clean, dry beaters, whisk the egg whites and salt together until frothy. At high speed, whip, slowly dusting in the remaining sugar, until the whites are stiff and glossy.

Mix one third of the whipped egg whites into the yolk mixture to lighten and aerate it. Then gently fold in the remaining whites, in 2 batches, to incorporate but not deflate the whites.

Gently pour the batter into the prepared pan and place in the oven. After 10 minutes, reduce the heat to 325° and bake until done (30 to 45 minutes) or until the cake seems just firm when lightly touched.

continued

Cool the pan by inverting onto a large plate. Cake will eventually unmold itself without losing much of its height this way.

A Thousand and One Sponge Cakes: Variations on a Theme

SPICE CAKE: With the matzoh meal, add 1 teaspoon ground cinnamon, ½ teaspoon ground cloves, ¼ teaspoon each grated nutmeg, ginger, and ground mace or allspice. You may also use brown sugar instead of white.

WINE AND NUT SPONGE: Replace the orange or lemon juice with sweet, red, kosher wine. Add ½ cup finely ground toasted nuts with the cake meal and potato starch, *or* sprinkle the top of the unbaked cake with 2 teaspoons sugar and ¼ cup sliced almonds.

GRATED CHOCOLATE SPONGE CAKE: Add ⅓ cup grated, frozen chocolate flakes to the batter just before pouring it into the pan.

CHOCOLATE CHIP SPONGE: Fold ⅓ cup finely grated semi-sweet chocolate into the batter before pouring it into the pan.

CRANBERRY ORANGE: Grate ⅓ cup frozen cranberries into fine bits and fold into the batter before pouring into the pan.

COCONUT CAKE: To the cake meal and potato starch, add ⅓ cup shredded coconut to the batter. Top the unbaked cake with another ¼ cup coconut shreds and ¼ cup chopped macadamia nuts, if desired. Serve with sliced fresh mangoes and strawberries.

"I Can't Believe This Is a Passover Cake" Yellow Cake

Makes 8 to 10 servings

*This recipe is a cross between a true sponge cake, a classic genoise, and a chiffon cake.
I like it because I do not have to separate the eggs and yet I get a well-textured cake. It keeps well
and is a good foundation for fresh fruit, pareve Passover mousse, or a chocolate ganache topping.
Although the eggs are not separated, you must treat them with care. Another must is a good,
stationary, electric mixer (such as a Kitchenaid, Rival, or Sunbeam) with a whisk or
whip attachment that will properly mount the warmed, whole eggs. For people who loathe
dry cakes and think Passover cakes are suspect at best, this is a must.*

8 large eggs
⅓ cup matzoh cake meal
⅓ cup potato starch, not packed, plus extra for
 dusting
1 tablespoon lemon juice
3 tablespoons unsalted Passover margarine,
 melted, or kosher for Passover oil
¾ cup granulated sugar
1 tablespoon Passover vanilla sugar
½ teaspoon salt
1 tablespoon finely minced lemon or orange zest

Preheat the oven to 350°F. Generously grease a 10-inch springform pan or a 9 by 13-inch rectangular pan. Dust it with potato starch and line the bottom with parchment paper.

Warm the eggs (still in their shells) by placing them in a bowl and covering them with very hot water for 1 to 2 minutes. (The water should be hot enough to warm them up but not so hot as to crack the eggs and cook them. Do not leave the eggs in the water longer than 1 or 2 minutes.) This is the most important step. *Do not omit it.* Heat a mixing bowl by filling it with very hot water, then dry it completely.

Meanwhile, sift together the cake meal, potato starch, and ¼ teaspoon salt. Combine the lemon juice and melted margarine or oil in a small bowl. Set these ingredients aside.

Break the warmed eggs into the bowl of an electric mixer along with granulated sugar, vanilla sugar, ¼ teaspoon salt, and citrus zest. Using the whip attach-

continued

ment, beat on low speed very briefly just to combine the ingredients. Then increase to high speed and beat for 12 minutes. The batter will be extremely voluminous.

Pour the batter into a very large mixing bowl. Stir in the potato starch/matzoh cake meal mixture, then gently fold this mixture into the egg batter, taking care not to deflate the mixture too much (some deflation is impossible to avoid). Gently drizzle and fold in the lemon juice and melted margarine or oil.

Pour the batter into the prepared pan and bake for 30 to 35 minutes, until the cake is set in the center or until it seems just firm when lightly touched. Cool well before removing from the pan.

VARIATIONS:

FOR MARBLE CAKE, omit the lemon juice. Mix 2 tablespoons unsweetened cocoa powder with 2 to 3 tablespoons water. Stir this into one third of the vanilla batter. Spoon alternating dollops of white and chocolate batter into the pan.

FOR STRAWBERRY OR RASPBERRY CAKE, prepare fresh berries by mashing and mixing them with a bit of sugar. Serve in dollops over a slice of cake. For dairy occasions, serve with whipped cream.

FOR DOUBLE LEMON CAKE, add ½ teaspoon citric acid (usually available for Passover in the kosher food section) along with the juice. This gives an extra lemony kick without upsetting the liquid balance in the recipe. Garnish with lemon zest threads. Serve the cake with prepared Passover lemon curd and fresh raspberries.

FOR CINNAMON NUT CAKE, replace the matzoh meal with ⅓ cup ground toasted nuts and add 1 teaspoon ground cinnamon. Garnish the top of the cake with 1 tablespoon ground nuts before baking.

FOR SPICE CAKE, add ½ teaspoon ground cinnamon and up to ¼ teaspoon ground cloves, allspice, and grated nutmeg along with the cake meal and potato starch.

FOR JELLY-ROLL YELLOW CAKE, you can also bake this cake in a jelly-roll pan or on a small cookie sheet. Roll into a log while the cake is warm, using a clean tea towel as an aid (dust the towel first with potato starch). Once the cake is set in a roll shape, gently unroll it. Fill it with lemon curd, Passover mousse or jam, or whipped cream, as desired. You can also drizzle melted semi-sweet chocolate on it to dress it up.

Chocolate Spice Cake

Makes 10 servings

A chocolate cake with a difference. Or is it a spice cake with a difference? Delicious, any way you look at it.

10 eggs, separated
2 cups sugar
⅓ cup Passover wine or warm coffee
¼ cup unsweetened cocoa powder
¼ teaspoon plus a pinch of salt
¼ teaspoon ground cloves
1½ teaspoons ground cinnamon
1⅓ cups matzoh cake meal
¼ cup potato starch, plus extra for pan
1¼ cups finely chopped toasted almonds

Preheat the oven to 325°F. Line a 10-inch tube or angel food pan with parchment paper. Lightly grease and dust the sides with potato starch.

In a medium bowl, beat the egg yolks with 1¼ cups of the sugar until very thick and pale yellow, about 5 to 7 minutes. Stir in the wine or coffee, the cocoa powder, salt, cloves, and cinnamon. Stir in the matzoh cake meal, potato starch, and the chopped almonds.

In another large bowl, with clean, dry beaters, gently whisk the egg whites with a pnch of salt to break them up. Increase the speed to high, and, gradually dusting in the remaining ¾ cup sugar, beating until the whites are stiff and glossy but not dry. Briskly and thoroughly fold about one third of the beaten whites into the yolk mixture to lighten it. Then, in 2 separate batches, fold in the remaining egg whites, taking care not to deflate the egg whites but to blend the batter properly.

Pour into the prepared pan and bake for about 55 minutes, or until the cake springs back when gently touched. Cool by inverting onto a serving plate. Cake will unmold itself as it cools.

Chocolate Hazelnut Torte

Makes 8 to 10 servings

This versatile cake can be decorated with a simple chocolate glaze or a whipped chocolate frosting.
If not being served with the meal, offer this elegant torte with vanilla-scented whipped cream.

CAKE
1½ cups (6 ounces) coarsely chopped semi-sweet chocolate
¾ cup (1½ sticks) unsalted Passover margarine or butter, at room temperature
¾ cup sugar
¼ teaspoon salt
6 eggs, separated
2 teaspoons Passover vanilla powder
1¼ cups finely ground toasted hazelnuts

CHOCOLATE GLAZE
1 cup semi-sweet chocolate chips or chopped semi-sweet chocolate
2 tablespoons unsalted Passover margarine
1 cup raspberry or apricot jam, warmed
Chopped toasted hazelnuts, for garnish (optional)

Preheat the oven to 375°F. Generously grease a 9-inch springform pan with vegetable shortening and line the bottom with a circle of parchment paper or greased wax paper.

CAKE: Melt the chocolate for the cake in the top of a double boiler over simmering water. Set it aside to cool. Meanwhile, cream the butter or margarine, add the sugar and salt, and blend until fluffy. Then beat in the egg yolks, melted chocolate, and the vanilla powder. Stir in the ground nuts.

In a large bowl, with clean, dry beaters, whip the egg whites until they hold peaks but are not dry (they should still be glossy). Stir a large spoonful of whites into the chocolate mixture to loosen it. Then fold in the remaining whites in 3 batches. It does not matter if bits of egg white are still visible. Pour into the prepared pan and bake for 20 minutes. Reduce the heat to 350° and bake for another 20 to 25 minutes. Do not overbake—the top will look light and crusty but the interior will be moist. Cool in the pan on a wet kitchen towel for 20 minutes. Cut away edges that may have baked up and adhered to the pan's inner edges and invert on a cake rack. Unmold carefully. Place in the freezer while preparing the glaze.

GLAZE: Melt the chocolate and margarine slowly in the top of a double boiler over simmering water, stirring to melt. Cool to room temperature. Spread the top of the chilled cake with warmed apricot or raspberry preserves. (Note: Use a piece of cardboard to lift the cake without breaking it.) Place the cake gently on a wire cake rack set over a cookie sheet. Using a spouted measuring cup, pour the cooled chocolate glaze directly onto the center of the cake and allow it to run down the sides. Remove the cake to a serving platter and garnish it with chopped toasted hazelnuts, if desired.

Espresso Truffle Torte

Makes 14 to 20 servings

There are many recipes for this type of torte. Mine is adapted from a recipe called Torta di Cioccolata alla Santa Cohen from a very early issue of the renowned Chocolatier magazine. Cookbook author Lora Brody is known for her Bête Noire, yet another version of this chocolate "experience," and almost every pastry chef I ever worked with had a version of this, tucked in his or her files. Suffice it to say, it is a winner. Low slung, yet sophisticated, this cake tastes somewhat like cheesecake (although it contains no cheese). It can be made ahead and frozen until an hour or so before serving. Serve it dusted with cocoa or with pureed strawberries on the side. This is rich and suitable for a large Seder crowd.

TORTE
2 cups (4 sticks) unsalted butter or unsalted
  Passover margarine
1 cup brewed, warm coffee
16 ounces semi-sweet chocolate, coarsely
  chopped
8 eggs, at room temperature
1 cup granulated sugar
2 tablespoons Passover vanilla sugar
¼ teaspoon salt

GLAZE
1 cup semi-sweet chocolate chips
2 tablespoons unsalted butter or Passover
  margarine

Preheat the oven to 350°F. Line the bottom of a 9-inch springform pan with parchment paper.

TORTE: In a heavy saucepan set over low heat or in a double boiler, melt the butter or margarine with the coffee, mixing well. Remove from the stove and add the chocolate, stirring to melt. Cool the chocolate very well before proceeding.

Meanwhile, in the bowl of an electric mixer, whip the eggs with the granulated and vanilla sugars, and salt on high speed for 10 minutes. Whisk in one third of the cooled, melted chocolate into the egg mixture until thoroughly incorporated. Add the remaining melted chocolate and blend the batter gently but well. Pour into the prepared pan and bake for 50 to 55 minutes. The cake is done when the top has a slight crust and seems set. If it rises too fast, reduce the heat to 325°. The cake may rise and fall, but that is fine.

Cool the cake to firm it up, then refrigerate for several hours.

GLAZE: In a double boiler, melt the chocolate chips with the butter or margarine, stirring to melt evenly. Cool, then pour over the chilled cake before serving, or offer separately as a topping sauce.

Alternatively, serve the cake with pureed raspberries or strawberries. Or, dust the top with cocoa and garnish the center with sliced strawberries.

Passover Rich Chocolate Genoise and Buttercream Roll

Makes 8 to 10 servings

This makes a very rich cake with an exceptionally pretty presentation. The recipe looks complicated, but it is not—3 elements: a rich chocolate cake base, followed by a fluffy chocolate buttercream, and finished off with melted chocolate glaze. Can be made ahead and frozen or refrigerated until needed. Since the eggs are not separated in this recipe, you need a heavy-duty electric stand mixer such as a KitchenAid to get the most volume from the eggs.

CHOCOLATE GENOISE
8 large eggs
¾ cup granulated sugar
¼ cup matzoh cake meal
⅓ cup potato starch, not packed
¼ cup unsweetened cocoa powder, measured then sifted
1 tablespoon Passover vanilla sugar
¼ teaspoon salt
3 tablespoons unsalted Passover margarine, melted, or vegetable oil

CHOCOLATE BUTTERCREAM FILLING
1 cup (2 sticks) unsalted Passover margarine, softened
½ cup unsweetened cocoa powder, measured then sifted
2–3 cups Passover confectioners' sugar
2–4 tablespoons warm water, brewed coffee, or cola

CHOCOLATE GLAZE/TOPPING
1 cup (4 ounces) semi-sweet chocolate chips
Semi-sweet chocolate shavings, or slivered, toasted almonds
Passover confectioners' sugar, for dusting

Preheat the oven to 350°F. Generously grease a baking or jelly-roll sheet that measures about 11 by 7 inches. Line with parchment paper. (If you cannot find parchment paper for Passover, line the pan with aluminum foil and grease with unsalted margarine.) Generously grease the parchment paper (this will help release the cake later).

GENOISE: Warm the eggs (still in their shells) by placing in a bowl and covering with very hot water for 1 to 2 minutes (water should be hot but not so hot as to crack the eggs open and cook them but hot enough to warm them up. Do not leave eggs in water longer than 1 to 2 minutes). This is the most important step. Do not omit it. Heat the mixing bowl by filling with very hot water and then dry it completely. Place the eggs in an electric mixing bowl and, using the wire whip or whisk, mix on slow speed just to break up the eggs. Then increase the speed to high and beat for 10 minutes, dusting in the sugar gradually, as the eggs are being whipped. After 10 to 12 minutes, the batter should be extremely voluminous.

In a small bowl, sift together the cake meal, potato starch, cocoa, Passover vanilla sugar, and salt.

Gently transfer the batter into a very large mixing bowl. Dust in the dry ingredients in small increments, gently folding after each addition. Drizzle in the unsalted margarine or oil, taking care not to deflate the mixture unduly (some deflation is impossible to avoid).

Pour the batter into the prepared pan. Bake for 35 to 40 minutes, until the cake is set in the center or until the cake seems just firm when lightly touched. Cool for about 8 minutes, then remove the cake from the baking pan (still with the parchment paper attached). Using the parchment paper as an aid, roll up the cake into a jelly roll or log. Wrap the log in a new sheet of parchment paper and wrap in a clean, kitchen towel. Let the cake rest this way for 20 to 30 minutes to allow it to set or retain its log shape. (It will be filled and rerolled.)

FILLING: Using the whisk or whip attachment of an electric mixer, cream the margarine with the cocoa and most of the confectioners' sugar on slow speed. Increase the speed to high, stopping occasionally to scrape down the bowl, and whip to make a fluffy frosting, adding in a couple of tablespoons of water, coffee, or cola as required to achieve a proper consistency. The buttercream should be whipped for 2 to 4 minutes.

TO ASSEMBLE: Gently unroll the cake and, using a metal spatula, spread on the chocolate buttercream. Reroll the cake into a log. Trim the ends (about a ½ inch on each end to make them neat). Wrap snugly in parchment paper and place in the freezer while making the chocolate glaze. Before glazing, let the cake warm up to almost room temperature.

CHOCOLATE GLAZE: Melt the chocolate chips in the microwave (on high for 2 to 3 minutes). Stir the chocolate to make it smooth. Spread over the chilled cake (using a pastry brush or small metal spatula). Coat as evenly as possible. (If the cake is too cold, the chocolate will set very quickly and be hard to spread—but it will still be fine.) Top with chocolate shavings and a dusting of Passover confectioners' sugar or with toasted slivered almonds (and confectioners' sugar, if you wish).

Apple Rhubarb Cobbler

Makes 6 to 8 servings

*A brown sugar crumble topping and a fresh, springlike apple-and-rhubarb filling make
for a sweet and tart dessert. Good after a big meal or as a during-the-week reward. A refreshing change
from chocolate, nuts, and sponge cakes. Substitute cranberries or raspberries for the rhubarb, if you like,
for a rosy and tart filling, or substitute apricots (fresh or canned) for a sweeter filling. Almost any
combination of fruits will work.*

CRUMBLE TOPPING
1½ cups potato starch
1 cup matzoh meal
⅓ cup brown sugar
2 teaspoons Passover vanilla sugar
Pinch of ground cinnamon
½ teaspoon salt
½ cup (1 stick) unsalted Passover margarine or
  unsalted butter
¼ cup orange juice

APPLE RHUBARB FILLING
6 cups peeled and sliced apples
1 cup coarsely chopped rhubarb
¾ cup granulated sugar
1 teaspoon ground cinnamon
¼ cup orange juice
2 tablespoons potato starch

Preheat the oven to 350°F. Generously grease a 9 by
13-inch or 8 by 10-inch rectangular pan, or a 10-inch
springform pan.

CRUMBLE TOPPING: In a medium bowl, combine the
dry ingredients. Cut the margarine or butter into the
dry mixture. Stir in the orange juice to make a
crumbly topping that just holds together. Set aside.

APPLE RHUBARB FILLING: In a large bowl, toss all the
filling ingredients together.

Sprinkle half the crumble topping over the bottom
of the pan and press very slightly. Spoon on the fruit
filling. Sprinkle the remaining crumble topping over
the fruit. Bake until the fruit is bubbling and the top
is lightly golden (25 to 35 minutes). Cool well in the
pan before serving.

Brown Sugar Pecan Passover Cake

Makes 10 to 12 servings

The combination of nuts makes for a unique cake with a slightly crunchy, sweet top and a moist interior.
For another taste entirely, see the citrus variation. Kosher for Passover brown sugar is available.

9 eggs, separated
1⅓ cups granulated sugar
½ cup brown sugar
2 tablespoons Passover vanilla sugar
¼ teaspoon ground cinnamon
½ teaspoon plus a pinch of salt
⅓ cup matzoh cake meal
¼ cup potato starch
2 tablespoons unsalted Passover margarine, melted
½ cup lightly toasted ground almonds
½ cup lightly toasted ground walnuts
½ cup lightly toasted ground pecans

Preheat the oven to 375°F. Line the bottom of a 10-inch tube pan with baking parchment.

Set the egg whites aside in a clean, dry mixing bowl.

In another mixing bowl, combine the egg yolks, 1 cup of the granulated sugar, the brown sugar, vanilla sugar, cinnamon, and the ½ teaspoon of salt. Whisk very well to blend and lighten the egg yolks. Fold in the cake meal, potato starch, and melted margarine. Blend in the nuts and stir well. (The mixture may be thick.)

Add the pinch of salt to the egg whites and, with clean, dry beaters, slowly begin whipping the whites to foam. Increase the speed and dust in the remaining ⅓ cup of sugar. Whip until the whites form stiff, glossy peaks.

Stir a generous one third of the whipped egg whites into the yolk mixture to lighten and loosen it. Gently fold in the remaining whites.

Spoon the batter into the prepared pan. Place in the oven and immediately lower the heat to 325°. Bake until the cake springs back to the touch (50 to 55 minutes—the cake may rise, then sink—this is okay). Remove from the oven and cool well before inverting the cake and removing it from the pan. It helps to run a flat knife around the edge to separate the cake from the pan.

VARIATION: For Citrus, Cinnamon, and Nut Cake, replace the brown sugar with granulated sugar. Increase the cinnamon to 1 teaspoon, and gently fold into the batter 2 tablespoons *each* finely minced orange and lemon zest.

Glazed Chocolate Orange Torte with Berry Sauce

Makes 12 to 16 servings

Light citrus overtones in a fudge-like cake. This torte can be made ahead and frozen.

TORTE
¾ pound (1½ sticks) unsalted butter or unsalted Passover margarine (not whipped style)
¾ cup sugar
1 cup orange juice
12 ounces semi-sweet chocolate, coarsely chopped
6 large eggs

RASPBERRY OR STRAWBERRY SAUCE (OPTIONAL)
1 (10-ounce) package frozen strawberries or raspberries, defrosted
1–2 tablespoons sugar

TOPPING
Unsweetened cocoa powder, for dusting
Orange zest, in long shreds
Orange or rose leaves, washed and shined with vegetable oil
Fresh raspberries

Preheat the oven to 350°F. Line the bottom of a 9-inch springform pan with parchment paper.

TORTE: In a heavy saucepan over low heat, or using a double boiler, melt the butter or margarine, sugar, and orange juice, stirring to blend. Remove from the heat and add the chocolate, stirring to melt. Cool very well, then whisk in the eggs until thoroughly incorporated. Pour the batter into the prepared pan and bake for 35 to 45 minutes. The cake is done when the top has a slight crust and seems set. If the cake rises too fast (that is, if the top is forming a crust yet the center seems uncooked), reduce the heat to 325° and let the cake bake more slowly.

Cool to firm up the cake while still in the pan. Then place in the refrigerator for several hours. Serve cold or at room temperature.

BERRY SAUCE: combine the berries with the sugar in a food processor. Process until smooth. Taste, and add more sugar if you prefer a sweeter sauce.

Before serving, dust the cake with the cocoa. Sprinkle the top of the cake with the orange zest and citrus or rose leaves. Place a couple of raspberries in the center. Offer the berry sauce on the side, if desired. Alternatively, you can simply dust the cake with cocoa.

Apple Cherry Passover Kuchen

Makes 8 to 10 servings

This low-slung apple cake resembles an apple crisp more than a cake, but it is tasty, moist, and rippled with cinnamon. A "ladies auxiliary" classic, a cinch to make.

APPLE LAYER
5 large apples, such as Golden Delicious, peeled and sliced thin
1 teaspoon ground cinnamon
¼ cup granulated sugar
½ cup canned sour cherries, very well drained and halved

CAKE
3 eggs, separated
¾ cup granulated sugar
1 tablespoon Passover vanilla sugar
2 teaspoons finely minced lemon zest
⅓ cup matzoh cake meal
⅓ cup matzoh meal
¼ cup potato starch
½ cup vegetable oil
¼ teaspoon salt

TOPPING
⅓ cup finely chopped walnuts
2–4 tablespoons granulated sugar
2 teaspoons ground cinnamon

Preheat the oven to 350°F. Lightly grease a 9-inch springform pan.

APPLE LAYER: Toss the apples with the cinnamon and sugar. Set aside.

CAKE: In a mixing bowl, combine the egg yolks, granulated and vanilla sugars, lemon zest, matzoh cake meal, matzoh meal, potato starch, and oil and blend until smooth. In a separate bowl, whip the egg whites with the salt until stiff and glossy. Loosen the batter with a couple of generous dollops of egg white. Gently but firmly fold in the remaining egg whites.

Spoon half the mixture into the pan (a wet metal spatula works well for this). Arrange the apples on top. Dot with the cherries, and cover with spoonfuls of the remaining batter. The batter is thick and sticky. It is okay if it is spread somewhat unevenly.

TOPPING: In a bowl, combine the topping ingredients and sprinkle them over the cake.

Bake for 50 to 55 minutes, until the cake tests done—slightly browned and set. Cool well in the pan.

Mock Chestnut Torte

Makes 14 to 18 servings

This makes a rich but surprisingly light, torte.
An absolute, worth-the-price-of-the-book winner. Mashed sweet potatoes make a great substitute
for the traditional pureed chestnut paste. Chestnut puree is available kosher, but I have never been able
to find it "kosher for Passover." It may seem unusual, but I can assure you of two things—it tastes divine
and it is easier than buying fresh-in-the-shell chestnuts, roasting, poaching, and grating them to get them
ready for this cake. You can also serve this in squares, as French-style "petit fours." The glaze slicks this up
but is not necessary—a dusting of cocoa is just fine.

TORTE
½ cup (1 stick) unsalted Passover margarine
⅓ cup plus 2 tablespoons granulated sugar
6 large eggs, separated
1½ cups cooked and mashed sweet potatoes,
  fresh or canned
1 teaspoon Passover rum extract (optional)
10 ounces good-quality semi-sweet chocolate,
  melted and cooled
¼ teaspoon salt

CHOCOLATE GANACHE GLAZE
½ cup water
6 ounces semi-sweet chocolate, coarsely chopped

TOPPINGS (OPTIONAL)
Unsweetened cocoa powder, sifted
Curls of semi-sweet chocolate
Pureed strawberries or raspberries

Preheat the oven to 350°F. Line a 9-inch springform pan with baking parchment.

TORTE: In a mixing bowl, cream the unsalted margarine or butter with the ⅓ cup of sugar. Blend in the egg yolks, then the mashed sweet potatoes, rum extract (if using), and cooled chocolate.

In another bowl, with clean beaters, whip the egg whites gently until they are a bit foamy. Then add in the salt and whip on a higher speed, slowly dusting in the two tablespoons of sugar to form stiff, glossy (but not dry) peaks. Fold one third of the egg whites into the sweet potato/chocolate mixture and work them in well to loosen the batter. Then, gently fold in the remaining egg whites, blending well but taking care not to deflate the mixture. Spoon the batter into the prepared pan and bake for about 40 minutes. The cake rises and looks dry, and *slightly* cracked on top when done. The middle should be soft but firm. Cool in the pan for 20 minutes, then remove to a wire rack. At this point, the cake can be frozen for up to a month. Even if serving it the same day, chill the cake for an hour or two before finishing it with the ganache glaze.

CHOCOLATE GANACHE GLAZE: In a double boiler, bring the water to a gentle boil and add the chopped chocolate all at once. Remove from the heat and stir briskly with a wire whisk until all the chocolate melts and you have a thick glaze or sauce-like topping. Refrigerate for an hour or so. (You can also make this ahead and refrigerate it for up to a week or two. Simply warm it to the right temperature for glazing the cake.)

Invert the cake onto a cardboard circle or cake board so that the smooth, flat bottom faces up. Do not be dismayed if this is not a high cake—it is a torte and is meant to be a little less than statuesque. Pour the glaze over the cake and, using a metal spatula, even out the glaze and spread it along the sides.

Instead of the glaze, you can also simply sift some cocoa over the top of the cake or decorate it with curls of chocolate (using a vegetable peeler and a warmish chocolate bar). The cake can also be offered with a pureed raspberry or strawberry sauce, garnished with chocolate shavings, or left as is, with a citrus leaf, a sweetheart rose, or several berries in the center.

Passover Carrot Spice Torte

Makes 10 to 12 servings

You may not go back to conventional carrot cake after you try this delight. Nice and moist.

6 eggs, separated
¼ teaspoon salt
1½ cups granulated sugar
1 tablespoon Passover vanilla sugar
2 tablespoons orange juice
¼ cup matzoh meal
¼ cup matzoh cake meal
1¼ cups ground toasted nuts (almonds or
  walnuts)
1 teaspoon ground cinnamon
¼ teaspoon ground ginger
¼ teaspoon ground allspice
Zest of 1 lemon, finely minced
1 cup carrot puree (see Note)

NOTE: To make carrot puree, boil 4 to 6 medium carrots in water. Once they are tender, mash them with a fork or puree them in a food processor until smooth.

Preheat the oven to 350°F. Generously grease a 9- or 10-inch tube pan and line the bottom with a circle of parchment paper.

Place the egg whites in a large mixing bowl with the salt. Whip on slow speed, just to foam up the whites. Then increase the speed, and dust in ½ cup of the granulated sugar while beating the whites, until they hold stiff, glossy peaks. Set aside.

In a separate bowl, beat the egg yolks until they pale, then slowly add the remaining 1 cup of granulated sugar, beating until the mixture thickens. Blend in the vanilla sugar, orange juice, matzoh meal, cake meal, ground nuts, spices, and lemon zest.

Stir the carrot puree into the egg yolk mixture. Then fold one third of the whipped egg whites into the yolk mixture to lighten it. In 2 more additions, fold the remaining whites gently into the batter. Spoon the batter gently into the prepared pan.

Place the cake in the oven and immediately reduce the heat to 325°. Bake until the cake springs back when lightly pressed (50 minutes to 1 hour). Cool in the pan for 20 minutes before removing to a serving plate.

Seder Strudel Roll

Makes 2 to 3 dozen pieces

More of a cookie roll than a traditional strudel, this confection has "bubbie" written all over it.

PASSOVER STRUDEL DOUGH
½ cup vegetable oil
⅓ cup granulated or brown sugar
1 tablespoon Passover vanilla sugar
¼ teaspoon salt
2 eggs
2–4 tablespoons ginger ale
1¼ cups potato starch
1 cup matzoh meal

FILLING
1 cup raspberry, strawberry, or peach jam
1½ cups sweetened coconut
1 cup chopped semi-sweet chocolate or
   chocolate chips
1 cup coarsely chopped nuts
2 teaspoons ground cinnamon
1 cup either leftover macaroons; chopped
   Passover jelly candies; chopped Turkish delight;
   or chopped raisins

GLAZE/TOPPING
1 egg, beaten
Granulated sugar, for sprinkling

DOUGH: In a medium bowl, stir together the oil, granulated or brown sugar, vanilla sugar, salt, eggs, and most of the ginger ale. Stir in the potato starch and matzoh meal, adding enough ginger ale to make a soft, just rollable dough. Let the dough stand for 10 to 15 minutes to allow the matzoh meal to swell and absorb the liquid. Moisten it again with additional ginger ale if required. Divide the dough in half.

Preheat the oven to 350°F. Line a baking sheet with parchment paper.

On a sheet of parchment or wax paper dusted with potato starch, roll out one portion of dough at a time into a rectangle approximately 5 by 10 inches. (Alternatively, chill the dough for 15 minutes, dust your hands with potato starch, and instead of rolling the dough, press it out into a rectangle.)

FILLING: Spread half the filling ingredients over the dough. Using the paper as an aid, roll up the dough into a log. Brush the top with the beaten egg and sprinkle with sugar. Repeat with the remaining dough, filling, and topping.

Transfer the logs to the baking sheet and score them into 1-inch sections. Bake until lightly golden, about 35 minutes. Cool, then, using a very sharp knife, cut the scored sections into slices. (Or, freeze the log whole and cut it before serving.) This roll is pastrylike when freshly baked; storing it in plastic wrap will change the texture, making for a slightly moister pastry—delightful either way!

Decadent Fudge Brownies
with Glossy Fudge Frosting

Makes 30 squares

Just wonderful even when it is not Passover—fudgy, dense, delicious. Another "most requested" recipe.

BROWNIES
2 cups granulated or brown sugar
1 cup (2 sticks) unsalted butter or unsalted
  Passover margarine, melted and cooled
3 eggs
1 tablespoon brewed coffee
3/4 cup unsweetened cocoa powder, sifted
1/4 teaspoon salt
1 scant cup matzoh cake meal
1/2 cup finely chopped toasted walnuts (optional)

GLOSSY FUDGE FROSTING
2/3 cup water or brewed coffee
7 ounces semi-sweet chocolate, coarsely chopped
2 tablespoons unsalted butter or Passover
  margarine, softened

TOPPING
Finely chopped nuts (optional)

Preheat the oven to 350°F. Lightly grease a 7 by 10-inch rectangular baking pan, a 9-inch square pan, or an 8- or 9-inch springform pan.

BROWNIES: In a bowl, mix the sugar into the melted butter, then the eggs, coffee, cocoa, salt, cake meal, and toasted walnuts, if using.

Spoon the batter into the prepared pan and bake for about 25 minutes. Do not overbake. The brownies should be set and seem dry to the touch, but there should not be a crust around the sides. Cool in the pan.

FROSTING: Heat the water or coffee in a small saucepan. As it comes to a boil, reduce the heat and stir in the chopped chocolate. Remove the pan from the stove and stir until the chocolate is thoroughly melted. Cool in the refrigerator for about 30 minutes. Whisk in the softened butter or margarine and spread the frosting on top of the cooled brownies. Decorate the top by running the tines of a fork through the frosting and sprinkle with additional chopped nuts, if desired. Cut into squares or (if baked in a round pan) into wedges.

Extraordinary Macaroon Fudge Bars

Makes about 30 squares

This recipe should be subtitled, "what to do with those leftover macaroons from the second Seder."
Take some of those store-bought macaroons (chocolate for chocolate addicts; vanilla for a nice contrast)
and dice them up. They bake up into sweet and chewy little nuggets of flavor in a dense, fudgey bar—sort
of like a Mounds bar in a brownie. Leave them plain or frost them with Glossy Fudge Frosting (page 298)
or Chocolate Glaze (page 224), if you wish. This is another recipe to make year round.

6 ounces semi-sweet chocolate
1 cup (2 sticks) unsalted butter or unsalted
  Passover margarine
1¼ cups granulated or brown sugar
1 tablespoon Passover vanilla sugar
3 eggs
¾ cup matzoh cake meal
¼ cup potato starch
¼ teaspoon salt
1½ cups lightly packed quartered or coarsely
  chopped Passover macaroons (any brand
  or flavor)

Preheat the oven to 350°F. Lightly grease an 8 by 10-inch or 7 by 11-inch brownie pan or (in a pinch) a 9 by 9-inch baking pan will do.

In a saucepan, melt the chocolate and butter or margarine over low heat. Cool to room temperature. Stir in the brown and vanilla sugars, eggs, cake meal, potato starch, and salt. Stir in the macaroon pieces.

Spoon the batter into the prepared pan and bake for 40 to 50 minutes, until the top seems set and is beginning to take on a crackled appearance. Do not overbake. The brownies should be set and seem dry to the touch, but there should not be a dry crust around the sides.

Cool the brownies in the pan until serving time or, let them cool to room temperature if frosting. Cut into squares.

Double Chocolate Chip Cookies

Makes about 4 dozen cookies

Extra chocolate chips entice chocolate lovers; the cookie crunch is satisfying for all noshers.
If you prefer, substitute raisins for the chocolate and add chopped nuts. If you are not serving these
for a Seder supper, I would strongly suggest you use the butter rather than all margarine.

1 cup (2 sticks) unsalted butter or unsalted
  Passover margarine, plus 2 extra tablespoons
  margarine
1½ cups brown sugar
2 tablespoons honey
1 tablespoon Passover vanilla sugar
¼ teaspoon salt
2 eggs, at room temperature
1½ cups matzoh cake meal
¼ cup matzoh meal or finely ground walnuts
3 cups semi-sweet chocolate chips

Preheat the oven to 350°F. Lightly grease 2 baking sheets or line them with parchment paper.

In a mixing bowl, cream the butter and/or margarine with the brown sugar, honey, vanilla sugar, and salt. Add the eggs and blend very well. Fold in the cake and matzoh meal or ground nuts. Stir in the chocolate chips.

Drop onto the baking sheets in large tablespoonfuls 2 inches apart. *Press down* with the back of a wet spoon to flatten. Bake until slightly golden, 12 to 15 minutes. These cookies are fragile just after baking but firm up as they cool. Cool well on the baking sheets, or chill in the refrigerator for easier handling.

Crisp and Chewy Chocolate Chip Cookies

Makes 4 to 5 dozen cookies

A delicate, oversized, thin-but-chewy cookie that is addictive. You can add spices if you like, or use miniature chocolate chips or chopped chocolate. Yes, this recipe really calls for 1 cup of potato starch.

1⅓ cups brown sugar
½ cup granulated sugar
1 tablespoon Passover vanilla sugar
¾ cup (1½ sticks) unsalted butter or unsalted Passover margarine
2 eggs
½ teaspoon salt
1 cup matzoh cake meal
1 cup potato starch
2 cups chocolate chips

In a large mixing bowl, cream the brown, granulated, and vanilla sugars with the butter or margarine. Blend in the eggs. Stir in the salt, matzoh cake meal, and potato starch. Fold in the chocolate chips. Chill the dough for 1 hour or overnight for chewy-style cookies; do not chill for thin and crisp cookies.

Preheat the oven to 350°F. Line 2 baking sheets with parchment paper.

Scoop out generous teaspoonfuls of dough or roll marble-sized balls. Place on the baking sheet, leaving room for the cookies to spread. If using cold dough, press it a little; if using fresh dough (not chilled), do not press down.

Bake for 12 to 15 minutes, then cool on the baking sheets for 20 to 30 minutes. Use a metal spatula to remove the cookies to a serving platter. (Or, if you have room, place the baking sheets in the refrigerator to hasten cooling.)

VARIATION: For Pecan Sandies, replace the chocolate chips with chopped pecans. Replace the granulated sugar with an additional ½ cup brown sugar.

Passover Blondies

Makes 30 to 40 blondies

A rich bar with a smooth caramel taste. Especially good cold.

1½ cups brown sugar
¼ cup granulated sugar
1 tablespoon Passover vanilla sugar
1 cup (2 sticks) unsalted butter or unsalted
  Passover margarine
2 eggs
½ teaspoon salt
1 cup matzoh cake meal
1 cup potato starch
1 cup coarsely chopped semi-sweet chocolate
1 cup coarsely chopped walnuts or pecans

Line an 8 by 10-inch brownie pan with greased foil, leaving enough overhang to lift out the baked blondie.

In a large mixing bowl, cream the brown, granulated, and vanilla sugars with the butter or margarine. Blend in the eggs. Stir in the salt, cake meal, and potato starch. Then fold in the chocolate and nuts. Chill the batter for 20 minutes.

Preheat the oven to 350°F.

Spread or press the batter into the prepared pan. Bake for 35 to 40 minutes, until the center is just set, not jiggly. Cool well, then use the foil to lift the blondie from the pan. Cut into serving-sized squares.

Passover Puff Rings
or Passover Paris Brest

Makes 12 to 15 puffs

Reminiscent of classic French pastries, these can be made ahead and completed just before serving. Fill them with fresh fruit, nondairy tofu sherbet, or mousse for an elegant and easy dessert.

1 cup water or orange juice
$\frac{1}{4}$ teaspoon salt
2 tablespoons Passover vanilla sugar
1 tablespoon fresh finely minced orange zest
$\frac{1}{2}$ cup vegetable oil
$1\frac{1}{4}$ cups matzoh meal
4 eggs

FILLING AND TOPPING
Fresh fruit, berries, nondairy mousse, or frozen
   nondairy sorbets suitable for Passover
Pureed berries or purchased chocolate syrup

NOTE: If not using a pastry bag, use an oiled hand, or a large soup spoon to ladle the dough onto the pan.

Preheat the oven to 400°F. Line a cookie sheet with parchment paper.

In a medium saucepan, combine the water or juice with the salt, vanilla sugar, orange zest, and oil and stir over medium heat to dissolve the sugar. When the mixture reaches a brisk boil, add the matzoh meal all at once, stirring well with a wooden spoon until the mixture pulls away from the sides of the pan. Shake the pan over the heat a little more to dry out the "dough" (it should be a rounded, paste-like mass).

Transfer the dough to a mixing bowl and let it cool for 5 minutes. Add the eggs, one at a time, mixing vigorously by hand or with an electric mixer after each addition.

Using a pastry bag fitted with a large plain or star tip (see Note), deposit rounded lumps of dough on the prepared baking sheet. Bake until puffed up and doubled in size (50 to 60 minutes). Cool well on the baking sheet.

TO ASSEMBLE CREAM PUFFS: Split each cream puff in half. Spoon or pipe in the filling of your choice, cover lightly with the top half of the pastry, and drizzle on pureed berries or chocolate syrup.

Pesach Sugar Cookies

Makes 2 to 3 dozen cookies

Don't be surprised by the crushed potato chips.
They give the cookies their delicate taste and short crumb. Substitute nuts, if you prefer. This is a light and buttery sugar cookie that is ideal for the Passover cookie jar or as an elegant sweet for coffee or tea. You can also use this recipe to make jam sandwich cookies.

½ cup (1 stick) unsalted butter or unsalted
  Passover margarine, softened
⅓ cup granulated sugar, plus additional for
  sprinkling
1 tablespoon Passover vanilla sugar
1 egg
½ cup crushed salted potato chips (see Note)
1 teaspoon finely minced lemon zest (optional)
½ cup potato starch
¼ cup matzoh meal
½ cup matzoh cake meal

NOTE: If you use nuts instead of potato chips, add ¼ teaspoon salt to the batter.

Preheat the oven to 350°F. Line a baking sheet with parchment paper.

In a mixing bowl, cream the butter or margarine with the ⅓ cup granulated sugar and the vanilla sugar until very fluffy. Blend in the egg, then fold in the remaining ingredients. Blend until the mixture is smooth and holds together.

Chill for several hours or overnight.

Roll out to ¼ inch thick on a board sprinkled with potato starch. Cut into 3-inch rounds and sprinkle with additional granulated sugar, if desired. Alternatively, roll the dough into walnut-sized balls and press down with the bottom of a drinking glass dipped in sugar to flatten.

Bake on the prepared sheet until lightly golden (14 to 16 minutes). Cool on the sheet for 8 to 10 minutes, then remove to a wire cake cooling rack.

VARIATIONS: For Spice Cookies, replace the granulated sugar with brown sugar. Add ½ teaspoon ground cinnamon, and ¼ teaspoon ground cloves, allspice, or mace along with the matzoh meal.

For Chocolate Chip or Jam Thumbprints, make an indentation in the center of each cookie and press in either a few chocolate chips or a small dollop (½ teaspoonful) of apricot or strawberry jam.

Make the cookies miniature-sized (¾-inch rounds), bake and toss in Passover confectioners' sugar (regular or mix with some cinnamon).

For Chocolate Dipped Cookies, dip half of each cookie in melted semi-sweet chocolate after the cookies have cooled.

Passover Honey Nut Cake
in Soaking Syrup

Makes 10 to 12 servings

*The Middle Eastern tone is part of this cake's appeal.
A very nutty cake is suffused with a honey-citrus soaking syrup, much like baklava in concept but
flour-free, making it suitable for Passover. A little goes a long way. For large Seder crowds, you can
double the recipe and bake it in a 9-inch springform pan or a 9 by 13-inch rectangular pan.
I serve this cake cut into small squares or diamonds placed in small muffin liner cups. Copeland Marks,
in his book* Sephardic Cooking, *attributes this to Turkish cuisine. Joan Nathan calls it "Tishpishiti"
in her book,* Jewish Cooking In America *and points to Syrian, as well as Turkish roots as does
Claudia Roden in her book,* Mediterranean Cookery. *A nutty classic indeed! My version is
inspired by a recipe simply called "Nut Cake," found in* From My Grandmother's Kitchen,
*by Viviane Alcheck Miner with Linda Krinn. If you are interested in Sephardic recipes
along with a very engaging family history, this book is a real find.*

CAKE
³/₄ cup granulated sugar
¹/₄ cup brown sugar
¹/₄ cup vegetable oil
3 eggs
3 tablespoons orange juice
1 teaspoon finely minced orange zest
¹/₄ teaspoon salt
¹/₄ teaspoon ground cinnamon (or ¹/₂ teaspoon
  for a more pronounced cinnamon flavor)
¹/₂ cup matzoh cake meal
¹/₂ cup finely chopped hazelnuts or almonds
1 cup finely chopped walnuts

SOAKING SYRUP
²/₃ cup granulated sugar
¹/₄ cup honey
¹/₃ cup orange juice
¹/₄ cup water
1 tablespoon lemon juice
¹/₄ teaspoon ground cinnamon

continued

Preheat the oven to 350°F. Generously grease a 7-inch round layer cake pan (if you do not have one, you can use a round foil pan of the same or similar size available in the supermarket baking aisle).

CAKE: In a medium-sized mixing bowl, using a wire whisk, beat the granulated and brown sugars with the oil and eggs until the mixture is thick and pale yellow. Stir in the remaining batter ingredients. Turn the batter into the prepared pan.

Bake for 35 to 40 minutes, or until the top is light brown and set. Cool for at least 20 minutes. Meanwhile, prepare the Soaking Syrup.

SOAKING SYRUP: In a medium saucepan, combine the ingredients. Heat to dissolve the sugar and simmer for 5 to 10 minutes, until the mixture becomes syrupy. Cool well.

Pour the cooled syrup over the cooled cake, poking holes in the cake with a fork, to permit the syrup to penetrate. Allow it to stand for 2 to 4 hours to absorb the syrup. I prefer to refrigerate this cake so that while it is absorbing the liquid, it is also firming up. Also, chilling the cake offsets its sweetness and makes it easier to cut. Serve it on splayed muffin liners.

Light and Crisp Meringue Mandelbrot

Makes 20 to 25 slices

This exceptionally crisp and light nut, chocolate, and raisin cookie contains no oil.
Rather sophisticated and unique.

3 egg whites, room temperature
½ cup granulated sugar
2 teaspoons Passover vanilla sugar
⅓ cup potato starch
Zest of 1 orange, finely minced
Zest of 1 lemon, finely minced
1 teaspoon Passover almond extract (optional)
Good pinch of ground cinnamon
⅓ cup finely ground almonds, preferably toasted
½ cup blanched whole almonds
¼ cup blanched whole hazelnuts
½ cup raisins (plumped [page 22], dried, and chopped)
¼ cup chocolate chips

Preheat the oven to 350°F. Grease a small loaf pan (about 7 by 3½ inches—a small foil one works well but any loaf pan will do). Line the pan with greased foil leaving enough overhang to lift out the loaf after baking.

In a large bowl, with clean, dry beaters, whip the egg whites slowly, dusting in the granulated and vanilla sugars gradually. As the egg whites begin to foam increase the speed and whip until stiff and glossy. Fold in the remaining ingredients.

Spoon the batter into the prepared pan and bake until lightly browned on top (35 to 45 minutes). Cool in the pan, then remove, using the foil overhang to assist you, and wrap the loaf tightly in foil. Refrigerate or freeze it overnight.

The next day, preheat the oven to 325°F. Line a baking sheet with parchment paper.

Using a very sharp, serrated knife, cut the loaf into ½ inch slices. Places the slices on the baking sheet and bake to dry out, about 15 minutes per side. These will crisp as they cool.

Seder Kamishbrot

Makes 2 to 2½ dozen cookies

*You may use any liquid to replace the ginger ale in this recipe—cola, wine, lemonade, or orange juice.
My friend Heidi Cooney tested this and claims it is just "great"!*

1 cup vegetable oil
¾ cup granulated sugar
2 tablespoons finely minced lemon zest
2 tablespoons Passover vanilla sugar
3 eggs
½ cup ginger ale or lemony soda
2½ cups matzoh cake meal
2 tablespoons potato starch
¼ teaspoon salt
¼ teaspoon ground cinnamon
1 cup semi-sweet chocolate, coarsely chopped
1 cup ground walnuts

FOR SPRINKLING (OPTIONAL)
¼ cup granulated sugar
2 teaspoons ground cinnamon

Preheat the oven to 350°F. Line a large baking sheet with parchment paper.

In a large bowl, whisk together the oil, granulated sugar, lemon zest, vanilla sugar, and eggs and beat well for 3 minutes. Stir in the ginger ale, then fold in the cake meal, potato starch, salt, and cinnamon. Fold in the chocolate and nuts.

Using lightly oiled hands, shape the batter into two logs, 10 to 12 inches long by 3 inches wide. Place the logs on the baking sheet and bake until lightly colored (25 to 30 minutes). Cool on the baking sheet 10 to 15 minutes. Reduce the oven temperature to 325°. Slice the logs about ¾ inch thick. Place the slices on the baking sheet and bake for 15 to 25 minutes more, until the cookies begin to color. Turn once during baking.

Cool the cookies, then toss in the sugar and cinnamon, if desired, or leave plain.

VARIATION: For chocolate cookies, substitute cola or brewed coffee for the ginger ale. Add 2 tablespoons of unsweetened cocoa powder with the dry ingredients. You can dip the cooled cookies in melted semi-sweet chocolate, if desired.

Passover Double Chocolate Biscotti

Makes about 2 dozen slices

¾ cup vegetable oil
½ cup granulated sugar
½ cup brown sugar or granulated sugar
1 tablespoon honey
1 tablespoon Passover vanilla sugar
¼ cup unsweetened cocoa powder
3 eggs
2 tablespoons brewed coffee
¼ teaspoon of salt
¼ cup matzoh meal
1¼ cups matzoh cake meal
2 tablespoons potato starch
¾ cup coarsely chopped semi-sweet chocolate
¼ cup finely ground walnuts

Preheat the oven to 350°F. Line a large baking sheet with parchment paper. Alternatively, generously grease an 8 by 4½-inch loaf pan.

In a large bowl, whisk together the oil, granulated and brown sugars, honey, vanilla sugar, and cocoa. Whisk in the eggs, then stir in the coffee, salt, matzoh meal, cake meal, and potato starch. Let stand for 10 minutes, then fold in the chocolate and nuts.

Using lightly oiled hands, shape the batter into two logs and place them on the baking sheet. If using the loaf pan, pour or spoon the batter into the pan. For logs, bake until set (25 to 30 minutes). For the loaf, bake until the top seems set and is slightly cracked (35 to 40 minutes). Refrigerate the logs or loaf, well wrapped in foil, for a couple of hours to firm up.

Preheat the oven to 325°F. Cut the log or loaf into slices about ¼ inch thick. Place the slices on a parchment-lined baking sheet and bake for 15 to 20 minutes to dry out, turning once mid-way.

Passover Pecan Bars

Makes 3 to 4 dozen bars, depending on size

Bake these in a 9 by 13-inch pan for a great bar.
Bake in a smaller pan for a square reminiscent of pecan pie.

BASE
½ cup matzoh meal
1 cup matzoh cake meal
½ cup ground toasted pecans
1 cup brown sugar
¼ teaspoon salt
½ teaspoon ground cinnamon
1 cup (2 sticks) unsalted butter or unsalted
   Passover margarine
1 egg yolk

FILLING
4 eggs, lightly beaten
2 tablespoons unsalted butter or unsalted
   Passover margarine, melted
1⅓ cups brown sugar
Pinch of salt
½ cup Passover maple table syrup
1 teaspoon lemon juice
1 tablespoon Passover vanilla sugar
½ cup chopped pecans
½ cup shredded coconut (optional)

Preheat the oven to 350°F. Lightly grease a 9 by 13-inch loaf pan or an 8 by 11-inch brownie pan.

BASE: In a large mixing bowl, combine the matzoh meal, cake meal, pecans, brown sugar, salt, and cinnamon. Cut or work in the butter or margarine to make a crumbly mixture. This can be done in a food processor. Stir in the egg yolk. Press the dough firmly into the prepared pan and bake for 20 to 25 minutes, until the edges are just starting to brown. Let cool for 15 minutes. Do not turn off the oven.

FILLING: In a bowl, whisk together all the ingredients. Pour over the baked and cooled base. Bake for 20 to 25 minutes. Cool well, then chill in the refrigerator until serving time. Cut into small squares to serve.

Sticky Cherry Compote

Makes about 8 servings

This compote is a baked rather than stewed fruit mixture that fairly shines with a cherry and wine gloss.

2 cups pitted prunes
1 cup dried apricots
1 cup dried peaches or pears
1 cup yellow raisins
1 (19-ounce) can cherry pie filling (see Note)
1 (10-ounce) can mandarin orange segments
1 (14-ounce) can pineapple chunks
2 cups red wine

NOTE: If you require kosher cherry pie filling and cannot find it, this recipe can be made with canned sweet or sour water-packed cherries. Drain the canned cherries, reserving the juice. Heat the cherries in a saucepan with two thirds of the reserved juice and ⅓ cup sugar (or less, depending on how sweet the cherries are). In a small bowl, mix the remaining juice with 2 to 3 tablespoons potato starch. As the cherries come to a gentle boil, stir in the starch mixture. Allow the mixture to return to a boil, reduce the heat, and stir gently until the mixture thickens. Cool well before using. Then continue with the recipe using the cherries in place of the canned pie filling.

In a medium saucepan, combine the dried fruit (not the raisins). Cover with water and simmer over low heat to plump (about 5 minutes). Drain, reserving the liquid.

Preheat the oven to 350°F.

In a medium-sized oven-proof dish with a lid, stir together the drained dried fruit with the remaining ingredients. Bake for about 40 minutes to meld the flavors. If, after baking the mixture seems too thick, loosen it by adding a small amount of reserved liquid from the simmered fruit.

Serve warm or chilled, in wine or cognac glasses.

Passover Praline-Covered Truffles

Makes about 2½ dozen truffles

My Matzoh buttercrunch gets a revamp in this recipe. Crushed into a crumbly meal, the matzoh butter-crunch makes a fine praline-like coating for these truffles. Serve in miniature paper candy or chocolate cups (available at candy-making supply stores or gourmet kitchen supplies). These taste nutty—but are not—and are the most elegant Passover item you may ever make.

COATING
4–6 unsalted matzoh sheets
1 cup (2 sticks) unsalted butter or unsalted
  Passover margarine
1¼ cups firmly packed brown sugar

TRUFFLES
1½ cups water, cola, or brewed coffee
2 cups (8 ounces) coarsely chopped semi-sweet
  chocolate

Preheat the oven to 350°F. Line a cookie sheet completely with foil. Cover the bottom of the pan with baking parchment, on top of the foil. This is very important since the mixture becomes sticky during baking.

Line the bottom of the pan evenly with the matzoh, cutting extra pieces of matzoh, as required, to fit any spaces on the cookie sheet as evenly as possible.

COATING: In a 3-quart, heavy-bottomed saucepan, combine the margarine or butter and brown sugar. Cook over medium heat, stirring constantly, until the mixture comes to a boil. Boil for 3 minutes, stirring constantly. Remove from the heat and pour over the matzoh.

Place in the oven and bake for 15 to 20 minutes, checking every few minutes to make sure the mixture is not burning (if it seems to be browning too quickly, remove from the oven, lower the heat to 325°, and replace).

Remove from the oven and stack the matzoh on a plate and place in the refrigerator or freezer to chill very well. When very chilled, break up the matzoh and grind to a medium coarse meal in a food processor. Set aside.

TRUFFLES: In a medium-sized saucepan, heat the water, cola, or coffee to a gentle boil. Stir in the chopped-up chocolate. Reduce the heat and whisk well to melt the chocolate into a thick, smooth consistency. Pour into a heat-proof bowl and cool for about 20 minutes. Cover lightly and freeze or refrigerate several hours or overnight.

To make the truffles, use a melon baller, miniature ice-cream scoop, or a teaspoon. Dig out the balls (about a tablespoon of truffle mixture) and round into a ball about ¾ inch thick. Toss or coat in the matzoh praline crumbs. Repeat until all of the chocolate mixture is used up. Place the truffles in a candy cup and store in a covered container in the refrigerator or freezer until ready to serve.

VARIATIONS: Truffles can be tossed in cocoa powder instead of matzoh praline crumbs. (Or do some in each, for eye appeal.)

For Double-Dipped Truffles, coat the truffles once in matzoh praline crumbs. Chill well. Dip each truffle into room temperature, melted, semi-sweet chocolate. Leave as is or recoat in matzoh praline crumbs.

Imberlach Passover Farfel Nut Candy

Makes 4 to 6 servings

This Passover-style "peanut brittle" is guaranteed to evoke many memories. Matzoh farfel, a kind of "chunky-style" matzoh, is often used in Passover dishes. Here it is the main component of the recipe.

2 cups honey
1 cup sugar
½ cup chopped walnuts
3 cups matzoh farfel
¼ to ½ teaspoon ground ginger
¼ teaspoon ground cinnamon

Line a cookie sheet with parchment paper or cover it with lightly greased foil.

In a medium-sized saucepan, stir together the honey and sugar. Over very low heat, melt the honey and sugar and allow the mixture to bubble gently or come to a boil. Stir in the walnuts, farfel, ginger, and cinnamon and cook until just amber colored. The mixture cooks quite quickly at this point; do not allow it to become too brown.

Spread out on the prepared pan 1 inch thick. As it sets, mark the candy into portions with a knife. Chill until completely hardened and cut into squares.

Homemade Matzoh

A few years ago, when my kids were in nursery school,
I made it my business to sign up for the "make-your-own-matzoh" field trip to the local matzoh factory.
Actually, the "factory" was a seasonal endeavor. Special Passover matzoh bakers leased a space in a large
synagogue kitchen and prepared the "matzoh shemurah." As a community courtesy, they also took the time
to teach avid young bakers the secrets to homemade—or noncommercial—matzoh.
This matzoh is certainly not in accordance with Passover law.
To be "kosher for Passover" the wheat must come from special, well-guarded fields
and be processed in special flour mills; and the process of making the matzoh dough must not take more
than eighteen minutes. Longer than eighteen minutes would mean that fermentation might occur, via
natural means. A nice, fun, pre-Passover baking project.

2 cups all-purpose flour
1 cup whole-wheat flour

Preheat the oven to 450°F. Line 2 large baking sheets with parchment paper.

In a large bowl, mix the 2 flours and add water until you have a soft, kneadable dough. Knead for about 5 minutes. Let the dough rest for a couple of minutes.

Break off egg-sized portions of dough. Stretch each portion as thin as you can before rolling it into even thinner, oval slabs. Prick each slab with a fork or pastry docker. Place them on the baking sheets and, as soon as the sheet is filled, place it in the oven. Bake until the matzoh is crisp and buckled, about 3 minutes. Cool and eat.

Passover "Rolls"

Makes 12 puffs

Serve these with butter, jam, or cream cheese, or fill them with any sandwich filling you like. These "rolls" can also be made into oblong Passover "hot dog" buns for children. Miniatures are called "soup nuts."

2 cups water
4 teaspoons salt
4 teaspoons sugar
1 cup vegetable oil or unsalted Passover margarine, melted
2⅔ cups matzoh meal
8 eggs

Preheat the oven to 425°F. Line 2 baking sheets with parchment paper.

In a medium-sized saucepan over low heat, combine the water, salt, and sugar and stir to dissolve the sugar. Add the oil or melted margarine and heat until the mixture reaches a brisk boil. Add the matzoh meal all at once, stirring well with a wooden spoon until the mixture pulls away from the sides of the pan. Shake the pan over the heat a little more to dry out the "dough" (it should be a rounded, paste-like mass). Transfer the dough to the bowl of a food processor and let it cool for 5 minutes. Meanwhile, break the eggs into a small bowl.

With the motor running, and using the feed tube of the processor, add the eggs, one at a time, allowing each one to be thoroughly incorporated before adding the next one. Or, beat the matzoh meal mixture vigorously with one egg at a time, using a wire whisk, a wood spoon, or an electric mixer.

Use a medium-sized oiled ice cream scoop or soup spoon to dispense dollops of dough onto the prepared baking sheets or oil your hands and form dough into rounded mounds. You can also use a pastry bag fitted with a large plain tip to dispense batter in mounds or hot dog bun oblongs. Place the baking sheets in the oven. After 20 minutes, reduce the heat to 400°.

Bake until the mounds puff and double in size (45 to 50 minutes). (For lighter puffs, bake longer; for moister puffs, bake a little less.) Cool well.

9. Shavuot

Festival of Weeks

Their innate majesty impresses every heart; their warnings reverberate in every conscience. Jew and Gentile alike confess their power. These commandments are written on the walls of Synagogue and Church; they are the world's laws for all time.

—M. JOSEPH, 1903

No religious document has exercised a greater influence on the moral and social life of man than the Divine Proclamation of Human Duty, known as the Decalogue. These ten brief commands speak not only of outer actions, but also of the secret thoughts of the heart. In simple, unforgettable form, this unique code of codes lays down the fundamental rules of Worship and of Right for all time and for all men.

—J. H. HERTZ, 1930

And He gave us this land, a land flowing with milk and honey.

—THE TORAH

THE FEAST OF WEEKS

WHEN ❀ In the Hebrew calendar, seven weeks after the end of Passover, the sixth and seventh day of Sivan. The period between Passover and Shavuot is called "Omer," after the early maturing grain, the first crop, barley.

CORRESPONDING TO ❀ May-June.

HOLIDAY CONTEXT ❀ This holiday has dual roots founded in both the agricultural calendar and in Jewish history.

The earliest references to Shavuot, also known as *Hag Habikkurim* or Festival of the First Fruits, describe it as a celebration of the first harvest. Many, many years ago, the farmers of Israel would bring a portion of this first harvest to Jerusalem to honor God and as a symbolic gesture of thanksgiving.

An explanation with more religious overtones came many years later. This explanation for Shavuot is that it celebrates Moses' bringing down the Ten Commandments from Sinai. In a way, since Shavuot follows Passover, it is seen almost as an extension of the observance. When the Jews wandered for forty years following their flight from Egypt, they were given the two tablets inscribed by Moses as he, according to the Bible, documented God's word that, in a brief 120 Hebrew words, were to guide them in every facet of human interaction.

The Jews, having received the Commandments, were about to experience their first kosher meal, but they had no time to kosherize their cooking implements. Logistically, therefore, it was easier to prepare a dairy meal. Another possible explanation for eating dairy is that the new land where the Jews ended their trek, was rich with "milk and honey," as it is mentioned in the Talmud. Dairy foods, therefore, symbolize this happy discovery.

ACTIVITIES/CUSTOMS ❀ Shavuot-related liturgy is recited in synagogue at Shavuot services, which include reading the Book of Ruth. In general, Shavuot does not call on the same food symbols as other holidays (at least in North America), but its association with the eating of dairy foods is quite strong. Shavuot seems like celebration of the very best of Jewish dairy recipes. Dishes such as blintzes and dairy kugels, rich in milk, cheese, and butter, are typical Shavuot fare. With research, one may also find recipes for cookies made in the shape of tablets in honor of the Commandments. Cheesecakes are appropriate, as are any recipes that rely on dairy products.

Malai, or Romanian Cottage Cheese and Cornmeal Kugel Casserole

A couple of years ago, my mother handed me a recipe on an index card, entitled "Mrs. Pesner's Johnnycake." Mrs. Pesner was an old and dear family friend. Apparently, well into her eighties, she still entertained friends, albeit modestly, and would serve this dish. The recipe was both intriguing and simple—a cornmeal batter base and a slightly sweetened cottage cheese filling. Very unusual. Why would a recipe with the American appellation of "Johnnycake" be in Mrs. Pesner's file? And what about the cottage cheese filling? In any case, unfortunately, I misplaced the recipe. Then I got to writing this cookbook and remembered it. I described the recipe to a friend who seemed at once to know what I was talking about. "Of course," she said. " 'Malai,' that's absolutely delicious!" Well I asked more people, and some had heard of it. The rest, like me, couldn't begin to imagine what it would taste like. Cornmeal and cottage cheese? Exotic, to say the least.

So I researched it and, soon enough, recipes in old Jewish cookbooks revealed similar dishes called either "malai" or "mamaliga with cheese." The former referred to a dish with a cornmeal base, swirled with either a salty or sweetened cheese and sour cream or yogurt filling. The latter, mamaligina with cheese, seemed to be a Jewish version of polenta, the Italian cooked cornmeal dish. "With cheese" signified a variation that added cheese on top of the cooked cornmeal. More often than not, the references mentioned that the dish was a Romanian specialty. Interestingly, the various recipes were significantly different from one another. Some layered cornmeal batter alternately with cheese batter; some simply topped the baked cornmeal with melted cheese; some called for baking powder in the cornmeal batter, while others relied on yeast; some called for several eggs; others called for but one, or asked that the whites be mounted and folded in separately. The common thread was the cornmeal and cheese.

I culled several recipes to come up with a definitive malai. Some called for quite a bit of butter (too rich, I thought), some relied on skim milk (okay, but not as luscious as a sour cream–based malai). It turns out that malai is quite easy to make and yields something absolutely ambrosial. Malai whips up as fast as Jell-O and results in a casserole or cheese kugel–type dish that is outstanding. It is a foundation of moist corn cake, topped or marbleized with a sweetened cottage cheese filling. You can make it in a variety of ways, but you wind up with something that looks like a cross between a cheesecake and a kugel and tastes like a blintz or a cheese bagel. Malai was a major success. I took one to my neighbor Brenda and shared much of it with our surrogate bubbie, Doris Leibovitch. Kudos and "may-I-have-the-recipe?" rang in my ears immediately.

And then . . . I called my mother-in-law in Florida. "Ever hear of malai?" I ventured. She called out to her sister, my aunt Florence (aka, Faigie). "Faigie, listen, ever hear of this dish called malai made with cornmeal and cottage cheese?" "Why, that's johnnycake and cottage cheese!" she replied. Full circle.

Malai can be served for Chanukah or to break the fast on Yom Kippur, but it is especially appropriate for Shavuot since it is cheese based.

This dish can be made ahead and microwaved to serve hot, with sour cream or yogurt, or served at room temperature, in wedges, with cherry topping or sour cream. Call it whatever you like, but try it. It's a gem.

Malai Romanian Cottage Cheese Cornmeal Kugel

Makes 8 to 10 servings

A great dish for after the fast. Easily made ahead, can be served hot or cold.

BATTER
1/3 cup unsalted butter, melted, or vegetable oil
1/3 cup sugar
2 eggs
1/4 cup milk
1/3 cup sour cream or plain yogurt
1 cup all-purpose flour
1 cup cornmeal
2 teaspoons baking powder
1/4 teaspoon salt

CHEESE FILLING
1 pound dry cottage cheese
1/3 cup sugar
1 teaspoon vanilla extract
2 eggs
1/2 cup sour cream or plain yogurt
Pinch of salt

TOPPING
Sour cream or plain yogurt
Cherry pie filling, warmed (optional)

Preheat the oven to 350°F. Grease an 11 by 7-inch rectangular dish. (If using Pyrex, reduce the oven heat to 325°.) You can also make this dish in a 9- or 10-inch springform pan.

BATTER: In a large mixing bowl, stir together the butter or oil and sugar. Blend in the remaining ingredients to make a smooth batter. Set aside.

FILLING: In a bowl, cream the cottage cheese with the sugar. Blend in the remaining ingredients.

Spoon half the cornmeal batter into the prepared pan. Top it with half the cheese filling, then finish with more cornmeal batter and cheese filling. You can marbleize this, if you wish, by gently swirling a butter knife through the mixture.

Bake until the casserole seems set, (40 to 50 minutes). Serve it warm or cold, cut in generous squares, with sour cream or yogurt spooned on top, or warm cherry pie filling. To reheat, microwave individual portions on a serving plate, (35 to 45 seconds).

Smoked Salmon, Dill, and Cream Cheese Brunch Pizza

Makes three 9-inch pizzas

This is perfect for lunch, brunch, or early supper, combining 2 of the best flavors in Jewish cuisine: lox and cream cheese. Hold the bagels—bring on the pizza! Usually, I make the dough for this in the bread machine.

QUICK PIZZA SPONGE
1 cup warm water
¾ teaspoon dry yeast
2 teaspoons sugar
1¼ cups unbleached all-purpose flour

PIZZA DOUGH
All the sponge from above
½ cup warm water
1¼ teaspoons salt
2 tablespoons olive oil
½ teaspoon baking powder
2½ cups bread flour

TOPPING (FOR 1 PIZZA, TRIPLE FOR ENTIRE RECIPE)
2 teaspoons olive oil
1 small clove garlic, finely minced
Salt and pepper to taste
⅓ cup crumbled feta cheese
¼ cup cream cheese
1 small red onion, sliced thin
¼ cup sliced black olives (any type)
2 small plum tomatoes, sliced
1 tablespoon chopped fresh dill
Approximately 2 ounces lox, minced
Sesame seeds, for sprinkling

QUICK PIZZA SPONGE: In a bowl, whisk together the water, yeast, and sugar. Let the mixture stand for a couple of minutes, then stir in the flour to make a soft, puddinglike batter. Cover the sponge with plastic wrap and let it stand anywhere from 30 minutes to overnight (the longer the better, but even a half hour will make for a better-flavored and -textured pizza).

DOUGH: Stir down the sponge mixture and add the dough ingredients. Knead for 8 minutes to make a soft dough. Cover and set aside to rise for 30 minutes. Gently deflate the dough and let it rise again until needed (1 to 3 hours).

To make the pizza, divide the dough into 3 pieces. Flatten each one to make a 9-inch disc. Cover with a tea towel and let rest for a few minutes. Preheat the oven to "Broil," (though the pizza goes in the oven not the broiler). Place the pizza on a baking sheet and set it on the lowest rack in the oven. (Check often to ensure it does not burn.) Allow the pizza to bake for a few minutes so that the top surface chars a bit (5 to 8 minutes). Remove it from the oven. Reduce the oven temperature to 475°.

TOPPING: On the charred surface, spread the olive oil and garlic, salt, and pepper. Spread out the feta and cream cheese (in dollops). Top with the remaining ingredients. brush the rim with olive oil and sprinkle on the sesame seeds. Bake on the middle rack of the oven until the top is bubbling and the rim is colored, (7 to 12 minutes).

Delicatessen-Style Classic Sour Cream Coffee Cake

Makes 14 to 16 servings

One of the nicest, tallest, richest, most statuesque renditions of a typical Jewish-style sour cream coffee cake. It is also one of the first cakes I ever made. On nothing-to-do days, my next-door neighbor and I would often decide to bake. Our first effort was cream puffs; our second was this sour cream coffee cake. To us, it seemed like such an adventure! But it turned out beautifully. At that time, I thought sour cream coffee cake was incredibly original, but of course, it is a Jewish kitchen classic, although you will see a myriad of different versions—some with more sour cream, some with less, some with less flour, some with more butter, and so on. All good, all trouble-free. This cake is moist and tender and keeps fresh for days—another one of those melt-in-your-mouth types. The recipe can be halved, or make two 9 by 5-inch loaves and freeze one. Also good for Yom Kippur or a dairy Sabbath meal, this cake is rich in the good dairy flavors that celebrate Shavuot.

CAKE
1 cup (2 sticks) unsalted butter
2½ cups granulated sugar
4 eggs
1 tablespoon vanilla extract
1–2 drops almond extract (optional)
2 teaspoons very finely minced lemon zest
4 cups all-purpose flour
½ teaspoon salt
1 teaspoon baking soda
4 teaspoons baking powder
Pinch of grated nutmeg
1¾ cups sour cream
¼ cup milk

STREUSEL FILLING/TOPPING
½ cup brown sugar
2 tablespoons granulated sugar
2 teaspoons ground cinnamon
¼ teaspoon ground mace or grated nutmeg (optional)
½ cup chopped walnuts

Preheat the oven to 350°F. Generously grease a 10-inch tube or angel food cake pan or two 9 by 5-inch loaf pans, or a Bundt cake pan. Line the pan(s) (except the Bundt pan) with parchment paper. For the Bundt pan, make sure each fluted crevice is extra well greased.

CAKE: In a bowl, cream the butter with the sugar until light and fluffy. Blend in the eggs, vanilla, almond extract (if using), and lemon zest. In another bowl, whisk together the dry ingredients. Fold them into the egg mixture, alternating with the sour cream and milk to make a smooth batter. Scrape the sides and bottom of the mixing bowl to ensure no globs of butter and sugar remain uncombined.

STREUSEL FILLING/TOPPING: In a small bowl, combine all the ingredients and set aside. Spoon one third of the batter into the pan, toss on one third of the filling, repeat with more batter, more filling, and more batter, ending with more filling on top.

Bake tube, angel food, or Bundt cakes for 60 to 70 minutes, until the top is set and slightly crusty; 55 to 60 minutes for loaf cakes. Cool for 30 minutes in the pan before removing to a serving plate.

Montreal Cheese Bagels

Makes about 1 dozen cheese bagels

This dough is flaky and delicate. If you are in a hurry, substitute store-bought puff pastry dough. This recipe is similar to the one by Montreal Jewish cooking maven, author, and cooking teacher, Norene Gilletz. Her book, Second Helpings, *is a part of many kitchen libraries in these parts. These bagels freeze well.*

MOCK PUFF DOUGH
½ cup (1 stick) unsalted butter, cut into chunks
2 cups unbleached all-purpose flour
¼ teaspoon salt
2 teaspoons baking powder
1 tablespoon sugar
½ cup sour cream
1 egg

FILLING
1 pound dry cottage cheese (also known as hoop or baker's cheese or no-curd, dry cottage cheese)
1 egg
2–6 tablespoons sugar (to taste)
Pinch of salt
Squirt of lemon juice
1 tablespoon flour

TOPPING (OPTIONAL)
1 egg
Fine sugar, for sprinkling

DOUGH: Place the dry ingredients in a food processor. Pulse to blend. Add the butter chunks and pulse to cut the fat into the flour. Add the sour cream and egg and process to form a soft dough. Wrap the dough in plastic wrap and chill for about 20 minutes.

FILLING: In a bowl, blend all the ingredients and chill for 10 minutes.

Preheat the oven to 350°F. Line a baking sheet with parchment paper.

To form cheese bagels, divide the dough in half. On a lightly floured board, roll out one portion in an oblong ¼ inch thick. Place half of the filling along one edge. Roll halfway, then cut the roll you have formed away from the remaining body of the dough. Repeat. Cut into 8-inch lengths and place on the baking sheet. Curve the rolls into horseshoe shapes, pinching the ends together to seal a bit.

TOPPING: Brush (if desired) with beaten egg and sprinkle very lightly with fine sugar.

Bake for about 40 minutes, or until the cheese bagels are lightly browned.

BABKA BASICS

Homemade babka is one of those things that will surprise you. First, it looks as professional—no matter how inept you think you are—as bakery babkas. Second, it is the most versatile, supple, easy-to-work-with dough in the world. Third, babka is rarely as rich and flavorful from a bakery as it is when made at home. This is because many babkas from the bakery are made with leaner, cheaper "coffee cake" dough—simply a sweet yeast dough. Butter, egg, and sour cream–laced babkas are not inexpensive for the commercial baker. Few bakeries, save only a couple of very elite ones, can afford to offer this sort of product anymore. They would have to charge inordinate amounts of money for what looks like a very unassuming cake. So, if you want a real, old-fashioned babka, it's best to make it yourself.

You make babka dough by hand, creaming the butter with the sugar, blending in the dissolved yeast and the eggs, then the other ingredients. You can also make babka by hand by cutting the butter into the dough, much like preparing pie dough.

Other options for making babka include the bread machine or food processor, providing you have a large-capacity processor (eight to ten cups). Bread machines also make perfect babka dough.

Both methods are explained below.

Babka dough is fine with all-purpose flour, and that is what I have stipulated in the recipes in this book. If you have a choice, however, it is wise to use some bread flour in a babka recipe, as it is sufficiently higher in protein than all-purpose flour and will offer the strength this rich dough needs. When I make babka for my family, I use either two thirds all-purpose flour, and one third bread flour or half bread, half all-purpose flour for optimal tenderness and chewiness. Try these flour combinations if you want a babka that is truly reminiscent of a professional bakery.

Babka Better Than the Bakery's Chocolate, Cinnamon, or Poppy Babka

Makes 1 large or 2 medium babkas

*This ridiculously easy babka tastes like chocolate swirl danish.
It can be made with poppy seed paste or cinnamon glaze as well (see page 176). This babka calls for
dry milk powder (a professional baker's trick). Since yeast does not dissolve very well in milk,
the pros use water and add the richness of milk in its dry form later on. Milk powder (or skim milk
powder) helps with dough texture and strength.*

BABKA DOUGH
1½ cups water
2 tablespoons dry yeast
¾ cup plus a pinch of sugar
2 eggs plus 2 egg yolks
1 teaspoon vanilla extract
1 teaspoon lemon juice
2 drops almond extract
1 teaspoon salt
⅓ cup milk powder
1 cup (2 sticks) unsalted butter, softened, in
    small pieces
Approximately 6 cups all-purpose or bread flour
    or equal amounts of the two

FILLINGS
Chocolate, Cinnamon, Almond, Poppy, or Prune
    (see page 330)

EGG WASH/TOPPING
1 egg, beaten
Sugar, for sprinkling

**NOTE: This recipe requires a machine
with a one-and-a-half-pound capacity or
larger. If you have a smaller machine, you
will have to divide the dough in two and
knead in two shifts.**

DOUGH: In a large mixing bowl, whisk together the
water, yeast, and pinch of sugar. Let the mixture
stand for about 5 minutes to allow the yeast to swell
and dissolve. Stir in the eggs, yolks, vanilla, lemon
juice, almond extract, ¾ cup of sugar, salt, and milk
powder. Fold in the softened butter and the flour.
Mix the dough, then knead as it becomes a mass
(with a dough hook or by hand), for 8 to 10 minutes,
until it's smooth and elastic.

Processor Method for Large-Capacity Processor

Bread dough made in a processor can be dense, but babkas, since they are rich coffee cakes rather than lean breads, do quite well using this method. If you have an eight- to ten-cup-capacity food processor, you can use it to make this babka dough. In a measuring cup, stir together the water, yeast, and pinch of sugar. Allow the mixture to stand for a few minutes. In a medium bowl, whisk together the eggs and yolks, vanilla, lemon juice, and almond extract.

Place the flour, salt, and ¾ cup of sugar, and milk powder in the food processor work bowl. Add the butter, then process, to cut the butter into the flour, pulsing until the mixture is grainy. Add the dissolved yeast and the egg mixture and pulse to incorporate the liquid and dry ingredients to form a soft mass of dough. This should take under a minute. Remove from the work bowl and turn out onto a lightly floured board. Knead for 5 minutes by hand to make the dough smooth.

Bread Machine Method for Babka Dough

Set your machine on the Dough cycle. Place the water, yeast, and pinch of sugar in the bread machine pan. Let the machine heat up while the yeast is dissolving in the water.

Add the eggs, vanilla, lemon juice, almond extract, ¾ cup of sugar, the salt, milk powder, and any other additions, and a cup of the flour. On top of the flour, place the cut-up chunks of softened butter. Add the remaining flour.

Often, rich doughs, such as babka dough, and/or those exceeding four cups of flour need assistance in the initial part of the Dough cycle. Using a rubber spatula, move the flour from the sides or corners into the center and make sure the dough is being mixed. Once a mass is formed, the dough will begin to make a ball that is more cohesive. Dust in additional flour as required to make a soft, bouncy ball. Let the dough rise in the machine, then remove and gently deflate the dough before proceeding with the recipe as written.

Place the dough in a well-greased bowl and place the entire bowl in a plastic bag. Seal the bag and allow the dough to rise until puffy (45 to 90 minutes). (You can also refrigerate the dough overnight and continue with the recipe the next day, allowing the dough to warm up a bit first).

Divide the dough into 2 equal parts. (To use all the dough to make 1 large babka, see below.) Cover them with a tea towel and let them rest for 10 minutes. Line a large baking sheet with parchment paper or generously grease two 9-inch springform or layer cake pans. If making one large babka, generously butter a 10-inch tube pan.

On a lightly floured board, roll one piece of the dough into a 16-inch square. Arrange or spread the filling of your choice all over the dough surface. Roll up the dough into a large jelly roll. Cut the roll in half. Place the 2 pieces side by side in the prepared pan—it doesn't matter if they are a little squished. Brush the top with egg wash and sprinkle it with some sugar. Place the pan in a plastic bag and let the dough rise until it is flush with or over the top of the pan (45 to 60 minutes).

Repeat with the other half of the dough, using the same or a different filling, as you prefer.

Preheat the oven to 350°F.

To use all the dough in 1 large babka, roll all the dough into a 20-inch square and proceed as above. A large babka is especially dramatic, but 2 smaller ones give you 2 flavor and assembly options.

Bake the babka for 35 to 45 minutes (50 to 70 minutes for the large babka), until the babka is medium brown. Cool in the pan for 15 minutes before removing the babka(s) to a rack or serving plate.

Variety Fillings for Your Basic Babka

I call these fillings my babka "wardrobe." A simple change of filling and your babka becomes a new coffee cake. Each filling makes enough for 1 medium babka. Double the recipes if making a large babka.

CHOCOLATE SMEAR

1¹/₂ cups semi-sweet chocolate chips
¹/₂ teaspoon ground cinnamon
¹/₄ cup unsweetened cocoa powder
¹/₂ cup granulated sugar
3 tablespoons unsalted butter or margarine

Grind all the ingredients in a food processor to make a loose paste. You can also use a chopped-up, imported Swiss semi-sweet or milk chocolate bar.

CINNAMON SMEAR

¹/₄ cup (¹/₂ stick) unsalted butter
1 cup brown sugar
2 tablespoons corn syrup (or maple syrup)
2–4 teaspoons ground cinnamon
³/₄ cup chopped walnuts (optional)

In a food processor, process all the ingredients to make a loose paste.

ALMOND FILLING

¹/₄ cup (¹/₂ stick) unsalted butter, in bits
¹/₄ cup apricot jam
1 cup almond paste cut into small chunks
¹/₂ cup slivered almonds

For almond babka, arrange the butter bits, dollops of jam, and chunks of almond paste over the dough. Sprinkle on the slivered almonds. After the egg wash, sprinkle on a few more slivered almonds.

POPPY SEED OR PRUNE FILLING (See Hamantaschen Fillings, pages 254–256.)

Options in Babka Toppings

Babkas change appearance depending on how you finish them. Here are some classic options.

EGG WASH AND EXTRAS FOR EACH BABKA

1 egg, beaten, brushed over top
Coarse sugar (optional, available at decorating stores, bakeries, or by mail order)
Ground walnuts
Slivered almonds
Poppy seeds (if filling with poppy-seed filling)

CRUMB TOPPING FOR EACH BABKA

2 tablespoons unsalted butter or margarine, melted
1/4 teaspoon ground cinnamon (optional)
1/3 cup confectioners' sugar
1/4 cup flour

In a bowl, mix all the ingredients together to make a crumbly topping. Sprinkle this over the risen babka *before* baking.

CHOCOLATE DRIZZLE

1/2 cup semi-sweet or milk chocolate, melted and slightly cooled

This is drizzled over the *baked* babka and is especially good with a Chocolate Smear–filled loaf.

CONFECTIONERS' SUGAR Dust the *baked, cooled* babka with confectioners' sugar.

APRICOT GLAZE

1/2 cup apricot preserves

Warm the preserves and strain out any fruit pieces. Brush lightly over the baked, cooled babka.

Blueberries 'n Cream and Lemon Lime Curd Tart

Makes 8 servings

*A modest cheesecake in a pastry crust, topped with tangy lemon lime curd and blueberries.
The creamy filling together with the snappy yellow topping make this summery and light. You may use
raspberries to replace the blueberries.*

½ recipe My Favorite Pie Pastry (page 135) or
prepared pastry for a single 9-inch crust

FILLING
1 pound cream cheese, softened
½ cup granulated sugar
1 tablespoon finely minced lemon zest
3 eggs
1 teaspoon vanilla extract
1 tablespoon lemon juice
Tiny pinch of salt

ZESTY LEMON LIME CURD (SEE NOTE)
1½ cups water
1 cup granulated sugar
4 egg yolks
6 tablespoons cornstarch
½ cup fresh lemon juice
¼ cup fresh lime juice
1 tablespoon finely minced lemon zest
1 tablespoon unsalted butter

TOPPING
2 cups blueberries
Confectioners' sugar
Lemon shreds
Lemon leaf (optional)

Preheat the oven to 350°F. If you want a more browned tart shell, prebake the tart bottom for 8 minutes at 400°. Allow it to cool well before filling. (This is optional.)

FILLING: In a mixing bowl, cream the cheese with the sugar and lemon zest. Add the eggs and blend well. Stir in the vanilla, lemon juice, and pinch of salt. Spoon the filling into the prepared crust and bake for 30 to 35 minutes. Remove from the oven and chill for 2 hours.

LEMON LIME CURD: In a medium saucepan, heat together 1¼ cups of the water and ¾ cup of the sugar. In a medium bowl, stir together the egg yolks, the remaining ¼ cup of sugar, the remaining ¼ cup of water, and the cornstarch. Bring the sugar and water to a boil and stir in the egg yolk mixture, whisking constantly to blend the ingredients and prevent scorching. Stir over medium heat until the curd has thickened and reached a custardlike consistency, 1 to 2 minutes. Remove from the heat and stir in the lemon and lime juices and the zest. Last, stir in the butter and cool to room temperature (if using right away) or cover with plastic wrap and refrigerate.

Spread the lemon lime curd on the chilled tart. Top with fresh berries, dust with confectioners' sugar and lemon shreds, and a lemon leaf, if desired.

NOTE: You can use purchased lemon pie topping, packaged lemon pie filling, or a jar of lemon curd.

Yogurt Banana Cake

Makes 12 to 16 servings

*I make this cake with sour cream, buttermilk, or yogurt,
depending on what I have on hand. A tender, moist, cake.*

CAKE
1 cup (2 sticks) unsalted butter
2 cups granulated sugar
4 eggs
1 teaspoon vanilla extract
¼ cup warm, brewed coffee
½ cup plain yogurt (or sour cream or
  buttermilk)
1 cup mashed bananas
3 cups all-purpose flour
½ teaspoon salt
1 tablespoon baking powder
1 teaspoon baking soda

CHOCOLATE CREAM CHEESE ICING (SEE NOTE)
4 ounces cream cheese, softened
¼ cup (½ stick) unsalted butter
1 teaspoon vanilla extract
⅓ cup unsweetened cocoa powder, sifted
3–4 cups confectioners' sugar
2–8 tablespoons brewed coffee or water,
  as required

NOTE: You can also use a plain chocolate frosting, as for Chanukah Gelt Double Fudge Chocolate Layer Cake, page 230.

Preheat the oven to 350°F. Generously grease a 9 by 13-inch rectangular pan or a 10-inch tube pan.

CAKE: In a large mixing bowl, cream the butter with the sugar. Add the eggs one at a time, until well blended. Stir in the vanilla, coffee, yogurt, and bananas. Fold in the dry ingredients. Spoon and spread the batter into the pan and bake until the cake springs back when gently touched or pressed (50 to 55 minutes). Cool for 15 minutes in the pan then move to a wire rack until the cake reaches room temperature.

ICING: In a mixing bowl, blend the cream cheese and butter together. Stir in the vanilla, cocoa, and enough confectioners' sugar to obtain a spreadable consistency. Blend on medium speed, adding brewed coffee or water as required to make a light frosting. Spread on the cooled cake.

New Wave Chocolate Tunnel Cake

Makes 12 to 16 servings

*A luscious "tunnel" of cream cheese and chocolate chips make this cake
the most talked-about item on any sweet table. The cake is easily mixed by hand and the
glaze is optional, since the cake is magnificent alone. The original Tunnel of Fudge Cake was a
Pillsbury Bake-Off winner and featured a fudgey layer running through a chocolate butter cake.
The cake inspired Pillsbury to launch a line of Bundt cake mixes.*

CAKE
1 cup granulated sugar
1 cup brown sugar
1 cup vegetable oil
2 large eggs, lightly beaten
2 teaspoons vanilla extract
2 teaspoons baking soda
2 teaspoons baking powder
½ teaspoon salt
¾ cup unsweetened cocoa powder, sifted
3 cups flour
1 cup buttermilk
1 cup warm, brewed coffee

TUNNEL FILLING
¼ cup granulated sugar
1 (8-ounce) package cream cheese, softened
1 teaspoon vanilla extract
1 egg
1 cup miniature semi-sweet chocolate chips

GLAZE (OPTIONAL)
1 cup confectioners' sugar
3 squares unsweetened chocolate, melted and
   cooled
2 tablespoons unsalted butter
Hot water to thin, if needed

Preheat the oven to 350°F. Generously grease a 10-inch Bundt or tube pan (a Bundt is better).

CAKE: In a large mixing bowl, combine the sugars, oil, and eggs and beat for 1 minute until smooth. Add the remaining cake ingredients and beat on medium for 2 to 3 minutes (use a whisk if doing this by hand). Set the cake batter aside.

FILLING: In another bowl, cream the sugar with the cream cheese, then add the vanilla, egg, and chocolate chips and blend until smooth. Ladle half the batter into the pan. Spoon the filling evenly over this layer. Cover with the remaining batter. Bake for 70 minutes, or until the top springs back when touched.

Let the cake cool for at least 30 minutes before removing it from the pan. If the cake sticks, place it on a warm burner to loosen it up and help release it. The cake firms up as it cools.

GLAZE: In a bowl, combine all the ingredients to form a pourable glaze, thinning with water if necessary. Pour over the cooled cake.

This cake freezes well wrapped airtight, and keeps for several days, covered, at room temperature.

CHEESECAKE 101

"The artichokes in vinaigrette were passing fair, the smoked quail was nice, and the auberges au gratin, pleasant but oh . . . that *cheesecake!"*

What is it about cheesecake that immediately inspires glamour? Is it the decadence of pure, rich cream cheese baked until just set and held within a light buttery crust, or is it the crown of crimson summer strawberries, shimmering under a halo of light apricot glaze? Whatever it is, there is definitely something about cheesecake, homemade or served in restaurants, that strikes even a hard-core anti-dessert person's fancy. "Oh no, I'm too full for dessert" is somehow forgotten as guests mysteriously regain their appetite (or forget their diet) and offer forth their plates for a slice.

Most chefs, both domestic and professional, will claim to have the absolute best cheesecake. No other recipe, save perhaps, Toll-House cookies, can account for such disproportionate culinary ego. Long after even a Cordon Bleu meal fades to Cheshire-cat-like memory, the taste of a superb cheesecake seems forever recorded on one's tastebuds. In all honesty, however, I have never tasted a truly "bad" cheesecake, providing it was made with quality ingredients. The rivalry is not between the good and bad cheesecakes, but rather between the superlative, the phenomenal, and the extraordinary. What determines the quality of cheesecakes seems to be based on three components: the recipe; the technique; and finally, the finishing of the baked cake.

The basic premise is to start with the best ingredients cold cash can procure, since cheesecake is essentially a cake of few, but choice ingredients. The cake can be made with ricotta cheese, cottage cheese, and tofu with admirable results. But for that truly classic texture, pure fluffy cream cheese is a must.

Depending on your location, cream cheese may be offered by several reputable companies. Search out those companies whose cream cheese is without chemical additives and has a light appealing texture to start with. Avoid cream cheese that seems gluey or compacted.

Now that you've invested in the cheese, consider those other ingredients. Eggs, unless otherwise specified should be size large. *Extra*-large eggs might offset a presumably perfect balance of liquid to solid. As for sugar, generally granulated white sugar is called for, although additions of honey and/or brown sugar do wondrous things for maple or pumpkin cheesecakes. Most recipes require anywhere from three quarters of a cup of sugar to upward of double that amount, according to the size and type of recipe. This can be altered to suit personal taste without compromising the final results. These three ingredients, cream cheese, sugar, and eggs, occur in almost all cheesecakes. Everything else, including the crust or bottom (some cakes are made without one), is a variable.

Additions of sour cream, whipping cream, preserves, nuts, and liqueurs are all happily subject to each recipe or chef's creative intervention. Cheesecake technique is another matter altogether, for the best recipe improperly prepared may be tasty but not outstanding.

Special cakes demand special pans, and cheesecake is a perfect example of "special." Cheesecake or "springform" pans allow the chilled cake to be properly unmolded for serving without marring the cake surface or gouging out its sides. A good choice is the American-made Hillside springform pan, as it has particularly high sides, which provide necessary support for large cheesecakes and also allow you to garnish the top of the cheesecake with the pan as a support to the cake side or edges. Pans made of tin tend to bend more easily and are less durable overall. If you have this sort of pan, make sure you clean and dry it very well after use, and take care to handle the clip mechanism carefully.

Preparing the crust and bottom is generally a short and easy task, but one that should be done before you begin the cheesecake batter. The only issue here is whether or not to grease the pan. Logic dictates that a greased pan would help when unmolding the cake. Experience tells me that the cake rises higher if you allow the delicate batter to cling to ungreased sides.

Preparing cheesecake batter begins with one absolute must, which is to work with all ingredients at room temperature. This allows for the proper incorporation of eggs and will ultimately result in the best texture and maximum volume. Properly creaming the cheese with the sugar and eggs is another absolute must. Do not undercream the cheese—make sure it is smooth and pliant, and add the eggs one by one until thoroughly blended. The batter should be as homogenous as possible. Do not be alarmed if it seems too liquid. At this point, an electric mixer becomes a virtual necessity; food processors and blenders just don't perform as well here. Resist the temptation to mix on the highest speed and settle instead for a conservative slow to medium speed. This prevents too much air from being incorporated into the batter, which only causes irreconcilable rifts and cracks in the surface of your finished product.

Most recipes call for a moderate oven, although some start with relatively high heat for a short, initial period of time with substantial reductions soon after. It is best to adhere to the particular recipe you are using.

The important issue here is how to avoid the greatest of all cheesecake evils: cracks—hairline, San Andreas, and otherwise. There are two methods of prevention, one popular, one much less so. Method number one subscribes to the notion of cooling the cake gradually. First the oven heat is turned off and the cake "rests" in the closed oven for an hour. Then, it either rests some more at room temperature or is placed in the refrigerator. Gradually cooling the cake should help prevent cracking, since the changes in temperature occur slowly.

Method number two, which works best for me, but which alarms most people, is to refrigerate the baked cake immediately. Again, most bakers regard this as sheer heresy, but success, however illogical, is difficult to criticize.

Yet another ploy, which works well in that it produces a crack-free, creamy, luscious cheesecake is to bake your cheesecake in a water bath. Not everyone wants to bother with this step, but it does produce an outstanding cake. For baking a cheesecake within a water bath, cover the outside of your cheesecake pan with a double layer of aluminum foil to protect against possible leaks. Fill a large, shallow roasting pan with water. Place the filled cake pan in this water—the water should reach to two thirds of the way up the sides of the pan—and bake, as per recipe instructions.

It is now twenty-four hours later and your cheesecake is no longer an infant dessert but a mature gateau. (Incidentally, refrigeration for a minimum of twelve hours, preferably twenty-four, is a must, for the cake must be thoroughly "set" and chilled before decorating and serving.) All that remains is to top your triumph. Canned cherry topping is the usual, and while it is not novel, I have never seen anyone avoid a cheesecake because of it—in fact, it gets devoured first. Cheesecake is rich, and fruit toppings are especially appealing. Aside from canned cherry (or blueberry, pineapple, apple, and so on) you can opt for fresh fruit toppings (slices of fresh fruit glazed with strained, warmed apricot jam), or try nut-crunch topping for pumpkin or pecan cheesecakes. A dark chocolate glaze makes a marble cheesecake a visual delight. Grand desserts take grand finales, and professional bakers will always find the time and imagination to remember the light dusting of ground nuts or chocolate shavings or to furnish a lace doily. The way the cake tastes is the final test, but its visual impact is prime, especially as it sits on a dessert trolley or party buffet.

The final frontier: cutting the cheesecake. Again, one has a choice of two noble alternatives. The first choice is to cut the cake with a long knife (not serrated) dipped in hot water and cleaned before each cut. The second method is to cut the cake using unwaxed dental floss held taut across the cake. Cuts are made by simply lowering the dental floss through the cake and pulling away the cord, much like using a wire to cut through potter's clay. Either method yields perfect, cleanly executed cake portions.

Unless they are garnished with fresh fruit, most cheesecakes freeze exceptionally well. And finally, no matter what the holiday, cheesecake, like bagels and babkas, is always appropriate.

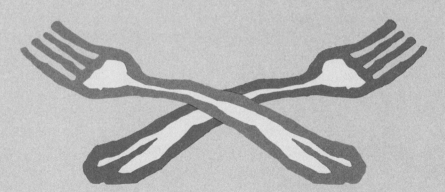

Hungarian Cheesecake

Makes 10 to 12 servings

I don't know why this style of cheesecake is called "Hungarian." But it is delicious.

SWEET TART CRUST
1/4 cup granulated sugar
1 1/2 cups all-purpose flour
1/4 teaspoon salt
1 egg yolk
1 tablespoon lemon juice
1/2 cup (1 stick) unsalted butter, softened

CHEESE FILLING
1 1/2 pounds dry cottage cheese
Pinch of salt
3/4 cup granulated sugar
2 tablespoons all-purpose flour
2 tablespoons cornstarch
1 cup sour cream
1 teaspoon vanilla extract
4 eggs plus 1 egg yolk
1/2 cup yellow raisins, plumped (see page 22) and chopped
1/2 cup well-drained crushed pineapple

TOPPING
Confectioners' sugar, for dusting

Preheat the oven to 350°F. Generously grease a 9-inch springform pan or a 9-inch deep quiche or tart pan with a removable bottom.

CRUST: In a medium-sized bowl, combine the sugar, flour, and salt. Make a well in the center and stir in the egg yolk, lemon juice, and butter. Mix with your fingertips until the dough is blended and pat into a flattened disc. Wrap the disc in plastic and chill for 10 minutes. Roll out half the dough to cover the pan bottom, patching in any areas that tear. Prick the dough with a fork in several places and bake for 15 to 20 minutes, or until the crust is golden brown. Remove from the oven and let cool.

FILLING: In a mixing bowl, cream the cottage cheese with the salt and sugar. Then, fold in the flour and cornstarch and blend well. Stir in the sour cream, vanilla, eggs, and yolk. Fold in the raisins and pineapple. Spread the filling over the cooled crust. Roll the remaining dough into 12 pencil-thin strips. Arrange the strips on top of the cake in a lattice pattern. Bake for 8 to 10 minutes, until light golden brown on top. Chill for several hours or overnight.

Dust with confectioners' sugar before serving.

White Chocolate Truffle and Raspberry Cheesecake

Makes 14 to 16 servings

*This cake is over the top—both in appearance and taste. Don't let the components intimidate you—
it can be made in steps, over a day or two. You can even freeze the baked cheesecake and garnish it with the
white chocolate topping and raspberries an hour or so before serving. The big tip here is to work with
melted white chocolate at room temperature. A version of this recipe of mine first appeared in Bon Appetit.*

CRUST
1¼ cups finely ground shortbread cookie
  crumbs
2 tablespoons granulated sugar
¼ cup ground almonds
⅓ cup unsalted butter, melted
2 drops almond extract

FILLING
4 ounces white chocolate, melted and cooled
2 pounds cream cheese, at room temperature
1¼ cups sugar
3 tablespoons flour
1 teaspoon vanilla extract
¼ teaspoon almond extract
4 large eggs
1 cup seedless raspberry preserves

WHITE CHOCOLATE GLAZE
¾ cup light cream
4 ounces white chocolate, coarsely chopped
¼ teaspoon vanilla extract

GARNISH
Warmed apricot jam (about ¼ cup)
Toasted slivered almonds (optional, to decorate
  sides)
Raspberries
White chocolate shavings

RASPBERRY SAUCE
1 (10-ounce) package frozen raspberries
1–2 tablespoons confectioners' sugar

Preheat the oven to 350°F.

CRUST: In a large bowl, mix all the ingredients lightly with a fork. Press into the bottom of a 10-inch springform pan.

FILLING: Melt the white chocolate over simmering water or in the microwave and allow it to cool. In a bowl, cream the cream cheese with the sugar and flour until smooth. Stir about ⅓ cup of the cheese mixture into the melted white chocolate (this tempers the chocolate). Then add this mixture to the main cheese mixture and add the vanilla and almond extract. Beat in the eggs, one at a time. Pour half the batter into the prepared pan. Gently place half the raspberry preserves on top, then cover with the remaining batter. Bake until the cake is set and the top starts to brown lightly (45 to 50 minutes). Refrigerate the cake immediately for at least several hours or overnight.

GLAZE: In a saucepan, bring the cream to a gentle boil. Reduce the heat and add the chopped chocolate. Over low heat, stir to melt the chocolate into the cream. Remove the glaze from the stove, add the vanilla, and allow the glaze to cool very well. It will thicken as it cools. Pour over the center of the cake, allowing the excess to drip down the sides. Allow the glaze to set at room temperature.

GARNISH: Paint the sides of the cake with warmed apricot jam and, if you wish, press toasted slivered almonds all around. Garnish the cake with fresh whole raspberries and white chocolate shavings.

RASPBERRY SAUCE: Puree the raspberries and sugar in a blender. Strain to remove any seeds, if desired. Pass the sauce separately.

Deluxe New York–Style Strawberry Cheesecake

A large and luscious cheesecake, meant for big, festive gatherings. Creamy but not cloying,
this is a classic that takes well to many variations. Use the easy graham crust or try the Sweet Tart Crust
from the Hungarian Cheesecake (page 339) or a traditional graham crumb crust.

EASY GRAHAM CRUST
1½ cups graham cracker crumbs
¼ cup (½ stick) unsalted butter, melted
2 tablespoons brown sugar
¼ teaspoon ground cinnamon

FILLING
2½ pounds cream cheese, softened
1½ cups granulated sugar
¼ cup all-purpose flour
6 eggs plus 2 egg yolks
1½ teaspoons vanilla extract
1 tablespoon lemon juice
⅓ cup whipping cream
2 teaspoons *each* finely minced lemon and
    orange zest

SOUR CREAM TOPPING
2 cups sour cream
½ teaspoons vanilla extract
2 tablespoons granulated sugar

GLAZE/TOPPING
½ cup apricot jam
2–4 tablespoons water
1 pint fresh strawberries, hulled

Preheat the oven to 425°F.

GRAHAM CRUST: In a large mixing bowl, toss all the ingredients together to combine. Press into the bottom of a 10-inch springform pan. Chill while preparing the filling.

FILLING: In an electric mixer bowl, cream the cheese on slow speed and add the sugar and flour. Add the whole eggs, then the yolks, one by one, until thoroughly incorporated. Stir in the vanilla, lemon juice, cream, and zests. Pour the filling over the cooled crust and bake for 15 minutes, then reduce the heat to 225° and bake for an additional 55 to 60 minutes, until the cheesecake is just set but not browned. Do not let the cheesecake color or bake too long so that the sides begin to rise and show cracks.

SOUR CREAM TOPPING: In a small bowl, combine the sour cream, vanilla, and sugar and set aside.

Remove the cake from the oven and raise the oven temperature to 350°. Gently spread the sour cream topping over the cake and return it to the oven to bake for 8 minutes more. Transfer the cake immediately to the refrigerator to chill overnight.

GLAZE: In a saucepan, heat the jam on low with a little water. When the jam has melted and thinned, strain it through a fine mesh sieve and return it to the saucepan. Keep warm over low heat until needed, thinning it with additional tablespoons of water if the mixture thickens.

Unmold the chilled cake and brush the top with the apricot glaze. Arrange the strawberries in concentric circles, making sure all the cake surface is covered. Using a small pastry brush, gently brush additional apricot glaze over the fruit topping. Chill until serving time.

VARIATION: For Mixed Fruit Topping, instead of strawberries alone, garnish the cake with these fruits for an outstanding visual presentation: 1 pint fresh strawberries, sliced in half; 2 kiwi, sliced; and/or 1 (10-ounce) can mandarin orange slices, drained.

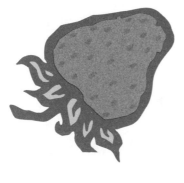

Caramel Cheesecake

Makes 10 to 12 servings

There are chocolate people and there are caramel types like me.
This is an ultra-smooth, caramel-laced cheesecake that takes only minutes to prepare. You can use any
chocolate-covered toffee bar in this recipe—Heath Bars are fine and, if you can find them,
Skor Bars are excellent.

CRUST
1¼ cups graham cracker crumbs
3 tablespoons brown sugar
¼ cup (½ stick) unsalted butter, melted
¼ cup butterscotch chips

FILLING
1½ pounds cream cheese, at room temperature
1 (14-ounce) can condensed milk
4 large eggs
2 teaspoons vanilla extract
1 tablespoon lemon juice
Very tiny pinch of salt
15 caramels, minced or quartered

SOUR CREAM TOPPING
1½ cups sour cream
½ teaspoon vanilla extract
1 tablespoon granulated sugar

GARNISH (OPTIONAL)
⅓ cup coarsely chopped chocolate-covered toffee
  bar, such as Heath or Skor

Preheat the oven to 375°F.

CRUST: In a food processor, pulse the ingredients together to make a crumbly mixture. This should take a few seconds. Press the mixture into the bottom of a 9- or 10-inch springform pan.

CHEESECAKE: Using an electric mixer, cream the cream cheese with the condensed milk until smooth. Beat in the eggs, one at a time, then the vanilla, lemon juice, and pinch of salt. Fold in the minced caramels. Pour the batter over the crust in the pan. Place in the oven and immediately reduce the temperature to 350°. Bake until the cake is set (about 45 minutes). Meanwhile, prepare the topping.

TOPPING: In a small bowl, stir together the sour cream, vanilla, and sugar. Remove the cake from the oven and gently spread this mixture over the top. Bake for an additional 5 to 8 minutes. Remove the cake from the oven and immediately refrigerate it for several hours or overnight. Sprinkle with the chopped toffee bar before serving.

VARIATION: For Creamy Vanilla Cheesecake, omit the butterscotch chips in the crust and the toffee garnish.

Fudge Top Marble Cheesecake

Makes 12 to 15 servings

*A dramatic version of a chocolate marble cheesecake: semi-sweet chocolate swirls
with a glossy fudge glaze.*

CRUST
1½ cups chocolate wafer cookie crumbs
¼ cup (½ stick) unsalted butter, melted
2 tablespoons brown sugar

FILLING
1 cup semi-sweet chocolate chips or coarsely
  chopped semi-sweet chocolate, melted and
  cooled to room temperature
2 pounds cream cheese, softened
¾ cup granulated sugar
2 tablespoons all-purpose flour
5 large eggs
1 teaspoon vanilla extract
⅓ cup half and half

SWISS FUDGE GLAZE
1 cup heavy cream
¾ cup coarsely chopped semi-sweet Swiss or
  imported chocolate
½ teaspoon vanilla extract

Preheat the oven to 425°F.

CRUST: In a bowl, mix the ingredients together until
evenly moistened. Press into the bottom of a 9- or
10-inch springform pan.

FILLING: In a double boiler, melt the chocolate and
set it aside to cool. In a bowl, cream the cheese with
the sugar and flour. Beat in the eggs, one by one, until
thoroughly incorporated. Stir in the vanilla and half
and half. Pour one third of the batter over the crust in
the pan. Pour another third into a mixing bowl and
stir in the cooled, melted chocolate. Pour this
chocolate batter into the springform pan, then add
the remaining vanilla batter. Create a marbleized
effect by gently swirling a knife through the batter.
Bake for 15 minutes at 425°, then reduce the heat to
225° and bake for another 45 to 50 minutes until the
cake seems set and not unduly jiggly. Immediately
refrigerate the cake for several hours or overnight.

GLAZE: In a saucepan, heat the cream to just
bubbling. Stir in the chopped chocolate all at once
and stir to blend the cream and chocolate. Remove
the pan from the heat and stir with a whisk until all
chocolate is melted. Stir in the vanilla. Cool to room
temperature before using.

When ready to serve, remove the cake from the
pan and pour the chocolate glaze over the cake
surface, spreading it evenly with a small spatula to
cover the top and sides. Let the glaze set for
15 minutes before serving.

Milchidig Marble Cake

Makes 12 to 16 servings

A superb butter cake with a swirl of chocolate throughout, topped by a glossy chocolate glaze. One of my favorite cakes, this appeals to all age groups and is great for any and all occasions, not just for Shavuot. Full of fresh dairy flavor, this cake is perfect at a milchidig brunch or anytime someone asks you to "bring something."

CHOCOLATE SYRUP

Scant ⅓ cup unsweetened cocoa powder
½ cup sugar
½ cup water
½ teaspoon vanilla extract

CAKE

1 cup (2 sticks) unsalted butter
2 cups sugar
2½ teaspoons vanilla extract
5 eggs
1 cup milk
3¼ cups all-purpose flour
½ teaspoon salt
1 tablespoon cornstarch
1 tablespoon baking powder

CHOCOLATE TOPPING

6 tablespoons unsalted butter
⅔ cup semi-sweet chocolate chips
½ cup sugar
½ cup half and half or evaporated milk
1 tablespoon cornstarch
Confectioners' sugar, for dusting (optional)

Preheat the oven to 350°F. Generously grease and flour a 9- or 10-inch tube or angel food cake pan. Line the bottom with parchment paper. You can also use a large Bundt pan, making sure each fluted indentation is well greased with shortening.

CHOCOLATE SYRUP: In a saucepan, combine the cocoa, sugar, and water. Simmer gently for 5 minutes. Remove from the heat and cool a minute. Stir in the vanilla and set aside.

CAKE: In a large mixing bowl, cream the butter until softened, then blend in the sugar until the mixture is light and fluffy. Stir in the vanilla, then the eggs, one at a time (if the batter seems curdled, stir in a little flour from the measured quantity). Stir in half the milk, then fold in the flour, salt, cornstarch, and baking powder, then the remaining milk, until the batter is smooth and well blended. Be sure to scrape down the bottom and sides of the bowl to incorporate all of the mixture.

Remove one third of the batter to a small bowl and stir in the cooled chocolate syrup. In dollops or large spoonfuls, ladle about two thirds of the vanilla batter into the prepared pan. Top this with big dollops of chocolate batter, then the remaining white batter. It really doesn't matter how you place the 2 batters—it all comes out in a nice design during the baking. Swirl a knife through the batter, if desired, or leave it as is. Do not stir or mix. Bake for about 1 hour, 10 minutes, until the cake springs back when pressed gently. Cool in the pan.

CHOCOLATE TOPPING: In a saucepan over low heat, heat the butter, chocolate, sugar, and ¼ cup of the half and half or evaporated milk to melt the chocolate. Stir to blend and bring to a gentle boil (just until beginning to bubble). Meanwhile, in a small bowl, stir together the remaining half and half and the cornstarch. Add the cornstarch mixture to the chocolate mixture, whisking as it cooks and thickens, reducing the heat as it does this. Stir until the glaze thickens, 2 to 3 minutes. Remove from the stove and cool to room temperature. This can be made in advance and stored in the refrigerator. Reheat it slightly before using.

When ready to serve, remove the cooled cake from the pan and drizzle the glaze over the top. Or decorate with only a light dusting of confectioners' sugar.

THE ROAD TO RUGELACH

Ask anyone, Jewish or not, about the best of Jewish baking, and you'll hear a familiar refrain: bagels, challah, cheesecake, and deli-style rye bread—just some of the most mainstream examples of Jewish baking. Add one more item, a little harder to pronounce, but definitely on everyone's list—rugelach. Also known by several aliases: roggles, ruggles, rogulah, rugulach, and sometimes "yeasted kipful" or "Hungarian crescents," but wonderful under any name.

Rugelach, in their definitive form, are delicate and pastrylike (but easy, easy, easy, to make) and usually fashioned in crescents. I have sometimes seen them rolled up in a jelly roll, cut into small slices, and baked in rounds. My friend Janet Goldstein, who tested a huge portion of this book, makes them as small twists. You can also make them as big as danish.

Jewish baking is full of legend, such as who's Mom makes the best honey cake, which Aunt made outstanding cheesecake, and who's Grandmother's challah is like velvet. Rugelach also inspires such legends. Whole companies make nothing but rugelach of all shapes, flavors, and descriptions. They will even mail you rugelach if you are desperate. But it is not necessary. Homemade rugelach is a snap to make with a dough that can be adapted to anyone's schedule.

The dough is the most versatile, easiest-to-work-with pastry on the planet. It can be yeasted or not. With yeast, and a short rise, you get a mini-danish-style pastry. Without yeast you wind up with a more flaky-crusted treat. The dough can also be cream cheese–based (see Cream Cheese Hamantaschen Dough, page 250) or enriched with milk or cream, or—most popular—enhanced with sour cream. Extra butter, ultra-rich doughs (like the Double Raspberry Sour Cream Rugelach, page 166) make for exceptional, pastrylike rugelach. Don't get too confused by all these choices. Just remember that even modestly buttery doughs (such as the recipe that follows) yield exceptional treats. Sour cream, yogurt, or milk tenderize the dough, butter makes it tasty and flavorful, eggs hold things together, and flour provides the bulk. You can always add extras such as lemon zest, vanilla, or almond flavoring. And then we get to the inside, the filling . . . now there's a dilemma.

What filling to choose? Traditional cinnamon, raisins, sugar, and nuts; or apricot butter and pecans; almond paste or chocolate chips; chunks of Turkish delight or a sprinkling of coconut; sour cherries and cranberries; tidbits of dates or prune butter? Choices, choices, choices—may all our problems be this big.

Traditional Rugelach

This is an excellent basic recipe that works with any filling.

DOUGH
3 cups all-purpose flour
½ teaspoon salt
¼ cup sugar
1¼ cups (2½ sticks) unsalted butter, cut into
    1-inch chunks
3 egg yolks
1 cup sour cream or plain yogurt

FILLINGS
Apricot or raspberry jam
Brown or granulated sugar
Ground cinnamon
Chopped nuts
Miniature chocolate chips
Shredded coconut
Dried cherries, raisins, or cranberries

GARNISH
Egg white or whole egg, beaten
Granulated or coarse sugar (optional)

In a large bowl, mix together the flour, salt, and sugar. Cut the butter into the dry ingredients until the mixture is crumbly. Make a well in the center and stir in the egg yolks and sour cream or yogurt to make a soft dough.

FOOD PROCESSOR METHOD: This dough can also be done in a food processor, which is usually the way I make it. Place the flour, salt, and sugar in the work bowl. Place the butter chunks on top and pulse until the mixture is crumbly. Stop the machine and add the egg yolks and sour cream. Pulse a few times, then process until the mixture sticks together or forms a mass.

Smooth or pat the dough out on a lightly floured work surface. Divide it into 2 to 3 portions (2 portions for larger pastries; 3 portions for smaller ones). Wrap each portion well and chill the dough for an hour. You can also freeze it until needed.

Preheat the oven to 350°F. Line a large, doubled-up baking sheet with parchment paper. Rugelach can be very sticky and parchment paper is essential.

Roll 1 portion of dough into a 12-inch circle. Spread the jam, sprinkle with white or brown sugar and cinnamon or with ground nuts, miniature chocolate chips, raisins, or whatever filling you choose.

Cut the dough into 12 to 14 portions or wedges. Roll up each portion, starting from a point, to form small crescents. Place the rugelach on the baking sheet. Brush with the beaten egg and sprinkle with sugar, if using. Repeat this process with the remaining dough and your preferred fillings.

Bake until lightly golden (25 to 35 minutes, depending on the size of the rugelach). Cool on baking sheet for 10 minutes, then remove to a wire rack to complete cooling.

Sconalahs

Makes 10 to 14 scones

While on a family holiday in Cape Cod, I tasted some terrific scones.
They were buttery and properly crumbly, with little sweet nuggets of cinnamon tucked into the flaky layers.
I found that they were in fact "cinnamon chips" and, of course, only available to commercial bakers. But a
little ingenuity works here, in the form of butterscotch chips and cinnamon. The result is pure coffee klatch
heaven—a cross between a cake and a pastry, actually—or, as one of
my sons puts it, "It tastes like rugelach, only better!" Hence the appellation, "Sconalahs,"
a hybrid. A food processor makes this recipe a snap. A soft flour, such as
White Lily's All-Purpose White Flour, makes it very tender.
Regular all-purpose flour works well, too.

CINNAMON SMEAR
½ cup butterscotch chips
⅓ cup brown sugar
3 tablespoons unsalted butter
1 tablespoon ground cinnamon

DOUGH
3 cups unbleached all-purpose flour
⅓ cup sugar
1 tablespoon baking powder
½ teaspoon salt
½ cup (1 stick) unsalted butter, cut into chunks
1 egg
1 teaspoon vanilla extract
1 cup half and half or evaporated milk

TOPPING
1 egg white, beaten, for brushing
⅓ cup sugar mixed with 2 teaspoons ground
  cinnamon

Preheat the oven to 425°F. Lightly grease a baking sheet or line it with parchment paper.

CINNAMON SMEAR: Place the ingredients in the work bowl of a food processor. Pulse until the mixture is rough and pasty looking. Set it aside in a small bowl.

DOUGH: Wipe the work bowl with a paper towel and add the flour, sugar, baking powder, and salt. Pulse to blend. Add the butter chunks, and process to form a mealy, crumbly mixture. Transfer this mixture to a large mixing bowl.

Combine the egg, vanilla, and half and half or evaporated milk in a small bowl, then add the liquid mixture to the dry mixture and stir with a fork until the dough just comes together. Turn the dough out onto a floured work surface and knead it gently, pressing in the cinnamon smear throughout the dough. It will look marbleized, this is fine.

TOPPING: Roll or pat the dough into a 10 by 6-inch rectangle or a 10-inch circle. Cut it into 12 to 14 squares or wedges. Place these on the baking sheet, brush each one with beaten egg white, then sprinkle them with the cinnamon sugar.

Bake in the preheated oven for 12 to 15 minutes, or until the bottoms are browned and the tops are lightly golden. Cool on a rack or on the baking sheet.

VARIATION: For Chocolate Sconalahs replace the Cinnamon Smear with this Chocolate Smear: ½ cup chocolate chips, ⅓ cup brown or granulated sugar, 1 teaspoon unsweetened cocoa powder, ½ teaspoon ground cinnamon, and 3 tablespoons unsalted butter.

For the topping, omit the cinnamon and add 1 tablespoon unsweetened cocoa powder to the sugar.

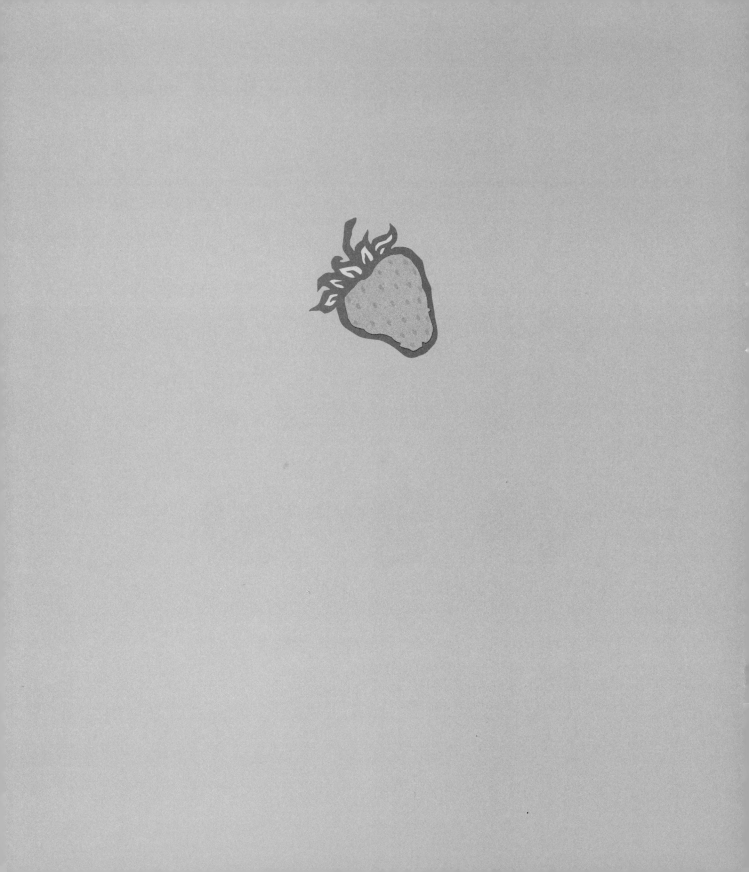

SOURCE GUIDE:

Equipment, Tools, and Ingredients

The following sources supply most of the ingredients, and equipment I work with. These companies and individuals are very helpful to all cooks and bakers.

J. K. ADAMS CO.

Rte. 30
P.O. Box 248
Dorset, VT 05251
1-800-451-6118
(802) 362-2303

Solid hardwood rolling pins, plastic (not metal) bearings, as well as pastry boards and spice racks.

AMERICAN SPOON FOODS

P.O. Box 566
1668 Clarion Avenue
Petoskey, MI 49770
(616) 347-9030
1-888-735-6700
1-800-222-5886
1-800-220-5886

This company is dedicated to preserving the bounty of the Heartland and offers some of the best dried fruits to be found. Sweet dried cherries, as well as zesty sour cherries and cranberries, dried blueberries (perfect in scones) and strawberries are some of the essentials. Renowned for their concentrated, hallmark "Spoon Fruits," the company also specializes in chutneys, jams, barbecue sauces, and vinaigrettes, as well as gift baskets.

ARES EQUIPMENT INC.

2355-A Transcanada Highway
Pointe Claire (Montreal) Quebec
H9R 5Z5
(514) 695-5225
(514) 695-0756 (fax)
1-888-624-8008 (toll-free)
Web site: www3.sympatico.ca/ares/
email: ares@sympatico.ca

A retail store that is unparalleled in its (often discounted) offerings for the home and professional chef, Ares is a good source for both Canadians and Americans looking for specialty items with a very wide range of upscale domestic culinary items as well as commercial or trade items. A full range of Wilton products, pizza stones (great for bagel-making too), decorating tools, Hillside cheesecake pans, Cooper timers, and All Clad Cookware. Also a large range of smallwares (from Norpro, Progressive International, Fox Pro), Canadian Paderno/Padinox cookware, Michigan Maple butcher blocks (in a variety of sizes), Wustoff Trident and Victorinox knives, Cambro and Rubbermaid commercial storage products, Edgecraft sharpeners, KitchenAid mixers and processors (a complete selection), and the Porkert Poppy Seed Grinder. Although this is a retail store, Ares is happy to fill mail orders throughout North America. If you are in Montreal, check this store out, it is almost a tourist attraction for visiting foodies.

BERYL'S CAKE DECORATING EQUIPMENT

P.O. Box 1584
N. Springfield, VA 22151
1-800-488-2749
(703) 256-6951
Web site: Beryls@Beryls.com

Among the extensive line of British, European, and American cake and decorating supplies, including Judaic decorating molds, Beryl's also carries a fine, kosher, "Anna Bach's Marzipan." This is just about the best marzipan I ever tasted. It is very fresh and has a long shelf life, staying soft, malleable, and richly flavorful for a very long time. If there is anything you need—advice, ingredients, products—Beryl will make sure Beryl's Cake Decorating can help you. If it is not in the catalogue, it can be procured, or Beryl herself will direct you to a source. One of the most comprehensive sources for cake decorating and specialty items.

FERMIPAN

Consumer Products Division
151 Skyway Avenue
Rexdale, Ontario M9W 4Z5
1-800-387-3876
(416) 674-6484
Web site: www.betterbaking.com

Leading manufacturer of dry instant yeast. Invented instant yeast, also kosher yeasts for Passover wines. Sister company Lallemand makes fresh yeast.

EGGOLOGY LIQUID EGG WHITES

This company specializes in fresh, bacteria-free, liquid egg whites that are shipped within hours of the eggs being laid. I use Eggology to replace whole eggs when I want to reduce fat and they are great for Passover sponge cakes or egg white omelettes as well. This product also has great shelf life: four months, refrigerator or freezer.

1-888-No-Yolks
1-818-991-8088
www.eggology.com

FLEISCHMANN'S YEAST
Specialty Brands
Burns Philip Food, Inc.
San Francisco, California 94108
1-800-777-4959

Specializing in fresh, active, and instant dry yeast products for retail and wholesale market. Their consumer help line is very helpful, their own recipes are always contemporary and well tested.

HODGSON MILL
P.O. Box 430
201 W. Main Street
Teutopolis, IL 62467
1-800-525-0177
(217) 347-0105
Web site: customservice@hodgsonmill.com

Excellent stone-ground cornmeal, as well as many other flours and mixes for home baking. Largely available in supermarkets, nationally, or write the company for mail order and catalogue information.

HOLLINGSWORTH CUTOM WOOD PRODUCTS INC.
296 North Street
Sault Ste. Marie, Ontario
P6B 2A4
(705) 759-8464
www.betterbaking.com

This company is renown in the trade for their incredible butcher block and other specialty wood products. Their butcher block counter tops are heirlooms—and contribute much to success in baking and pastry tasks. They also manufacture unique bread machine storage and work units, master baker tables, butcher block chef's carts, and customized rolling pins of incomparable design and craftsmanship. Mail order available and made-to-order–size butcher block counters and dining room tables are also available.

HULMAN COMPANY
P.O. Box 150
Terre Haute, IN 47808
no tel. # for consumers

Rumford and Clabber Girl baking powder. Recipe booklets available on request.

KING ARTHUR FLOUR BAKER'S CATALOGUE
P.O. Box 876
Norwich, VT 05055
1-800-827-6836

A unique source for professionally inclined, dedicated home bakers, this flour company's other life revolves around a marvelous catalogue of bakeware including muffin, loaf, cake, and specialty pans, as well as durable commercial cookie sheets. Also "Best" whisks, Zyliss professional ice cream scoops, and ingredients such as superb kosher King Arthur flours: their trademark all-purpose "Special" for bread; white whole wheat flour; and outstanding rye flours that make all the difference in Jewish rye breads. King Arthur is also a source for European yeasts such as fermipan and Saf, as well as some yeasts from Fleischmann's and Red Star that are not always available in regular supermarket baking sections. This is also where you can get buttermilk powder, coarse sugar (for babkas and other pastries), Nielsen Massey and other quality vanillas, Boyajian citrus oils (a must!), dried fruits, baker's caramel, Parrish bakeware, Edgecraft's serrated bread knives, the Magic Mill Mixer DLX—a large-capacity mixer that can take between 24 and 28 cups of flour for big batches of challah, and Zojirushi bread machines. New products are constantly being added.

LA CUISINE
323 Cameroun Street
Alexandria, VA 22314
1-800-521-1176
Web site: lacuisine@worldnet.att.net

An excellent source for upscale bakeware, decorating equipment, and anything associated with the art and craft of baking and cooking. La Cuisine prides itself on importing the "best of the best," and you can count on them to stock the latest in classic French, as well as other European items, such as poppy seed grinders; mandolins; Matfer bakeware; and tools such as nested, durable Exoplas cookie cutters; and specialty cake and pastry molds. They also carry Chicago Metallic and Lockwood commercial bakeware, and are a source for fermipan yeast. La Cuisine, as with other top-league mail order culinary sources, is a storehouse of solid advice from people with hands-on experience. If they don't have it, they will find it.

MANN LAKE LTD.
501 South 1st Street
Hackensack, MN 56452-2001
1-800-233-6663

These folks specialize in beeswax candle-making supplies. One item they always stock, and I could not do without, is the "skep honey jar." This acrylic honey server, complete with a matching honey spoon that swirls and twirls honey into challah dough or onto English muffins and bagels, is a beehive-shaped vessel that is the perfect home for your honey. It is decorative, nostalgic, classic, and a good gift at Rosh Hashanah, along with a freshly baked sweet challah.

MATFER INC.
1-800-766-0333

This manufacturer of kitchen and bakery equipment does not directly sell to consumers but can direct you to a source in your area.

MIGDAL MARGARINE
World Cheese Company Inc.
Kosher Food Products
178 28th Street
Brooklyn, NY 11232
(718) 965-1700

Among other quality kosher dairy products, World Cheese supplies a very good, unsalted margarine that is recommended for Passover baking. If you cannot find Migdal unsalted margarine in your town, contact the company for the source nearest you.

NATIONAL HONEY BOARD
390 Lashley Street
Longmont, CO 80501-6045
(303) 776-2337
1-800-553-7162
Web site: www.nhb.org

An ideal resource for honey information and additional, superb honey recipes—many with a Jewish holiday bent.

NIELSEN MASSEY VANILLA INC.
1550 Shields Dr.
Waukegan, IL 60085
1-800-525-PURE

Nielsen Massey vanillas are certified kosher and come in single or double strength, and in Madagascar, Bourbon, Mexican, or Tahitian extracts and vanilla blends. Nielsen Massey vanillas can also be ordered from the King Arthur's Baker's Catalogue. A family-run, well-established company. The people at Nielsen Massey know almost everything about producing *the* best vanilla I have ever worked with. Equally helpful to avid consumers as they are to large commercial bakers. I recommend their double-strength or double-fold vanillas for mandelbrot, cookies, and dairy-free cakes; single-strength vanillas for most other baking; I use their dry, brown vanilla powder for preparing home mixes, such as pancake mix.

PASKESZ COMPANY
4473 First Avenue
Brooklyn, NY 11232
(718) 832-2400

Full line of kosher snack and confectionary products, ranging from nut and chip snacks, cookies, candies (both retail and bulk pack), chocolates (including Chanukah gelt—pareve, milk chocolate, and semi-sweet varieties), specialty Israeli and Swiss products, and baking supplies. Paskesz is not a consumer supplier but can direct you to retailers in your region if you are looking for a particular product or hard-to-find kosher item.

PENZEYS LTD. SPICE HOUSE
P.O. Box 1448
Waukesha, WI 53187
(414) 574-0277
Web site: www.penzeys.com

A terrific source for wonderfully fresh and fragrant *ground* poppy seeds (for hamantaschen and babka filling) as well as for pungent, intense, makes-all-the-difference cinnamon, mixed cake spices (add a tad to banana cake for extraordinary results), apple pie spices (try some in apple strudel), as well as superb vanillas and specialty spice blends for cooking and baking, including a "Baker's Assortment" to start you out or a "Deluxe" model.

PROGRESSIVE INTERNATIONAL INC.
6111 South 228th Street
Kent, WA 98032
1-800-426-7101

A full line of exceptional, innovative culinary products, largely available from the mail order companies listed here but also in gourmet shops and houseware departments. I like all of their products but specifically recommend two, unbeatable items: their long-handled, stainless-steel measuring spoon set (includes ⅛ teaspoon) and a comparable, companion set of stainless-steel measuring cups.

RED STAR YEAST
Universal Foods Corporation
1-800-445-4746

Specializing in fresh, active, and instant dry yeast for the consumer and trade markets. As with Fleischmann's, Saf, and fermipan, this is another extremely helpful company that offers information and recipes for their home bakers.

RYCRAFT CERAMIC STAMPS INC.
4205 SW 53rd Street
Corvallis, OR 97333
1-800-479-2723 (Orders)

An unusual source for unique, heirloom ceramic cookie stamps, suitable for shortbread cookies for Chanukah, Purim, and Yom Kippur. A broad range of designs, including a particularly artful Star of David stamp, as well as a King David's crown stamp. Also suitable are seasonal motifs (for Sukkot) such as a sheaf of wheat, fruit, and flowers.

SACO FOODS
6120 University Avenue
Madison, WI 53562-0616
1-800-373-SACO
Web site: Sacofoods@aol.com or
www.betterbaking.com

Makers of Saco Buttermilk blend, cocoa powder, and incredible semi-sweet chocolate chunks that are perfect in cookies and cakes. Saco products are available nationwide. The company also offers an extensive series of recipe cards (that utilize their Buttermilk Blend) to consumers who write in for them.

SAF PRODUCTS
400 S. Fourth Street, Suite 310
P.O. Box 15066
Minneapolis, MN 55415
1-800-641-4615

This French yeast is carried by La Cuisine as well as King Arthur Flour. For other sources or availability in your area, contact the company directly. An excellent dry yeast, especially good for sweet yeast cakes and pastries. Information and bread machine recipes are available on request.

SOKOL COMPANY
5315 Dansher Road
Countryside, IL 60525
(708) 482-8250

Makers of Solo cake and pastry fillings, such as poppy seed, nut, and cherry, as well as glazes (for cheesecakes), and Simon Fischer prune and apricot butters. Also manufacture a kosher almond paste and marzipan. Usually available in kosher food stores, as well as in mainstream supermarkets nationwide. Contact the company for a retail source in your area.

THE SOURCE FOR EVERYTHING JEWISH
Hamakor Judaica, Inc.
P.O. Box 48836
Niles, IL 60714-0836
1-800-426-2567

If you need a Sesame Street video for Passover, a great bar mitzvah gift, or a Marc Chagall print, modern as well as traditional menorahs, Seder plates, challah boards, juvenile Judaica toys and symbols, or unique skullcaps and prayer shawls, this is the place. Their catalogues follow holiday themes and are available on request.

SULTAN'S DELIGHT
P.O. Box 090302
Brooklyn, NY 11209
(718) 745-2121
1-800-852-5046
Web site: www.sultansdelight.com

Carries a variety of wooden ma'maoul molds for date- and walnut-filled cookies (recipe in Sukkot section) as well as other Middle Eastern supplies, such as pomegranate molasses, sumac spice, and za'ataar.

SUR LA TABLE
1765 Sixth Avenue South
Seattle, WA 98134-1608
1-800-243-0852

This extraordinary mail order company has an extensive selection of culinary. Sur La Table's most recent catalogue is a special baker's issue in which you will find items from Matfer, such as their nested cookie cutters, as well as other tools; heavy-duty aluminum cake pans; gugelhuph molds; Zojirushi bread machines; hardwood rolling pins; rolling pin covers; handmade ceramic pizza stones (for great bagels); Progressive International measuring spoons and cups; bench scrapers; and many other items. For cooks as well as bakers. Check out the regular seasonal catalogues.

SWEET CELEBRATIONS INC.
P.O. Box 39426
Edina, MN 55439-0426
(612) 943-1661
1-800-328-6722

This mail order company, formerly known as Maid of Scandinavia, has everything for the home baker who wants to shop at home for basics as well as hard-to-find items. Various Star of David cookie cutter sets (in graduated sizes), Judaic cake decorations, candy molds for Chanukah, and blue and white Star of David baking cups, cookbooks, supplies, and so on. Carries many unique bakery-related items other mail order sources do not, such as loaf cake pan liners. Made of oven-proof parchment paper, these liners fit 9 by 5- and 8½ by 4½-inch loaf pans. I use them when making honey cakes as gifts, but also for all sorts of quick breads, such as marble cake, carrot, and lemon poppy seed.Unusual bakery and pastry-related items, as well as standard but hard-to-find necessities.

THORPE ROLLING PIN COMPANY
336 Putnam Avenue
P.O. Box 4124
Hamden, CT 06514
1-800-344-6966.

Classic, quality hardwood rolling pins with ball bearings, available nationwide in culinary stores, or contact the company for the retailer nearest you.

VIC FIRTH/BANTON MANUFACTURING
49 High Street
Newport, ME 04953
(207) 368-4358

Specializes in outstanding rolling pins—all hardwood with metal ball bearings, as well as pepper mills of all descriptions. Order directly or contact the company for a retailer in your area.

THE WHITE LILY FOODS COMPANY
P.O. Box 871
Knoxville, TN 37901
(423) 546-5511

Superb soft wheat flours, excellent for cakes, scones, biscuits, pies, and pastries. I use this flour exclusively for Sconolahs (Shavuot section). Information, mail order, and recipes available.

WILTON INDUSTRIES
2240 West 75th Street
Woodridge, IL 60517
1-800-772-7111

Wilton offers a full line of specialty and standard cake pans that are suitable for a variety of baking purposes. Offers a few different lines including "Performance Pans," nonstick, anodized aluminum, and "Wilton Pro," a more heavy-duty baking pan. Available nationwide in cake decorating stores, gourmet shops, and houseware departments. Wilton is a premium cake pan manufacturer and a good choice for layer cake, 9 by 13-inch pans, as well as sheet and brownie pans. Its annual decorating catalogue has many good and fun ideas for holiday baking, such as Chanukah theme cakes and bar mitzvah cakes.

BIBLIOGRAPHY

Books quoted from, or found useful and recommended for further reading:

The Book of Esther, excerpts, translated and revised by Rabbi Simon Glazer Ktav Publishing House Inc., New York, n.d.

A Book of Jewish Thoughts, new and revised edition, edited by Dr. J. A. Hertz, Office of the Chief Rabbi, London, England, Lowe and Bydrone Printers Limited, London, England, 1941. A collection of selected writings intended for His Majesty's Jewish sailors, soldiers, and airmen.

The Code of Jewish Law. Rabbi Solomon Ganzfried (translated by Hyman E. Goldin), Hebrew Publishing Company, New York, 1961.

A Complete Family Guide to Jewish Holidays, Dalia Hardof Renberg, Adama Books, New York, 1985.

A Dictionary of Yiddish Slang and Idioms, Fred Kogos, Citadel Press, Carol Publishing Group, 1995 (original published 1966).

The Hallah Book: Recipes, History and Traditions, Freda Reider, KTAV Publishing House Inc., New York, 1987.

The Jewish Holidays, A Guide and Commentary, Michael Stassfeld, Harper & Row, New York, 1985.

The Joys of Yiddish, Leo Rosten, Pocket Books, New York, 1970 edition (first published 1968).

My Glorious Brothers, Howard Fast, Blue Heron Press, New York, 1953.

Passover Haggadah, Rabbi Nathan Goldberg (based on Haggadah by Rabbi Z. Harry Gutstein), Ktav Publishing House Inc., New York, 1949.

The Pastry Chef, William Sultan, Avi Publishing Company, Inc., Westport, Connecticut, 1983.

Practical Baking, William Sultan, Van Nostrand Reinhold, New York, 1990.

This Is My God, Herman Wouk, Doubleday and Company, New York, 1960.

Yiddish Wisdom, Yiddishe Chochma, illustrated by Kristina Swarmer, compiled/published by Chronicle Books, San Francisco, 1966.

INDEX